W9-DED-243

#76900-1

AUTHOR, READER, BOOK:
MEDIEVAL AUTHORSHIP IN THEORY
AND PRACTICE

EDITED BY STEPHEN PARTRIDGE
AND ERIK KWAKKEL

Author, Reader, Book

Medieval Authorship in Theory and Practice

UNIVERSITY OF TORONTO PRESS
Toronto Buffalo London

© University of Toronto Press 2012
Toronto Buffalo London
www.utppublishing.com
Printed in Canada

ISBN 978-0-8020-9934-1

Printed on acid-free, 100% post-consumer recycled paper with vegetable-based inks.

Library and Archives Canada Cataloguing in Publication

Author, reader, book : Medieval authorship in theory and practice / edited by Stephen Partridge and Erik Kwakkel.

Includes bibliographical references and index.
ISBN 978-0-8020-9934-1

1. Literature, Medieval – History and criticism.   2. Authorship –
History – To 1500.   3. Authors and readers – History – To 1500.
I. Partridge, Stephen   II. Kwakkel, Erik, 1970–

PN671.A97 2012   809'.02   C2011-906090-6

This book has been published with the help of a grant from the Canadian Federation for the Humanities and Social Sciences, through the Aid to Scholarly Publications Program, using funds provided by the Social Sciences and Humanities Research Council of Canada.

University of Toronto Press acknowledges the financial assistance to its publishing program of the Canada Council for the Arts and the Ontario Arts Council.

   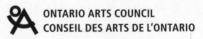

Canada Council Conseil des Arts   ONTARIO ARTS COUNCIL
for the Arts   du Canada   CONSEIL DES ARTS DE L'ONTARIO

University of Toronto Press acknowledges the financial support of the Government of Canada through the Canada Book Fund for its publishing activities.

Contents

Acknowledgments   vii

Illustrations   ix

Introduction: Author, Reader, Book, and Medieval Authorship
in Theory and Practice   3
STEPHEN PARTRIDGE

1 The Trouble with Theology: Ethical Poetics and the Ends of
Scripture   20
ALASTAIR MINNIS

2 Wit, Laughter, and Authority in Walter Map's *De nugis curialium*
(Courtiers' Trifles)   38
SEBASTIAN COXON

3 Late Medieval Text Collections: A Codicological Typology Based
on Single-Author Manuscripts   56
ERIK KWAKKEL

4 The Censorship Trope in Geoffrey Chaucer's *Manciple's Tale*
as Ovidian Metaphor in a Gowerian and Ricardian Context   80
ANITA OBERMEIER

5 'The Makere of this Boke': Chaucer's *Retraction* and the Author
as Scribe and Compiler   106
STEPHEN PARTRIDGE

6 Reading for Authority: Portraits of Christine de Pizan and Her
   Readers   154
   DEBORAH MCGRADY

7 Vernacular *Auctoritas* in Late Medieval England: Writing after the
   Constitutions   178
   KIRSTY CAMPBELL

8 Master Henryson and Father Aesop   198
   IAIN MACLEOD HIGGINS

9 Erasmus's *Lucubrationes*: Genesis of a Literary Oeuvre   232
   MARK VESSEY

Bibliography   263

Notes on Contributors   289

Index   291

Index of Manuscripts   303

Acknowledgments

The editors wish to thank, above all, their fellow contributors for their essays and for their patience as this collection made its way through preparation, revision, evaluation, and production. Suzanne Rancourt of the University of Toronto Press likewise has been most patient and supportive. We are grateful also to two anonymous readers for the Press, whose perceptive and rigorous readings helped to make this a better book. Most essays in this collection grew out of papers delivered at the Thirty-Fourth Medieval Workshop at Green College, the University of British Columbia, in 2004, and we are happy to thank again those who helped make that occasion possible: the Committee on Medieval Studies; the Office of the Vice President, Research; the Dean of Arts; the Departments of English, History, and Central, Eastern, and Northern European Studies; the Leon and Thea Koerner Foundation; and SSHRC. As ever, the editors are indebted to their spouses, Ruth Davison and Elise Partridge.

Illustrations

Figure 6.1 *Le livre de la cité des dames*: Christine in her study and building the walls of the 'city of ladies.'   163

Figure 6.2 Christine offering her collected works to Queen Isabeau de Bavière.   165

Figure 6.3 *Proverbes moraux*: Christine seated in a lectern before an open book speaks with an all-male audience.   166

Figure 6.4 *Livre du duc des vrais amans*: Christine in her study receives the duke who commissions the present work.   167

Figure 6.5 *Epistre Othea*: Diane reading from a book while members of her audience consult their copies.   170

Figure 8.1 Steinhöwel's Aesop. Aesopus, *Fabulae*, trans. Heinrich Steinhöwel ([Augsburg], [Günther Zainer], [ca. 1477/8]), frontispiece.   202

Figure 8.2 Caxton's Aesop . . . . *[T]he book of . . . fables of Esope . . .* translated . . . by wylham Caxton ([Westminster: William Caxton, 1484]), fol. 1v.   203

Figure 8.3 Bassandyne's Aesop. *The morall fabillis of Esope the Phrygia[n]* (Edinburgh: Thomas Bassandyne, 1571), from the title-page (A1r).   204

Figure 9.1 Title-page of the *Lucubrationes* (Strasbourg: Matthias Schürer, 1515).   234

Figure 9.2 Sig. 4v of the *Lucubrationes* (Strasbourg: Matthias Schürer, 1515), facing the first page of the *Enchiridion militis christiani*.   242

Figure 9.3 Verso of the title-page *Lucubrationes* (Strasbourg: Matthias Schürer, 1515).   253

AUTHOR, READER, BOOK:
MEDIEVAL AUTHORSHIP IN THEORY
AND PRACTICE

Introduction: Author, Reader, Book, and Medieval Authorship in Theory and Practice

STEPHEN PARTRIDGE

The editors of the present volume prompted the conversation which it records in response to two related phenomena of recent scholarship on the Middle Ages. The first consists essentially of a single book, Alastair Minnis's *Medieval Theory of Authorship*, and its status, more than two decades after its publication, as one of the most-cited points of reference for medieval literary studies.[1] Minnis devotes much of his book to the development of medieval ideas about pre-medieval *auctores* – biblical, classical, and patristic. In a concluding chapter, however, Minnis points out some of the ways that the academic tradition he outlines affected how the 'familiar' vernacular writers of the later Middle Ages presented themselves and were received by their readers. By joining the history of a set of ideas developed largely in the medieval Latin tradition with illustrations of that tradition's contact with vernacular writing, Minnis's book helped to enable an increased sophistication in studies of medieval literature. We may measure its influence by the frequency with which scholars consider, for example, the relative statuses of Latin and vernacular, or compilation as a medieval mode of writing – whether or not such issues are at the centre of their inquiries.

The second aspect of the scholarly discourse which drew the editors' interest was that, beginning at about the same time Minnis's book on the theory of authorship appeared, there have also been published, in ever-increasing numbers, monographs, articles, and collections of essays which emphasize the practical manifestations and consequences of medieval ideas about authority, the author, and authorship.[2] These studies have been more specific than Minnis's, as they have usually focused on a single national literature or a single writer. Such studies approach the practice of authorship in several ways, often in combination though sometimes emphasizing one aspect or another of the issue. First, they may seek to discover strategies of authorship by reading texts; such readings often take prologues, epilogues, or other passages in which medieval writers directly discuss their circumstances and agendas as a major object of inquiry. Textual approaches may also find implicit authorial self-reference elsewhere, as in patterns of allusion to models and antecedents, or in narrative episodes or characters which seem intended as emblems of the author and his or her situation. A second strand of scholarship on the medieval author is codicological. This approach considers, for example, whether the author serves as a rationale for collecting works together in a manuscript; or where a manuscript's paratext, such as its rubrics or titles, might name the author of works collected therein; or how a manuscript's illustrations represent the author(s) of works it contains. A third route of inquiry considers an author's relationship to his or her readers. The evidence for how readers perceived an author's project and status may be codicological, but may also be found, for instance, in literary allusions and imitations, in patterns of patronage, or in monarchical or ecclesiastical censorship or licence.[3]

Our goal in the workshop out of which this collection grew was to bring together people working on related aspects of medieval authorship but in scholarly spheres which had tended to remain rather separate. In the first instance, this meant inviting Minnis to offer reflections based on his continuing work with medieval literary commentary and theory as the framework for a series of specific studies of practice. We had other aims as well. One was to consider Latin texts together with those in the vernacular, in part to challenge notions sometimes underlying work on vernacularity – that writing in Latin automatically garnered authority, or that the authority of Latin was a fixed and static value. Thus our specific studies begin with Walter Map and conclude with Erasmus, in order to show that Latin writers of the Middle Ages employed strategies to define and secure their authorship which were very similar to those used by writers in the vernacular. These two essays also serve to extend the chronological scope of debate about medieval authorship, which has usually focused on the thirteenth through fifteenth centuries, by including in our conversation Map, who wrote in the twelfth, and Erasmus's self-compilations of the early sixteenth.

There was also much to be gained from bringing into dialogue those working on several vernaculars, since studies and collections have tended to confine themselves to works in a single language.[4] Thus Sebastian Coxon, although writing here on Map, brings to the issue a conceptual force based in a well-developed, but not widely enough known, theoretical discourse developed from studies of Middle High German writing. Moreover, Deborah McGrady's essay on Christine de Pizan provides an example of the rich vein of scholarship on the theory and practice of authorship in late medieval France. One of the collection's two essays on Chaucer suggests that we can understand the manuscripts' references to Chaucer's compiling of the *Canterbury Tales* by taking into account not only the academic tradition traced by Minnis, but also the French literary culture represented by Christine, through which English writers' experience of the academic tradition may have been mediated. And Erik Kwakkel, considering manuscripts of Middle Dutch writers, brings to attention a literary culture with an underrecognized influence on Middle English, including the tradition of vernacular theology explored in Kirsty Campbell's essay on Reginald Pecock.

A further goal of the present collection is to demonstrate similarities between devotional authors such as Pecock and literature which was primarily secular in nature. With Pecock in the former category we might include most or all of the Dutch writers whose manuscripts are analysed by Kwakkel, as well as Robert Henryson, whose 'Morall fables' are the subject of Iain Higgins's essay, and Erasmus, whose vision of theology as poetry is discussed by Mark Vessey. On the other hand, the collection also considers the wonderfully urbane (and sometimes profane) Walter Map, and Christine and Chaucer, who while writing some devotional works seem to have identified primarily with a secular tradition. Minnis's essay on the relationship of theology to poetry shows that it was sometimes difficult for medieval thinkers to separate the sacred and secular even when considering them on the theoretical plane.

While this collection aims to transcend certain linguistic and generic boundaries, two recurrent interests help to bind its essays. One of the collection's persistent themes is the relationship of authorship to readership. One aspect of this relationship is the activity of authors as readers. A number of contributors consider how medieval writers define their authorship by representing, in various ways, their relationships to their predecessors – thus portraying themselves as sensitive and sometimes critical readers of established authorities such as Ovid, Aesop, and Jerome. Another essay shows that Christine defines herself as an author in part by demonstrating her mastery of multiple techniques of reading. In addition, medieval writers' relationships to their readers are discussed in several essays. Christine is concerned with constructing her audience, by illustrating a model of readership to which she hopes her readers at court will conform. Chaucer designs his 'book of the tales of Canterbury' in order to create the illusion of physical contact with his readers, as part of his imparting his authority to copies of the *Tales*. Writing in the charged context of Henry II's court, Map employs wit to deflect and undermine the potential rage of powerful readers. Finally, Chaucer and Pecock seek in different ways to negotiate their authorship within more formal regimes of censorship – a circumstance illustrating the less attractive consequences of endeavouring to make the vernacular author more visible.

A second strong area of interest in this collection is the relationship of authorship to the book. For example, Kwakkel's study of Dutch manuscripts provides codicological evidence that the author was a category around which manuscript production was organized, perhaps in more instances than have heretofore been recognized. Other essays show that Christine and Chaucer exploited the possibilities offered by manuscript production to define and assert their places in the Anglo-French literary system. Vessey's study shows that Erasmus worked in a remarkably similar way, though in the new medium of print, as successive collections of his work reflect his evolving ideas about his authorship. It is through their concern with reading, defined in various ways, and with the shapes of manuscripts and early printings – with social and material circumstances of authorship – that these essays make the case that we can understand medieval literature by reference not only to the ideas of authority and the author, but also to a set of practices that served to constitute authorship.

Our collection opens with its most wide-ranging and consistently theoretical essay, Alastair Minnis's account of the relationship between theology and secular poetics in the high and later Middle Ages. That relationship was mutually informing and enriching, but also created anxieties. Did using the techniques and terms of secular poetics when describing the various books of the Bible threaten the unique status of theology in the hierarchy of the disciplines? Medieval considerations of that question were particularly influenced by Hermann the German's Latin translation (1256) of Averroes's 'Middle Commentary' on Aristotle's *Poetics*. Averroes/Hermann revises Aristotle by replacing the concept of mimesis with representation 'of a kind that arouses people's emotions in a way that encourages them to follow virtue and flee from vice.' The popularity of the established *accessus* tradition's 'notions concerning the ethical aims and affective methods of poetry,' Minnis believes, helps explain medieval thinkers' attraction to this revision of Aristotle. The 'Averroes/Hermann emphasis on affectivity' seems to have influenced the poetics of Roger Bacon, who brings theology and poetics especially close when he claims 'that Scripture and moral philosophy rely on the same kind of poetical argument' and 'draws parallels between the poetical modes used by secular writers and those found in' scripture.

Other writers valued scripture's ways of appealing to men's minds and its end of inculcating piety above those 'lesser' sciences which use logical methods of analysis to educate the intellect, even though this approach seems to contradict Aristotle's judgment in the *Organon* that affective poetics and rhetoric were the least of those 'lesser' sciences. It appears, however, that medieval scholars never brought into direct conflict these apparently divergent ways of ranking rhetoric and poetics in relation to logic, but instead 'managed to think in compartments.' The potential for conflict was heightened by the medieval reception of Aristotle's *Ethics*. If the Bible and Aristotleian ethics shared similar means and ends, did this mean that the Bible was an ethical book, like the secular (and often pagan) texts of the grammar curriculum, and that theology was a branch of the lesser discipline of ethics? Bacon classified both theology and moral philosophy as 'practical sciences,' and thought that they pursued the same ends as poetic rhetoric. Bonaventure, by contrast, kept theology distinct from lesser sciences such as ethics and poetics, in part by insisting on the uniquely divine authorship of the Bible – in his eyes more important than the fact that human authors might employ the same narrative modes as did scripture. Bonaventure also insisted that theology sought to instill a goodness more comprehensive than the practical, exterior goodness of Aristotle's *Ethics*, and others emphasized that theology dealt with an affection far superior to the intellect.

In the realm of secular poetics, however, the similarities, in both ends and means, between theology and ethical poetics were invoked by Petrarch, Boccaccio, and others as they strove to elevate the status of poetry. While Minnis sees Bacon as an especially close precedent for their thinking, they drew on a pervasive and influential tradition of describing scripture; Boccaccio, for example, made use of patristic defences of scripture's obscurity and fictiveness to justify secular poetry that shared these characteristics. This conjunction of poetics and theology provoked a sharp reaction from Savanarola – an extreme response, but one which brought into sharp relief a widely perceived problem with theology. '[I]f the difference between poetry and theology were reduced significantly,' theology might be reduced to ethics. On the other hand, theology's unique position required that it also remain distinct from the higher logical sciences. Late medieval thinkers therefore returned, 'again and again, to confront the poetical qualities of scriptural style' in order to show that theology had sources of knowledge surpassing those of speculative science. The 'trouble' caused by theology's similarities to poetry was never to be finally resolved, however, and revealed tensions within the church that have extended beyond the Middle Ages.

The collection's more specific case studies, arranged roughly in chronological order of their subjects, then begin with Sebastian Coxon's discussion of Walter Map's *De nugis curialium*. Coxon shows how Map carefully shaped and placed anecdotes portraying his antagonistic wit, including in them the authorizing laughter of those who heard his bon mots when he delivered them. While such episodes seem far from the theoretical debates about theology and poetics that Minnis traces, and are formed in part by the pressure of Map's specific historical circumstances, Coxon argues that passages in which Map portrays himself as an outstanding court wit offer especially rich opportunities for understanding his relationship to fundamental issues of authorship and authority. They serve to increase the force of Map's commentary on the most serious issues of his day, such as heretical dissent, the secular abuse of ecclesiastical office, and the need for monastic reform. Such passages bolster Map's authority by leading the reader to trust in his comic flair, but also support his licence to comment on the Angevin court, since the witty speech of which he was an expert practitioner was an important aspect of court culture. Map portrays himself as an *auctor* of memorable sayings, and since such *dicta* were a recognized genre of the 'ancients,' collecting his own 'goes some way to compensating the modern writer for his lack of time-honoured *auctoritas.*'

In the final, long passage Coxon discusses, Map's authority is reinforced by the status of his adversary, an illegitimate son of the king, and by the thoroughness of Map's triumph over him – of which we are persuaded by Map's fearless wit, his adversary's 'impotent rage, and the approving laughter of courtly society.' Map artfully shapes this passage to show his adversary's diminution and also, by shifting from his usual first-person narration to the third person, creates an opportunity to name himself a good dozen times; it is 'the most privileged site of authorial naming in the whole work.' Coxon proposes that Map may have 'elected to use the third person to increase the chances of a record of his authorship being preserved for posterity.' This was apparently part of Map's project as a self-compiler, 'the first collector of his own bonmots,' which served specific functions in shaping his literary afterlife. Such third-person discourse in the *De nugis*, Coxon proposes, may have provided the basis and model for similar accounts of his wit that supported Map's posthumous author-mythology. As Coxon points out, after Map's death, in addition to helping create a specific mode of discourse which alluded to and extended Map's reputation as a brilliantly witty clerk, this author-mythology exercised a kind of gravitational force on works he had not in fact written, and resulted in false attributions to Map.

Erik Kwakkel's essay addresses compilation in a more specifically material context, as he explores how the idea of the author could influence the ways that scribes, perhaps sometimes in collaboration with their patrons, organized and produced Middle Dutch manuscripts. Kwakkel proposes a codicological typology for late-medieval text collections with a specific focus, which became more popular during the later Middle Ages in the Latin scholastic tradition as well as in the vernacular. After reviewing the definition of a composite manuscript, which was marked by discontinuities in production and sometimes in use, Kwakkel defines several new terms in order to make more precise our analysis of the genesis of single-author collections. These terms are the 'production unit,' similar to but distinct from the familiar 'booklet'; the 'extended production unit,' which has been modified in a further stage of production; the 'usage unit,' an element in a composite manuscript that had an independent history of use before being incorporated into the larger book; and 'usage phase,' which refers to any given stage of a unit's use, whether on its own or after its incorporation into the composite manuscript. Using these terms, Kwakkel distinguishes four common types of text collections – two types produced without interruptions and two others for which production was discontinuous.

In the course of establishing this codicological taxonomy, Kwakkel shows how many Middle Dutch writers were treated as authors, in that common authorship became the organizational principle for entire manuscripts or significant parts thereof. His analysis takes up manuscripts containing works by such writers as Jan van Ruusbroec, Meister Eckhart, and Hadewijch of Brabant. The examples Kwakkel discusses range from codices of over a hundred folios devoted to one author, carefully planned to collect the entire oeuvre of a writer and group his or her works by genre, to single quires or small groups of quires which might reflect more intermittent and opportunistic gathering of works by a single author. Codicological examination can reveal the significant histories of 'books' of the latter type as independent 'usage units,' before they were incorporated into composite manuscripts containing works by other writers. The varying forms of composite manuscripts, Kwakkel concludes, therefore must be taken into account by literary historians who study the texts transmitted in these manuscripts.

Anita Obermeier's essay on the *Manciple's Tale* returns to several of the issues addressed in Coxon's study of Map, but Obermeier focuses on what this tale reveals about Chaucer's relationship to a particular ancient *auctor*, Ovid, and to one specific reader and potential censor in his court audience – the monarch himself, Richard II. Obermeier reads the *Manciple's Tale* as an element of Chaucer's self-criticism which offers a veiled critique of Richard's behaviour in the turbulent final years of his reign, as well as a warning to his fellow poet John Gower about his criticisms of the king. As Chaucer chose and adapted a tale from the *Metamorphoses*, she argues, he had in mind also Ovid's exile at the hands of the emperor Augustus. Chaucer intended, she believes, 'to mark himself as an Ovidian descendant' vulnerable to censorship by the unpredictable Richard II. Ovid's story concerns a raven who observes the infidelity of Apollo's lover and is punished by the god when he reveals this to him. In Chaucer's version, the raven becomes a crow, Apollo's lover becomes his wife, and the story becomes one 'about authorship, power, and its abuses.' Obermeier sees parallels between this pair – Phebus and the crow – and two other pairs, Richard II/Chaucer and Augustus/Ovid. In his poems of exile, Ovid suggests he was banished both for writing the *Ars Amatoria* and because he had seen something he should not have (as did his raven and Chaucer's crow). In these poems, Ovid pleads with an Augustus who is portrayed as harshly angry, and 'laces his accolades with subtle and not so subtle criticisms of his censor.' Obermeier interprets Phebus's crow – accused by the god of lying and punished, when he has merely told the truth – as a symbol for the medieval translator and compiler. His fate reminds us of Chaucer's in the *Legend*, where he is censured by Cupid for simply translating authoritative 'old books' – Cupid perhaps representing a Richard II whose literary sensitivity, like Augustus's, is portrayed as flawed. Like Cupid, Phebus shows little judgment 'in killing his wife and punishing the messenger for the message before verifying the crow's story.'

Obermeier argues, however, that unlike Chaucer, the crow provides no introductory context or apology for his bringing of distasteful news, and thus misuses 'Apollo's divine gift of speech.' The crow therefore represents, more specifically, the medieval poet who misuses language, who carelessly forgets his relationship to temporal and divine power. This does not mitigate the guilt of Phebus, for Chaucer seems to bring out the criticisms implicit in Ovid's portrayal of Apollo. Moreover, as Obermeier argues by exploring the late fourteenth-century associations of Apollo, together with contemporary views of Richard's reign, Chaucer would have expected a perceptive reader to recognize his Phebus as a mirror of Richard II. Obermeier sees a thematic continuity between the story of Phebus and a long, concluding passage of moralizing attributed to the tale-teller's 'Dame,' since these lines revisit 'the problems and pitfalls of the medieval poet and performer,' and imply that a writer's salvation can hang in the balance depending on whether or not he uses language for proper Christian ends. The crow of the *Manciple's Tale*, she reminds us, 'is thrown out the door for the devil to take.' Returning in her conclusion to the very specific historical context, Obermeier proposes that Chaucer, whose 'metaphoric critique of Richard' contrasts with Gower's more direct protests, intends to warn his fellow poet 'to be more cautious in his own criticism of Richard II.'

The following essay continues to explore Chaucer's conception of his authorship, this time by examining the *Retraction*, with special attention to its appearance in the manuscripts of the *Canterbury Tales*. This study thus returns to Kwakkel's codicological approach to authorship, but shifts the focus to how an author can define himself by asserting control over the manuscript presentation of his works. It proposes that for Chaucer, as for the French predecessors and contemporaries whose literary culture so shaped him, portraying himself as involved in the design and production of manuscripts was an integral aspect of authorship. Specifically, a detailed survey of the manuscript rubrics to the *Retraction* yields two main findings. First, a number of scribes, when encountering an incipit which attributes the *Retraction* rather ambiguously to 'the makere of this boke,' modified the rubric to make clear that what follows are Chaucer's words, rather than their own. This scribal reading of the rubric helps bring to our attention similarities in position and language between the *Retraction* and scribal colophons. Second, the ambiguous incipit, and an explicit which states that Chaucer 'compiled' the 'boke of the tales of Caunterbury,' can be attributed to Chaucer himself; these work together with the *Retraction* to ascribe several roles to Chaucer – author, scribe, and compiler. Comparisons with rubrics in roughly contemporary French manuscripts show that 'compile' in this concluding rubric is not a term of modesty suggesting Chaucer has simply assembled material by others in the *Tales*, though Chaucer, like other late Middle English writers, uses the word in this 'disclaiming' sense elsewhere. Rather, in the contexts of the *Retraction* and a literary culture in which one became an author by book-making and compiling one's work, to state that Chaucer 'compiled' 'this boke' expands the scope of Chaucer's authorship and lends his authority to the copies of his own book which are all that survive to readers. The rubrics thus contribute to the effect the *Retraction* achieves of making Chaucer present to his readers at the close of his book.

In the next essay, Deborah McGrady continues to approach authorship through codicology, as she shows how Christine de Pizan, through texts, rubrics, and manuscript images, sought to identify herself as a reader and to shape the reading practices of her audience. Christine drew on both clerkly and lay reading identities to define herself as an author who 'straddled the two realms' of male, clerical culture and the less learned, amateur reading culture at court. In addition, she imagined a new type of lay reader for her writings, a reader she hoped would bring to them some of the reading practices traditionally associated with clerks. From the beginning of her career, Christine portrayed herself as one who read widely and thoughtfully, and she claimed that the nobility valued her works because they combined her extensive learning with her lived experience at court. Although she had referred to herself skimming the *Roman de la Rose* – a way of reading associated with France's newly expanded non-clerical literate community – she shows herself paying close attention to and reflecting in more clerical fashion on more deserving *auctores* such as Boethius, Augustine, and Aristotle. Christine offers the most fully developed portrait of herself as a reader in the opening of the *Cité des Dames*, which 'vividly details the author's mastery of a full range of reading skills,' including the highest levels of understanding outlined by Hugh of

St Victor's *Didascalicon*. An opening illustration that appears in several manuscripts of the *Cité* expresses the dynamic aspects of this opening scene of reading, as Christine's meditative study 'affords her the authority to challenge respected authors and fellow readers who have misconstrued women's role in society.'

While she thus distances herself from antifeminist clerical culture, however, Christine also sets herself apart 'from the lay culture that formed and educated her.' Although she was the social inferior of her patrons and many in her initial audience, Christine implies that she is their superior in her mastery of books. Her writings and miniatures in her manuscripts often portray those at court as patrons, listeners at oral readings, or 'spectators before the written artefact' rather than private, meditative readers. Yet her works and their manuscripts also reflect Christine's evolving effort to reshape her lay audience as literate and 'text-bound.' She appears to have revised the format of *Epistre Othea* manuscripts, for example, in order to insist on what McGrady calls a 'material reading' of the text, which 'would entail holding the book, gazing on its images, and studying its text.' This does not mean that Christine expected her audience at court to read as she did. Rather, she invites them 'to engage in a hybrid form of reading' which could include listening and discussion, but in a quiet setting that allowed respectful attention to her writings. This new, hybrid reading model was perhaps intended especially for the women in Christine's audience, and could be used for devotional and didactic works as well as her 'courtly' writings. Eustache Deschamps's verse epistle to Christine offers compelling evidence of her success in establishing herself as 'a reader of learned works *and* as a producer of books intended for study.'

Kirsty Campbell considers Reginald Pecock's theorizing and practice of vernacular authorship in the shadow of Archbishop Arundel's 1409 *Constitutions*, designed to extirpate Lollard heresy. She revises views of Pecock as sharply constrained by this much-discussed act of censorship, proposing instead other explanations for his 'apparent self-censorship.' While Pecock's writings reveal clearly that he was aware of the *Constitutions*, he nevertheless traverses a wider realm of inquiry and debate than Arundel had permitted. For example, he opens up to rational proof topics which the church had decreed were to be treated simply as articles of belief. Campbell sees even his use of Latin to discuss certain topics not as a retreat from vernacular theology but rather as a self-authorizing strategy on Pecock's part. Some of Pecock's choices that have been seen as responses to the *Constitutions*, Campbell proposes, sometimes resulted instead from his teaching methods. Pecock's example, she argues, suggests that the production of vernacular theology in fifteenth-century England was less affected by the *Constitutions* than Arundel and the other churchmen who sought to enforce them would have hoped.

A second challenge Pecock faced was establishing authority for his vernacular works in the face of the official position that Latin writing, especially on his topics, would be superior. Yet Pecock seems confident about his vernacular authority, 'boldly asserting that his theological works are the best choice of reading material for lay readers.' As a bishop, Pecock aimed to educate the laity and to convert Lollard heretics to orthodoxy with his vast corpus of writing. His works reflect a strong sense of authorial identity, for Pecock suggests that they may convey doctrinal truth more effectively to his audience than the Bible itself; he offers numerous cross-references from one of his works to another, and 'envisions his own work as a source for compilers.' While deferring to Jerome and other *auctores*, Pecock states that their authority is not unquestionable, for 'even the fathers did not always comprehend and give proper expression to the timeless, universal truths for which they were supposed to be searching.' In terms of authority, his vernacular theology, contemporary English writing, and the revered *auctores* are all to be measured by the same standard, of whether they are 'properly grounded in the truths of reason and faith.' Through the vision which he 'describes as the impetus to the creation of his' *Reule of Christian Religion*, Pecock expresses alarm about illegitimate writings by clerks who were led astray from doctrinal truths by imaginative descriptions such as allegories. Any work, he insists – even those of the Latin *auctores* – must be in accord with such doctrinal truth in order to be genuinely authoritative. Campbell points out that in a fascinating passage echoing some of the arguments surveyed by Minnis, Pecock declares that the 'writings of the *auctores* merely witness and rehearse the timeless truths that exist . . . in "the largist book of autorite that ever God made, which is the doom of resoun."' In essence, God is the only author, and all human writers are merely scholars, translators, or compilers – an idea reflected in Pecock's comparisons of himself to a forester, a merchant, and a gardener. Thus, somewhat like Christine, Pecock grounds his vernacular authority in his ability as a reader, not only of the Bible but also of the book of reason. Campbell concludes that Pecock's anxious efforts to authorize his own works over others in the vernacular imply that he was writing in an atmosphere where vernacular theology continued to develop despite Arundel's attempts to inhibit it.

Iain Higgins's essay, 'Master Henryson and Father Aesop,' traces the Scottish poet's relationship in his *Morall Fabillis* with his ancient, Latin, and (significantly) pagan *auctor*. Though he addresses them rather differently, Henryson's concerns in the *Fabillis* thus offer some points of comparison with Chaucer's in his Ovidian tale of the crow, and Higgins suggests that Henryson is defining his relationship to his medieval vernacular predecessor as well as to his ancient *auctor*. Higgins focuses on Henryson's dream-vision encounter with Aesop, which he embeds at the midpoint of his fable-collection. That placement, in Higgins's reading, is part of the encounter's meaning, since Henryson sees 'the rich thematic implications of form and structure – in this case, for matters of moral as well as literary authority in the vernacular.' When Henryson first mentions Aesop in his Prologue to the *Fabillis*, the ancient is a 'received authority' cited to defend the seriousness of fable, but Henryson also begins to modernize that authority into a medieval (clerkly) figure and make him his own. After opening with two Aesopian fables, Henryson moves to three Reynardian tales, thus transforming Aesop's book into a medieval one. These Reynardian fables focus on 'problems of achieving earthly justice,' a theme that carries over to the next Aesopic fable, 'The Sheep and the Dog.' Comments in that fable also extend Henryson's developing portrayal of himself as what Higgins calls an 'ear-witness' to the actions and speech recounted, an innovation that suggests he is a more direct authority for the fables, rather than simply a rewriter of Aesop – that he, not Aesop, 'is each tale's nearest intermediary.'

After 'The Sheep and the Dog,' Henryson brings Aesop back into view in dramatic fashion, inserting the scene 'in which the narrator meets his writing master and gets him to tell in "his own voice" a tale.' The prologue in which this meeting occurs interrupts the sequence of tales and confirms that Henryson has reached a crisis in his work as a fabulist. This midpoint moment of hesitation allows Henryson to shift 'the very ground on which he stands' and ultimately assert more forcefully his own Christian identity. The dream-vision presents a scene of instruction, a 'passing on of the patriarchal line in moral fabulation,' in which iconographic details related to the academy and to the materials of writing (which might remind us of Chaucer and Christine) depict Aesop as a figure of 'embodied intellectual power.' The details of the two writers' interaction, however, undermine any sense of a hierarchical relationship, as the ancient author seems familiar with Henryson. In one of Henryson's apparently original touches, Aesop is portrayed as a saved pagan visiting from heaven. His 'prudence and moralitie' authorize him to critique Christian society, but he holds out little hope that the fable Henryson invites him to tell will secure his audience's attention. In response, Henryson asks Aesop to instruct him, confirming his crisis as fabulist and also placing Henryson 'on the same level as his audience.' Aesop's 'Lion and the Mouse' and his 'morality' express the secular idea that injustice will come back to haunt those who exercise power indifferently, but in his parting words before the narrator awakes, 'Aesop implicitly acknowledges the limits of his pagan wisdom' as he proposes that 'kirkmen' pray for an end to treason and the return of justice to Henryson's country. The following tale offers an implicit rebuke to Aesop's strictly secular moralizing, as it features a prologue and a vision (now a waking one) but a Christian setting and moral. The 'increasingly bleaker sequence of tales' that closes out the collection continues to portray the secular world as harsh, making it all the more necessary that Henryson supplement (and thus 'master') his received authority and 'pray for a Christian end,' including in the collection's closing words.

From the title-page of a 1515 volume of Erasmus's works, Mark Vessey develops several related ideas about Erasmus's influences, development, and self-presentation. Vessey traces three narratives – lexicographical, bibliographical, and biographical – which he sees converging in this volume. He begins with the word, *Lucubrationes*, which served as title for the volume, and which he translates as 'Works' or, more literally, 'Wakes' or 'Exertions by Lamplight.' This word and its cognates belong to classical and late-antique Latin prose, though 'the idea of burning the midnight oil' in order to read and write reaches back to Hellenistic poets and their Latin imitators. Vessey assumes these precedents made the idea 'part of the stock-in-trade of Latin writerly self-presentation' among Renaissance humanists, but proposes that 'Erasmus's talk of lucubration . . . has a distinctly, originally Erasmian accent.' In support of this idea, he explores the many uses of *lucubratio* and its cognates by Jerome, the early Christian writer whom Erasmus most admired. In addition, Vessey draws a connection between Aulus Gellius's use of *lucubratiunculae* ('trimmings of a late-burning lamp') to refer to the *Noctes Atticae* and Erasmus's use of the same word for a collection of his works published in 1503 (or 1504), a forerunner to the 1515 volume.

Turning from the lexicographical to the bibliographical, Vessey first outlines the contents and arrangement of the 1503 volume, which included works in 'a range of edifying genres.' The various contexts in which elements of this volume were published throughout Erasmus's career help to illuminate changes in how Erasmus conceived of himself as an author. While scholars have described Erasmus as shifting from poet to theologian in the first decade of the fifteenth century, Vessey argues that Erasmus would not have seen poetry and theology as opposed in the way this scholarly formula suggests they are. The *Lucubratiunculae* of 1503, he proposes, 'announced Erasmus's maturing sense of Christian, literary, and theological vocation' by invoking Christ as his Apollo and professing 'theology-as-poetry.' Vessey focuses on the 1500 *Adagiorum Collectanea* – referred to as *lucubrationes* in the volume's commendatory letter – as 'the advent of a new, more eclectic conception of humanist literary oeuvre.' The 1503 *Lucubratiunculae* confirms this development, for 'Erasmus presents himself as a humanist poet for whom poetry and humanism now represent a multigeneric, ultimately theological enterprise of textual instruction, conducted chiefly through print and largely in prose.'

This theory of scriptual poetics also informs the 1515 *Lucubrationes*, to which Vessey returns. The contents, arrangement, and even pagination of this volume, which contains about twice as many items as that of 1503, make all the clearer Erasmus's emphasis on prose. His collected editions of Seneca and Jerome, which appeared in print in 1515 and 1516, show that Erasmus now understood and used *lucubrationes* in a more capacious sense than his predecessors' (and than his own earlier) usage, 'to stand for the totality of a multigeneric oeuvre, as now critically edited and issued in print.' Together these editions 'established the profile of a learned, eloquent, and morally persuasive author-in-print to which Erasmus was now conforming his own output.' Not surprisingly, soon thereafter Erasmus was referring to his own collected oeuvre in similar terms; Martens in 1519 published a comprehensive list of Erasmus's writings under the title *Lucubrationum Erasmi Roterodami index*. Within a few years, Erasmus was outlining for correspondents his plans for a collected edition of his own works, a newly conceived *Lucubrationes Erasmi*, and those plans indeed became the basis for the organization of the posthumous *Opera omnia* and later collected editions, into the twentieth and current centuries.

Any number of ideas taken up in earlier essays reappear in Vessey's, thus demonstrating significant continuities between the Middle

Ages and the Renaissance in the theory and practice of authorship. For example, Erasmus looks to Jerome as an authorizing model, as had Pecock and other medieval predecessors. This relationship to Jerome is connected to Erasmus's desire to draw on classical texts and their poetics in a Christian context, as he sought ways to reconcile the authorities of the pagan classical and Christian patristic traditions – a project explored in its broad outlines by Minnis and by Higgins in the specific instance of Henryson. Vessey shows that Jerome made use of very specific language to identify his own writings with those of a prestigious literary culture, while he also enlarged the possible meanings of that language through his uses of it – as Chaucer seems to have done with his references to book-making and compilation. The mixture of modesty and self-assertion visible in Erasmus's use of *lucubratio* and its cognates reminds us of how often writers in this volume have perceived those attitudes together in medieval authors' references to their roles. The diversity of Erasmus's writings, together with his clear sense of them as an authorial canon, finds precedents in the careers of medieval writers as different (from him and from each other) as Chaucer, Christine de Pizan, and Reginald Pecock. Finally, as Erasmus used print as a means to define his authorship and his audience, medieval authors such as Christine had seen the advantages of shaping all aspects of the books that transmitted their works. Erasmus's new medium undeniably differed in important ways from the manuscript books which had preceded it, and the sixteenth century certainly brought major developments in intellectual and literary history. One imagines, however, that his age's books and their authors would not have seemed totally alien to the writers of early centuries, had they lived long enough to see them.

NOTES

1 Minnis, *Medieval Theory of Authorship*.
2 A partial list would include Brownlee, *Poetic Identity in Guillaume de Machaut*; Huot, *From Song to Book*; Watson, *Richard Rolle and the Invention of Authority*; Justice and Kerby-Fulton, *Written Work*; Andersen, *Autor und Autorschaft im Mittelalter*; Holmes, *Assembling the Lyric Self*; Zimmerman, *Auctor et auctoritas*; Coxon, *The Presentation of Authorship*; Minnis, *Magister Amoris*; Poor, *Mechthild of Magdeburg and Her Book*; Greene, *The Medieval*

Author in Medieval French Literature; Ascoli, *Dante and the Making of a Modern Author*; and Hobbins, *Authorship and Publicity Before Print*.

3 These approaches to medieval authorship of course resemble and are related to broader trends in literary scholarship. To choose only a few of very many possible examples, one may see points of sympathy and contact with such studies of the early modern period as Helgerson, *Self-Crowned Laureates*; Loewenstein, *Ben Jonson and Possessive Authorship*; and Pask, *The Emergence of the English Author*. For two recent studies that argue for greater continuity between the later Middle Ages and the early modern period than previous scholarship has tended to acknowledge, see Gillespie, *Print Culture and the Medieval Author*; and Griffiths, *John Skelton and Poetic Authority*. For two helpful, if selective, accounts of how medievalists have regarded the author, and of the relationship of this scholarship to broader trends in literary theory and criticism, see 'Introduction: The Author in the Text,' in Coxon, *The Presentation of Authorship*; and Virginie Greene, 'What Happened to Medievalists after the Death of the Author?'

4 While they cite a number of the same sources on the theory of the author and authorship, one notices how little overlap, in terms of specific studies, there is in the bibliographies of Justice and Kerby-Fulton, *Written Work*; Coxon, *The Presentation of Authorship*; and Greene, *The Medieval Author in Medieval French Literature*.

1 The Trouble with Theology: Ethical Poetics and the Ends of Scripture

ALASTAIR MINNIS

In May 2005, the medieval volume of the *Cambridge History of Literary Criticism* was published, edited by myself and Ian Johnson.[1] The general brief for this history was to produce an account of Western literary criticism which would deal with both literary theory and critical practice; such fields of knowledge as history of ideas, linguistics, philosophy, and theology were deemed 'related' but not essential, to be drawn upon when necessary but not forming part of the central core of the enterprise. The main consequence of this remit for the medieval volume was the omission of a substantial treatment of Bible commentary. This omission was unfortunate but inevitable, particularly given the limited amount of space allowed to cover some thousand years of textual commentary and controversy. It was dictated by the exigencies of publishing rather than ideological reasons. Any ideological attempt to exclude biblical exegesis from medieval literary-critical history must be contested. No book was more assiduously studied during the Middle Ages than the Bible; no text received more careful exegesis. Many crucial theoretical issues enjoyed full development, or indeed achieved initial definition, within medieval exposition of the 'sacred page,' whence they passed into secular poetics. Far from 'theological thinking' being essentially antithetical to 'literary criticism' (as O.B. Hardison has claimed),[2] on many occasions it served as a major stimulus to it.

The converse was also true. Interpretative techniques and exegetical discourses characteristic of secular poetics often had a considerable impact on biblical exegesis. Within a tradition of textual classification formalized in the early thirteenth century by Alexander of Hales O.F.M. (c. 1186–1245), and followed enthusiastically by many of his successors, the different styles and didactic modes deployed in the various books of the Bible were itemized and described at considerable length, with the 'poetic,' 'affective,' and 'imaginative' nature of certain types of writing being recognized and justified.[3] But this trend brought with it major anxieties. Were such means of enlisting human emotions unworthy of the superlative branch of knowledge, and – given that poetry was generally supposed to 'pertain to ethics' – was the queen of the sciences[4] in danger of being reduced to one of her subject disciplines? Such are the anxieties which this essay seeks to address.

There is no better method of tapping into the deep sources, the fundamental assumptions, of poetic theory in medieval Latin than to consider what the *accessus ad auctores* have to say.[5] These formal introductions to the authoritative writers taught in medieval grammar schools took on many forms; the most germane to our purpose are those which include the question typically formulated as: *cui parti philosophiae supponitur*, what part of philosophy is being taught in this particular text? And the most typical answer was: *ethice supponitur*, it pertains to ethics, serves as an agent of moral instruction. Concomitant with this classification was the identification of the end or objective (the *finis* or *finalis causa*) of a given poem, which frequently was defined as the motivation of its audience to flee from vice and follow virtue. There is no need to rehearse here the history of how this moralizing program was applied to a wide range of classroom texts, thereby promoting an 'ethical poetic.'[6] Many parts of that story have frequently been told, by myself and others. Suffice it to offer by way of example a late example of the genre, the *Prohemia poetarum* of Thomas Walsingham (died c. 1422), an English Benedictine based mainly at St Albans in Hertfordshire. Walsingham, although best known nowadays as a chronicler, was a classical (or, better, 'classicizing') scholar of some substance. His moralizing commentary on Ovid's *Metamorphoses*, the *Archana deorum*, has received at least some attention and is available in a modern edition.[7] In contrast, Walsingham's *Prohemia poetarum* is little known, the only available edition taking the form of a 1992 doctoral thesis.[8] It is essentially a collection of *accessus*, or rather a first draft of such a collection. Apparently Walsingham had planned to fill in more material later but never got round to it.[9] Perhaps we are dealing with the (very welcome) survival of only the first stage of an ambitious project.

Here, then, are the monk's *auctores,* listed according to the sequence followed in the *Prohemia* as we have it:

1 Virgil (*Aeneid, Bucolics, Georgics*)
2 Horace
3 Persius
4 Prudentius
5 Avianus
6 Statius (*Achilleid, Thebaid*)
7 John of Hanville (*Architrenius*)
8 'Theolulus'
9 Claudian
10 Alan of Lille (*Anticlaudianus*)
11 The *Pamphilus*
12 Bernardus (Palponista)
13 Maximian
14 Homer (*Ilias latina*)
15 Peter Riga
16 Sedulius (only two sentences)
17 Arator (only one sentence)
18 The *Tobias* (again, a single sentence)
19 Prosper (name only, no comment whatever: presumably Walsingham meant to insert material later)
20 Juvenal
21 Martianus Capella
22 Tibullus (a brief *vita*, the incipit, and a single quotation)
23 Walter of Chatillon (*Alexandreis*)
24 Aesop
25 Terence
26 Lucan
27 Martial (*Epigramata*; consisting mainly of quotations)
28 Statius (again – cf. item 6 above. Here Walsingham draws heavily on the commentary of Lactantius Placidus)
29 Ovid (a *vita* followed by an introduction to the *Metamorphoses*)
30 Seneca (*Hercules Furens, Thyestes, Thebais / Phoenissae, Ypolitus / Phaedra, Oedipus, Troades, Medea, Agamemnon*)
31 Claudian

The biggest surprise here is the inclusion of Seneca's tragedies – made even more intriguing by the fact that Walsingham seems ignorant of the extensive commentaries on those texts which his fellow-countryman Nicholas Trevet O.P. had produced in the early fourteenth century. (But that is hardly a surprise, given that this work had been commissioned by an Italian cardinal, Nicholas of Prato, and enjoyed a largely Italian reception.)[10] Trevet had brought the analytical techniques of the *accessus* tradition to bear on this new subject of scholastic commentary;[11] Walsingham does not attempt to do so, restricting himself to mere plot summary. The traditional 'ethical poetics' which permeates the *Prohemia poetarum* is, therefore, better illustrated by Walsingham's introduction to Persius. The mythic satyrs went about naked; in like manner satire is naked, because it reprehends the vices without ambiguity and in a naked and open style. Moreover, this genre functions in a derisory manner inasmuch as it laughs aloud at vice.[12] A discussion like this – which is typical of the *accessus ad satiricos* – evinces considerable respect for the emotive or 'affective' punch which a poem can pack.[13] It is supported by the later *accessus* to Juvenal, wherein the poet's intention is seen as castigating the Romans' wicked vices, and in particular warning the emperor about how deep-rooted they were.[14] John of Hanville is praised for continuing the tradition of satiric reprehension;[15] Prudentius's *Psychomachia* is identified as describing the hard-fought battle between the virtues and the vices.[16] In line with one of the standard *vitae Ovidii*, the poet is said to have made a great mistake in promoting immoral behaviour in his *Ars amatoria*; subsequently he sought to assuage the emperor's anger by writing the *Remedia amoris*.[17] And so on and so forth. All quite standard fare.

Such a belief in the moral purchase of poetry, as achieved through its characteristic affective and imaginative styles of writing, goes some way toward explaining one of the puzzles of the history of medieval literary theory and criticism: why was Averroes's *Middle Commentary* on Aristotle's *Poetics* (as translated into Latin by Hermann the German in 1256) preferred to the impressively accurate translation which William of Moerbeke produced in 1278?[18] Such success as Averroes/Hermann did enjoy (initially within a mainly Parisian milieu, though in the fourteenth and fifteenth centuries it was used by an impressive array of Italian schoolmen and protohumanists) may in large measure be attributed to the fact that medieval thinkers found this treatise more comprehensible within their hierarchies of the sciences, and in respect of long-established notions concerning the ethical aims and affective methods of poetry. Here, I believe, is where the cultural significance of the Averroes/Hermann *Poetics* commentary is to be located.

Rather than confining our attention to the extent of its influence (a question which, quite understandably, has received much attention), we should appreciate the ways in which it is symptomatic of crucial developments in medieval thought concerning poetics which indubitably *did* achieve considerable cultural penetration. The *Middle Commentary*'s affective 'ethical poetic' was consonant with other crucial hermeneutic developments of the later Middle Ages.

In Averroes/Hermann's reading of Aristotle, the concept of imitation (*mimesis*) has largely been replaced with that of imagination (*imaginatio*) or imagistic 'likening' (*assimilatio*), this being representation (*representatio*) of a kind that arouses people's emotions in a way that encourages them to follow virtue and flee from vice. Averroes/Hermann declares that since all *assimilatio* involves what is either becoming or base, the art of poetry must have as its purpose 'the pursuit of what is becoming and the rejection of what is base.'[19] Good men are to be praised and evil men are to be blamed, whence tragedy is defined as 'the art of praise' and comedy, which is reduced to satire, is defined as 'the art of blame' or vituperation. It follows that poetry should imaginatively heighten certain natural qualities relating to what is fair and what is foul, thus ensuring that the audience is in no doubt concerning its correct moral response.

This crucial reconfiguration of Aristotle's treatise at once explains and affords a rationale for Averroes/Hermann's move from a genre (drama) that enacts its performance in the theatre to a genre (poetry) that enacts its performance in the mind, from stage business to oral recitation or private reading. Dramatic plot-structure and strategy is transmuted into a pattern of affective textual messages. Applying these ideas in his commentary on Dante's *Commedia*, Benvenuto da Imola (d. 1388) described how the poem begins with representation of blameworthy sinners in Hell, proceeds with representation of the inhabitants of purgatory (who have some redeeming qualities), and ends with those who, having received their heavenly reward, are unqualifiedly worthy of praise and emulation. 'No other poet knew how to praise or blame with more excellence,' declares Benvenuto.[20]

Dante himself, however, seems to have been quite innocent of such Averroistic theory, and the same may be said of other major vernacular poets of the period, including Geoffrey Chaucer and the writers of romance in Middle High German. On the other hand, material from Hermann's Averroistic *Poetics* does appear in many intriguing, and sometimes quite unexpected, places, proof positive of what I have proposed here as a major reason for its relative success – i.e., its compatibility with prevailing cultural norms. As far as poetics in particular is concerned, Horace's *Ars poetica* did much to set such a norm, given its status as a school text attended by a fairly substantial commentary tradition. It is revealing therefore to observe Hermann and Horace being brought together without any apparent sense of strain in the *Poetria* of Matthew of Linköping, who is best known nowadays as the confessor and amanuensis of St Bridget of Sweden. This treatise, which seems to date from the 1320s, when Matthew was studying at the University of Paris, starts out with the Horatian comparison of the *poeta* with the *pictor*. 'The skilful painter, by the appropriate arrangement (*conuenienciam disposicio*) of the different parts and colours of the picture,' produces an agreeable representation of something that would not in itself be agreeable to look at.' 'In the same way,' Matthew continues, 'the perfect poet gives pleasure (*delectat animam*) by making us imagine a thing in accordance with its characteristics (*faciendo rem secundum suas proprietates imaginari*).'[21] Poetic imagination is accomplished by three means, representation (*representatio*), intonation (*tonum*), and metre (*metrum*) – here the influence of Averroes/Hermann is evident – but only *representatio* is of the very essence of poetry. Matthew defines *representatio* in terms which correspond to Hermann's account of *assimilatio*. Whereas other sciences attain their ends by means of rational arguments (*raciones*), poetry accomplishes its end by means of representation. And poetic representation seeks to move rather than prove; hence *laus poetica* is defined as 'something said in verse that incites to the virtues.'[22]

Moving further back, to the early days of the study of the 'new' Aristotle by Christian scholars, it may be noted that the Averroes/Hermann emphasis on affectivity also seems to have exercised a considerable influence on the poetics of Roger Bacon (c. 1220–c. 1292) – despite the fact that Bacon questioned Hermann's competence as a translator.[23] This criticism does not involve any distaste for the Aristotelian ideas in question; on the contrary, Bacon's point is that the philosopher's translators lack the skills to do his thought full justice. Referring to poetry in particular, he laments the fact that 'we do not have the full thinking of Aristotle in Latin.'[24] And there speaks a scholar who knew the Moerbeke *Poetics* as well as the Averroes/Hermann exposition. Bacon wanted to hear more on the subject rather than less.

Bacon shares with Averroes/Hermann an appreciation of how poetry can move the souls of its audience members to good. He draws upon Aristotle's great Arab commentators in emphasizing the extent to which 'moral science' (*moralis sciencia*) can make profitable use of what we might call 'literary' methods to enlist human emotions in the pursuit of the good. Sublime and decorous words have the power to carry away the soul to love the good and detest the bad, Bacon argues. He goes so far as to claim that scripture and moral philosophy rely on the same kind of poetical argument.[25] To prove this challenging point, he draws parallels between the poetical modes used by secular writers and those found in holy scripture. The beauty of metrical and rhythmical texts is vigorously defended, with support from Averroes/Hermann, Avicenna, and Al-Farabi. In short, the notion that Bacon 'attacked poetry' for, *inter alia*, its 'resistance to logical paraphrase' is very wide of the mark.[26]

Although Bacon stands out as something of an intellectual 'loner' in his academic milieu, many of his great scholastic contemporaries also expressed considerable interest in the wide range of didactic styles to be found in scripture, though their theoretical language differed from Bacon's, in that they considered them together under such headings as *modi agendi/tractandi/procedendi* and *formae tractandi*, and frequently placed them under the general heading *causa formalis*, this being one of the Aristotelian 'four causes' which frequently appear as an analytical device in thirteenth-century prefaces to a wide range of authoritative texts. An excellent example is found in the prologue to the *Breviloquium* which St Bonaventure O.F.M. wrote between 1254 and 1257. Discussing the *modus procedendi* of holy scripture, Bonaventure explains:

Among all the many kinds of wisdom which are contained in . . . holy scripture, there is one common way of proceeding: by authority. Grouped within it are the narrative, perceptive, prohibitive, exhortatory, instructive, threatening, promising, supplicating, and laudatory modes. All these modes come within the scope of that one mode, proceeding by authority, and quite rightly so.

This doctrine exists in order that we should become good and be redeemed, and this is not achieved by deliberation alone, but rather by a disposition of the will. Therefore, holy scripture had to be handed down to us in whatever way would dispose us best [to goodness]. Our affections are moved more strongly by examples than by arguments, by promises than by logical reasonings, by devotions than by definitions. Scripture, therefore, had to avoid the mode of proceeding by definition, division, and inferring to prove the properties of some subject, as do the other sciences. It had rather to adapt its own modes to the various dispositions of men's minds which incline those minds differently. Thus, if a man is not moved to heed precepts and prohibitions, he may at least be moved by the examples narrated; if someone is not moved by these, he may be moved by the benefits which are pointed out to him; and if he is not moved by these, he may be moved by wise warnings, by promises which ring true, by terrifying threats; and thus be stirred to devotion and praise of God, and therefore receive grace which will guide him to the practice of virtuous works.

These narrative modes cannot proceed by way of certainty based on reasoning, because particular facts do not admit of formal proof. Therefore, lest scripture should seem doubtful, and consequently should have less power to move [men's minds], instead of certainty based on reasoning God has provided it with certainty based on authority, which is so great that it rises high above the most acute human mind.[27]

Here Bonaventure is building on the highly influential distinction between the two kinds of *modus* which Alexander of Hales had made in his *Summa theologica*. Behind Bonaventure's commendation of the stylistic abundance and flexibility of holy scripture, which exploited every means possible (precepts, prohibitions, examples, etc.) to appeal to the diverse dispositions of men's minds, lies Alexander's assertion that the Bible may not be judged 'unscientific' or doubtful in its truth-claims because it 'proceeds' in a way which 'is poetic or historical or parabolical,' these being methods which are not appropriate to any human art or science 'which operates by means of the comprehension of human reason.'[28] Biblical science, as Alexander eloquently explains, has the special task of inculcating a pious disposition (*affectus pietatis*), whereas the lesser sciences are concerned only with educating the intellect to know the truth, and therefore they use the standard logical methods of analysis (definition, analysis, deduction, and so forth). The supreme science of theology has a far more important end in view – the redemption of men. Is its *multiplex modus*, then, capable of certain verification, i.e., can we be sure that its doctrine is in some sense true?[29] Of course, the answer is 'yes' – true in terms of experience and disposition rather than investigation and intellect, and certain in respect of that knowledge which is transmitted 'through God's spirit' rather than that which is transmitted merely though the 'human spirit.'[30]

These excursus by Alexander and Bonaventure seem to up-end the traditional hierarchy of knowledge as elaborated by Islamic and

Christian commentators on Aristotle's *Organon* – i.e., the corpus of logical texts – and give affective poetics and rhetoric pride of place. The *Rhetoric* and the *Poetics* were deemed the seventh and eighth parts of this collection, far inferior to the *Prior* and *Posterior Analytics*, which are concerned with syllogisms that proceed from true and necessary premises (as in metaphysics).[31] What, then, do rhetoric and poetics offer? The former seeks to persuade and employs the enthymeme and the *exemplum*; the latter has imaginative representation as its purpose and the imaginative syllogism as its characteristic device.

This is hardly a ringing recommendation of the truth value of rhetoric and poetry, which have, as their stock and trade, those very devices which, as our citation from Bonaventure has exemplified, were listed in the context of discussions which established theology as the queen of the sciences. Why not, then, simply denigrate the higher texts within the *Organon*'s hierarchy as serving those merely human sciences which proceed by 'definition, division, and inferring,' and elevate the humble *Rhetoric* and *Poetics*, just as Christ himself had elevated the poor and the lowly? After all, had not Christ and the apostles preached to people from all walks of life through language which was common, broad, and gross (*grossus*), making excellent use of affective, figurative, metaphorical, and indeed poetic methods, in many cases originating (or at least adopting) those *modi* which generations of theologians identified as the Bible's distinctive, and therefore prestigious, *formae tractandi*?[32]

No theologian (to the best of my knowledge) was quite prepared to go that far. There was no desire to call in question a system of instruction in argumentation that had been in place for many centuries, and that, after all, could be put to good use in scriptural exegesis; no one called for logic's superior position in the schools to be ceded to poetics, so that the scriptural *modi* might better be understood. Whether by accident or design (it is hard to tell), in this instance medieval scholars managed to think in compartments, thereby preventing these different systems of valuation from coming into direct confrontation. Poetry continued to be demoted within the *Organon*, even as it was promoted within theologians' accounts of the *multiplex modus* of scripture.

This situation was exacerbated by other doctrine derived from Aristotle – not from the *Organon* this time, but from the *Nicomachean Ethics*. As Aristotle 'writes in the second book of the *Ethics*, we undertake moral study not for the sake of abstract contemplation, nor to gain knowledge, but in order that we may become good.'[33] Thus Giles of Rome draws on Aristotle at the beginning of his highly popular *De regimine principum* (c. 1285). He continues:

> ... the end (*finis*) in this science [i.e., ethics][34] is not to gain knowledge concerning its own matter, but [moral] activity (*opus*); it is not truth but goodness. Since subtle arguments, therefore, are more effective in illuminating the intellect, while those that are superficial and broad (*superficiales vero et grosse*) are more effective in stirring and firing the affections (*affectus*), in the speculative sciences, where the main aim is the illumination of the intellect, one must proceed by way of proof and in a subtle manner, but in moral matters (*in negocio morali*), where the goal is an upright will and that we should become good, one must proceed by way of persuasion and the use of figures (*persuasive et figuraliter*).[35]

This Aristotelian justification of ethics serves well Giles's purpose of introducing a treatise wherein a 'broad and figurative' mode of procedure is used. But it bears a troubling resemblance to Bonaventure's justification of the *modus procedendi* of sacred scripture, as quoted earlier. This is not coincidental, since Bonaventure clearly has in mind the very same passage of Aristotle's *Ethics* that is cited explicitly by Giles of Rome in his account of the *modus procedendi* followed in the instruction of princes. Further evidence of Bonaventure's debt to Aristotle is afforded by his assertion that 'particular facts do not admit of formal proof,' from which the theologian infers that scripture's narrative modes, being concerned with particular facts, are not susceptible of such proof, it being impossible to gain 'certainty based on reasoning' in such a case. This derives from Aristotle's statement in book ii, chapter 2 of the *Ethics* that 'things pertaining to actions ... do not have anything fixed about them,' and thus are uncertain (and hence unprovable) in scientific terms. Indeed, Giles of Rome had quoted that very same passage a little earlier in his introduction to *De regimine principum*, noting that 'the subject-matter of morals ... concerns individual matters, matters which, as is shown in the *Ethics*, book ii, are very uncertain because of the variability of their nature.'[36]

Apparently, both the Bible and Aristotelian ethics have as their goal moral action, making men good, and the correct disposition of the human will rather than the illumination of the intellect. May it be concluded, then, that the ends (and the means to those ends) of ethics and theology are the same, indeed that the Bible may be deemed an ethical book, judged to fall within the scope of morals and classified under 'practical' (as opposed to 'theoretical') philosophy as defined by Aristotle? Or, in other words, that it 'pertains to ethics,' just like all those lesser texts which served the curricula of medieval grammar schools? Quite a lot for the queen of the sciences to swallow, surely, despite the sugar put on the pill by Aristotle's powerful celebration of ethics.

This problem seems to have arisen whenever the 'new' Aristotle was brought into contact with *doctrina Christiana*, as may be illustrated with reference, once more, to Roger Bacon. Bacon asserts that the speculative procedures of dialectic and demonstration are unsuitable for moral philosophy because, as Aristotle says in the *Ethics*, its end is not that we should contemplate grace, but rather that we should become good.[37] A much better job is done by a kind of rhetoric which deals with subjects that move us to labour in the service of 'divine worship, laws, and virtues.' This kind of rhetoric, Bacon explains, is called 'poetic' by Aristotle and other philosophers, because, rightly understood, poets have as their true mission the direction of men to the honesty of virtue. While the speculative sciences delight in argument, opinion, and knowledge for its own sake, the 'practical sciences' consider arguments *ad praxim*, with the aim of inciting men to good works. Likewise, poetical argument pursues vice and honours virtue in order that men may be attracted to honour and moved to hatred of sin. Crucially, for Bacon the 'practical sciences' are theology and moral philosophy.[38] This bringing together of these two sciences is quite understandable in view of Bacon's exceptionally high opinion of *moralis sciencia*, an opinion which few of his Parisian successors shared in such an extreme form. And they were more aware of the dangers of appearing to reduce theology to ethics than their cantankerous but brilliant predecessor had been.

Such an anxiety may be discerned in Bonaventure's *Breviloquium*, in the passage quoted on pp. 26–7 above. He addressed it emphasizing where true authority lay, by referring all the narrative modes of the Bible back to its ultimate *auctor*, God. Holy scripture has 'one common way of proceeding: by authority.' And grouped within this multiple *modus* are all the specific, individual narrative modes. 'All these modes come within the scope of that one mode, proceeding by authority,' Bonaventure says, and quite rightly so – the implication being that, no matter how those modes are employed by other (merely human) authors, no matter how humble they may be in other hands and in other contexts, in holy scripture they are under divine control, at the disposal of God. And therefore their prestige – in the Bible at least – is unquestionable. Bonaventure's solution, then, is to appeal to unique authorship, rather than seek to valorize the specific modes themselves. That way, a decorous distance is maintained between ethics and theology, between poetics and sacred science.

And yet – the apparent similarities between them could be exploited to great effect by innovative literary theorists of trecento Italy, including Petrarch and Boccaccio, as they laboured to elevate the status of poetry. 'Poetry is not at all inimical to theology,' Petrarch declares. 'I would almost say that theology is poetry written about God. When Christ is called, now a lion, now a lamb, and again a worm, what is that if not poetic? You will find a thousand more instances in holy scripture . . .' He goes on to argue that the Saviour's parables in the Gospel employ discourse wherein the meaning differs from the normal sense of the words, 'to which we give the more usual name of allegory,' a device regularly used by the poets.[39] A fuller version of this argument is offered in Boccaccio's *Genealogia deorum gentilium*, where it is emphasized that many literary devices – including pure fiction – are shared by secular and scriptural authors. Of all the thirteenth-century theologians I have read, the one who seems to anticipate this position most fully is Roger Bacon, who, as we have seen, claimed that scripture and moral philosophy often relied on the same kind of poetical argument, and, to prove it, pointed to many parallels between the poetical modes used by secular writers and those found in the Bible. But Bacon was just one among many schoolmen who furthered the tradition of describing the *multiplex modus* of holy scripture (to revert once again to Alexander of Hales's discourse) in ways which highlighted its affective, imaginative, figurative, and even fictive properties.

That tradition was pervasive and highly influential; Boccaccio draws on it to great effect in constructing a comprehensive relationship between poetry and theology, which powerfully serves the cause of poetry. Of course, as he freely admits in his *Trattatello in laude di Dante*, 'the holy and the secular writings do not . . . have a common end (*fine*; cf. the Latin term *finis*) in view.' All that the poets can show us is 'how we may, by behaving virtuously, achieve that end (*fine*) which they, not knowing the true God aright, believed to be the supreme salvation.'[40] In other words (though Boccaccio does not actually put it like this), their poetry pertains to ethics, and its end is limited by the pagans' ignorance of revealed Christian truth. But these (very real) differences do not drive a firm wedge between poetry and theology; the lesser end of poetry is certainly not antithetical to the greater end of theology. And there is no doubt that they 'share a common mode of treatment (*modo del trattare*; cf. the Latin *modus tractandi*).'[41]

In his *Genealogia*, Boccaccio brilliantly builds on the common ground which poetry and theology supposedly share, directing theological discourse to serve the cause of poetry. The argument that the obscurity of poetry is no reason for condemning it is supported by theological defences of the obscurity of holy scripture. Here Augustine is cited to good effect, as 'a man of great sanctity and learning' who freely admitted his inability to understand the beginning of Isaiah (this being a means of claiming textual obscurity as empowering of scripture).[42] Furthermore, Boccaccio supports his declaration that the poets are not really liars with theologians' affirmations that the Bible is never false or mendacious, though it sometimes uses fictions and even on occasion seems to recount blatant lies.[43] Here once again Augustine appears, and a particularly trenchant argument is developed from the use of 'not literally true' discourse by St John (in the Apocalypse) and the other prophets:

> My opponents will add that their [the prophets'] writings are not fiction but rather figures, to use the correct term, and their authors are figurative writers. O silly subterfuge! As if I were likely to believe that two things to all appearances exactly alike should gain the power of different effects by mere change or difference of name.[44]

A mere change of name does not make the problem go away, or airbrush away the evident fact that both sacred and secular writers are using one and the same literary technique.

Not everyone approved of this method of dignifying poetry, however, as is made abundantly clear by the vigorous reaction of Girolamo Savonarola (d. 1498),[45] who sought to make a bonfire of such vanities. It cannot be argued, he declared, that just because poetry and theology both use metaphors, therefore 'poetry is nothing else than theology.' Offering a more stringent version of the distinction which Thomas Aquinas had made between metaphor in poetry and metaphor in theology,[46] he asserts that it is one thing 'to use metaphors because of necessity and the magnitude of the subject,' as in the Bible, and quite 'another to use them for pleasure and weakness of truth,' as in pagan poetry.[47]

Here, then, was the trouble with theology. The fact that it shared certain styles and methods of literary procedure with the writings of the poets, who habitually were branded as liars, obliged generation after generation of medieval theologians to defend the epistemological and moral credentials of their subject and the 'scientific' basis of its knowledge. The tradition that poetry 'pertained to ethics' offered some help, which could hardly be accepted (indeed, I know of no explicit medieval address of the matter) because it threatened to replace one problem with another. For, if the difference between poetry and theology were reduced significantly, the status of the higher science would be questioned, the spectre raised of theology being reduced to ethics, a branch of merely practical philosophy. (But what was problematic for theology was good news for poetics. In trecento literary theory such a reduction of difference between them was asserted and exploited for the greater glory of poetry, as argued above.) If, on the other hand, one wished to emphasize the more ratiocinative and intellectual aspects of theology, then that tended to place theology within the same category as the higher logical sciences (with their characteristic *modus procedendi* of definition, division, and inference). While this was a more elevated position within the classifying system of the *Organon* – the same system that placed poetics at the very bottom of its epistemological hierarchy – it was insufficiently elevated for the supreme science of theology, which had sources of knowledge that even the cleverest of pagan thinkers knew nothing about, the revealed and eternal truths of Christianity. Such pearls could not, should not, be cast before swine. And yet – during his earthly ministry the Son of God, Jesus Christ himself, had preached with humble and homely parables, thereby rendering his message accessible to all, even the most lowly.

Little wonder, then, that late medieval thinkers should return, again and again, to confront the poetic qualities of scriptural style. They could invoke the unique (because divinely inspired) authorship of the Bible, emphasize the more comprehensive and infinitely more important end of theology (which seeks salvation rather than moral goodness), and indeed use a positive term like 'figure' in their scriptural exegesis instead of a negative one like 'fiction' (to recall Boccaccio's astute remark). By such means, they sought to affirm the superiority of Holy Writ over the texts discussed in (for example) Thomas Walsingham's *Prohemia poetarum*, that representative repository of ethical poetics with which this paper began. But whatever they did, this particular trouble would not go away. Nor could it go away. For the debate was fundamentally about substance rather than style, ultimate goals and final causes rather than formalism and fine expression. It was about what separated Christianity from the Roman paganism it had superseded; whether it belonged to the many or the few; if its definitive language was basically exclusive or inclusive, élitist or demotic; or whether it embraced all of those attributes, given that the one and only true faith was not susceptible to containment and restriction by sublunar categories.

It would seem, then, that this investigation of the fraught relationship between poetry and theology in late medieval thought has led us to the major underlying question of what sort of pedagogy the great medieval schoolmen believed to be appropriate to Christianity – how they quantified its mission as a catholic (i.e., universal) and apostolic movement, and what the consequences were for how believers were to be instructed, the ways in which theology's 'own modes' should be adapted 'to the various dispositions of men's minds' (here I return one last time to my extensive quotation from Bonaventure's *Breviloquium*). In their time, and far beyond their time, no issue has proved more troublesome within the history of the church.

NOTES

1 Minnis and Johnson, *Cambridge History of Literary Criticism*. Henceforth referred to as *CHLC* 2.
2 Hardison, 'History of Medieval Literary Criticism.'
3 On these accounts of the various styles and didactic modes characteristic of theology, and their place within inquiries into the 'scientific' basis of theology, see especially Chenu, *La Théologie comme science*; and Köpf, *Die Anfänge der theologischen Wissenschaftstheorie*. Köpf's listing of the topics discussed in some twenty-six prologues to *summae* and *Sentences* commentaries, along with relevant collections of *quaestiones* (276–85), makes very clear the central importance of the *modus sacrae scripturae* within this type of investigation.
4 Here, and throughout this paper, I use 'science' to translate the Latin *scientia*, meaning simply a body of knowledge in contrast with the main contemporary use of the term as designating experimental science.
5 The bibliography on this subject has grown rapidly. The three important initial studies are: Przychocki, '*Accessus Ovidiani*'; Quain, 'Medieval *Accessus ad auctores*'; and Hunt, '*Artes* in the Twelfth Century.' For a particularly interesting collection see Huygens, *Accessus ad auctores*, 19–54; see also

Elliott, '*Accessus ad auctores*: Twelfth-Century Introductions to Ovid.' For further bibliography see *CHLC* 2.

6 Here I use the term popularized by Judson B. Allen's magnum opus, *The Ethical Poetic of the Later Middle Ages*.

7 Thomas Walsingham, *De archana deorum*. On Walsingham see further Rigg, *Anglo-Latin Literature*, 297–8, and Clark, 'Thomas Walsingham Reconsidered.'

8 Heriot, '*Prohemia poetarum Fratris Thome de Walsingham*.'

9 Revealingly, the *Prohemia* is extant in a single manuscript (British Library, MS Harley 2693), which may be in the monk's own hand, and which displays clear evidence (not least the blank spaces where, presumably, material was to be inserted) of a text in the very process of composition.

10 On Trevet's Seneca commentaries, see Minnis and Scott, *Medieval Literary Theory*, 324–8 and 340–60.

11 Trevet says that Seneca composed his tragedies so he might 'instill into tender minds ethical teachings wrapped in *fabulae*, while at the same time amusing them, and might through these teachings root out vices, sow his seed, and reap a rich reward in the form of the various virtues.' The *causa finalis* of the *Hercules Furens*, in particular, is said to be 'the enjoyment (*delectatio*) of its audience – or else, insofar as there are narrated here some actions which are praiseworthy and some which deserve censure, the book can in a certain manner be placed in the category of ethics.' Hence, in this latter case, the end of Seneca's text may be described as 'the correction of behaviour by means of the examples set out here.' Tr. Minnis and Scott, *Medieval Literary Theory*, 342 and 346.

12 Heriot, '*Prohemia poetarum*,' 46.

13 On medieval commentary on Roman satire, see Kindermann, *Satyra*; Miller, 'John Gower, Satiric Poet'; and Reynolds, *Medieval Reading*.

14 Heriot, '*Prohemia poetarum*,' 60–2.

15 Ibid., 50–1.

16 Ibid., 47–8.

17 Ibid., 91–2.

18 On this work, see Minnis and Scott, *Medieval Literary Theory*, 277–307; Gillespie, 'Study of Classical Authors,' 167 and 171–7; and Minnis, 'Medieval Imagination and Memory,' 252–5.

19 Tr. Minnis and Scott, *Medieval Literary Theory*, 283.

20 Cf. Preminger, Hardison, and Kerrane, *Classical and Medieval Literary Criticism*, 346–7.

21 Matthew of Linköping, *Testa nucis* and *Poetria*, 46–7. See further Minnis, 'Acculturizing Aristotle.'

22 Matthew of Linköping, *Testa nucis* and *Poetria*, 54–5.
23 On Bacon's poetic theory, see the excellent account by Gillespie, 'Study of Classical Authors,' 161, 169–71 and 174. See further Hackett, 'Roger Bacon.'
24 *Moralis philosophia*, pars VI, 4, p. 267, translated and discussed by Gillespie in 'Study of Classical Authors,' 171.
25 Cf. Gillespie, 'Study of Classical Authors,' 170.
26 Preminger, Hardison, and Kerrane, *Classical and Medieval Literary Criticism*, 311.
27 *Breviloquium*, Prologue, 5, tr. Minnis and Scott, *Medieval Literary Theory*, 235–6.
28 *Summa Alexandri*, tractatus introductorius, qu. 1, cap. 4, art. 1; tr. Minnis and Scott, *Medieval Literary Theory*, 212–15.
29 *Summa Alexandri*, tract. int., qu. 1, cap. 4, art. 2; tr. Minnis and Scott, *Medieval Literary Theory*, 215–17.
30 Tr. Minnis and Scott, *Medieval Literary Theory*, 217.
31 Cf. Minnis and Scott, *Medieval Literary Theory*, 279–81.
32 Such doctrine was characteristic of the medieval *artes praedicandi*. Cf. Minnis, *Medieval Theory of Authorship*, 136–8.
33 Giles here is citing the *Nicomachean Ethics*, ii.2 (1103b, 26–8).
34 Ethics as applied here in the education of princes. Giles's treatise also offers instruction in other branches of practical philosophy (economics or family management and politics) as understood within medieval Aristotelianism.
35 *De regimine principum libri III*, lib. I, cap. 1: *Quis modus procedendi in regimine principum* (Rome, 1556), fol. 2r–2v; tr. Minnis and Scott, *Medieval Literary Theory*, 249.
36 Tr. Minnis and Scott, *Medieval Literary Theory*, 248.
37 Bacon, like Giles, cites the *Nicomachean Ethics*, ii.2 (1103b, 26–8); see Gillespie, 'Study of Classical Authors,' 170, for a paraphrase and discussion of this passage from Bacon's *Moralis philosophia*, pars V, cap. 2.3.
38 Cf. Gillespie, 'Study of Classical Authors,' 170.
39 *Letters on Familiar Matters*, x.4, to his brother Gherardo; tr. Minnis and Scott, *Medieval Literary Theory*, 413. Petrarch immediately admits that poetry and theology differ in their subject matter: the subject of holy scripture is God and matters divine, whereas in poetry (evidently he is thinking of pagan poetry) it is man and the gods. But even here an empowering connection may be found. 'The poets were the first theologians,' as Aristotle says (*Metaphysics* i.2; 982b); that elementary knowledge of things divine which is found in secular poetry came to enjoy its full flowering in poetry

about God. The subject matters of theology and poetry are not, it seems,
utterly opposed.

40 *Trattatello in laude di Dante,* red. 1, tr. by David Wallace in Minnis and Scott,
    Medieval Literary Theory, 494–5.
41 *Trattatello,* tr. Wallace, 495.
42 *Genealogia* xiv.12, tr. Minnis and Scott, *Medieval Literary Theory,* 428–31.
43 *Genealogia* xiv.13, tr. Minnis and Scott, *Medieval Literary Theory,* 431–6.
44 *Genealogia* xiv.13, tr. Minnis and Scott, *Medieval Literary Theory,* 433.
45 See Minnis, 'Fifteenth Century Versions of Literalism.'
46 'Poetry employs metaphors for the sake of representation, for this is some-
    thing which naturally gives men pleasure' (here the influence of Aristotle's
    Poetics is evident, probably in the version of Averroes/Hermann the Ger-
    man). 'But sacred instruction uses metaphors because they are necessary .
    and useful . . .' *Summa theologica,* 1a 1, art, 9, ad 1um; tr. Minnis and Scott,
    Medieval Literary Theory, 240.
47 Cf. Hardison, *The Enduring Monument,* 7.

2 Wit, Laughter, and Authority in Walter Map's *De nugis curialium* (Courtiers' Trifles)

SEBASTIAN COXON

The following anecdote concerning Walter Map, for many years a clerk at the Angevin court of Henry II, is included in a collection of stories entered by 'a 13th-century hand'[1] in Oxford, Corpus Christi College MS 32:

> A clerk of King Henry, rich in revenues but miserly, said to Walter Map in jest: 'Master Walter, you wear your age well.' He replied: 'What do you mean?' to which the former said: 'To wear your age well is to be old and not to seem it.' Walter Map replied: 'In the same manner you carry your revenues. For you have much and spend little.' (fol. 95r)[2]

One suspects that Walter Map would have been very pleased with this image of himself: the witty clerk who occupies the higher moral ground but, on being provoked, is not afraid to use his intellect and eloquence to strike back in exemplary rhetorical fashion, turning the words – and force – of an antagonistic joke back against his opponent.[3] Map might also have approved of this anecdote as evidence of a new-found authorial status regardless of the historical veracity of the incident thereby recorded. If true, then the very fact that the incident is written up in this way presupposes that the sayings of Map are worth collecting,[4] that he has an authority (*auctoritas*) of some kind.[5] If not true, then Map's name was clearly considered appropriate as an authorial tag for such a witticism, legitimizing the circulation and transmission of this material for the benefit of subsequent generations.[6]

The free-standing anecdote itself seems to anticipate the kind of *facetum dictum* or witty saying which late medieval humanists liked to collect,[7] and which on occasion could give rise to an author-mythology.

This is most famously the case with Dante whose wit is attested to in exactly this form by the papal secretary Poggio Bracciolini (1380–1459) in his *Liber facetiarum* (earliest extant print 1471). Here brief accounts of Dante's devastating wit serve to consolidate the authority of the preeminent yet vulnerable poet in exile who excites envy and hostility in the mean-minded, is the subject of unwarranted verbal attacks and pranks, and is consequently granted the licence to be as cutting as he pleases in response.[8] Viewed in this light the (isolated) Map anecdote in the Corpus Christi manuscript might also be read as an instance of author-mythology that fixes Walter Map in the analogous role of the disadvantaged yet brilliantly witty clerk.[9] The decades following Map's death in 1209 or 1210 thus not only witnessed the considerable exaggeration of his authorial output, but also the onset of a distinctive mode of discourse concerning Map the historical persona.[10] What is particularly intriguing about this is the possibility that Map himself set this whole process in motion in the work for which he is best known today: *De nugis curialium* (Courtiers' Trifles).

Authorship has always been a focal point of scholarly interest in *De nugis*. Indeed, the work, both as a material object and as a literary text, may be held to illustrate many of the most important issues and problems associated with authorship in the Middle Ages. In codicological terms a handful of rubrics assert and maintain Map's authorship at various points.[11] At the same time the single extant fourteenth-century copy of the work preserves the text in an extremely dishevelled state.[12] It seems likely that Map wrote the bulk of his text in a space of a few years in the early 1180s, adding to it many times in the years that followed, before undertaking, but never completing, a reorganization of the whole. The role that scribes may have played in the production of a (relatively) fair copy, either under his supervision or posthumously, is equally unclear. The text remains full of inconsistencies, repetitions, and gaps, which evoke an image of Map as an author who struggled to exercise control over his highly varied material that included satirical commentary, a host of colourful (and in some cases masterful) short narratives, and historiographical reportage. As Siân Echard has observed, the glue which holds this disparate collection together is Map's projection of himself in the text by means of a mass of authorial comment, intervention, and self-reference.[13] Quite apart from his self-presentation as eye-witness and participant in important historical events surrounding the court of Henry II, Map reflects at length on the roles of writer and reader, that is to say, on the respective processes of literary authorship and reception. He compares the ideal reader to the industrious bee,[14] and likens himself, rather more comically, to a braying ass,[15] a huntsman,[16] a naked unarmed fighter,[17] and, most tellingly of all, to a modern writer who has only to die to be better received as an author:

> My only offence is, that I am alive; it is, however, one which I have no intention of correcting – by dying . . . I know what will happen when I am gone. When I have begun to rot, the book will begin to gain savour, my decease will cover all its defects, and in the remotest generations my ancientness will gain me dignity: for then, as now, old copper will be of more account than new gold. (IV, 5 [313])

Echard argues that Map's overriding concern in such passages is the provocative subversion and assertion of authority.[18] This reading is doubtless correct, but it may also be usefully developed with reference to Map's narrative depiction of himself as an 'actor' in various court scenes, and quite specifically those which revolve around outstanding moments of wit. Walter Map was evidently the first collector of his own bon mots. It remains to be seen what form these take in *De nugis*, and what exactly their text-internal functions are, before considering how they might relate to the author-mythology suggested by the subsequent separate transmission of Map's witty sayings in the thirteenth century.

The anecdotal accounts of Map's own wit are spread unevenly throughout *De nugis*, clustered in the first and fifth books or *distinctiones* of the text as it now stands. The comic incidents described are drawn from both of the major phases in Map's career as a clerk in public life, the first of which places him at the court of Gilbert Foliot, bishop of London (1163–87):[19]

> So also, two white abbots were conversing about Bernard [of Clairvaux] in the presence of Gilbert Foliot, bishop of London, and commending him on the strength of his miracles. After relating a number of them, one of the abbots said: 'Though these stories of Bernard are true, I did myself see that on occasion the grace of miracles failed him. There was a man living on the borders of Burgundy who asked him to come and heal his son. We went, and found the son dead. Dom Bernard ordered his body to be

carried into a private room, turned everyone out, threw himself upon the
boy, prayed, and got up again: but the boy did not get up; he lay there
dead.' 'Then he was the most unlucky of monks,' said I; 'I have heard
before now of a monk throwing himself upon a boy, but always, when the
monk got up, the boy promptly got up too.' The abbot went very red, and
a lot of people left the room to have a good laugh. (I, 24 [81])

In this, the most aggressive of all of his bon mots, Map indirectly pours
scorn on the sanctity of Bernard of Clairvaux by deliberately usurping
the reverential Cistercian tale of the latter's occasional failure to per-
form a miracle in order to voice the (obscene) slur of the pederastic tendencies of monks. The Cistercian tale itself is phrased in terms of one of
the miracles of the prophet Elisha (2 Kings 4:34),[20] and it is feasible that
Map wanted his readers to perceive this as a further provocation, justi-
fying his remarkably profane response. That Map claims to have been
speaking with the approval of many of those present is made clear by
the detail of the collective laughter ('ut riderent plurimi') provoked by
his witticism, albeit away from the bishop's presence, the dignity of the
latter's office proving still to be a restraining force on those gathered
around him. Nevertheless, this anecdote is testimony to Map's desire
to arrogate for himself the licence to joke freely and to voice what others dare only to think. In the immediate context of *De nugis* this episode most particularly serves to establish Map's satirical credentials in
advance of his bitter review of 'monachia' (monkery) in the following
chapter (I, 25 [84–112]).[21]

The religious theme of the final chapters in *distinctio* I also provides
the context for the next relevant anecdote (I, 31) in which Map's wit is –
apparently – put to a more obviously serious purpose on the grander
ecclesiastical stage of the Third Lateran Council of 1179 (attended by
Map in the service of Henry II):

The bishop bade me try my hand against them [two Waldensians], and I
prepared myself to answer. First, therefore, I put to them very simple questions which ought to be unknown to no one, for I was aware that when an
ass eats thistles, his lips count lettuce unworthy of them. 'Do you believe
in God the Father?' They answered: 'We do.' 'And in the Son?' They answered: 'We do.' 'And in the Holy Ghost?' They answered: 'We do.' I said
again: 'And in the mother of Christ?' And they once more: 'We do.' And
by everyone present they were hooted down with universal clamour, and
went away ashamed . . . (I, 31 [127])

Map's verbal dexterity is a means to a political end here, or so we are meant to believe, enabling the Council to dismiss and greatly diminish the importance of the Waldensian heretics by holding them up for ridicule.[22] Rather than a single cutting response, Map's rhetorical craft lies in linguistic entrapment through a simple series of leading questions requiring the Waldensians only to affirm their belief in the Trinity. Lulled into a false sense of security, they then 'mechanically'[23] answer a fourth and quite patently ludicrous question in the same way, thereby appearing to believe in a Quaternity. Map may feel compelled to prepare the recipients of *De nugis* for this joke with the somewhat obscure reference to the stupidity of a donkey that cannot distinguish what is good from what is not: a lack of discrimination then that will be seen to characterize the foolish Waldensians as well. However, the collective raucous derision ('ab omnibus multiplici sunt clamore derisi') that Map describes as breaking out at this moment of the interview demonstrates once more the success of his joke *in situ*.

The moral imperative that informs Map's application of his wit in public also holds good to a certain extent in the second cluster of pertinent anecdotes occurring in *dist.* V, which depict Map at the Angevin court itself, although such an imperative is tempered by a number of other considerations arising from the more worldly context. This is exemplified by Map's record of his humorous banter with Ranulf de Glanville, chief justiciar to Henry II:

> And thus it happened once that after I had heard a concise and just judgement given against a rich man in favour of a poor one, I said to Lord Ranulf, the chief justiciar: 'Although the poor man's judgement might have been put off by many quirks, you arrived at it by a happy and quick decision.' 'Certainly,' said Ranulf, 'we decide causes here much quicker than your bishops do in their churches.' 'True,' said I, 'but if your king were as far off from you as the pope is from the bishops, I think you would be quite as slow as they.' He laughed, and did not say no. (V, 7 [509])

The dialogue is apparently recalled in fine detail. In truth, of course, it is heavily stylized in its stringent focus and movement toward Map's own punchline, delivered consummately to the appreciative laughter ('Ipse uero risit') of his friendly opponent. The point at issue, the relative merits of lay and ecclesiastical law courts, is decided urbanely and to the detriment of neither Map nor Ranulf. Clerk may gain the upper hand over layman in the sense that the former has the last (witty) word, but each graciously accepts the validity of the other's opinion. Joking in this scene is in effect conducted in accordance with the courtly virtues of wit and affability,[24] which, as *dist.* V repeatedly makes clear, are characteristic of the courtliest of noblemen, and of the best-functioning courts under the worthiest rulers.[25] Map and Ranulf de Glanville's interaction thus confirms that in spite of all the problems at the Angevin court, the target of satirical criticism in the rest of V, 7 (and I, 1–12), in certain respects Henry II's court is still laudable.

The basic function of all three of the episodes examined so far is to bolster the authority of Walter Map as the author of *De nugis*. On the one hand, the repeated narrative rehearsal of Map's ability to make others laugh, and not just anyone, but members of the courts of the bishop of London and the king of England, encourages the reader of *De nugis* to look out for and trust in the wit and comic flair of the authorial narrator in this work. On the other hand, these anecdotes support Map's opening claim to be 'of the court' ('in curia sum' I, 1 [2]). For in spite of his subsequent protestation of ignorance ('nescio, Deus scit, quid sit curia' I, 1 [2] [and what the court is, God knows, I know not]), Map can talk authoritatively about court life, not simply because he has witnessed it, but because he is well versed in its culture. Map, it turns out, is an expert practitioner of witty speech, an aspect of court culture, moreover, in which the clerically educated appear to excel; it should not be overlooked that ready wit in the presence of the king is epitomized elsewhere in the work by the figures of Bishop Hugh of Lincoln and a certain Benedictine monk, Dom Reric.[26] It is as if witty utterances have come to represent for Map a category of memorable speech (*dicta*) which may be justifiably attributed to 'moderns' as well as 'ancients' and which thus goes some way to compensating the modern writer for his lack of time-honoured *auctoritas*. Map's own witticisms are not statements of philosophical or theological import, but nevertheless they lay claim to an alternative authority by virtue of their socially grounded comic efficacy and successful prosecution and defence of a variety of causes.

The retrospective first-person point of view shared by the anecdotes from *dist.* I, chapters 24 and 31, and *dist.* V, 7, is entirely typical of Map's mode of historiographical reportage: a style of autobiographical writing, in other words, which is at once familiar and conveys a greater sense of immediacy. Not all of Map's bon mots are recorded in this way in *De nugis*, however. In fact the longest sustained narrative depiction of Map as court wit, which concludes the sixth and final proper chapter of *dist.* V,[27] belongs to a different formal category altogether:

> This lord king was served by a certain clerk, who has written these matters for you, whose surname was Map. He was dear and acceptable to the king, not for his own merits, but for those of his forebears who had been faithful and useful to the king, both before his accession and after it. The king had also a son named Geoffrey born to him, if it be lawful to say so, of a common whore named Hikenai (as was hinted before), and him he acknowledged as his own, contrary to his honour and to the wish of everyone. Between this man and Map quarrels often arose on slight provocation, both in the king's presence and elsewhere. The king had him elected to the see of Lincoln, and he kept that bishopric longer than he should, though the lord pope often pressed him either to resign it or to be consecrated bishop: he vacillated long, and would not do either or both. So the king, who beheld with anxiety so great a territory encumbered by such a barren figure, compelled him to take one or other course. He elected to resign. And resign he did, at Marlborough, where there is a spring of which they say that whoever tastes it speaks bad French; hence when anyone speaks that tongue faultily, we say that he is speaking Marlborough French. Map therefore, when he had heard Geoffrey say the words of resignation to lord Richard of Canterbury and the lord archbishop asked him: 'What are your words?' (wishing him to repeat what he had said, so that all might hear), and he held his tongue, and the archbishop asked again: 'What are your words?' Map answered for him: 'Marlborough French.' Everyone else laughed, but he went off in a rage.
>
> In the year immediately preceding his resignation he had with hard exaction, not like a shepherd but with violence, demanded from all the churches of his diocese tithes of all their incomings, and had assessed each one, and was extorting tithes according to his own estimate: and from Map's church, which was called Ashwell, he proudly and swaggeringly ordered four marks to be paid him, at the rate at which he was plundering the rest. Map would not pay, but complained to our lord the king, who took that elect one into an inner chamber and chastised him in fit phrase and with a notable thrashing, that thenceforth he should not vex the clerks in any way. Returning thence, soundly cudgelled, he hinted many a threat at all the members of the court, and particularly at his accuser: and happening to meet him, he swore by the faith he owed

the king his father that he would use him hardly. But Map, who knew that in his oaths he always used his father's name and also boastfully added 'the king' thereto, said: 'My lord, the apostle Paul says, "Be ye imitators of God, as dear children." Now our God, the Son of God, often used to name himself by his weaker part and call himself the Son of Man, saying nothing of the godhead of his Father. I wish you with like humility would sometimes swear by the profession of your mother, and keep back your father's royalty. That is the proper way to imitate God, who never did anything in arrogance.' Then he, shaking his head after his wont in royal fashion, roared out threatenings. Map added: 'I observe that I have corrected you with the same success as the archbishop did his wife.' 'What was that?' said one of the bystanders. Map whispered in his ear that the archbishop's wife when in bed with him, made a rude noise, and when the archbishop hit her, made another. The Elect, on hearing this, raged and scolded as if he had suffered the worst of injuries.

On the day of this man's resignation the lord king made him happy by the gift of his Chancery, and hung his seal about the neck of the joyful recipient. He showed it to the aforesaid Map, and said: 'So far everything has come to you at your call from the Seal gratis, but from this moment not the very least brief shall you have, but you shall pay fourpence for it.' To him, Map: 'Thank God! this step-up of yours is a gain to me. Some people's hurt is others' health: last year you wanted four marks; now it is four-pence.'

After this, however, when we were in Anjou, and this royal person had seen Walter of Coutances summoned to Lord Richard, archbishop of Canterbury, to be consecrated to the bishopric which he himself had resigned, envy opened his eyes, and he was dumbfounded, and eventually collecting his wits, he appealed. The lord king soothed him, and promised him the revenues which he had lost by the election. But he, who then saw for the first time that with the bishopric he had irrevocably lost everything (pined) for revenge. And catching sight of Map, who was canon of the prebend at London, which he had formerly enjoyed, he shouted at him: 'You shall give me back my prebend, whether you will or no.' *Map*: 'Nay, with the best of will, if you can devise any way of recovering all that you have lost for nothing.' (V, 6 [495–9])

This relatively large segment of text revolves around one particular antagonistic relationship, describing in a series of four encounters the repeated triumph of Map's wit over a mean, yet socially superior opponent: Henry II's illegitimate son Geoffrey Plantagenet.[28] The scenes are not presented in strict chronological order; the second confrontation described here actually occurs prior to the first. Instead, the sequence begins with Map's most spectacular jest on an important occasion in the life of the court (not to mention Geoffrey's ecclesiastical career) of Geoffrey's public resignation as bishop-elect of Lincoln (in 1182). The artificial arrangement of the various episodes seemingly ensures that Geoffrey, the butt of Map's jokes, is utterly discredited in the eyes of the recipients of De nugis, characterized as he is as a failure right from the start. At the same time Map's own behaviour is understood to be driven (once again) by a moral imperative. Thus, his spontaneous intervention in the ceremonial dialogue between Geoffrey and the archbishop of Canterbury is seen to be provoked by the former's apparent reluctance to cooperate fully in the public process of resignation in the hearing of all those present; and the three elements of Map's wit, Geoffrey's impotent rage, and the approving laughter of courtly society ('Ridentibus igitur aliis') are combined here to form an unambiguous point of comic reference for the anecdotes that follow. These in turn are unified further by the theme of money (Geoffrey's unjust and vindictive avarice) and a structure of 'diminishing returns' whereby Geoffrey threatens to extort ever smaller amounts of money from his arch enemy. Map, it would appear, knows almost no limits in his jibes, being afraid in the second episode neither to remind Geoffrey of his illegitimacy, nor to belittle him by means of an anticlerical (and mildly scatological) joke about an archbishop's haplessness when in bed with his wife.[29]

The choice of the third-person perspective may be read in the first instance as a function of the status of this passage as a type of closure to dist. V of De nugis and as the most privileged site of authorial naming in the whole work. After all, the surname Map is mentioned a further twelve times here once his identity as the author of De nugis has been reconfirmed with programmatic clarity. However disconcerting it may be to the modern reader, alternation between first-person and third-person modes of authorial self-reference is not uncommon in medieval Latin and vernacular literature.[30] As perhaps a more formal technique of self-naming Map may well have elected to use the third person to increase the chances of a record of his authorship being preserved for posterity. The distancing, objectifying, even historicizing effect of this perspective, however, clearly extends beyond the figure of Map the literary author to Map the witty courtly clerk. Thus, out of all of the relevant accounts of Map's bon mots in De nugis it is this one, rather than the three others related in the first person (I, 24; I, 31; V, 7), which evinces the greatest affinity with the anecdote transmitted separately in the Corpus Christi manuscript. The tone of humility which marks the introduction of Map in this part of V, 6 ('hic ipsi carus fuit et acceptus, non suis sed parentum suorum meritis' [494] [He was dear and acceptable to the king, not for his own merits, but for those of his forebears]) makes it seem even more likely that what might at first look like a foreign body in *De nugis* was actually penned by Map himself.[31] As a result it cannot be ruled out either that the Corpus Christi anecdote – also told in the third person – was originally by Map as well.[32] If indeed we are to assume that Map's preoccupation with sketching a bold image of his courtly witty self went further than the material contained in *De nugis*,[33] then the various incidents related here might be more properly regarded as just a few chapters from an extended (implied) narrative of Map's own life and memorable sayings.[34] If, on the other hand, the Corpus Christi anecdote was composed by someone other than Map, it is not infeasible that it was inspired by the kind of anecdotal material that went into V, 6 of *De nugis*. In these circumstances, intentionally or otherwise, Map would have created the basis and model for the later (posthumous?) development of his own author-mythology.

Appendix of Latin Passages Cited

Oxford, Corpus Christi College, MS 32, fol. 95r
Quidam clericus regis Henrici diues redditibus sed auarus ait Waltero Map cum ioco, 'Magister W(altere), bene portas etatem.' Respondit ille, 'Quid est hoc?' et ille, 'Bene portare etatem est habere multos annos et non apparere senem.' Respondit ei W. Map, 'Hoc modo tu portas redditus. Multos enim habes et parum expendis.' [515]

De nugis curialium: IV, 5
Hoc solum deliqui, quod uiuo. Verumptamen hoc morte mea corrigere consilium non habeo [. . .] Scio quid fiet post me. Cum enim putuerim, tum primo sal accipiet, totusque sibi supplebitur decessu meo defectus, et in remotissima posteritate michi faciet auctoritatem antiquitas, quia tunc ut nunc uetustum cuprum preferetur auro nouello. [312]

De nugis curialium: I, 24
Duo similiter abbates albi de predicto uiro colloquebantur in presencia Gilleberti Foliot, Londoniensis episcopi, comendates eum ex uirtute miraculorum. Euolutis autem multis, ait alter: 'Cum uera sint que de Barnardo dicuntur, uidi tamen aliquando quod ipsi gracia miraculorum defuit. Vir quidam marchio Burgundie rogauit eum ut ueniret et sanaret filium eius. Venimus et inuenimus mortuum. Iussit igitur corpus deferri dompnus Barnardus in talamum secretum, et eiectis omnibus incubuit super puerum, et oratione facta surrexit; puer autem non surrexit, iacebat enim mortuus.' Tum ego: 'Monachorum infelicissimus hic fuit. Nunquam enim audiui quod aliquis monachus super puerum incubuisset, quin statim post ipsum surrexisset puer.' Erubuit abbas, et egressi sunt ut riderent plurimi. [80]

De nugis curialium: I, 31
Iussit me pontifex experiri aduersus eos [two Waldensians], qui respondere parabam. Primo igitur proposui leuissima, que nemini licet ignorare, sciens quod asino cardones edente indignam habent labia lattucam: 'Creditis in Deum patrem?' Responderunt: 'Credimus.' 'Et in Filium?' Responderunt: 'Credimus.' 'Et in Spiritum sanctum?' Responderunt: 'Credimus.' Iteraui: 'Et in matrem Christi?' et illi item: 'Credimus.' Et ab omnibus multiplici sunt clamore derisi, confusique recesserunt [. . .] [126]

De nugis curialium: V, 7

Vnde cum ego semel ibi iudicium audissem compendiosum et iustum contra diuitem pro paupere, dixi domino Randulfo summo iudici: 'Cum iusticia pauperis multis posset diuerticulis prorogari, felici celerique iudicio consecutus es eam.' Tum Randulfus: 'Certe nos hic longe uelocius causas decidimus, quam in ecclesiis episcopi uestri.' Tum ego: 'Verum est; sed si rex noster tam remotus esset a uobis, quam ab episcopis est papa, uos eque lentos crederem.' Ipse uero risit, et non negauit. [508]

De nugis curialium: V, 6

Domino regi predicto seruiebat quidam clericus, qui uobis hec scripsit, cui agnomen Map; hic ipsi carus fuit et acceptus, non suis sed parentum suorum meritis, qui sibi fideles et necessarii fuerant ante regnum et post. Habebat eciam et filium Gaufridum nomine susceptum, si dicere fas est, a publica cui nomen Hikenai, ut est pretactum, quem contra fidem et animum omnium in suum aduocauit. Inter hunc et Map faciles aliquando lites coram ipso sed et alias ueniebant. Hunc rex ad Lincolnie sedem elegi fecit, qui iusto diucius episcopatum illum detinuit, domino papa sepius urgente quod cederet aut ordinaretur episcopus; qui diu tergiuersans neutrum et utrumque uoluit et noluit. Rex igitur qui sollicite considerabat multam terram occupatam a ficu tali, coegit eum ad alterutrum. Is autem elegit cedere. Cessit igitur apud Merleburgam, ubi fons est quem si quis, ut aiunt, gustauerit, Gallice barbarizat, unde cum uiciose quis illa lingua loquitur, dicimus eum loqui Gallicum Merleburge. Vnde Map, cum audisset eum uerba resignacionis domino Ricardo Cantuariensi dicere, et quesisset dominus archiepiscopus ab eo 'Quid loqueris?,' uolens eum iterare quod dixerat, ut omnes audirent, et ipso tacente, quereret item 'Quid loqueris?' respondit pro eo Map: 'Gallicum Merleburge.' Ridentibus igitur aliis, ipse recessit iratus.

Anno proximo renunciacionem precedente, districcione rigida, non ut pastor sed uiolenter, exegerat ab omnibus ecclesiis parrochie sue decimas omnium obuencionum suarum, et singulas taxarat, et secundum propriam estimacionem decimas extorquebat. Quatuor autem marcas ab ecclesia Map, que dicitur Eswaella, iactanter et superbe sibi iubebat afferri, racione qua spoliabat alias. Ille noluit, sed domino nostro regi questus est; qui ducens electum illum in thalamum interiorem castigauit eum dignis uerbis et fuste nobili, ne deinceps clericis molestus in aliquo fieret. Vnde uerberatus egregie rediens, in omnes curie socios minas multas intorsit, et in acusatorem suum precipue; cui cum forte fuisset obuiam, iurauit per fidem quam debebat patri suo regi, quod ipsum dure tractaret. Map autem sciens ipsum in iuramentis patrem suum ponere, sed et regem iactanter semper apponere, ait: 'Domine, Paulus apostolus dicit "Estote imitatores Dei, sicut filii karissimi"; Filius autem Dei Deus noster se frequenter secundum infirmiorem sui partem se filium hominis dicebat, tacita Patris deitate. Vtinam et tu consimili uelis humilitate iurare secundum matris officium aliquando, celata patris regalitate. Sic decet imitari Deum qui nil egit arroganter.' Tum ille, capite regaliter ut mos erat illi concusso, minas intonuit. Map autem adiecit: 'Audio quod uos emendaui, sicut archiepiscopus uxorem suam.' Quidam autem constancium: 'Quid hoc?' At ille sibi murmurauit in aure, quod uxor archiepiscopi dormiens cum illo strepuit, et ab archiepiscopo percussa restrepuit. Hoc cum audisset electus ab illo, tanquam ex illata quauis iniuria fremuit obiurgans.

Die cessionis predicti uiri beatificauit eum dominus rex cancellaria sua, sigillumque suum appendit collo gratulantis. Quod ipse predicto Map ostendens ait: 'Omnia cesserunt tibi ad nutum de sigillo gratis, at ex hoc nunc nec unum extorquebis inde breuiculum quod non redimas quatuor nummis.' Cui Map: 'Deo gracias! Bono meo gradum hunc ascendisti. Quorundam infortunium aliorum successus est. Anno preterito quatuor marcas exegisti, nunc quatuor denarios.'

Post hec autem, cum essemus in Andegauia, uidissetque uir ille regius Walterum a Constanciis ad dompnum Ricardum Cantuariensem archiepiscopum uocari, consecrandum ad episcopatum ab ipso resignatum, aperuit inuidia tunc oculos eius, et obstupuit, tandemque resumptis uiribus appellauit. Mitigauit eum dominus, et promisit ei redditus quos in eleccione perdiderat. Ipse uero, cui tunc primum uisum est se cunta cum episcopatu simul amisisse sine spe, talionem redibuisse [. . .] Videns ergo Map, qui sue quondam prebende canonicus erat Lundoniis, ingeminat: 'Reddes prebendam meam et nolens.' Map: 'Immo certe uolens, si potes omnia que gratis amisisti per aliquod ingenium recuperare.' [494–8]

NOTES

1 Map, *De nugis curialium*, 515.
2 Map, *De nugis curialium*, 516. Passages discussed in the main body of this article will appear first in English translation, while the (original) Latin citations may be found in an Appendix. Where passages are cited in notes both the Latin original and the English translation will be given. Unless otherwise indicated all citations of *De nugis*, as well as any English translations, are taken from the James, Brooke, and Mynors edition; page numbers in the edition are given in square brackets.
3 Cicero, *De oratore*, II, 277: 'Est bellum illud quoque ex quo is qui dixit irridetur in eo ipso genere quo dixit: [. . .]' [It is delightful too when a jester is requited in the identical vein in which he himself bantered].
4 In fact in the aforementioned Corpus Christi manuscript the preceding story begins with just such an authorial attribution to Walter Map: 'Ex dictis W. Map' [From the sayings of W. Map] (Map, *De nugis curialium*, 515).
5 For more on the concept of *auctoritas* in the Middle Ages, see Müller, 'Auctor – Actor – Author.'
6 For more on the role of authorship as a 'function' in medieval textual transmission, see Wachinger, 'Autorschaft und Überlieferung'; Bein, '*Mit fremden Pegasusen pflügen*.'
7 For an overview of this tradition, see the pair of articles by Bowen, 'Renaissance Collections of *Facetiae*, 1344–1490,' and 'Renaissance Collections of *Facetiae*, 1499–1528.'
8 Bracciolini, *Facezie*, No. 58: 'Huic ipsi inter seniorem aliquando iuniorem Canes prandenti, cum ministri utriusque, dedita opera, ante pedes Dantis ad eum lacessendum ossa occulte subiecissent, remota mensa, versi omnes in solum Dantem, mirabantur cur ante ipseum solummodo ossa conspicerentur. Tum ille, ut erat ad respondendum promptus, "Minime" inquit "mirum, si Canes ossa sua comederunt: ego autem non sum canis"' [The same man was once dining between the older and the younger Cane della Scala, when the servants of both, having finished their work, secretly threw bones in front of Dante's feet in order to slight him. When the table was removed all of them turned toward Dante and feigned amazement that bones were to be seen in front of Dante only. Then Dante responded with ready wit: 'It is hardly a marvel if the Dogs eat their bones: I, however, am not a dog' (my translation)]; cf. also nos. 57 and 121.
9 Map's reputation as a great wit is upheld by contemporaries such as Gerald of Wales; see Rigg, *Anglo-Latin Literature*, 88.

10 A wide range of Latin literature came to be (falsely) attributed to Walter
    Map in the subsequent course of the Middle Ages; see Wright, *Latin Poems
    Commonly Attributed to Walter Mapes*; Map, *De nugis curialium*, xix–xxiii.

11 See, for example, 'In libro magistri Gauteri Mahap de nugis curialium
    distinctio prima' (fol. 7r [2]); 'Incidencia magistri Gauteri Mahap de mona-
    chia' (fol. 17v [84]); 'Distinccio primi libri Magistri Mahap de nugis curia-
    lium' (fol. 72v [lvi]); 'Incidencia Magistri Gauteri Mahap de monachis' (fol.
    73r [lvi]); 'Explicit distinccio quinta libri Magistri Gauteri Mahap de nugis
    curialium' (fol. 73v [lxii]).

12 The following is based on Map, *De nugis curialium*, xxiv–xxxii; but see also
    Hinton, 'Plan and Composition.'

13 Echard, 'Map's Metafiction,' 292.

14 'Apis et dulcibus et amaris herbis insidet, et ex singulis aliquid cere uel
    mellis elicit; amator sapiencie quemlibet in aliquo poetam approbat, et ab
    omni pagina quam baiulauerit recedit doctior' (III, 3 [260]) [The bee settles
    upon sweet and bitter plants alike, and from each draws some wax or
    honey; the lover of wisdom relishes every writer in some point, and comes
    away the wiser from every page he has turned].

15 'Videris me calcaribus urgere Balaam quibus in uerba coegit asinam. Qui-
    bus enim aliis possit quispiam induci stimulis in poesim? At ualde timeo
    ne michi per insipienciam cedat in contrarium asine, et tibi in contrarium
    Balaam, ut dum me loqui compellis incipiam rudere, sicut illa pro ruditu
    locuta est, fecerisque de homine asinum, quem debueras facere poetam'
    (I, 12 [34]) [It seems to me that you are using Balaam's spurs on me – the
    spurs with which he drove his ass to speak: for what other would avail to
    drive anyone into writing poetry? I am much afraid that my stupidity will
    cause our parts – mine of the ass, and yours of Balaam – to be reversed,
    so that when you try to make me speak I shall begin to bray – as the other
    spoke instead of braying – and you will have made an ass out of a man
    whom you wanted to make into a poet].

16 'Venator uester sum: feras uobis affero, fercula faciatis' (II, 32 [208]) [I am
    but your huntsman. I bring you the game, it is for you to make dainty
    dishes out of it].

17 'Non enim fori lites aut placitorum attempto seria; teatrum et arenam in-
    colo nudus pugil et inermis, quem in armatos obtrectancium cuneos talem
    ultro misisti' (III, 1 [210]) [I do not touch upon the suits of the lawcourts
    or upon grave pleas: it is the theatre and the arena that I haunt, a naked
    unarmed fighter, and you have insisted on sending me forth in that guise
    to meet the armed squadrons of my detractors].

18 Echard, 'Map's Metafiction,' 313.

19 Map was most probably engaged in the service of Gilbert Foliot in the 1160s before becoming a royal clerk under Henry II in the early 1170s; see Map, *De nugis curialium*, xvi.

20 As pointed out by the editors of Map, *De nugis curialium*, 80.

21 It is notable in this context that I, 25 [84] is the only chapter in *De nugis curialium* to include the author's name in its title: 'Incidencia magistri Gauteri Mahap de monachia' [A Digression of Master Walter Map on Monkery]. I, 24 and I, 25 thus combine to place considerable emphasis on Map's status as a satirical author.

22 For more on this phenomenon in the Middle Ages, see Scharff, 'Lachen über die Ketzer.'

23 The comic effect of the 'mechanical' is of course explored most thoroughly by Henri Bergson, *Le Rire*: 'Les attitudes, gestes et mouvements du corps humain sont risibles dans l'exacte mesure où ce corps nous fait penser à une simple mécanique' (22–3).

24 See Müller, 'Lachen – Spiel – Fiktion,' 46–57; Jaeger, *Origins of Courtliness*, 161–73; Zotz, 'Urbanitas'; and Althoff, 'Zur Bedeutung symbolischer Kommunikation,' 379–83.

25 Cf. the depiction of the court of Henry I: 'Maturi uel etate uel sapiencia semper ante prandium in curia cum rege, uoceque preconia citabantur ad eos qui pro negocio suo desiderabant audiri; post meridiem et sompnum admittebantur quicumque ludicra sectabantur; eratque scola uirtutum et sapiencie curia regis illius ante meridiem, post, comitatis et reuerende leticie' (V, 5 [438]) [Those who were ripe in age or wisdom were always in the court with the king before dinner, and the herald's voice cited them to meet those who desired an audience for their business; after noon and the siesta, those were admitted who devoted themselves to sports; and this king's court was in the forenoon a school of virtues and of wisdom, and in the afternoon one of hilarity and decent mirth]; or that of the French king Louis VII: 'Waleranius ab Effria miles erat illiteratus, iocundissime tamen facundie, regique notus et carus [. . .]' (V, 5 [446]) [Waleran of *Effria* was a knight without letters, but of a most pleasant gift of speech, and was known and loved by the king].

26 More serious-minded churchmen might well have dismissed outstanding instances of clerical wit as recklessly frivolous (see Jaeger, *Origins of Courtliness*, 162), but Map casts them in an entirely favourable light: 'Hos [royal foresters] Hugo prior Selewude, iam electus Lincolnie, reperit repulsos ab hostio thalami regis, quos ut obiurgare uidit insolenter et indigne ferre, miratus ait: "Qui uos?" Responderunt: "Forestarii sumus." Ait illis: "Forestarii foris stent." Quod rex interius audiens risit, et exiuit obuiam ei' (I, 9

[10]) [Once Hugh, Prior of Selwood, now Elect of Lincoln, found these men [royal foresters] repulsed from the door of the King's chamber; and hearing them give vent to loud abuse, and observing their rage, he was surprised, and said: 'Who are you?' 'We are the keepers' they replied. Said he to them: 'Keepers, keep out.' The King within heard the words, laughed, and came out to meet the Prior]; 'Dominus rex Henricus secundus nuper, ut ei mos est, totam illam infinitatem militum et clericorum suorum precedens, cum domino Rerico monacho magno et honesto uiro uerbum faciebat, eratque eis uentus nimis, et ecce monachus albus in uico pedes negociabatur, respiciensque diuertere properabat; offendit ad lapidem, nec portabatur ab angelis tunc, et coram pedibus equi regii corruit; uentus autem uestes eius in collum propulit, ut domini regis et Rerici oculis inuitis manifesta fieret misera ueritas pudendorum. Rex, ut omnis facecie thesaurus, dissimulans uultum auertit, et tacuit. Rericus autem intulit secreto "Maledicta religio que deuelat anum!"' (I, 25 [102]) [The lord king, Henry the Second, of late was riding as usual at the head of all the great concourse of his knights and clerks, and talking with Dom Reric, a distinguished monk and an honourable man. There was a high wind; and lo! a white monk was making his way on foot along the street and looked round, and made haste to get out of the way. He dashed his foot against a stone and was not being borne up by angels at the moment, and fell in front of the feet of the king's horse, and the wind blew his habit right over his neck, so that the poor man was candidly exposed to the unwilling eyes of the lord king and Reric. The king, that treasure-house of all politeness, feigned to see nothing, looked away, and kept silence; but Reric said, sotto voce, 'A curse on this bare-bottom piety'].

27 In the text as it now stands V, 7 actually functions as an epilogue to the work as a whole, although this purpose was probably originally served by IV, 2. The editors of the text note that much of this chapter appears to be a first draft of I, 1ff. (see Map, *De nugis curialium*, 498) and this view is supported by its title: 'Recapitulacio principii huius libri ob diuersitatem litere et non sentencie' (V, 7 [498]) [A Recapitulation of the Beginning of this Book, Differing in Expression but not in Substance].

28 See Map, *De nugis curialium*, 478, note 2; and 496, note 1.

29 This last example is also notable for the 'stagecraft' Map displays in making his quips; here he uses the anticlerical joke to draw in a third party, representative of the Angevin court at large, thereby guaranteeing that the snub to Geoffrey unfolds in public.

30 For a detailed discussion of this phenomenon see Coxon, *Presentation of Authorship*, 17–25.

31 If this passage was not in fact penned by Map then at some point in its life *De nugis* was refunctionalized as a receptacle for further anecdotes relating to Map and the Angevin court. Although this would, in its own way, speak loudly for Map's status as a renowned wit in the society of his day, it is difficult to see what purpose would be served in this context by the (affected) modesty of the passage's opening lines.

32 It is not inconceivable that the authorial attribution ('Ex dictis W. Map') which opens the exemplum immediately preceding our anecdote in the Corpus Christi manuscript applies in fact to both texts.

33 That Map has one eye on posterity when he recounts his own jokes goes some way to explaining the presence of accompanying 'glosses,' his elucidation of the idiom 'Gallicum Merleburge' (Marlborough French) in V, 6 being the most obvious example.

34 Map's project, if we may call it that, would thus also seem to anticipate the late medieval interest in self-documentation which is reflected in the collections of *facetiae* of Poggio Braccidini, Heinrich Bebel, and others; see Röcke, 'Lizenzen des Witzes.'

3 Late Medieval Text Collections: A Codicological Typology Based on Single-Author Manuscripts

ERIK KWAKKEL

In his essay 'The Influence of the Concepts of *Ordinatio* and *Compilatio* on the Development of the Book,' Malcolm Parkes shows how the textual organization of scholastic books produced in the thirteenth and fourteenth centuries was different from that of manuscripts made in the twelfth century.[1] Due to a change in the model of reading, from monastic *lectio*, which was a spiritual exercise, to scholastic *lectio*, which was an intellectual undertaking, the contents of books became more regulated. In the academic milieu, for example, there was a growing tendency to copy related texts in each other's vicinity, which resulted in the creation of various kinds of well-planned compilations. Common denominators are texts of the same genre (philosophy, alphabetical indices), those with a particular theme (sermons devoted to a certain topic), texts from the same author (St Augustine, Aristotle), or collections with the same function (commentaries on a certain scholastic work). The creation of well thought-through collections was not limited to Latin, or to the academic milieu. Studies by Sylvia Huot and Sarah Westphal, devoted to French and German compilations respectively, show the same tendency in the vernacular traditions of the thirteenth and fourteenth centuries – possibly as an offspring of the older scholastic tradition.[2]

The study by Parkes suggests that compilations with a pronounced focus (hereafter called 'collection') became more popular in the later Middle Ages; or at least that they were produced in larger numbers.[3] The common thread of collections was sometimes clarified with the use of aids such as rubrics, paragraphs, running titles, and marginal enumerations that helped structure an argument. For example, in a rubric a scribe could emphasise the reason for including a text, such as in Vienna, Österreichische Nationalbibliothek, Cod. 13.708, a Middle Dutch collection of treatises devoted to Christian faith, where the following rubric is found at fol. 218r: 'Om dat hi van den geloeue sprect, so willickene hier setten' (I am putting this text here because it also discusses faith).[4] The studies of Parkes, Huot, and Westphal show how scribes in the later Middle Ages took on the role of compiler – though this trait was not shared by all scribes of the period, nor was it restricted to copyists of the later Middle Ages.[5] Copyists in the later Middle Ages, then, not only duplicated exemplars, but sometimes they would also take on different, more creative roles – for example, that of the compiler.

The present essay will take these observations of Parkes and others a step further. It aims to show how scribes not only adapted the structure and contents of texts in order to compose a coherent collection, but also undertook well-planned actions on a codicological level to this end. As will be shown, there are four different ways in which text collections were constructed physically. After the four types have been presented, I will attempt to shed light on the rationale behind the scribe's choice to opt for a certain codicological format. The central focus of this essay is the collection containing multiple texts by a single author. These collections were most likely the product of a plan envisioned by a scribe – although at times his work may also reflect the vision of a patron.[6] The codicological study of miscellanies and other text collections is best done in situ, although detailed manuscript descriptions may sometimes be sufficient. I will therefore present my case using examples from the Middle Dutch manuscript tradition, which has been an important focus of my research in the past. The types presented here are also encountered in other vernaculars, however, as well as in Latin, and from time to time examples from other traditions will be provided. Before the typology is presented, however, the codicology of composite manuscripts needs to be addressed. Whereas the best-known collection is perhaps the one that was copied 'in one go,' many collections were, in fact, copied discontinuously.

Composite Manuscripts

Catalogue descriptions of manuscripts use a variety of terms to denote that a surviving codex is composite: 'Latin works on science and mathematics assembled from several 13th-century booklets,' 'A miscellany of five separate manuscripts,' 'A set of five volumes,' and

Table 1
Schematic Representation of a Composite Manuscript

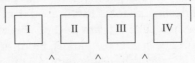

'Three independent manuscripts bound together.'[7] With phrases like these, the descriptions denote that the codex in question consists of several independently produced parts, usually called 'booklets,' which for some reason ended up in one volume.[8] Each individual part of a composite book represents a separate production process: the scribe or scribes involved in the production of a booklet usually worked independently from the copyists of other parts. The result is that the components of a composite manuscript often have varied physical appearances. Thumbing through such a volume one typically encounters alternations in *mise en page*, script, quire, and leaf signatures, and in the style of headings and running titles. A schematic representation of a composite manuscript consisting of four parts would look like table 1.

The four cubes in this scheme are the booklets; the horizontal line above them represents the present binding. The *caesurae*, indicated by wedges, point out locations in the volume where a discontinuity in the production process is encountered: they mark the end of a particular scribal undertaking, as well as the beginning of another. With the presence of *caesurae*, composite manuscripts are differentiated from books that have been copied 'in one go.' In such cases the production process, undertaken by either one or more scribes, resulted in a set of quires originally intended to form a single manuscript rather than part of a composite volume.

Apart from straightforward cases such as those illustrated by table 1 – a number of single units assembled in one volume – there are also composite books with a more complicated genesis: those in which *sets* of booklets (rather than single units) are bound together. A schematic representation of such a complex composite manuscript is found in table 2.

Again, the horizontal line on top represents the present binding. The horizontal line over cubes I and II, on the other hand, represents an earlier binding: it indicates these parts were used as a set prior to their ending up in the composite manuscript. The same goes for cubes III and IV. In other words, this particular codex is a combination of

Table 2
Schematic Representation of a Complex Composite Manuscript

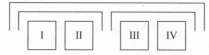

two batches of booklets, each used as a separate composite collection
until they were bound together.[9]

Understanding the genesis of composite manuscripts is useful, not
just for codicologists but also for literary historians. It influences, for
example, assessments of the relation between texts. A genesis of the
type presented in table 2 demonstrates that not all components of a
collection have equally strong ties. Some text clusters have always been
together (such as those found in booklet I), some have had a previous
life together but they were not always 'neighbours' (such as the texts in
booklets I and II), while the relation of others is even more distant, because they were united at an even later stage (such as the texts in booklets I and III). Furthermore, understanding the codicological structure
of a collection helps to profile its maker or makers. Complex composite
manuscripts such as the one in table 2 show that a collection may be
the product of not one but several individuals. The example in table 2
contains no less than four layers of composition: the first is found on
the level of the individual booklets (the contents of which were selected
at some point), the second covers the joining of part I and II, and the
third the joining of part III and IV (which could have taken place in a
different time and location). In the fourth compilation stage the two sets
were bound together, which produced the collection we study today in
manuscript departments of libraries. A complicated genesis like this,
which may be referred to as 'multilevel composition,' is frequently encountered among surviving manuscripts of the later Middle Ages.[10]

To fully understand the composition process behind a compilation
with a pronounced focus, for instance those with texts from a single
author, one needs to assess how the collection we encounter in libraries today evolved over time. A collection that is the result of multilevel
composition, and which represents the preferences and actions of multiple individuals, is obviously very different from the one that was
planned by a single person. Even when collections are studied from
a textual point of view, their physical construction needs to be taken
into account as well. This is the case not only when it is obvious from

palaeographical observations that the collection consists of parts made in different ages, which were obviously produced as separate units, but also when the handwriting of the scribes is contemporary. Even when a manuscript is copied by one hand, as many single-author collections are, it may still have a complex genesis, as will be shown. Our current terminology, which is limited to rudimentary phrases such as 'booklet,' 'Sammelbände,' 'composite,' and 'copied in one go,' is insufficient to discuss in detail the composition of complex composite manuscripts. Before we focus on single-author text collections, then, some useful terms need to be introduced.

Terminology

To address the genesis of composite manuscripts in a clear manner, four terms need to be introduced.[11] The first is 'production unit,' which denotes a set of quires that form a codicological unity. The quires of such a unity are linked by catchwords and they hold a single sequence of quire signatures, although there are many other markers.[12] A production unit is roughly the same thing as a 'booklet,' a term coined by Pamela Robinson in 1980, except there are three modifications.[13] First, a production unit is not limited in size. When a manuscript does not contain physical 'breaks' (*caesurae*) it will be called a single production unit. Second, production units in a codex may be of different ages, like booklets, but they may also have been copied by contemporary scribes, or even by one and the same hand. And third, unlike the booklet, a production unit is not necessarily self-contained in that it represents a complete textual unit. Texts with a natural subdivision, such as the Gospels or a literary work consisting of several books, are often divided over several production units.[14] The absence of catchwords is often the most prominent indicator that a manuscript, although consisting of a single text, was not copied continuously. The presence of multiple production units in a codex may be reflected by irregularities in the quire structure: the last quire of a production unit is often of a different size than the preceding ones, as scribes adapted the number of leaves in this quire according to the amount of text that remained to be copied (medieval scribes preferred to start copying a new textual unit in a new physical unit).

A special case of a production unit is the one that has been extended at a later stage. The last leaves of a production unit would often remain blank and it happened that at a later stage another scribe would start copying an additional text on these blank leaves. If no new leaves or quires were added we are dealing with quire filling. Although this also involves an additional production phase, the physical structure of the production unit was not altered. However, if a scribe needed more space to copy a text than was provided by the blank leaves, he would add new writing support material, either one additional singleton, a bifolium, a quire, or even several quires. Such a production unit, which was produced in several production stages, will be called an 'extended production unit.'

The third term that is useful for the analysis of composite manuscripts describes the relationship highlighted by the horizontal line over booklets: the line indicates the booklets in question were bound together prior to their ending up in the manuscript in which they survive today (part I and II, and III and IV in table 2, above). I will use the phrase 'usage unit' to denote such earlier gatherings. This level of the manuscript's genesis is more difficult to reconstruct, as there are usually no physical remnants left of earlier bindings (discussed below). In order to trace usage units in a composite book one has to focus on physical traits found in some but not all parts. Scribes who copied multiple production units meant for use as a single entity gave the parts certain traits that may not be present in the remaining production units of a composite manuscript. Users of these earlier gatherings sometimes did the same thing. For example, the existence of the usage unit that consists of parts III and IV in table 2 may become evident from the presence of an independent foliation (not found in I and II), running titles in a style that is different from those in parts I and II, or an independent set of quire or leaf signatures.[15] Another indication is the observation that two or more parts in a composite volume are contemporary while having the exact same *mise en page* (most notably the number of lines per page and the dimensions of written space). It is likely such parts were copied for combined use.

The fourth term introduced here is 'usage phase,' which is to denote the various stages of use of a production unit; first as a single unit, then combined with other units, and later possibly joined by even more. If we put the four terms into a scheme, the result is as follows in table 3.

Table 3 represents a composite manuscript that consists of three production units, which form two usage units: the first containing part I, the second parts II and III. Part I was copied with the intention to be used as a single unit, while it was anticipated that parts II and III would function together. In this case each production unit has two

Table 3
Composite Manuscripts and Terminology

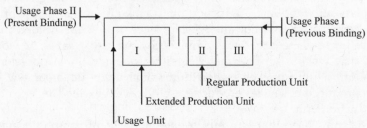

usage phases. Parts II and III were used as a set for some time, which is their first usage phase. The first usage phase of part I was the period when it was used individually. The second usage phase of both usage units started when the three production units were bound together.

A Typology of Late Medieval Text Collections

Now that we have tools at our disposal to dissect and analyse the codicological composition of medieval manuscripts we can shift our focus to the physical construction of single-author text collections. Among manuscripts surviving from the later Middle Ages four common types can be distinguished.[16] These four types form two codicological groups. Types 1 and 2 are collections that were produced without interruptions ('copied in one go'). Types 3 and 4, on the other hand, are intermittent in that they were produced in a discontinuous way: their production process contains interruptions.

Type 1: The Manuscript Copied in One Go

The least complex type of collection devoted to a single author is the manuscript that was copied continuously. In this case a significant number of texts were copied into a manuscript consecutively and without interruptions (table 4).

An example of type 1 is Leiden, Universiteitsbibliotheek, MS Ltk. 344, a paper codex of ninety-five folia copied in the fifteenth century by a single scribe. The book contains four texts from the mystical author Jan van Ruusbroec, whose work is remarkably often encountered in single-author text collections.[17] The texts were most likely copied in one go, which is indicated by the stable sequence of quires,

Table 4
Type 1

the fact that all catchwords are present, and the observation that the *ductus* of the handwriting is the same throughout the codex.

Collections of type 1 are often copied by a single hand, such as in MS Ltk. 344. However, they may also be the product of a group of collaborating scribes, although this scenario seems to be less common. One of them was usually the leader of the group: he divided the labour and often corrected the work of the others. An example of such a scenario is Zwolle, Stadsarchief, MS Emmanuelshuizen 7. The codex was copied around 1450 by two nuns in the convent of St John in Brunnepe near Kampen, in the eastern part of the Netherlands.[18] The manuscript is likely a single production unit, as no *caesurae* are found in the book (the quires are of the same size and all catchwords are present). The Zwolle manuscript contains three texts by Jan van Ruusbroec: *Vanden rike der ghelieve* (fols 3r–108v), *Boek der waerheit* (fols 108v–34v), and *Van vier becoringhen* (fols 135r–52r). Each text starts with a rubric identifying the title and author of the work; the title is repeated in the explicit ('Here ends . . .'). The first scribe wrote the *Rike* (fols 3r–108v) and part of the *Waerheit* (fols 108v–22v). Although this copyist put a catchword in the lower margin of fol. 122v, referring to the following quire, she did not continue her work on the book. Instead, a second scribe copied the remaining part of *Waerheit* (fols 123r–34v), as well as the complete *Becoringhe* (fols 135r–52v), which followed.[19] The latter was most likely the leader of the two: she corrected the work of the first hand, copied all rubrics in the book, and put an *ex libris* inscription of Brunnepe in the back of the codex.

The Zwolle manuscript shows that a compilation with a certain focus could be executed by several cooperating individuals.[20] As opposed to the types discussed below, collections of type 1 were built from scratch and their contents are most likely an accurate reflection of the textual profile envisioned by the (main) scribe – if the scribe had indeed compiled the collection himself, that is. We must not exclude the possibility, however, that she copied a selection of texts that was already in existence. For example, a (conjectural) collection of works by St Augustine in a house of Augustine Friars that had deteriorated because of its frequent use could be copied and presented in a new codex. In such cases a surviving manuscript mirrors the preference of an earlier scribe rather than that of the individual who made the copy.[21] The codex in which a collection survives today usually does not provide clues indicating whether or not the compilation is an 'echo' of an earlier manuscript. It is mostly impossible, therefore, to deduce what compilation scenario has led to a type 1 collection.[22]

Type 2: The 'Booklet' Copied in One Go

The second type of single-author text collection is a series of texts copied without interruptions that has survived as part of a composite manuscript (i.e., that does not form a complete codex by itself). Type 2 represents a cluster of texts from a single author that is found in the midst of one or more production units that contain texts by other authors (cases in which more than one production units in a composite volume contain works by a single author will be discussed under type 3). The collection at hand is usually of modest proportions; it often consists of no more than three or four quires, but it may also be limited to only one.

Such single-author 'booklets' come in two variants. First of all, there is the collection made for use with other units – all of which contained works by other authors (type 2a). In other words: single-author collections of this kind have had no independent life of their own. The schematics of this type is as follows in table 5 (in tables 5–8 below, filled-in boxes represent single-author production units).

An example of type 2a is Ghent, Universiteitsbibliotheek, MS 1374, a codex consisting of six production units from the same scribe. There are no indications the six production units, which are clearly marked by missing catchwords, were used separately as usage units: their fronts and backs are clean and undamaged, the parts have an identical *mise en page* (area of written space, number of lines), and the same style of running title is used throughout the six parts (the titles run continuously across the top of verso and recto in each opening). It is likely, therefore, that the units were anticipated for use as one collection. One of the smaller units is largely filled with brief texts of Jacob van Maerlant, a thirteenth-century author from the Low Countries (fols 102–28). On fols 102r–11r the three so-called '*Martijn*' (Martin) poems are found. Each is a discussion between Jacob and Martin on a specific theological theme. The poems are followed by a fourth discussion, often referred to as 'Martin 4.' This discussion is by an unknown

Table 5
Type 2a

Table 6
Type 2b

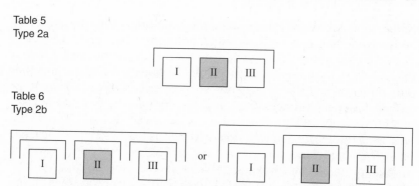

author, although the scribe may have thought it was written by Jacob van Maerlant.[23]

The other scenario covered by type 2 is more complicated. It would also happen that the single-author booklet was meant to be a separate usage unit (type 2b). That is, during the production of the physical unit the scribe anticipated it would be used as a separate entity. Usage units of such limited size were usually bound together with other units at a later usage stage (discussed below). *Ex libris* inscriptions found in the middle of such composite books are remainders of their earlier usage stage.[24] Two variants are encountered among type 2b collections (table 6).

As stated above, collections of type 2b are often bound together with other production units. In many cases these other 'booklets' had also had a previous life of their own (table 6, left). An example of such a scenario is Ghent, Universiteitsbibliotheek, MS 1330, part V (fols 50–82), copied around 1400 and consisting of sermons by Johannes Tauler.[25] The remaining twelve parts of the codex, which were made by different scribes in the fourteenth and fifteenth centuries, were all separate usage units at some point. This does not only follow logically from the fact that the booklets are of different ages, but it is also shown by the discolouring and wear-and-tear on the front and back of the units, and by the mismatch of *mise en page* they present.

The existence of single 'booklets' functioning as individual usage units is confirmed by documentary evidence. The will of Robert Norwich Esq., for example, mentions a 'little quire of paper, with the kings of England versified.'[26] Small usage units such as Robert's paper booklet and the fifth part of MS 1330 were not bound in wooden covers. They were obviously too thin to be fitted with a regular binding (the covers would be thicker than the leaves they supported).

Rather, they were given a so-called limp binding, a provisional cover without boards, composed of parchment, paper, or fabric. The quires were attached to the binding with small strips of parchment.[27] Because most of these usage units of modest proportions were bound together with other units at a later stage of their existence, few come down to us in their original bindings. A rare example of a production unit surviving individually is Oxford, Bodleian Library, MS Marshall 127 (c. 1375), with the Middle Dutch translation of Martinus Braga's *Formula honestae vitae*. The booklet measures no more than 120 x 90 mm and consists of a single quire of four bifolia (eight leaves). The limp binding consists of a parchment double leaf folded around the quire. The cover possibly dates from the fifteenth century, which is when a Latin and Middle Dutch title was added to the front cover (older sewing holes are still visible). The gathering is attached to the limp binding with small leather thongs. This is what a type 2b collection most likely would have looked like in its original state.[28]

Composite manuscripts in which type 2b collections survive are often a compilation of single usage units, like MS 1330. However, such composite volumes could also be a compilation of several *sets* of usage units. This is the second variant covered by type 2b (table 6, right). An example of this scenario is encountered in MS 3067–73, a Middle Dutch codex from the library of Rooklooster Priory near Brussels consisting of 179 leaves. This composite book consists of twelve production units with mystical texts and sermons, which were copied at different moments in the fourteenth century.[29] Each had been a usage unit in its first usage stage. Part three of the book, a single quire copied around 1350 (fols 42–9), consists of two sermons by Meister Eckhart. The unit functioned independently for a number of decades. This can be deduced, for example, from the fact that during its production part III had no relation with the units in its surroundings (which are a few decades older or younger), but also from the stains and damage on its first and last page, indicating these were once the outside pages of a usage unit. However, we are not dealing with an example of a type 2b collection discussed previously, which entered the composite codex directly from its independent life as a single unit; rather, unit III of MS 3067–73 was used as part of a bundle of production units before it ended up in the Brussels codex.

Although almost all of the twelve production units in MS 3067–73 functioned as separate usage units at some point in their lives, *ex libris* inscriptions found on pages within the book show that the individual who created the current codex joined several sets of pre-bound 'booklets,' each of which is still marked with an ownership inscription.[30] The part with the sermons by Eckhart belonged to a set of five production units, each consisting of only a few quires (now fols 2–79 of the codex). The aim of the individual who created this (pre-existing) usage unit seems to have been to combine texts that would provide devotional edification. For example, like the works by Eckhart, many texts in this older usage unit are sermons. On the first page the heading *quidam sermones* was placed (fol. 2r), and on the last page the same hand wrote an *ex libris* inscription of Rooklooster Priory (fol. 79v). With these actions essentially a new textual entity was constructed, which would then be placed in the library. Based on the handwriting of the individual who copied the inscriptions on the first and last page it can be deduced he was Arnold de Cortte, librarian of Rooklooster in the early fifteenth century. Cortte produced a significant number of such 'composite usage units,' both in Latin and the vernacular.[31] He was not the only librarian to do so: combining separate units of small proportions into a larger volume was common practice in monastic libraries of the fifteenth and sixteenth centuries. Such volumes were easier to handle, they were less fragile than single units, and they reduced the chances small parts would get lost among the 'real' books in the library. Like the little booklet in the Bodleian Library discussed above, usage units consisting of several booklets were often fitted with limp bindings, because they were still relatively thin. As their cover was removed when the sets of usage units were bound together into the composite codex in which they survive today, hardly any of these original bindings survive – which makes them difficult to trace in surviving codices.[32]

Types 1 and 2 represent collections copied in one go: the former consists of a large group of texts that filled an entire codex (or, alternatively, a small group of longer texts), the latter was a collection of modest proportions that ended up in a composite manuscript, either immediately after it was produced (type 2a) or at a later stage (type 2b). In both cases no *caesurae* are found within the collection itself. The production process of types 3 and 4, on the other hand, is discontinuous in that the collection was produced in several stages.

Type 3: Copied in Sessions – A Bundle of Production Units

Whereas type 2 represents a small collection of texts by a single author found in the midst of booklets containing texts by other authors, type 3 refers to cases in which a composite manuscript holds several

Table 7
Type 3a

production units with works of a single author. Just like type 2, there
are two possible scenarios: the individual production units were either
made with the intention of being bound together (type 3a), or the composite codex consists of production units that functioned individually
before being joined (type 3b). The first variant is as shown in table 7.

An example of type 3a is Brussels MS 2879–80. This Middle Dutch
codex consists of three production units that contain the collected
works of Hadewijch. Missing catchwords on fols 41v and 61v mark the
caesurae in the manuscript. Three production units can therefore be reconstructed: I. fols 1–41 (letters); II. fols 42–61 (visions); III. fols 62–101
(poems).[33] Two contemporary scribal hands are found in the codex.
The first hand wrote parts one and two, as well as the first quire of
part three (fols 1r–70v); the second copied the remaining quires of this
part (fols 70v–101v). It is likely the production units were meant to
function as a single usage unit. The primary indicator for this is the
observation that they have an identical *mise en page* (such as the number
of columns, the dimensions of written space, and the number of lines
per page). Additional support for this assessment is found in the observation that the outside leaves of the production units are undamaged
and clean.

Although MS 2879–80 contains multiple production units with texts
of a single author, their codicological features indicate they were most
likely intended to form a single collection. In spite of the fact that the
collection contains *caesurae*, then, it is likely that a single working plan
lies at its basis: the aim was to copy all known works of Hadewijch.
Another example of this procedure is Brussels MS 19295–97, which is
part two of a two-volume set that contained the collected oeuvre of
Jan van Ruusbroec (†1381); the first volume is not known to survive.[34]
The volumes were made in Groenendaal Priory, a community of Regular Canons near Brussels where Ruusbroec had been prior. They
were made shortly after the author had died. The Brussels codex consists of two production units: the first part contains Ruusbroec's *Tab-
ernakel* (fols 1–125); the second holds two shorter works (fols 126–71).
Two different scribes copied part I, while part II is copied by a third

Table 8
Type 3b

hand. The *mise en page* of the units is identical and the outside leaves (fols 125v and 126r) are clean and undamaged, which indicates the parts were likely meant for use as a single usage unit.[35]

MSS 2879–80 and 19295–97 show that collections divided among multiple parts are not necessarily made through multilevel composition. In spite of the presence of codicological *caesurae*, then, scribes may have worked as a team executing one master plan. The production of a type 3a collection is similar, in this respect, to the production of a type 1 collection. In both cases multiple scribes copied the texts, except that in type 3a collections the writing was divided over several independently produced parts (the possible rationale behind this approach is discussed below). However, a codex containing several production units with texts of a single author is not always the result of a single composition stage. Alternatively, a single-author collection could also be assembled from a number of production units that had already been in use. This is a collection of type 3b (table 8).

Prime examples of this type are the two related Middle English miscellanies, Cambridge, Trinity College, MSS R.3.19 and R.3.21 (1470s–1490s), filled with shorter works ascribed to John Lydgate and Geoffrey Chaucer. Combined, the books contain thirteen production units, most of which were copied by one and the same scribe. The units were used individually before they were joined, which becomes evident from the fact that each part has its own sequence of foliation.[36]

Type 4: Copied in Sessions – Extending an Existing Production Unit

The last type of single-author text collection discussed here is the production unit that was enlarged at a later phase through the addition of new leaves or quires. This is the 'extended production unit,' discussed previously.

Whereas type 4 collections are frequently encountered among medieval manuscripts in general, those containing texts from a single author are not very common. An example of type 4 is the production unit that covers fols 208–32 in Groningen, Universiteitsbibliotheek, MS 405,

Table 9
Type 4

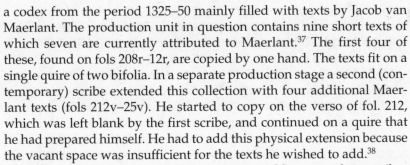

a codex from the period 1325–50 mainly filled with texts by Jacob van Maerlant. The production unit in question contains nine short texts of which seven are currently attributed to Maerlant.[37] The first four of these, found on fols 208r–12r, are copied by one hand. The texts fit on a single quire of two bifolia. In a separate production stage a second (contemporary) scribe extended this collection with four additional Maerlant texts (fols 212v–25v). He started to copy on the verso of fol. 212, which was left blank by the first scribe, and continued on a quire that he had prepared himself. He had to add this physical extension because the vacant space was insufficient for the texts he wished to add.[38]

At first glance, type 4 collections may resemble cases where scribes collaborated to produce a single text collection, such as in the Zwolle manuscript discussed under type 1 (one production unit copied by two hands), or MS 2879–80 under type 3 (three production units copied by two hands). However, type 4 is different. Whereas types 1 and 3 are 'single-level' compositions in that they reflect one selection process, collections of type 4 are the result of multilevel composition. That is to say, the collection as it survives today is the product of two independent selection rounds: first the original compilation was copied, while at a later stage an additional selection of texts was written on added leaves or quires.[39] It is not always possible to distinguish a type 4 collection from single-level compositions made by more than one scribe. Based on cases outside the range of this essay, books that do not contain texts from a single author, it can be deduced that an extended production unit usually involves a modest contribution from the second scribe: whereas the scribe writing the original collection copied a large number of quires, the individual who produced the extension often copied only a few leaves or quires – the example of the Groningen manuscript provided above seems to be a rare exception to this rule.[40]

Why Composite?

The production process of a manuscript consists of a sequence of decisions made by the scribe. Following his own preferences or those of his patron, a scribe had to decide what material to use (parchment or paper), what dimensions the page would have, in what type of script the texts would be copied, if he would add reading aids such as running titles and rubrics, and if the book would be decorated – to state a few of the most obvious choices.[41] Opting for a type of manuscript – composite or not, and if so in what manner – was another one of his decisions. The model presented here shows that text collections with a common denominator come in different formats. Texts from a single author could be copied, for example, in a single production unit. The unit could be extensive and form a codex by itself, which is perhaps the best-known type in current research, or it could be of modest proportions and become a 'booklet' that ended up as part of a composite manuscript, either immediately after its production or after it had been in use as a separate entity for a while. On the other hand, a text collection could also be split up and divided over multiple production units. It was up to the main scribe to decide which type of manuscript was most suitable for a collection. The motivation behind his or her choice may have varied significantly, as the following will show.

An important factor in the decision process of scribes will have been the size of the collection. If a collection with a common thread was limited to a few short texts, a scribe was likely to copy them into a production unit with a limited number of quires (type 2). When the collection was even more modest and consisted of one or two very brief texts, a scribe could decide to add them to an already existing usage unit with works from the same author, by means of adding the required amount of leaves to the original unit (type 4). When a text collection was extensive, on the other hand, and required a substantial number of quires, the scribe was likely to construct a regular manuscript (type 1). Related to the size of collections is the consideration of time. A manuscript consisting of two hundred folia (400 pages) and written in a good quality letter could easily take up to six months to produce.[42] If a scribe or a patron wished to have the collection quickly, the scribe could decide to divide the labour over multiple hands. Each scribe would be given a portion of the exemplars that formed the basis of the collection and the result would be a collection of type 3a. If it was necessary to 'fast track' the production of a collection a scribe might even decide to combine booklets that were already in existence rather than making new copies – a binder could subsequently be asked to fit the collection in a proper binding (type 3b).

Another important consideration is the availability of exemplars. It may have taken a scribe a while to acquire the exemplars needed to make a collection with a pronounced profile, such as those containing the work of a single author. Perhaps a scribe needed to visit certain institutional libraries to find suitable material. Some religious houses are known to have lent books to outsiders from time to time.[43] Or maybe the scribe needed to browse through the book collections of individuals, as the Utrecht-based surgeon Gerrit van Schoonhoven did in the 1460s. From colophons in his books it can be deduced that he visited the libraries of several townspeople to copy the medical texts he needed to practise his profession.[44] A scribe could decide to wait until he had acquired all the material he needed and copy everything consecutively. This procedure would result in a collection of type 1. On the other hand, he could decide to copy the collection in portions: he would save up enough material to fill a production unit of two or three quires, after which he picked up his quill. If he repeated this process a few times, and bound the production units together at a later stage, a collection of type 3a would ultimately be created; or type 3b if he used the existing parts in the meantime, which is the case in Cambridge, Trinity College, MSS R.3.19 and R.3.21, discussed above. If his explorations of local libraries did not turn up more texts of a particular author, he could decide to bind together the one production unit he had already made with existing units that contained other texts, which would result in a collection of type 2. Finally, if he found an extra text of an author when he had already finished copying a single-author collection, he could add his additional finding to an existing compilation, using an extra leaf, bifolium, or quire. Hence, a collection of type 4 was born.

Visual considerations were also important. It is unlikely that a single-author text collection that needed to look good, for instance because a wealthy patron had commissioned it, would consist of 'booklets' that had already been in use. Constructing a collection with 'recycled' usage units would, after all, lead to an inconsistent physical format. There could be considerable variation in the *mise en page*, style of rubrics and decoration, handwriting, as well as in the overall quality of the parts and the care with which the texts were copied. Moreover, with the booklets being of variable dimensions, it might not be possible to properly trim the pages so that a neat book block would appear.[45] A collection that was built from scratch – 'freshly' made copies of exemplars – would not only lead to a more consistent physical presentation of the texts, it would also allow the scribe to shape the presentation according to his own preferences, or those of his patron, as he was able to pick the size, script, number of columns, decoration, and alike. Cost, finally, will also have been a factor. Making a manuscript from scratch was far more expensive than 'recycling' units that were already in existence: copying the contents of the book-lets into a new volume (rather than binding them together) was considerably more costly given the additional expense of labour and materials.

The typology presented here is tangible evidence of the creativity of medieval scribes, some of whom were working according to a well thought-through plan and with a specific goal in mind. This essay focused on one particular aim, collecting texts from a single author, but the typology is also valid for other kinds of collections, such as those combining texts with a certain use (e.g., exegesis or commentary) and those with texts from the same genre (e.g., sermons or chronicles). To achieve their goal scribes would add new leaves and quires to existing units, combine collections that were already in circulation, and divide collections over multiple production units. Their products suggest the concepts of *ordinatio* and *compilatio* influenced the contents of late medieval manuscripts as well as their physical construction.

NOTES

1 Parkes, 'The Influence of the Concepts of *Ordinatio* and *Compilatio*.'
2 Huot, *From Song to Book*, and Westphal, *Textual Poetics in German Manuscripts*. A useful study related to the topic of this essay is Boffey and Thompson, 'Anthologies and Miscellanies.' Parkes, 'The Influence of the Concepts of *Ordinatio* and *Compilatio*,' 61, suggests the Latin academic tradition sparked a vernacular offspring, an observation that is supported by Westphal, 'The Van Hulthem MS,' especially at 77.
3 In current research various terms are employed to denote text collections. The choice of terms is based on a wide variety of criteria. A useful overview of terms and criteria is found in Wenzel, 'Sermon Collections,' 17–20, although the terminology presented in the opening essay is not used consistently throughout the volume. Frequently used terms in relation to text collections are 'miscellany,' 'anthology,' and '*florilegium*,' but none of these cover the type of collection at the heart of the present essay. Rather, the type of collection under discussion is what Denis Muzerelle calls a 'Recueil organisé,' which is a 'recueil rassamblant des texts ou des unités codicologiques dont la réunion répond à une intention quelconque' (Muzerelle, *Vocabulaire codicologique*, nr. 431.10). In the English translation project of Muzerelle's

dictionary, undertaken by Ian Doyle and others, the equivalent 'deliberate assemblage' is proposed – see http://vocabulaire.irht.cnrs.fr/vocab.htm under 431.10 (accessed 14 June 2010). However, as this term is not commonly used, I will use the neutral generic term 'collection' to denote compilations with a pronounced focus. The word 'collection' used in this article covers both new copies made by scribes and cases in which existing booklets with a certain focus (here: texts from a single author) were bound together, forming a composite collection (discussed in detail below).

4 See, for the aids used in (scholastic) collections, Parkes, 'The Influence of the Concepts of *Ordinatio* and *Compilatio*,' and Rouse and Rouse, '*Statim Invenire.*' Another example from the Middle Dutch tradition is '*Dit dichte oec iacob van marlant*' (This was also made by Jacob van Maerlant) placed above the last text in a collection of short works by Jacob van Maerlant (Ghent, Universiteitsbibliotheek, MS 1374, fol. 129r).

5 It should be noted that while the publications of these scholars indicate that compilations with a pronounced focus were gaining popularity during the later Middle Ages (notes 1 and 2, above), they are also encountered among surviving books from the high Middle Ages, although perhaps to a lesser extent. Some examples will be presented in the footnotes.

6 It is usually not possible to determine whether a text collection reflects the preference of the scribe or, when the book was made on commission, his patron. In this essay I will not attempt to assess which is the case. For argument's sake I am assuming the scribe who copied the collection is the one who made the selection. There are no indications that the cases discussed here reflect the preferences of patrons.

7 Taken from manuscript descriptions on the website of the Bodleian Library, Oxford (http://image.ox.ac.uk/) (accessed 14 June 2010). See Bodleian Library MS Digby 76; MS Arch. Selden B 26; and Balliol College MSS 238a and 350, respectively.

8 For 'booklets,' see Robinson, 'A Self-Contained Unit,' and Hanna, 'Booklets in Medieval Manuscripts.'

9 Composite manuscripts consisting of a series of booklets of which some (but not all) were bound together in an earlier stage are discussed in Kwakkel, 'Towards a Terminology,' and Gumbert, 'Codicological Units.'

10 Kwakkel, *Dietsche boeke*, Appendix.

11 A more detailed discussion of these terms is found in Kwakkel (note 9, above). I should like to add that the terms introduced here may not be very elegant; their primary purpose, however, is to promote clarity in a matter that is perhaps one of the most complex aspects of medieval codicology, that is, the physical construction of books that are not copied continuously.

12 Production units can be traced with the same criteria as those presented in Robinson, 'A Self-Contained Unit,' and Hanna, 'Booklets in Medieval Manuscripts,' both related to the booklet, although the two concepts of 'booklet' and 'production unit' are not entirely the same (discussed below).

13 Features attributed to the booklet by Robinson are the following: it is 'self-contained'; it 'originated as a small but structurally independent production containing a single work or a number of short works'; 'The beginning and end of a "booklet" always coincides with the beginning and end of a text or a group of texts.' See Robinson, 'A Self-Contained Unit,' 46 and 47.

14 An example from the Dutch tradition is Vienna, Österreichische Nationalbibliothek, Cod. 13.708. The Dutch translation of the second part of Vincent of Beauvais's *Speculum historiale* found in this codex is presented in seven production units, each holding one of the seven books of Beauvais's text. See Kwakkel, *Dietsche boeke*, 264–71. Brussels MS 2979 (c. 1350) and St Petersburg, Academy of Sciences, MS O 256 (1325–50) are Middle Dutch Gospel Books in which each Gospel is presented in a separate production unit; see 224–6 and 260–3, respectively.

15 For example, Edinburgh, National Library of Scotland, Advocates' MS 19.3.1 is a composite manuscript with various texts in Middle English. The only contemporary foliation in the book is found on fols 1–40, which indicates this section existed as a separate usage unit in an earlier usage stage. See Boffey and Thompson, 'Anthologies and Miscellanies,' 295–6. Other examples are Cambridge, Trinity College, MSS R.3.19 and R.3.21, two related Middle English miscellanies with thirteen booklets in all. Each of these parts has its own sequence of foliation (discussed below).

16 This typology covers nearly the full spectrum of vehicles in which late medieval text collections are found. Some 'exotic' cases, however, are not included, as they occur so infrequently they can hardly be called types. An example is the replacement of a folium or a quire by a later scribe, for instance to replace a flawed reading or damaged pages. Another example is the palimpsest, which can be regarded as a separate production phase, as new text was added to existing pages. It also happened that single folia from various manuscripts would be combined into a new physical entity because they were all devoted to the same topic. The Hague, Koninklijke Bibliotheek, MS 128 C 8, for example, consists of twenty-four leaves (taken from various Latin codices) with commentaries to various Bible books. The new entity was created in the early modern period. See for this case *Schatten van de Koninklijke Bibliotheek*, 91–2.

17 See, for MS Ltk. 344, De Vreese, *De handschriften van Jan van Ruusbroec's werken*, 163–4. Other examples of Ruusbroec collections of type 1 are Ghent, Universiteitsbibliotheek, MS 693 (eleven texts); Brussels MS 1165–67 (eight texts); Brussels MS 3416–24 (five texts); and The Hague, Koninklijke Bibliotheek, MS 73 H 17 (three texts); see 57–70, 44–55, 21–43, and 224–8, respectively. All are copied in one hand. A composite Ruusbroec collection will be discussed below (type 3a).

18 See the codicological description in De Vreese, *De handschriften van Jan van Ruusbroec's werken*, 330–4; and Hermans and Lem, *Middeleeuwse handschriften en oude drukken*, 34–5.

19 Hermans and Lem, *Middeleeuwse handschriften en oude drukken*, 34, presents an illustration of fols 122v–3r, where the second hand takes over from the first. Note that while the scribes use a similar *mise en page*, they employ different scripts: the first writes in a cursive hand, the second in a gothic book hand. This change of script is not a usual practice in the later Middle Ages.

20 Some older examples of this practice are the following: Valenciennes, Bibliothèque municipale, MS 170 (Fulgentius Ruspensis, *Opera*, ninth century); Vienna, Österreichische Nationalbibliothek, Cod. 808 (three texts by Alcuin, ninth century); Salzburg, St Peter Stiftsbibliothek, MS a VIII 29 (three texts by Augustine, ninth century). See Bischoff, *Die südostdeutschen Schreibschulen und Bibliotheken in der Karolingerzeit*, 99, 135, and 141, respectively. All three are copied by multiple hands.

21 An example of such a procedure is encountered in Cologne, Dombibliothek, MS 53 (late tenth century). The book contains Jerome's commentaries on the books of the little prophets. The codex combines the texts in Dombibliothek MSS 52, 54, and 55 (ninth century), which were used as exemplars in the creation of MS 53. See *Glaube und Wissen*, 87. See for this phenomenon also Gumbert, 'One Book with Many Texts,' 33.

22 The same goes for the other types of collections presented here. I will not attempt to make such a distinction in this essay; I assume the scribes of the manuscripts discussed made the selection themselves.

23 Kwakkel, *Dietsche boeke*, 242–5 for the contents and genesis of MS 1374. An example from the French tradition is Paris, Bibliothèque nationale de France, MS fr. 794. The codex consists of three production units copied by a single hand (thirteenth century): part I (fols 1–105) contains four texts by Chrétien de Troyes, part II (fols 106–83) and III (fols 184–433) hold work by other authors. The *mise en page* of the parts, which is identical, suggests the three units were made for use as a set. See the description in Careri et al., *Album de manuscrits français du XIIIe siècle*, 15–18. A minor part of part III is filled with texts by Chrétien.

24 This is the case, for example, in Paris, Bibliothèque Mazarine, MS 920 (five inscriptions); Brussels MS 3067–73 (five inscriptions, see also note 30, below); and Paris, Bibliothèque de l'Arsenal MS 8217 (one inscription). See Kwakkel, *Dietsche boeke*, 255, 228, 248, and 222, respectively.

25 Lieftinck, *De Middelnederlandse Tauler-Handschriften*, 74–6 (codicology) and 382–99 (edition of the texts).

26 Boffey and Thompson, 'Anthologies and Miscellanies,' 308.

27 See, for limp bindings, Szirmai, *The Archaeology of Medieval Bookbinding*, 285–319. A detailed study of limp bindings is Scholla, 'Libri sine asseribus.'

28 In modern times the original binding was fitted with a pasteboard (eighteenth or nineteenth century) and pastedowns (modern). I owe much of this information to Nigel Palmer (Oxford), whom I wish to thank for examining MS 127 and verifying some of my in situ observations. Another example of a booklet surviving as a single unit is Oxford, Corpus Christi College, MS 220. It consists of seven quires from the fifteenth century still fitted in their original limp binding. See Robinson, 'A Self-Contained Unit,' 12, 47, 52, and plate 3. It has been suggested that few single booklets have survived, 'because their shelf-life must have been comparatively short' (Boffey and Thompson, 'Anthologies and Miscellanies,' 290). It is more likely, however, that few of them have survived in their original physical form; many have come down to us in composite collections, for example of type 2b.

29 Manuscript description in Kwakkel, *Dietsche boeke*, 227–33.

30 Apart from *ex libris* inscriptions on the current flyleaves (fols 1r and 179r), such notations are found on fols 79v (two inscriptions), 133v, 154v, and 164r. The uncommonly complicated genesis of this codex is discussed in Kwakkel, *Dietsche boeke*, 227. A more detailed study is Kwakkel and Mulder, 'Quidam sermones.'

31 For the identification, see Kwakkel, *Dietsche boeke*, 21–4; plates 1 and 57 are illustrations of the heading and *ex libris* inscription in MS 3067–73. Many composite volumes surviving from monastic libraries were created in these centuries. They consist of a variety of texts from different ages. The main criterion for selection is usually the size of the booklets (an exception is mentioned in note 45, below).

32 An example is Darmstadt, Landes- und Hochschulbibliothek, MS 1088. The codex consists of three production units (thirty-seven leaves in total) that were copied by three different hands. The ruling and *mise en page* of the parts differ, and it is likely that each was produced to be used as a separate entity. See the description in Scholla, 'Libri sine asseribus,' 102–3. Although it is not a single-author collection, MS 1088 illustrates in what

physical format many type 2b collections were used (i.e., in limp bindings) before they ended up in 'real' manuscripts.

33 The genesis is discussed in Kwakkel, *Dietsche boeke*, 220–3.

34 See for the genesis of the twin-set, Kienhorst and Kors, 'Codicological Evidence.'

35 An example from the Latin tradition is Durham Cathedral, MS B. IV. 24 (1050–1100), which holds two production units with the *Regula S. Benedicti*, copied by two different hands: the first part is in Latin, the second in Old English. The parts were produced with the intention that they be bound together. See Gameson, *Manuscripts of Early Norman England*, 85.

36 Mooney, 'Scribes and Booklets,' 241–2 and table 1 at 242. See also Boffey and Thompson, 'Anthologies and Miscellanies,' 288–9. Although the Cambridge manuscripts combine the work of not one but two authors, and they are therefore factually outside the scope of this essay, it is evident that the aim of the main scribe was to collect texts from these two authors alone. The manuscripts can be regarded as collections and they therefore suitably underscore the argument made in this essay.

37 See, for the book's contents, Deschamps, *Middelnederlandse handschriften uit Europese en Amerikaanse bibliotheken*, no. 26. For its genesis, see Biemans, 'Het Gronings-Zutphense Maerlant-handschrift,' especially at 211–13.

38 After he finished copying the additional Maerlant texts the scribe added two short texts from an unknown author (fols 225v–32v). An example from the Latin tradition is Salisbury, Cathedral Library, MS 169. The first part of this codex contains six works by Augustine and was copied around 1100 (fols 1–77r). In the first half of the twelfth century, St Augustine's *Regula ad servos Dei* was added to this collection (fols 77v–91), probably by extending the original production unit. The genesis can be reconstructed from the facts provided by the description in Gameson, *Manuscripts of Early Norman England*, 153.

39 Some units were extended more than once. An example outside the scope of this essay is the seventh production unit of Paris, Bibliothèque Mazarine, MS 920. Originally it consisted of two letters by Hadewijch (fols 120r–6r), copied in the period 1325–50. The same hand added an excerpt from a Gospel Harmony, starting on the last blank page of the Hadewijch quire and adding new leaves (fols 126v–31v). At a later stage the same hand added three other excerpts from the Gospel Harmony (fols 132r–44v). The second extension was started on the blank remainder of the previous quire and was continued on newly prepared leaves. The stages of production can be deduced from the significant variation in ink colour and *ductus* as well as from variation in the type of parchment that was used for

the extensions, which varies in colour and structure. See Kwakkel, *Dietsche boeke*, 254–9 for the genesis of MS 920.

40 Examples from the Middle Dutch tradition are Brussels MS 1805–08, with Gregory the Great's *Dialogues* (extension consists of extra prologue); and Brussels MS 2873–74, in which four sermons were added, following a copy of Hugo Ripelin of Strassburg's *Compendium theologiae veritatis*. See Kwakkel, *Dietsche boeke*, 205 and 215, respectively.

41 The rationale behind the chosen physical appearance of a codex is explored in Kwakkel, 'Cultural Dynamics of Medieval Book Production.'

42 A scribe using a medium-quality book hand copied an average of four to six pages per day, while somebody using a high-grade script produced little over two pages. See Gumbert, 'The Speed of Scribes,' especially at 62–3 and 68–9.

43 From Bruges Charterhouse a list of lent-out manuscripts survives, dating from the late fourteenth century. The list names private individuals and monastic houses that borrowed books, and the titles of the objects. Returned books were crossed out. See Derolez, *Corpus Catalogorum Belgii*, 27–8.

44 The case of Schoonhoven is discussed in Kwakkel, *Dietsche boeke*, 162.

45 Leiden, Universiteitsbibliotheek, MS BPL 191 A is a Latin composite manuscript from the Benedict Abbey of St Jacques near Liège, Belgium. The book contains over ten production units copied independently in the thirteenth and fourteenth centuries. The dimensions of the parts vary significantly and as a result the binder was not able to trim the pages (if he had, the units with the largest dimensions would have lost a part of the area of written space). The bookblock is therefore uneven, and some parts stick out.

4 The Censorship Trope in Geoffrey Chaucer's *Manciple's Tale* as Ovidian Metaphor in a Gowerian and Ricardian Context

ANITA OBERMEIER

Two recent books partially take up the issue of Richard II's kingship. Samantha J. Rayner examines images of kingship in the literature of Chaucer, Gower, Langland, and the *Gawain*-poet written in the last quarter of the fourteenth century. Rayner postulates that 'Richard II's reign was marked by a particular concern to establish the king as a divinely confirmed ruler' and concludes that these 'poets reacted to their world by turning away from the monarch and restating the importance of the individual,' both politically and spiritually.[1] Jenni Nuttall illustrates how chroniclers, historiographers, and literary authors in the first decade of Henry IV's reign changed, solidified, and perpetuated the negative impressions of Richard II outlined in his bill of resignation.[2] Even though many of Richard II's purported shortcomings are attributable to Lancastrian propaganda, there is evidence from historical and literary records that suggests certain arrogant and absolutist tendencies in Richard II's royal persona that I see reflected in Chaucer's *Manciple's Tale*. Scholarship until the 1980s has often dismissed the *Manciple's Tale* as unsavoury and unimportant. More recent critics, such as Ann W. Astell and Brian Striar, focus on the *Manciple's Tale* as deeply concerned with Chaucerian poetics.[3] I argue that the tale occupies a pivotal place in the *Canterbury Tales* both as Chaucer's last tale before the Parson's didactic sermon and the *Retraction*, and in Chaucer's understanding of authorship. Therefore, in this essay I explore the discursive, metapoetic, and historical connections of authorship, power, and the literary trope of censorship in Chaucer's *Manciple's Tale* by linking Chaucer, Gower, Richard II, and the *Manciple's Tale's* source, Ovid, and his own censoring power, Emperor Augustus. I maintain that Chaucer adapts Ovid's *Metamorphoses* story for three purposes: to depict himself in the Ovidian auctorial tradition; to depict Richard as an irascible monarch, albeit in a veiled fashion that might not deter a real tyrant; and to caution his more outspoken fellow poet John Gower.[4] Before delineating these three purposes, I shall situate the *Manciple's Tale* in Chaucer's larger canon and against the authorship notions raised by my book, *The History and Anatomy of Auctorial Self-Criticism in the European Middle Ages*, specifically the notion that self-criticism might function as a mechanism to circumvent censorship.[5]

Chaucer looms large in the apology tradition's two primary ways to displace literary responsibility: apologies to God, or the religious establishment, and apologies to women.[6] Chaucer's self-criticism, his tactic of portraying himself in a humble light, often deprecating his poetic skills, stands as part of his masterful manipulation of the concepts of the medieval translator, the scholastic compiler, and the sinful author in the Christian cosmos. Chaucer's self-effacing bows to ancient authorities, to contemporary reality, and eventually to Christ – the Master Author – function as self-critical gestures found in *Troilus and Criseyde*, the Prologue to the *Legend of Good Women*, the *Astrolabe*, and the *Canterbury Tales*. These gestures allow Chaucer to construct an intertextual and intra-auctorial poet persona in order to achieve his poetic ends. Chaucer creates three distinct literary censorship scenarios, corresponding to, but not necessarily overlapping with, his three roles of translator, compiler, and author. In these three tableaus, the author has to face the consequences of his text production: first, the dreamer's encounter with the pagan God of Love in the *Legend*; second, the *Retraction* and its implied judgment in the Christian cosmos; and third, the *Manciple's Tale* and the crow's punishment at the hands of Phebus, the God Apollo. From my viewpoint, the *Manciple's Tale* can be read as a veiled and encompassing metaphor about the quandary offensive authors face unless they employ apology strategies; the tale paints a metaphoric picture of a medieval poet's precarious relationship to a potentially irascible monarch, which we might see in Chaucer's and Gower's relationships to Richard II. By choosing and modifying Ovid's story of the punished and exiled crow, Chaucer alludes to Ovid's own exile at the hands of Caesar Augustus in order to illuminate patronage and metapoetic issues and to mark himself as an Ovidian descendant.[7] In the context of Chaucer's two censorship scenarios prior to the *Manciple's Tale* as well as Ovid's two versions of the crow story and his own exile and power problems with Caesar

Augustus, I illustrate Chaucer's and Gower's metaphoric and historical connections to Richard II in the *Manciple's Tale*.

The first censorship tableau appears in the palinodic *Legend of Good Women*, a work supposed to atone for Chaucer's portrayal of Criseyde's faults in *Troilus*. In the Prologue to the *Legend*, Chaucer devises a self-critical frame of literary translation to validate his prior poetic production, to submit to the judgment of a deity – albeit a flawed literary critic and meant to represent Richard II[8] – and to subvert that submission into another auctorial licence. As Jacqueline T. Miller illustrates: 'The author may accept authority that is conferred upon him; he may simply posit and assert his authority; he may deny or abdicate, his authority . . . Furthermore, a poet may disclaim his autonomy only to provide himself with a beneficial type of authorial anonymity: the formal acknowledgment of a higher authority may allow the imagination to roam freely under the guise of authoritative sanction.'[9] The prologue to the *Legend* is an ironic microcosmic rendition of the dilemma the medieval author faces. In this mythological dream-vision structure, the poet recreates the archetypal role of the author whose text is threatened by censure. The medieval author should avoid angering patron and God, as the prologue evokes notions of authority, patronage, and censorship – concerns dealt with more lightly and ironically in a dream vision with a mythological god than with a real patron. Chaucer also depicts the only way the author can act: submit to the constraint of censorship and then manipulate the circumstances to his benefit. At the command of the God of Love, Chaucer will compose the stories of classical women 'That were trewe in lovynge al here lyves' (*LGW* G, 475),[10] but who were tellingly often killed or committed suicide.

Inherent in Chaucer's portrayal of Cupid's censorship is an indictment of the God of Love, by means of which Chaucer suggests the inability of Richard II to understand and to censor the author's art. Chaucer's excuse through his translator role preempts the accusations of the God of Love and challenges his ability as a literary critic long before he appears on the stage. Since it is questionable how a translation of the *Roman de la Rose* (*LGW* G, 246–50, 255–60) could incriminate Chaucer as a disobedient servant of Love, this accusation serves more aptly to demonstrate the ineptitude of Cupid as a reader. As a literary critic, he knows less about books than he thinks and his understanding of *translatio* is dubious.[11] The God of Love is only interested in stories that further his case; thus, he faults Chaucer for writing the wrong kind of truth. The *Manciple's Tale*, as we shall see, criticizes Apollo – also the God of Truth – for punishing the crow for exactly this crime.

The second censorship scenario, in the *Retraction*, transfers the mythological microcosmic aspect and application of the poet's dilemma presented in the *LGW* to the macrocosmic situation of the medieval poet in the Christian cosmos. Chaucer's encounter with the angry God of Love in the *Legend of Good Women* serves as his mythological dress rehearsal for the realities of medieval Christianity. As Chaucer leaves the literary realm ruled by the God of Love for the new literary landscape of fourteenth-century verisimilitude, he changes his allegiance from the God of Love to the God of Salvation and to a scenario that could truly harm him as an author. In this short *Retraction*, Chaucer emerges from behind his other rhetorical persona to acknowledge his literary creation and his responsibility for it. Some scholars argue for deathbed repentance, based on Thomas Gascoigne's *ex post facto* account of Chaucer's death, an account that recently has been severely challenged by Míceál F. Vaughan.[12] Chaucer's *Retraction* should be viewed as the logical continuation of persistent, pervasive, and thoroughly typical Chaucerian self-criticism. Only this time, he plays the role of the penitent author, who, in the medieval Christian cosmos based on the sacramental nature of language, seems to disavow those of his literary creations that do not express a Christian truth, thereby rejecting pagan and medieval stories of human and sexual love.[13]

Nevertheless, purposeful and unmitigated vagueness permeates his ostensible repentance and especially the list of works. The syntax of the *Retraction* reinforces its relative indeterminacy even as it seems to affirm its penitent purpose. Chaucer has arranged the first two thirds of the passage in a loose pattern of chiasmus, the rhetorical scheme of the cross, of the Christ he invokes, of Christianity. He, however, also begins the whole chiastic pattern with two conditional clauses ('if ther be any thyng in it that lyketh hem ... if ther be any thyng that displese hem,' 1081–2) that destabilize the apparent certainty of the *Retraction*. Although Chaucer now behaves like a sinful author in the Christian cosmos, accepting accountability for his literary actions and deeming them irreversible, the *Retraction* comes after the fact – the reader has already gone through the entire work before reading it – and Chaucer extends an invitation to revisit and to re-evaluate his writings, and thereby to remember the author. Chaucer takes responsibility for writing his works but not for readers reading them.[14]

The *Manciple's Tale* provides Chaucer's third censorship situation, once more couched in the form of a classical tale.[15] The author, who has bidden farewell to the God of Love in the *Legend of Good Women*, has not yet said goodbye to the God of Poetry. To me, the *Manciple's Tale* forms the nexus for many auctorial concerns, even though its characters can only be linked to Chaucer and Gower metaphorically, with the support of historical and literary parallels. Following the *Canon's Yeoman's Tale*,[16] Chaucer's *Manciple's Tale* is the penultimate story in the *Canterbury Tales*, preceding the *Parson's Tale*.[17] Opening with a sordid interchange between the Manciple and the Cook in the Prologue, it is presumably a short retelling of Ovid's *Metamorphoses* etiology of how the once white crow was turned black. A quick summary of Ovid's story is in order. Adapting the story from Callimachus,[18] Ovid actually writes two stories in which ravens, sharing the traits of speech and garrulity, interact with Apollo; neither story has a good outcome for the ravens. The *Metamorphoses* story is multilayered, starting with an exhortation about how the raven's tongue spelled his demotion. The raven observes the tryst of Coronis, Phoebus Apollo's lover, with another man, and eagerly wings it to Apollo with this information. On his journey, he is followed by a crow that, using herself as an example in a long digression of an inset tale, tries to warn off the raven from his plan to tell Apollo the truth about his unfaithful mate. The crow had similarly tattled to the goddess Minerva and had not been rewarded but punished with black feathers. The tale adds another layer when the crow recounts her metamorphosis from human girl to bird to escape the advances of Neptune. The raven, however, eschewing the crow's warning, snitches anyway because he expects a reward from his master. The angry Phoebus shoots the pregnant Coronis with his bow, killing her, although he ends up saving the child, Aesculapius. Losing his laurels and dropping his pen, Apollo turns his hatred on the raven for bringing this true message and punishes him with blackness.[19]

Chaucer condenses Ovid's *Metamorphoses* tale into a story about authorship, power, and its abuses. The raven has now become a crow.[20] Phebus, living on earth like a medieval knight, possesses a caged crow, which he has taught to speak. This bird, too, observes the unfaithfulness of Phebus's wife in Chaucer's version with a man of inferior station. Eager to tell his master, the crow tactlessly informs Phebus, who reacts angrily and rashly, killing his wife, breaking his musical instruments, and tossing the crow into the street after turning it black and depriving it of song.[21] The tale ends with the Manciple's editorializing on the dangers of garrulity. Some critics have previously pointed out that the *Manciple's Tale* comically portrays Chaucer's potential predicament as a court poet or that it is Chaucer's farewell to his poetic art.[22] Little in this rather mean-spirited and brutal story is comical; and the tale does not necessarily advocate never to write again. Instead, Chaucer intends to depict the consequences that non-contextualized writing entailed, especially since in all the previous examples, we have seen Chaucer's adeptness at avoiding punishment for his potential offences by defusing potential censorship with self-censorship.

Chaucer uses the classical past to evoke the parallels between Ovid, the crow, and himself, as well as Phebus, Caesar Augustus, and Richard II, as it is much safer to explore the problems of authorship and power in a classical myth. Ovid was one of the most important models for medieval writers in general and for Chaucer in particular. Peter L. Allen, in his discussion of medieval arts of love, asserts that the medieval love poet in some way must become 'a Naso novus' or 'a new Ovid.'[23] Striar claims that the *Manciple's Tale* is 'Chaucer's ultimate expression of his debt to Ovid,' especially in the placement of the tale in the CT order and his characterization of Apollo.[24] Michael Calabrese, although not mentioning the *Manciple's Tale*, discusses how certain Chaucerian works imitate Ovidian strategies. Calabrese maintains that 'Chaucer the vernacular poet could not have seen Ovid as the poet of love without seeing him as the poet of exile.'[25] If this is the case, we can infer that Chaucer intends for Ovid's tale, or the fate of his crow, to point to both Ovid's exile and his subsequent poetic production in *Tristia* and *Epistulae ex Ponto*.

How much did Chaucer actually know about Ovid's exile works? John Fyler and Henry Ansgar Kelly claim that Chaucer did not know the *Tristia* and *Ex Ponto*, mainly because there are no straight language borrowings.[26] I contend, however, that Chaucer cleverly imitates Ovid's life and literary strategy metaphorically with his Ovidian rewrite in the *Manciple's Tale*, a structuralism that needs no explicit language reference. Ralph J. Hexter proposes that Ovid's exile elegies 'suffered no lack of readers during the Middle Ages' and were used in the medieval curriculum, as 'students were expected to keep the reality of Ovid's exile very much in mind as they read the poetry.'[27] Up to the twelfth century, the *Ex Ponto* was slightly more widely owned than the *Tristia*; in the thirteenth century, the *Tristia* manuscripts outnumbered *Ex Ponto*.[28] Dorothy M. Robathan provides a list of medieval writers who penned elegies based on Ovid's *Tristia* and *Epistulae ex Ponto* in the eighth century, such as Modoin, bishop of Aubin (nicknamed 'Naso'), Theodolph, bishop of Orléans (who wrote in Ovid's style in his own exile), and Aquitainian monk Ermoldus Nigellus, after living in Strassburg. In the eleventh century, Bishops Baudry and Hildebert, of Bourgueil and Tours respectively, availed themselves of Ovid's exile poetry as well.[29] Hexter maintains that medieval textual communities knew the extent of Ovid's oeuvre and the place of the exile poetry within it.[30] Furthermore, Kathryn L. McKinley demonstrates that by the fifteenth century more copies of *Epistulae ex Ponto* existed in England than of the *Ars Amatoria*; one such copy in the fourteenth century was in the Hospital of St Thomas in London.[31] Copies of the *Tristia* are, among other libraries, also documented in Canterbury, Winchester, and Cambridge.[32] Robathan also mentions that Nicholas Trivet's (late thirteenth, early fourteenth century) commentary on Seneca's ten tragedies reveals direct quotations from Ovid's *Metamorphoses, Heroides, Fasti, Tristia*, and *Epistulae ex Ponto*.[33] Lastly, Gower both adapts lines from *Tristia* and 'borrows extensively from this and other poems of Ovid's exile as he broods on his solitude.'[34] While I cannot prove that Chaucer had access to a manuscript of Ovid's exile works, I doubt that he did not know about Ovid's own exile story.

Within the context of Ovid's exile stories and the *Manciple's Tale*, the pairs Phebus and the crow, as well as Richard II and Chaucer, parallel Augustus and his banishment of Ovid. Although it is uncertain why Ovid was expelled by Caesar Augustus, in his *Tristia*, Ovid blames his deportation on 'duo crimina, carmen et error' (*Tristia* II. 207 – two crimes, a poem and a blunder).[35] The supposedly offensive *Ars Amatoria* was used mostly as a pretext since the banishment did not happen until ten years after its publication. Exactly what the blunder was has been heatedly debated.[36] John C. Thibault depicts three scenarios: Ovid had an inappropriate liaison with an important female in Augustus's household, possibly his only daughter, Julia, or one of her four daughters; Ovid got entangled in a political faction that had fallen out of favour with Augustus; Ovid had observed something in the royal household, possibly an illicit sexual act by a top member of the royal family – perhaps Augustus himself – which, if divulged, would have caused great scandal during a time when Augustus was trying to counteract loose Roman mores.[37] In *Tristia*, Ovid bemoans:

cur aliquid vidi? cur noxia lumina feci?
cur imprudenti cognita culpa mihi?

inscius Actaeon vidit sine veste Dianam:
praeda fuit canibus non minus ille suis.
scilicet in superis etiam fortuna luenda est,
nec veniam laeso numine casus habet.   (II.103–8)

[Why did I see anything? Why did I make my eyes guilty? Why was I
so thoughtless as to harbour the knowledge of a fault? Unwitting was
Actaeon when he beheld Diana unclothed; none the less he became the
prey of his own hounds. Clearly, among the gods, even ill-fortune must be
atoned for, nor is mischance an excuse when a deity is wronged.]

Indeed, the ocular emphasis in this passage makes for an ironic parallel
between Ovid's life and his tale of the crow in *Metamorphoses*.[38] Ovid
would be censored for the literary message in *Ars Amatoria* and for the
potential voyeuristic information still to be divulged.

Most of these biographical theories about Ovid's exile are drawn
from his own writings and parallel the Apollo and Richard II connections. Although relegated outside the door of Roman civilized space to
the barbaric Black Sea by 'Caesar's anger' (*Tristia* I.ii 62 – Caesaris ira),
Ovid returns to his poetic craft and in atonement writes fervent appeals to Augustus in the *Epistulae ex Ponto* and *Tristia*.[39] Angry divinity
becomes Ovid's leitmotif: 'me deus oppressit' (I.v 75 – a god crushed
me) and 'me Iovis ira premit' (I.v 78 – Jove's wrath crushes me); the
angry Augustus reminds us of the irascible Apollo and of Richard II,
whose tyranny and discursive influence on politics and writing in the
late fourteenth century will be considered shortly. Unlike Chaucer,
who faces the fictional God of Love in the *Legend*, Ovid can implore
his deified exiler only from afar, mainly in *Tristia* II, an epistle, in which
Ovid for the first time addresses a contemporary.[40] In *Tristia* I.ii, Ovid
employs the same conditional sentence structure as Chaucer does in
the *Retraction*: 'immo ita si scitis, si me meus abstulit error, / stultaque
mens nobis, non scelerata fuit . . . ita parcite divi!' (99–100, 105 – Nay, if
such your knowledge, if a mistake of mine has carried me away, if stu-
pid was my mind, not criminal . . . then spare me, gods!). No admission
of fault here, and Ovid even implies that his case was unusual:[41]

nec mea decreto damnasti facta senatus,
nec mea selecto iudice iussa fuga est.
tristibus invectus verbis – ita principe dignum–
ultus es offensas, ut decet, ipse tuas.   (II. 131–4)

[Thou didst not condemn my deeds through a decree of the senate nor was my exile ordered by a special court. With words of stern invective – worthy of a prince – thou didst thyself, as is fitting, avenge thine own injury.][42]

Both Ovid and Chaucer construct literary situations in which they are confronted by their offended prince deities.

Like Chaucer, Ovid laces his accolades with subtle and not so subtle criticisms of his censor.[43] Since he cannot be more specific about the nature of his crime, Ovid's oscillating allusions focus on the imputed offensiveness of his writing – 'the charge that by an obscene poem I have taught foul adultery' (II. 211–12 – qua turpi carmine factus / arguor obsceni doctor adulterii). Searching for exoneration, Ovid defends himself in a number of ways: first, he contextualizes and thus downplays his *Ars Amatoria* as a poem of 'no serious mien . . . not worthy to be read by so great a prince' (II. 241–2 – non esse severae / scripta, nec a tanto principe digna legi) – a typical move of poets in the apology tradition. Then, Ovid points out that he wrote it for courtesans, specifically excluding married women from its readership. Third, he states that any piece of literature can offend a corrupt mind, and pillories theatre and mime performances as morally bankrupt but state sanctioned. Even temples are ill fit for women to attend because in them are told the tales of Jupiter's many extramarital exploits. In his *Metamorphoses*, often Ovid criticizes Jupiter and Apollo 'because they were the chosen gods of Augustus,' and sometimes the emperor and Apollo were even associated.[44] In the previous passage, Ovid downgrades Augustus's purported *deus* status with the earthly address, 'prince.'

On the one hand, Ovid tries to lessen his guilt by saying that his offence does not match his punishment (II. 578 – 'ut par delicto sit mea poena suo') and that Augustus has not shown Ovid his customary mercy. Augustus should read Ovid's entire oeuvre to see how many times the author extols his virtues, Ovid suggests. On the other hand, all this *captatio benevolentiae* is laced with criticism similar to that which Chaucer uses for the Ricardian God of Love; with the Apollo/Augustus connection, maybe it is not such a big leap to Richard, as we will see shortly:

fas ergo est aliqua caelestia pectora falli,
et sunt notitia multa minora tua;
utque deos caelumque simul sublime tuenti

non vacat exiguis rebus adesse Iovi,
de te pendentem sic dum circumspicis orbem,
effugiunt curas inferiora tuas.
scilicet imperii princeps statione relicta
imparibus legeres carmina facta modis?   (II. 213–20)

['Tis possible then, somehow, for divine minds to be deceived, for many things to be beneath thy notice. As Jove who watches at once o'er the gods and the lofty heaven has not leisure to give heed to small things, so whilst thou dost gaze about upon the world that depends upon thee, things of less moment escape thy care. Shouldst thou, forsooth, the prince of the world, abandon thy post and read songs of mine set to unequal measure?][45]

Ovid implies that 'what Augustus lacks is not merely or even primarily the time to give to poetic *ioci* like the *Ars Amatoria*, but rather the literary sensibility needed for their real appreciation,'[46] which Chaucer claims of his censor as well. For the God of Love in the *Legend* to accuse Chaucer of treason for translating the *Roman de la Rose* is equally ludicrous. Both Ovid and Chaucer face their accusers on the authors' own discursive turf, exerting a certain control over their opponents. Jo-Marie Claassen argues that 'Ovid's exile marks the beginning of a new phase in the story of exile: the wielding of literary power, and attempts at its suppression'[47] – maybe we are seeing an equivalent in Chaucer's time as well.

Richard II's two-decade, highly contentious reign was characterized by political and discursive antagonisms. Marion Turner examines this antagonistic discursive climate with its 'language of betrayal, surveillance, slander, treason, [and] rebellion.'[48] In the 1380s, the young king was faced with a number of scarring situations that were not helped by his inflexible adolescent behaviour: the Great Rising of 1381 and its fallout; the power grab by the Appellants, the Merciless Parliament, and his humiliation between 1387 and 1389; the factionalized London city government;[49] and his reclaiming of royal power at the end of the decade. Turner proposes that a 1387 royal proclamation represents Richard's attempt at silencing his critics by controlling discursive power on all spoken and written levels.[50] During the Appellant crisis, Chaucer had wisely withdrawn to Kent, as more than one Ricardian supporter had lost his life; for instance, author Thomas Usk was decapitated in 1388. With some exceptions, Richard spent the years between 1389 and 1397 'calm and generally consistent,' although he would not conclude his revenge on the magnates until 1397.[51] His world received a severe blow when Queen Anne died unexpectedly in 1394 at Sheene; subsequently, he had the manor destroyed. Richard's ire is documented when at Anne's funeral in Westminster Abbey he inflicted a bloody head wound on the disrespectful Earl of Arundel, one of his Appellant nemeses.[52]

Starting in 1397, Richard II 'began to tyrannize' his people, writes chronicler Thomas Walsingham.[53] Even before, the king, known for exercising his arbitrary will and cult of personality, projected an image of a 'ruler-in-majesty, a remote, godlike monarch to whom obedience was due,' Nigel Saul states.[54] But in the second decade of his reign, the 1390s, Richard both cultivated 'a loftier and more exalted image of himself as king' and encouraged 'new and more elaborate forms of address' – prince, your majesty – because of his dramatic flair, the blows he took from the Merciless Parliament, and the need to be regarded as 'supra-mortal' and godlike.[55] He was depicted 'as a sacred icon, supreme and all-powerful,' purposefully promoting connections to the Godhead.[56] Richard was extremely touchy about personal criticism, threatening imprisonment for offenders, and in the 1397 royal declaration pronounced disparagement of his person as treason and thus a capital offence.[57] In his overall assessment of the king, Saul remarks: 'there was a yawning and, almost certainly to observers, obvious gulf. Richard aspired to be an English Solomon; but in reality he was an English Rehoboam. It was not wisdom and prudence that were the characteristics of his rule; it was chastisement and tyranny.'[58]

The wielding of power is also encapsulated in the Prologue to the *Manciple's Tale*, where the Manciple tries to lord it over the drunken Cook, who is called upon for a tale.[59] This plan gets ambushed by the Manciple, who unleashes his mean-spiritedness on the Cook, maligning his tale-telling skills and his physical person in the vilest terms. The Cook, dumbstruck ('For lakke of speche' – *MancPro* 48) at this outburst, gets so upset that he falls off his horse. The Host, frequently employing conciliatory gestures, intercedes preemptively by cautioning the Manciple that the Cook might divulge his shady dealings (*MancPro* 71–5). The Manciple reconsiders and contextualizes his own censoring tongue lashing of the Cook as a 'bourde,' a jest, prompting the Host to repeat one of the *Canterbury Tales* leitmotifs, the need not to turn 'game' into 'ernest' (*MancPro* 81, 100). Donald R. Howard understands Ovid's tale as an exemplum that matches the circumstances of the prologue, while R.D. Fulk expands this idea and interprets the crow as representing the Cook, the Manciple, and the Wife in the story: 'The tattling crow reveals her misdoings, just as the Cook will expose the Manciple's, if the tale does not have its intended effect.'[60] Chauncey Wood argues that the silencing of the Cook in the Prologue mirrors that of the crow in the tale.[61] Given that, the Manciple takes on the role of Apollo, but the teller cannot act in the same unilateral fashion as Apollo because the Host reins him in. In the tale, no one reins in Apollo's rage with dire consequences for the crow. This aspect of unmitigated power points to tyrannical Ricardian events of 1397, which will be discussed below.

Chaucer employs Phebus in the *Manciple's Tale* as a mirror of Richard II, a *Fürstenspiegel* on how not to act, even if that critique was primarily addressed to an idealized reader rather than the monarch himself. On the surface, Ovid's Phoebus Apollo and Chaucer's Phebus seem rather different, but criticism lurks under the surface of Ovid's narrative as well. Ovid's Phoebus comes with heroic and divine attributes of the Sun God – the promoter of music, prophecy, and truth – that appear to have been demythologized and downgraded to ludicrous levels in the *Manciple's Tale*, where he is a pre-God, residing on earth like Richard. Chaucer may have done that to poke fun at Richard's aspirations to divinity. Phebus kills the serpent Phitoun, 'as he lay / Slepynge agayn the sonne upon a day' (*MancT* 109–10). Phebus is depicted both as a medieval knight and as the jealous – and soon to be cuckolded – husband of the *fabliau*; John P. McCall calls him Sir Thopas, the trite knight of Chaucer the Pilgrim's story.[62] But this comical designation obscures the fact that we see the god at his worst here, 'mean and arbitrary,' James Dean claims,[63] as Chaucer chooses not to equip his Phebus with the traditional garland of mercy.[64] Michael Kensak explains that Chaucer represents not the positive classical images of the Sun God but the 'counter-trend in medieval mythography which depicts a violent Apollo . . . as a despotic prince,'[65] and thus an obvious fit with Richard's 1390s personality.

Further evidence from the *Manciple's Tale* points to a connection between Phebus and Richard. David Wallace asserts that the Chaucerian reader should be able to recognize both the tyrannical Phebus and Lombard despots from these lines that are actually uttered in conjunction with the wife of Phebus: 'Right so bitwixe a titlelees tiraunt / And an outlawe or a theef erraunt, / The same I seye: there is no difference'

(*MancT* 223–5).[66] I postulate that the contemporary English audience was primarily supposed to recognize Richard in this passage. In January of 1397, Richard was greatly annoyed with the petition of Thomas Haxey that had been presented in Parliament, specifically his questioning of the size and cost of the royal household. True to the discursive power issues discussed above, the clerk Haxey was 'sentenced for treason but later pardoned.'[67] In July of 1397, Richard demanded that *carte blanche* loans be made to him and he arrested the Appellants Arundel, Gloucester, and Warwick in order to try, execute, or imprison them for life, and confiscate their property.[68] I argue that Chaucer alludes to these actions in the passage above. Richard's revenge against the Appellants and his *carte blanche* taxation scheme of 1397 demonstrate the aspects both of the tyrant, who destroys his subjects, and of the thief, who helps himself to others' property.

Moreover, Richard and Phebus the Sun God can be linked through the fact that a young Richard jousted in 1378–9 and in 1386 'in armor decorated with Edward III's famous sun badge'; sunbursts were also imprinted on his tomb effigy.[69] According to the *Middle English Dictionary*, Chaucer is credited with the first reference to (*MkT* 1375) and the most references to Phebus in Middle English.[70] He uses the term Phebus or Apollo seventy-five times in his entire corpus, most of them pedestrian metaphors for the sun. The actual Sun God is referenced in the *Monk's Tale*, the *Franklin's Tale*, the *Complaint of Mars*, the *House of Fame*, *Troilus*, and the *Legend*, but primarily in the *Manciple's Tale*.[71] The appearance of Apollo in Middle English literature occurs simultaneously with Richard's kingship. The initial associations intended with this pairing may have been positive ones, but by the later 1390s they were surely negative and exploited by Chaucer as such.

Chaucer also depicts the Manciple and the crow as metaphors for the medieval author generally, and himself and Gower specifically. The Manciple, like Chaucer in *Troilus*, mentions 'olde bookes' (*MancT* 106) and the writings of 'olde clerkes' (*MancT* 154) and apologizes for his own unseemly language:[72] 'Certes, this is a knavyssh speche! / Foryeveth it me' (*MancT* 205–6). Wearing the Chaucerian self-critical humility cap, the Manciple protests that he is 'a man nought textueel' (*MancT* 235, 316).[73] The crow echoes Chaucer's 'Blameth nat me if that ye chese amys' from the Prologue to the *Miller's Tale* (*MillPro* 3181) with his 'I synge nat amys' (*MancT* 248) before he tattles on the tryst he had just observed. Furthermore, the crow metaphorically represents the punished author because only in Chaucer's version is the crow bereft of his speech and song. This punishment is ironic because the ecclesiastical hierarchy often rebuked medieval authors for telling *fabulae*, instead of truths, just as the Parson in the Prologue to his tale condemns fables.[74] But the crow's truthful account is interpreted by Phebus, the censoring authority figure, as a 'false tale' (*MancT* 293). The crow, who 'countrefete the speche of every man / He koude, whan he sholde telle a tale' (*MancT* 134–5), represents the medieval translator and compiler, as he simply relates his observations, much like the Chaucerian narrator of the *General Prologue* does (*GP* 726–33), but he is treated like the author in the *Retraction*. Unlike in the other analogues, the Manciple does not criticize the crow and seems to think of it as 'an alter-ego.'[75] Dean argues that both the crow and Phebus represent Chaucer the author, who in the *Manciple's Tale* takes leave of his book by imitating the God of Poetry, breaking the instruments of his song.[76] But given the hierarchical power relationship between the crow and Phebus, they cannot, I contend, represent the same principle, especially since Apollo breaks his instruments out of sorrow for his bad judgment, but the crow is forced into his silence.

Both this Ovidian tale and the character of Phebus are important for Chaucer's self-critical intentions. Phebus mimics the *Legend's* God of Love as well as the Christian Master Author of the *Retraction* in his power over the crow/Chaucer.[77] However, just as the God of Love is implicitly criticized for his literary judgment, the God of Poetry, who himself was the willing participant in many illicit love affairs, shows little common sense in killing his wife and punishing the messenger for the message before verifying the crow's story. Chaucer's translator and compiler roles illustrate that the message should not implicate the messenger, as it is not his or her individual and original creation. In the delivery of his text, the crow provides no introductory context, no apology to the effect that he merely reports distasteful news, such as Chaucer supplies in the *General Prologue* and the *Miller's Prologue*. In fact, the crow's brazen tone is insulting, and thus would especially have required the mitigating contextualization of an auctorial apology to ensure sympathetic reception of his text:

> This crowe sang 'Cokkow! Cokkow! Cokkow!' . . .
> 'Phebus,' quod he, 'for al thy worthynesse,
> For al thy beautee and thy gentilesse,
> For al thy song and al thy mynstralcye,
> For al thy waityng, blered is thyn ye

With oon of litel reputacioun,
Noght worth to thee, as in comparisoun,
The montance of a gnat, so moote I thryve!
For on thy bed thy wyf I saugh hym swyve.'   (*MancT* 243, 249–56)

The crow seems to relish in his master's misfortune, emphasizing his blindness – not a great calling card for the God of prophecy. This insult smarts painfully because only in Chaucer's version had Phebus taught the bird to speak.[78] The crow's misuse of Apollo's divine gift of speech, a gift that parallels medieval poets' power to imitate the creative logos, constitutes a betrayal similar to the medieval poet's misuse of language.

One medieval dictum states that a garrulous tongue is a dangerous tongue, especially that of a 'jangler,' defined by the *MED* not only as a chatterer, but also as 'an eloquent person, a speech maker,' 'a raconteur, teller of dirty stories,' 'a professional entertainer.'[79] This terminology reflects value judgments of Chaucer's society and foregrounds the problems and pitfalls of the medieval poet and performer. 'A jangler is to God abhomynable' (*MancT* 343) and 'A janglere speke of perilous mateere' (*MancT* 348), ironically preaches the Manciple, echoing a prevailing sentiment of the fourteenth century that was backed by Matthew 12:36–7: 'But I say unto you, that every idle word that men shall speak, they shall render an account for it in the day of judgment. For by thy words thou shalt be justified, and by thy words thou shalt be condemned.'[80] A twelfth-century manuscript illumination glosses Matthew and reflects the medieval view of how use of language affects salvation. The Prüfening manuscript of Isidore of Seville's *Etymologiae* (Clm 13031) depicts on the first page the self-portrait of the scribe Ingelard: he lies on the ground dead while above him the archangel Michael holds the 'soul scale' and another angel places Ingelard's book on the scale; at that point the devil flees and the soul of the deceased is transported to heaven.[81] The illumination affirms the positive power literary creation can have on the poet's salvation; however, it could also have the opposite effect, evidenced by the devil's waiting in the wings. That the crow in the *Manciple's Tale* is thrown out the door for the devil to take clearly points to the fate of the author who does not measure up in the eyes of church hierarchy, patron, and God. The crow is not just expelled by Apollo; the god leaves the bird for the devil to take, apparently assuming it deserves damnation. These are the underlying ideas reflected in the manuscript illumination.

The white bird's unceremonious metamorphosis into the black and silenced crow[82] is accompanied by the raconteur's last warning on garrulity, authorship, and self-censorship. The Manciple reaffirms the dependency of the author – already expressed in the crow's Chaucer-specific captivity in a cage – with a comparison of the author to a 'thral' (*MancT* 357). David Raybin paradoxically argues that 'reasoned speech liberates the crow,' raising poignant questions about authorship, authority, freedom, and patronage,[83] just as the ventriloquist exhortation of the Manciple's mother does: 'My sone, be war, and be noon auctor newe / Of tidynges, wheither they been false or trewe' (*MancT* 359–60). One problem with authorship is reception, as an author never knows if text will be welcomed. Emphasizing that truth is a problematic principle, Chaucer seems to indict both the God of Truth, Apollo, and the censoring linguistic regime of Richard's reign that the Manciple seems to imitate. Chaucer thus equates the crow with a figure of the careless author, who is too sure of his position in the patron's household and who forgets his place, deference, and auctorial apology strategy. Immediately, Chaucer evokes Horace, writer of several apologies:[84]

> But he that hath mysseyd, I dar wel sayn,
> He may by no wey clepe his word agayn.
> Thyng that is seyd is seyd, and forth it gooth,
> Though hym repente, or be hym nevere so looth.   (*MancT* 353–6)

Authors cannot call their work back. They can either contextualize it with apologetic structures, such as Chaucer's, or if lucky, retract it later. The crow, however, is not so lucky.

Chaucer portrays both the God of Love and the God of Poetry as images of Richard II. Both gods act without being fully informed, behave rashly, and are easily prompted by anger. For instance, in the Prologue to the *Legend*, Alceste cautions the God of Love about 'wilfulhed and tyrannye' (*LGW* G, 355). Chaucer is not alone in that. Lee Patterson posits that in his *Book of Cupid*, 'Clanvowe's wilful Cupid is another . . . critique of Richard's tyranny.'[85] Also in the first recension of the Prologue to John Gower's *Confessio Amantis*, the author employs the 'Auftragstopos': Richard II invites Gower onto his barge on the Thames to request that he write 'Som newe thing.'[86] Subsequently, James Simpson perceives, a power struggle with an Ovidian root occurs in Gower's *Confessio*:

If the young Richard is described as tyrannical, it may be no coincidence that the rule of a tyrannical will generates Gower's *Confessio*. In the prologue the narrator speaks from a philosophical position of rationalism, to attack the division of the contemporary political world. In Book 1, however, the narrator himself falls prey to this very division, as he succumbs to the power of the boy-prince Cupid, and so abandons the matter of politics and history. These shifts in narratorial position invoke the opening of Ovid's *Amores*, where the narrator recounts that he was about to write powerful and historical matter, when Cupid laughed and stole a metrical foot, to produce elegiac couplets. The poet complains at this improper invasion of discursive fields rightly belonging to other deities, when Cupid shoots him and commands that Ovid's own pain be matter for his poetry. This leaves the poet both cut off from the public world, emptied of matter, but equally under a new and unremitting 'political' regime.[87]

Further literary authorship and potential censorship connections exist. Both Richard Axton and Richard Hazelton propose that in the *Manciple's Tale* Chaucer is specifically parodying Gower and his *Confessio*. Axton argues that Chaucer wants to question the moral qualities of Gower, who was viewed as the paramount 'provider of morals for stories from Ovid.'[88] Hazelton posits that Chaucer wanted to indict Gower 'as the chief purveyor of banal literary fare to the audience Chaucer wrote for'[89] with the phrase 'My sone' (359) from the *Manciple's Tale*, quoted above, which in the *Confessio* is employed by Venus to Amans, who is later identified as Gower. I suggest not a parody of, but instead a warning to, Gower, like that in the manuscript illumination of the *Etymologiae*, to be more cautious in his own criticism of Richard II. Despite the purportedly auspicious royal commissioning of the *Confessio*, Gower became so disillusioned with Richard that he rewrote the Prologue as early as 1392 and dedicated the *Confessio* to the future Henry IV. Gower had a penchant for speaking truth to power, such as in *Vox Clamantis* Book VII and the Latin 'social conscience' poems of the late 1390s, such as *Carmen super multiplici viciorum pestilencia*, pilloring Lollardy during the 'reign of Richard II.'[90] But while these two latter works chronicled social ills during Richard's reign, they did not attack him directly.

In another Latin social conscience poem, *O deus immense*, kings are even addressed in the second person singular, and thus the criticism is more blatant. Although universal sounding – the poem could apply to any king, even Henry IV – it highly chastises Ricardian behaviour, especially his arbitrariness, his unwillingness to listen to his subjects, and his discursive and monetary appropriations:

O Deus immense, sub quo dominantur in ense
Quidam morosi Reges, quidam viciosi,
Disparibus meritis – sic pax, sic mocio litis.
Publica regnorum manifestant gesta suorum:
Quicquid delirant Reges, plectuntur Achivi . . .
'Ve qui predaris,' Ysaias clamat avaris;
Sic verbis claris loquitur tibi qui dominaris.
Rex qui plus aurum populi quam corda thesaurum
Computat a mente populi cadit ipse repente.
Os ubi vulgare non audet verba sonare . . .
Ad vocem plebis aures sapienter habebis . . .
Absque Deo vana cum sit tibi cotidiana
Pompa; recorderis, sine laude Dei morieris . . .
Non ex fatali casu set iudiciali
Pondere regali stat medicina mali.

[O boundless God, under whom rule with the sword
Some moral kings, some vicious kings,
With diverse merits – now peace, now the agitation of strife–
Manifest the public deeds of their kingdoms:
For whatever folly the kings commit, the people are punished; . . .
'You who plunder,' Isaias cries out to the avaricious;
Thus in clear words he speaks to you who reign.
A king who reckons gold greater than the hearts of his people
Immediately falls from the people's mind.
When the people's voice does not dare to speak out loud . . .
You will wisely have ears for the voice of the people . . .
Since your daily splendor would be vain without God,
Remember: you will die without God's approval . . .
The remedy for evil consists not of fateful decree
But of judicial decree with royal gravity.][91]

This poem exists with two different headings. The earlier version's heading reads: 'Carmen quod Iohannes Gower tempore regis Ricardi dum vixit ultimo composuit' [A poem that John Gower recently composed in the time of King Richard, while he lived],[92] while the final version omits the reference to King Richard. The discrepancy in head-ings suggests that Gower did indeed write *O deus immense* during Rich-ard's reign. The poem has generally been dated to 1399, but R.F. Yeager suggests that it could have been started during the intensification of Richard's 'autocracy in 1397–98' when Gower was still hoping that Richard could be taught to see the error of his ways.[93] Thus, Chaucer's warning about 'tydinges . . . false or trewe' could have been meant for his friend Gower, who might have been too bold for Chaucer in this auctorial approach: writing poetry critical of the monarch with unob-scured auctorial identity. Even that most antagonistic poem toward the upper class, *Piers Plowman*, seems to have been penned by some-one sporting the *nom de plume* William Langland because its contents were too controversial, as John Bowers suggests;[94] the highly critical *Richard the Redeless* was anonymous. Chaucer's metaphoric critique of Richard within the *Manciple's Tale* corresponds to his general auctorial *modus operandi*. Unlike Gower, who approaches Richard directly in both the Ricardian commission narrative and the critical *O deus immense*, Chaucer interacts with Richard via the God of Love in the *Legend* and via Phebus Apollo in the *Manciple's Tale*; Kathryn McKinley points out that medieval authors had to mask criticism of their monarch 'under a cloak of silence, often resorting to classical story-material as a type of code to veil their intentions.'[95] The crow's and Gower's directness may have made Chaucer uneasy because of the restrictive discursive climate.

Lastly, based on my discussion of 1397 events and the dating of and connection to Gower's *O deus immense*, through which similar issues of tyranny and fiscal irresponsibility echo as in the *Manciple's Tale*, I suggest a circumscribed date for the *Manciple's Tale*. The dating of the tale is contested, as those critics who think it a poor tale have consid-ered it a product of Chaucer's early years. For critics seeing the tale as a more accomplished work or a parody of Gower's version, these features suggest a date post-1390; Donald C. Baker argues for a date between 1388 and 1399.[96] Based on my discussion of 1397 events and their echoes in the *Manciple's Tale*, I suggest that even if Chaucer started the tale earlier, he may not have finished it until 1397 or after.

The many-skeined intertextual threads relating to literature, author-ity, and the trope of censorship attest to the longevity and consistency of auctorial vicissitudes from classical to late medieval, and even to modern times, if we consider the *fatwa* pronounced on Salman Rushdie for his *Satanic Verses* in 1989. Ovid, Gower, and Chaucer grappled with their literary creative energy while dealing with a censoring political power; nevertheless, they portray poets in defiance. In *Tristia* III.vii, Ovid demonstrates his greatest defiance of imperial power: 'ingenio tamen ipse meo comitorque fruorque: / Caesar in hoc potuit iuris habere nihil . . . me tamen extincto fama superstes erit' (47–8, 50 – my mind is nevertheless my comrade and my joy; over this Caesar could have no right . . . when I am dead my fame shall survive).[97] Ovid clearly rejects Augustus, his desire for propagandistic uses of poetry,[98] and his censorship. A.M. Keith theorizes that in each of the stories in *Metamorphoses* Book 2, 531–835 (which includes the first raven story), 'mortal speech' is divinely censored and punished. Furthermore, the *Fasti*, containing the second raven tale, have been interpreted as examining 'the limits of speech under tyranny.'[99] In the *Manciple's Tale*, Chaucer revives this classical past and issues of censorship raised by Ovid's life and work in order to reflect on these same issues in late fourteenth-century England, where Gower openly criticizes the wayward monarch. The author who has provided numerous auctorial apologies to contextualize his works gives us a glimpse of the poetic world without the protection of auctorial apologies. Chaucer, like the crow and Ovid, is a survivor: the crow gets booted out, but not killed; Ovid, banished but not executed, still writes; and Chaucer, even though he had gone into self-imposed exile in Kent during the Ricardian magnate power struggle and the Merciless Parliament, returned and with a renewed sense of purpose embarked on the *Canterbury Tales*. The poets Ovid, Gower, and Chaucer have the last laugh: the power of Apollo, Augustus, and Richard II, along with them, has turned to dust – they themselves subjected to the poets' 'allusively mocking pen.'[100] As Ovid triumphantly declares, 'I shall be read' ('legar,' *Tristia*, III. vii. 52) – and so he, Gower, and Chaucer still are.

NOTES

1 Rayner, *Images of Kingship*, 160 and 161.
2 Nuttall, *Creation of Lancastrian Kingship*. For an assessment of Richard's masculinity, see Fletcher, *Richard II*. For a view of censorship in the Lancastrian reign, see Kirsty Campbell's essay in this volume, 'Vernacular *Auctoritas* in Late Medieval England: Writing after the *Constitutions*,' which challenges the notion of the chilling effect of Arundel's *Constitutions* on vernacular literary activity, especially religious writings; see also Kerby-Fulton, *Books Under Suspicion*.

3 Astell, 'Nietzsche, Chaucer, and the Sacrifice of Art'; and Brian Striar, 'The "Manciple's Tale" and Chaucer's Apolline Poetics.'

4 Helen Cooper points out that 'Chaucer was first compared to Ovid in his own lifetime by Eustache Deschamps' and later by Dryden ('Chaucer and Ovid,' 71). For general studies of Chaucer's use of Ovid, see Fyler, *Chaucer and Ovid*; Fyler, 'Ovid and Chaucer'; and Hoffman, *Ovid and the Canterbury Tales*.

5 Obermeier, *Auctorial Self-Criticism*. My work chronicles the European apology tradition from the sixth century BCE to 1500 by examining the vernacular and Latin tales, lyrics, epics, and prose compositions of Arabic, English, French, German, Greek, Italian, Spanish, and Welsh authors.

6 For an extended discussion of Chaucer's participation in the apology tradition and for literature reviews on Chaucer's works, see Obermeier, *Auctorial Self-Criticism*, 185–220.

7 For another poet with anxieties of origins, see Iain Macleod Higgins's essay 'Master Henryson and Father Aesop' in this volume.

8 John M. Bowers suggests that Chaucer may have found his 'model for the God of Love as Richard II's fictional alter ego in the Prologue to the Legend' in John Clanvowe's *Boke of Cupid* (*Chaucer and Langland*, 24).

9 Miller, *Poetic License*, 3–4.

10 All quotations from Chaucer are taken from Benson, *The Riverside Chaucer*, and documented by line numbers in the text.

11 See also Jamie C. Fumo, who developed my ideas further in 'The God of Love and Love of God.'

12 Dean, 'Chaucer's Repentance: A Likely Story'; Wurtele, 'The Penitence of Geoffrey Chaucer'; and Vaughan, 'Personal Politics and Thomas Gascoigne's Account of Chaucer's Death.'

13 See also Obermeier, 'Chaucer's "Retraction."'

14 Thus, he seems to intend to continue writing – we cannot infer from anything in the *Retraction* that he never intends to write again – nor does he call for the destruction of his works. In fact, in the tradition, even Christian self-criticism like that expressed in the *Retraction* usually becomes a pretext for further writing. Generally, self-critical Christian writers promise to redeem their sin of having celebrated physical love with a didactic work pleasing to God and the religious establishment. For a discussion of the posthumous manuscript tradition of the *Retraction* in Chaucer's canon formation, see Stephen Partridge's essay in this volume, '"The Makere of this Boke": Chaucer's *Retraction* and the Author as Scribe and Compiler.'

15 For an overview of criticism on the tale, see Baker, *A Variorum Edition, The Manciple's Tale*, 19–38; and Benson, *The Canterbury Tales: Complete*, 952–4. Most recently, *Studies in the Age of Chaucer* 25 (2003) devoted its Colloquium section to the *Manciple's Tale*.

16 For connections between the *Canon's Yeoman's Tale* and the *Manciple's Tale*, see Hill, *Chaucerian Belief*, 62–76.

17 For connections of the *Manciple's Tale* to the *Parson's Tale*, see Allen, 'Penitential Sermons, the Manciple, and the End of *The Canterbury Tales*'; Howard, *The Idea of the Canterbury Tales*; Jeffrey, '*The Manciple's Tale*'; Pitard, 'Sowing Difficulty'; Powell, 'Game Over'; and Wood, 'Chaucer's Tales of the Manciple and the Parson.'

18 Keach, 'Ovid and "Ovidian" Poetry,' 187.

19 Ovid, *Metamorphoses*, 96–105. In his *Fasti*, an unfinished work on the Roman calendar, Ovid gives a brief vignette about a lazy raven who is remiss in bringing water for Apollo's religious rite; he is punished with temporary water deprivation for his lies (Ovid, *Fasti*, II.243–66). For a detailed discussion of Ovid's raven stories, see Keith, *Play of Fictions*, 9–61. Some scholars contend that Chaucer may have known only the *Ovide Moralisé*, but others argue that Chaucer had access to Ovid's version as well (Baker, *A Variorum Edition, The Manciple's Tale*, 6). Truthtelling became a major issue in the usurpation events of 1399; see Nuttall, *Creation of Lancastrian Kingship*, 22–4.

20 Fumo has painted a fascinating mythographic tableau on the importance of Chaucer's switch from raven to crow ('The *Manciple's Tale* and Ovidian Mythography').

21 Chaucer probably knew Gower's version, the 'Tale of Phebus and Cornide,' in Book 3 of *Confessio Amantis*, with the stories against backbiting and fault-finding. Gower omits and emphasizes different, less authorship-oriented, aspects from Chaucer: Coronis is back to a lover, not a wife, and there is no mention of Phebus's status as the God of Poetry, nor any breaking of instruments. The bird is identified as treacherous and belonging to Cornide, the lover, hence the larger betrayal. Phebus kills Cornide with a sword, and the bird is turned into a raven. No silencing is discussed but a warning on speech is offered. For a discussion of sources and analogues to the tale and how Chaucer's version differs, see Baker, *A Variorum Edition, The Manciple's Tale*, 4–11; and Wheatley, 'The Manciple's Tale.'

22 James Dean sees the *Manciple's Tale* as 'an integral part of Chaucer's developing quarrel with fiction making and poetry' ('Dismantling the Canterbury Book,' 754). But I agree with Michaela Paasche Grudin, who questions that the *Manciple's Tale* negates 'the assumptions about

discourse and poetry that shaped' the *Canterbury Tales* (*Chaucer and the Politics of Discourse*, 150). See also Ginsberg, *Chaucer's Italian Tradition*, 58–104; and Storm, 'Speech, Circumspection, and Orthodontics in the *Manciple's Prologue*.'

23 Allen, *Art of Love*, 2–3.

24 Striar, 'Chaucer's Apolline Poetics,' 193. For a comprehensive treatment of Apollo, see Fumo, *The Legacy of Apollo*.

25 Calabrese, *Chaucer's Ovidian Arts of Love*, 15.

26 Fyler, *Chaucer and Ovid*; and Kelly, *Chaucerian Tragedy*, 61–5.

27 Hexter, 'Poetry of Ovid's Exile,' 41 and 56.

28 Ibid., 41–2.

29 Robathan, 'Ovid in the Middle Ages,' 192–3.

30 Hexter, 'Poetry of Ovid's Exile,' 50.

31 McKinley, 'Manuscripts of Ovid in England,' 41–85, 45–6, and 82. Also, about the same time as Chaucer translated the *Roman de la Rose*, Robert Holkot penned the *Moralia super Ovidii Metamorphoses* in England (Robathan, 'Ovid in the Middle Ages,' 200).

32 McKinley, 'Manuscripts of Ovid in England,' 81–3.

33 Robathan, 'Ovid in the Middle Ages,' 205–6.

34 Harbert, 'Ovid and John Gower,' 96.

35 All references to *Tristia* and *Epistulae ex Ponto* are taken from Ovid, *Tristia; Ex Ponto*, and documented by line numbers in the text.

36 Green, 'Carmen et Error'; Radulescu, *Ovid in Exile*, 49–68; Syme, *History in Ovid*, 192–229; and Thibault, *Mystery of Ovid's Exile*.

37 Thibault, *Mystery of Ovid's Exile*, 38–72.

38 For notions of Chaucer's poetic craft as voyeurism, see Spearing, *Medieval Poet as Voyeur*, 139.

39 For the theory that Ovid had not actually been exiled, see Claassen, *Displaced Persons*, 34. Translations in this sentence and the next are mine.

40 For further discussions of *Tristia* and *Ex Ponto*, see Barchiesi, *The Poet and the Prince*; Block, 'Poetics in Exile'; Claassen, *Displaced Persons*; and Williams, *Banished Voices* and 'Ovid's Exile Poetry.'

41 For a definition of Roman exile, see Claassen, *Displaced Persons*, 11.

42 I have emended the Loeb's translation of this passage, which reads 'degree' through an apparent typographical error.

43 For a discussion of Ovid as a pro-Augustan or an anti-Augustan poet, see Williams, *Banished Voices*, 154–62.

44 Striar, 'Chaucer's Apolline Poetics,' 194. Interestingly, Apollo was 'the favored deity of the Augustan age,' symbolizing 'Augustus's cherished ideals' (Rand, *Ovid and His Influence*, 91). On the divinity of Roman emperors, see Evans, *Ovid's Books from Exile*, 12.

45 Gareth Williams points out that *Tristia* II. 213–38 may parallel Horace's attitude toward Augustus in *Epistulae* 2.1 ('Ovid's Exile Poetry,' 239–40). See also Barchiesi, *The Poet and the Prince*, 30.

46 Williams, *Banished Voices*, 181–2.

47 Furthermore, Ovid imitates and perfects 'a literary form established by the exiled Cicero' (Claassen, *Displaced Persons*, 59 and 181). For a discussion of Richard II as a patron of the arts, see Bennett, 'The Court of Richard II and the Promotion of Literature'; Burrow, *Ricardian Poetry*; Eberle, 'Richard II and the Literary Arts'; and Strohm, *Social Chaucer*, 24–46. Richard Firth Green details through his discussions of the administrative structure and specific vicissitudes of Richard's deposition why there is a dearth of records on the king's possible patronage of the flowering poets of his reign (*Poets and Princepleasers*). See also Storm, 'Speech, Circumspection, and Orthodontics,' 110–11.

48 Turner, *Chaucerian Conflict*, 1. See also Bowers, *Chaucer and Langland*.

49 For a panegyric view of Richard's reconciliation with the city of London, see Richard Maidstone's *Concordia* (*The Reconciliation of Richard II with London*).

50 Turner, *Chaucerian Conflict*, 8–9.

51 Saul, *Richard II*, 202.

52 Wallace, *Chaucerian Polity*, 372.

53 Saul, *Richard II*, 366. On the topic of Lancastrian propaganda and for comparisons of Richard's public image in a number of chronicles, see Stow, 'Richard II in Thomas Walsingham's Chronicles'; and Nuttal, *Creation of Lancastrian Kingship*, 9–40.

54 Saul, *Richard II*, 238.

55 Saul, 'Richard II and the Vocabulary of Kingship,' 854 and 861–2.

56 Saul, *Richard II*, 239.

57 Grudin, *Chaucer and the Politics of Discourse*, 21–3; and Turner, *Chaucerian Conflict*, 10–11.

58 Saul, *Richard II*, 465.

59 Some think that this might indicate the journey back because the Cook has already told a tale, albeit an incomplete one (Baker, *A Variorum Edition, The Manciple's Tale*, 15), and, because as Stephen D. Powell points out, Chaucer was still revising the tales ('Game Over,' 43). For an extensive treatment of the Cook, see Kolve, *Chaucer and the Imagery of Narrative*, 257–84. Also see Astell for a treatment of the Dionysian prologue and the Apollonian tale ('Nietzsche, Chaucer, and the Sacrifice of Art,' 323–9).

60 Howard, *Idea of the Canterbury Tales*, 299; and Fulk, 'Reinterpreting the Manciple's Tale,' 492. See also Cox, *Gender and Language in Chaucer*, 47–52.

61 Wood, 'Chaucer's Tales of the Manciple and the Parson,' 220.

62 McCall, *Chaucer Among the Gods*, 129.

63 Dean, 'Ending of the *Canterbury Tales*,' 26. Dean expounds further: 'If Chaucer had intended to subvert Apollo's traditional (classical) mythic qualities, he could not have done it better: in Greek antiquity Apollo was essentially the god who provided purification (*katharsis*) after cases of homicide and the blood pollution (*miasma*) resulting from it' (27). But the murder of Coronis, Phebus' wife – not named by Chaucer – is already in Ovid, pointing to Ovid's own problems with arbitrary deities. For much needed feminist discussions on *Manciple's Tale*, see Cox, *Gender and Language in Chaucer*, 97–112; and Raybin, 'The Death of a Silent Woman.' Also, see Wallace for connections to the *Tale of Melibee* and women's council (*Chaucerian Polity*, 247–60).

64 Cited in Allen, 'Penitential Sermons,' 90, note 21.

65 Kensak, 'Apollo *exterminans*,' 143 and 144. For a Christianized reading of Apollo, see Allen, 'Penitential Sermons,' 89. This brutal medieval Apollo may originate from Ovid's portrayal of Apollo as vicious throughout the *Metamorphoses* (Kensak, 'Apollo *exterminans*,' 150). Ovid also shows a cowardly side of Apollo in *Metamorphoses* V.329, where Apollo turns himself into a crow to hide from giants trying to overthrow the gods.

66 For a discussion of tyranny, see Nuttall, *Creation of Lancastrian Kingship*, 11–12.

67 Saul, *Richard II*, 369.

68 Ibid., 366–7.

69 Patterson, *Chaucer and the Subject of History*, 187; and Wallace, *Chaucerian Polity*, 257 and note 31.

70 'Phebus' in the *Middle English Dictionary* (2001) [http://quod.lib.umich. edu/cgi/m/mec/med-idx?type=byte&byte=141968843&egdisplay=open &egs=141974348, accessed 10 June 2008].

71 *Chaucer Concordance at eChaucer* [http://www.umm.maine.edu/faculty/ necastro/chaucer/concordance/ accessed 10 June 2008].

72 A number of critics view the tale as essentially commenting on the nature and dangers of speech and language: Fradenburg, 'The Manciple's Servant Tongue'; Patton, 'Politics of Language in Chaucer's *Manciple's Tale*'; Pelen, 'Manciple's "Cosyn" to the "Dede"'; and Scattergood, 'Manciple's Manner of Speaking.'

73 Marianne Børch argues that the Manciple is 'arguably aligned with Chaucer in his least attractive role as a poet, a Chaucer in need of priest and Grace' ('Chaucer's Poetics and *The Manciple's Tale*,' 296).

74 See Obermeier, *Auctorial Self-Criticism*, 115 and 121; and Furrow, 'Chaucer, Writing, and Penitence,' 250.

75 Hazelton, 'Parody and Critique,' 27.

76 Dean, 'Ending of the *Canterbury Tales*,' 28–9.

77 See Hines, ' "For sorwe of which he brak his mynstralcye." '

78 Harwood, 'Chaucer's Manciple,' 270.

79 'Janglere' in the *Middle English Dictionary* (2001) [http://quod.lib.umich.
    edu/cgi/m/mec/med-idx?type=id&id=MED23775, accessed 10 June
    2008]. For a discussion of janglery, see Westervelt, 'Janglery in *The
    Manciple's Tale*.'

80 Douai-Rheims Bible [http://www-rohan.sdsu.edu/%7Eamtower/
    matthew.htm, accessed 10 June 2008].

81 Klopsch, *Dichtungslehren des lateinischen Mittelalters*, 5–6.

82 Chaucer leaves out the major metamorphosis of Ovid's tale. Apollo's lover,
    Coronis, pleads for her unborn child, Aesculapius, whom Apollo saves.

83· Raybin, 'The Death of a Silent Woman,' 35.

84 Harriet Seibert identified Horace as the source of this passage ('Chaucer
    and Horace').

85 Patterson, 'Court Politics and the Invention of Literature,' 11 and 13.

86 Gower, *Confessio Amantis*, 3, Prol. *50. Coleman argues for the historical
    veracity of the Gower barge scenario in the context of the Prologue to
    Chaucer's *Legend of Good Women* ('Royal Patronage, the *Confessio*, and the
    Legend of Good Women'). See also Mahoney, 'Gower's Two Prologues to
    Confessio Amantis.'

87 Simpson, 'Ricardian and Henrician Ovidianism,' 334. On Gower and
    authorship, see Butterfield, 'Articulating the Author.'

88 Axton, 'Gower – Chaucer's Heir.'

89 Hazelton, 'Parody and Critique,' 22–5.

90 Yeager, *John Gower: The Minor Latin Works*, 3. Gower, *Carmen super
    multiplici viciorum pestilencia*, 17, subtitle. For a discussion of these works,
    see Coffman, 'John Gower, Mentor for Royalty.'

91 Gower, *O deus immense*, lines 1–5, 19–23, 64, 77–8 and 95–6; trans. R.F.
    Yeager.

92 Yeager, *John Gower: The Minor Latin Works*, 69.

93 Ibid., 7 and 69.

94 Bowers, *Chaucer and Langland*, 56–7.

95 McKinley, 'Lessons for a King,' 108.

96 Baker, *A Variorum Edition, The Manciple's Tale*, 11–13.

97 At the end of the *Metamorphoses*, Ovid has a similar statement about
    the permanence and perseverance of his poetry and poetic fame
    (XV. 871–9).

98 Claassen, *Displaced Persons*, 210.

99 Keith, *Play of Fictions*, 135–6.

100 Claassen, *Displaced Persons*, 228.

5 'The Makere of this Boke': Chaucer's *Retraction* and the Author as Scribe and Compiler

STEPHEN PARTRIDGE

Chaucer's *Canterbury Tales* concludes with a passage traditionally known as the *Retraction*, in which the author addresses his readers, asking that they give thanks to Christ for anything in 'this litel tretys' (X.1081) that pleases them and forgive the writer for anything that displeases them.[1] He declares that his intentions are good and that any faults in the work result from his imperfect abilities, and asks that his readers pray that Christ forgive him his 'giltes,' which he goes on to specify as his 'translacions and enditynges of worldly vanitees' (X.1084–5). These include what a modern reader recognizes as the bulk of the Chaucer canon: the *Book of the Duchess*, the *House of Fame*, the *Parliament of Fowls*, *Troilus and Criseyde*, the *Legend of Good Women*, 'the tales of Caunterbury, thilke that sownen into synne,' and what Chaucer even more vaguely refers to as 'many a song and many a leccherous lay' (X.1086–7). These, he says, 'I revoke in my retracciouns' – perhaps the most frustratingly ambiguous phrase in the entire passage (X.1085). For other works, however – his translation of Boethius and 'othere bookes of legendes of seintes, and omelies, and moralitee, and devocioun' – he gives thanks to Christ, Mary, and the saints; he asks them to grant him 'grace to biwayle my giltes and to studie to the salvacioun of my soule' (X.1088–90). Specifically, he asks for 'grace of verray penitence, confessioun and satisfaccioun' (X.1090), and then concludes by remembering Christ's glory and sacrifice, and expressing hope that he may be saved on Judgment Day.

Anita Obermeier's scholarship on authorial self-criticism of the classical and medieval periods has significantly advanced our understanding of the *Retraction* by exploring two of its contexts.[2] First, Obermeier demonstrates, more clearly than any previous study has done, how the *Retraction* follows a tradition of apology in which ancient and medieval authors participated for many centuries. To take just one specific example, Obermeier shows how thoroughly traditional and well-recognized was the division into amorous and Christian writings that Chaucer makes in the *Retraction*. Second, Obermeier traces Chaucer's self-criticism through several works, including *Troilus and Criseyde*, the Prologue to the *Legend of Good Women*, the Prologue to the *Treatise on the Astrolabe*, and parts of the *Canterbury Tales* that precede the *Retraction*. In these passages where Chaucer discusses his own writing, Obermeier sees both repetition and development, and thus views the *Retraction* as the 'culmination of Chaucer's self-critical intra-auctorial approach' and 'a logical continuation of persistent and pervasive and thoroughly conventional Chaucerian self-criticism.'[3]

In what follows I will attempt to develop Obermeier's valuable observations by exploring two additional contexts for the *Retraction*: first, the 'career' of the *Retraction* in the manuscripts of the *Canterbury Tales*, and second, the contemporary French literary culture which so immediately shaped Chaucer's sense of himself as an author. I propose to 'import' the codicological approaches that have shed such light on late-medieval French writing, in order to show that certain features of Chaucer's *Retraction* become more fully visible when we consider how the manuscripts present this passage. I will argue that the *Retraction* and its rubrics work together to emphasize the status of Chaucer's works, including the *Tales*, as *books*, in order to assert Chaucer's status as author. Moreover, the rubrics to the *Retraction* imply that Chaucer himself participated in producing copies of the *Tales* because they blend his authorial identity with that of a book artisan or 'maker of books.' Even if this blending might always have been primarily fictional and figurative – part of what Sebastian Coxon, in his essay in the present volume, calls an 'author-mythology' – it nevertheless fulfilled an important function, as it helped create the illusion of Chaucer's presence and agency in any copy of the *Tales* a reader was holding.[4] This illusion of presence was itself a way of conveying Chaucer's authority to scribal copies of the *Tales*, conjuring a picture of the author's control over his text even as he professed to surrender his creation to his readers and to Christ – and even as, in historical reality, circulation of the work extended in space and (eventually) in time beyond the range of Chaucer's direction. In the concluding part of this essay, I will propose that the language of the rubrics to the *Retraction* implies that Chaucer's role in the *ordinatio* of the *Tales* was not only a matter of 'author-mythology,' but also involved actual design of the pages presenting his text.

Late-Medieval French Writers and the Book

Perhaps the best way to introduce recent codicological studies of Chaucer's French predecessors and contemporaries is to consider Deborah McGrady's essay in the present volume. McGrady appeals liberally to manuscript evidence in order to analyse Christine de Pizan's shaping of the readership and authorial status that she sought. Christine insists on what McGrady calls a 'material reading' of her work in part through certain aspects of her text – such as, for example, her use of anagrams which must be read on the page to be deciphered, and her 'detailed account,' in her dedication to Queen Isabeau in MS R, 'of the care she has personally put into the compiling, transcription, and decoration of the very codex she offers the queen.'[5] In addition, as McGrady shows, 'extratextual' aspects of manuscripts such as British Library MS Harley 4431 (MS R) offered opportunities for especially strong statements about what kind of audience Christine hoped to reach and to 'fashion,' and thus about what kind of author Christine aimed to be. For instance, 'the richly bound books . . . that take up a disproportionate amount of visual space' in the miniatures of MS R reinforce the dedicatory prologue's emphasis on the status of Christine's writings as books.[6] Similarly, the rubrics of MS R, most likely Christine's own, contribute to the same project by insisting 'on a "material reading" of the text that would entail holding the book, gazing on its images, and studying its text.'[7] This deployment of extratextual features to fashion Christine's authorship is by no means limited to MS R, but is a developing pattern through much of her career.[8]

Such arguments can be made about Christine with particular confidence because scholars have concluded that some manuscripts of her work were written by the author herself, and she is presumed to have overseen all aspects of these books and the production of others not in her own hand.[9] Thus in her case, at least, we can understand references to her writing, ordering, and presentation of books as direct historical evidence for her involvement in book production. Such references occur, for example, in Christine's dedicatory prologue in MS R. We can also, however, acknowledge as McGrady does that these references to Christine's involvement in book production constitute a kind of self-fashioning, as they are part of her project to ensure a 'material reading' of her works.[10] What modern scholars distinguish as mutually supporting categories of evidence, textual and bibliographical, would have been, in Christine's own day, mutually reinforcing ways to present herself as a specific kind of author. The textual references to her own book-producing activity would have told readers that elements of their manuscripts such as rubrics and illustrations reflected Christine's own direction and intentions. Moreover, McGrady argues that Christine hoped such readers would therefore interpret such extra-textual elements as part of an integrated artistic program and a guide to how Christine's works should be read.

As Jacqueline Cerquiglini-Toulet has written, 'Christine de Pizan was part of a movement among fourteenth-century poets to become more and more involved in the material production of their works.'[11] In her influential study, *From Song to Book*, Sylvia Huot has argued that Machaut and Froissart had likewise overseen production of their works and had used texts, rubrics, and programs of illustration to make their role in book production known to readers.[12] We might see Christine as taking these trends even further than her predecessors, since she was so closely involved in book production that she acted as her own scribe in presentation copies of her writings, and she referred so regularly to her earlier works and their reception. Awareness of this tradition in France helps us see that Christine's references to her book-making activity were not simply self-contained. Such references did function to authorize an entire manuscript as her 'work,' as McGrady proposes, but in addition they announced that she was the same kind of author as her male predecessors. In other words, to insert herself into the 'line' of clerk-poets who had raised the status of French poetry during the fourteenth century, Christine asserted control over virtually every detail of the material form of her work, but also stated, clearly and repeatedly, that she had done so. Such references helped to identify her with a specific and relatively new model of authorship; as Cerquiglini-Toulet has incisively stated, 'What the clerk-writer produced was books, not performances.'[13] This model of authorship so closely resembles our present one that we can easily underestimate how vigorously a 'clerical' status for vernacular literature had to be sought and argued for by Christine's predecessors.

How closely these writers' references to their compilation and ordering of their works reflect historical reality remains less absolutely certain than in the case of Christine, because for these authors we do not have the supporting, unanswerable evidence of manuscripts in their own hands. Instead, Huot bases her arguments for Machaut's and Froissart's oversight of some surviving manuscripts of their works on these manuscripts' early dates and textual accuracy, and on statements made in their prologues and rubrics. In addition, she argues in a way that might be described as circumstantial but that I nonetheless find persuasive, proposing that in each of these manuscripts we can discern an overall artistic project so coherent that it increases the likelihood that all aspects of that program are the products of a single intention, the author's. For example, Huot compares B. N. f. fr. 1586, a collection of Machaut's works prepared during the 1350s, with another collection in fr. 1584, which was produced about twenty years later. The later collection adds a *Prologue* which makes clear 'that the poet whose works we are reading is a writer' (as opposed to a performer like a *jongleur*), and includes a revised program of illustration for the *Remede de Fortune*.[14] Whereas the earlier manuscript's program 're-creates the experiential context of dream or oral declamation' and emphasizes the love story 'as the narrative context within which lyric composition and performance take place,' in the later manuscript's illustrations the *dit*'s songs are disassociated from performance.[15] Instead, 'they are conceived as written texts to be encountered in the context of the book, product of the poetic authority that is responsible for everything else in the book,' and the poet 'serves love less through amorous behavior than as an abstract poetic and intellectual ideal.'[16] Huot sees close parallels between these developments in the manuscript presentation of Machaut's works and his increasing identification of himself as a writer, rather than a performer or a lover, in the *dits* (including *Le Livre du voir dit*) he had composed between the dates of the two manuscripts.

Chaucer and the Book: Problems and Assumptions

Scholars have been hesitant to make similar arguments about Chaucer – that the 'extratextual' elements of the surviving manuscripts might reflect his intentions, and that he might have arranged such elements to help convey his ideas of himself and those works. Moreover, even when such assertions have been made, scholars have rarely drawn comparisons to the practices of Chaucer's French contemporaries.[17] There have been notable exceptions, however, such as Ardis Butterfield's study of rubrics in the manuscripts of *Troilus and Criseyde* and Laura Kendrick's essay on the *Canterbury Tales*, especially the Ellesmere manuscript.[18] Their studies offer models for a comparative project that could be considerably extended, but before I make my own attempt, it will be worthwhile to address some reasons for general reluctance to interpret features of the manuscripts as resulting from Chaucer's intentions.

In obvious and important ways it is more difficult to connect Chaucer directly with the surviving manuscripts of his works than it is for us to link the French poets with theirs. We have no manuscripts written by Chaucer himself (as we do for Christine), with the possible but disputed exception of an astronomical treatise, the *Equatorie of the Planetis*.[19] In fact, only a very small proportion of the surviving manuscripts of any of his works could even possibly be dated to within his lifetime, and in virtually every such specific case, there is room for disagreement about date and about whether Chaucer could have supervised production.[20] No early manuscript includes a prologue or rubric with specific information about date or occasion of production, and we have no presentation miniature of Chaucer – all forms of evidence we find in the manuscripts of his French contemporaries. Nor do we have specific 'external' documentation of Chaucer's publication or presentation of his poems. By way of contrast, consider the case of Froissart. In his *Chronicles* Froissart describes in detail an occasion on which he presented a manuscript of his poems to Richard II, and there survives a *de luxe* manuscript of his poetry with a rubric announcing that it was completed in 1394, the year before that in which, according to Froissart, the presentation took place. Though the manuscript rubric does not refer to that occasion, Huot has argued that this manuscript, B. N. f. fr. 831, probably is the very copy presented to Richard II.[21] Chaucerians can only envy such evidence and the inferences it makes possible.

What Chaucerians have instead are copies, all (or virtually all) produced at some distance from Chaucer himself, which must be compared in order to make judgments about what the author wrote, including whether any of the extratextual features in some or all manuscripts derive from him. Such analysis of the manuscripts of the *Canterbury Tales* is an especially vexed proposition. The reasons for the difficulties are of two kinds. First, even the earliest manuscripts differ, to some degree, in their order and contents, and in extratextual features such as rubrics and glosses. Second, the manuscripts agree in suggesting that Chaucer, in obvious ways, never finished the work. For example, the tales of the Cook and the Squire break off well short of their conclusions, and Chaucer apparently failed to provide tales for several pilgrims he introduces in the *General Prologue*.

Together these facts have led to conflicting hypotheses about the history behind the surviving manuscripts. The diversity of these hypotheses suggests how complex and ambiguous is the evidence for the early history of the *Canterbury Tales*, and how little consensus there is about the most fundamental questions.[22] Chaucerians have begun to debate once again their assumptions about how the surviving manuscripts were shaped, primarily as a result of Linne Mooney's discoveries about the London scribe Adam Pinkhurst.[23] In this essay I mean to contribute to that reassessment, but as I begin to explore one specific aspect of the textual tradition, I would invite my readers to suspend judgment, at least for the time being, about issues such as the following. Perhaps Chaucer circulated a significant number of tales and sequences independently; or perhaps he simply published the collection when it had reached its present size. Perhaps at the time of his death in 1400 he still envisioned adding more tales to those we have; or perhaps at some point in the 1390s he judged that he had completed as much of the collection as he was interested in writing. Perhaps the publication of the earliest surviving copies was a highly organized editorial undertaking, with Chaucer's 'literary executors' imposing order and *ordinatio* on his *nachlass* or on what scattered tales they could gather; or perhaps those producing the relatively numerous manuscripts of the fifteenth century's first decade were building, in a less centralized and critical fashion, on a circulation history for the collection that had begun in the last decade of the fourteenth.

It will not be possible to remain completely aloof from such fundamental issues, particularly that of the manuscripts' *ordinatio*, because the specific body of evidence I will consider, the *Retraction* and its rubrics, has been cited in support of at least two general hypotheses about the early history of the entire *Tales*. Charles A. Owen, Jr has focused on the manuscripts' treatment of the *Retraction* to argue that Chaucer intended it to belong with the *Parson's Tale*, but did not intend this unified, independent 'Treatise on Penitence' to be part of the *Canterbury Tales*.[24] Instead, in Owen's view, scribes added this 'Treatise on Penitence' as a conventional close to the collection, and manuscript variation in the treatment of the *Parson's Tale* and the *Retraction* reflects ongoing scribal uncertainty about their relationship to each other and to the rest of the *Tales*. Owen therefore interprets the presence of the *Parson's Tale* and *Retraction* in the manuscripts as an instance of what he argues was more general scribal compiling of individual tales and small groups of tales that Chaucer (in Owen's view) had only circulated piecemeal. Mícéal Vaughan has developed Owen's arguments with a more intensive exploration of the manuscript evidence for the *Retraction*, and therefore I will address my arguments more directly to Vaughan's presentation.[25] Derek Pearsall has emphasized the Ellesmere manuscript's concluding rubric to the *Retraction*, which states that 'the book of the tales of Caunterbury' was 'compiled by Geffrey Chaucer.' In Pearsall's view, this rubric helps to show that in Ellesmere, the unordered collection visible in the Hengwrt manuscript has been transformed by Chaucer's early editors into an imposing book, deceptively finished in appearance.[26]

We may begin to engage with such views of the *Retraction*, I suggest, by pursuing two general implications of Mooney's research. The first is that Pinkhurst's relationship with Chaucer may increase the authority of this scribe's manuscripts of the *Canterbury Tales*, Hengwrt and Ellesmere. Where they disagree, there will be much room for debate about whether those differences result from Chaucer's revisions or scribal interference, but the identification of Pinkhurst might help restrain the general tendency to assume from the outset that many features of Ellesmere, in particular, are scribal in origin. The second implication is that Chaucer's relationship with Pinkhurst made publication always a practical possibility. In my view, this increases the likelihood that as he was composing, Chaucer would have thought about how his works would be realized on the page. Whether or not we suppose Chaucer might have put the *Canterbury Tales* into circulation, his relationship with Pinkhurst – as well as his identification with the French literary culture of writers such as Machaut, Froissart, and Christine – may well have made *ordinatio* an integral aspect of composition for Chaucer, rather than an afterthought.[27]

I would therefore like to revisit the various manuscript rubrics for the *Retraction* with the assumption that their origins are still open to debate and their evidence can be subjected to textual criticism. That is, I will weigh such factors as the numbers and affiliations of witnesses for each form of these rubrics; the dates and relative general accuracy of those witnesses; and the direction of variation in manuscript readings. To determine this direction, I will consider such relevant information as the meanings of some words which the scribes seem to introduce or suppress, and the general practices of scribes when they present the *Retraction* as well as when they copy or supply rubrics at other points in the *Tales*. This analysis will lead to larger literary and cultural issues, for the variant rubrics tell us important things about the genres and status of the *Retraction*, the expectations of Chaucer's audience, and the model of authorship to which Chaucer was working. The manuscript history of the *Retraction* is clearly an instance where textual criticism and literary interpretation inform one another, and I will argue that we can understand that manuscript history more clearly by referring to aspects of the contemporary literary culture which, in this context, have received little attention.

The Text and Rubrics of the *Retraction* in the Manuscripts

By the simple measure of where the *Retraction* appears, the manuscripts give no support to hypotheses which propose either that the *Retraction* is not Chaucer's or that Chaucer intended it to appear somewhere other than at the close of the *Canterbury Tales*. The *Retraction* appears only in manuscripts and early prints of the *Tales* or, in one instance, after a copy of the *Parson's Tale* in a Chaucerian anthology, Pp, which clearly derives from a complete manuscript of the *Tales*.[28] Five *Tales* manuscripts never included the *Retraction* because they did not include (or in one case did not continue to the end of) the *Parson's Tale*. In theory, of course, it is possible that these manuscripts – which constitute fewer than a tenth of the relatively large surviving number of complete copies of the *Tales* – could weigh in favour of Owen's and Vaughan's arguments that Chaucer never meant to include the *Parson's Tale* and *Retraction* in the *Canterbury Tales*.[29] There are two kinds of evidence, however, that must be weighed against this possibility. First, there is the textual evidence of the *Parson's Prologue*, which has clear connections both to the *Manciple's Prologue* (which precedes it in the manuscripts) and to the *Parson's Tale*; this argues strongly that Chaucer intended Fragment X to conclude the work.[30] Second, we must consider the nature of the five manuscripts omitting (or abbreviating) Fragment X. Two of these manuscripts seem to have had access to good exemplars, but various features of both suggest that their omissions of Fragment X reflect the tastes of their patrons, rather than any 'deeper' history of the *Tales* circulating without it.[31] In the other three manuscripts where the final 'fragment' of the *Tales* is absent or discontinued, the situation could be due either to damaged exemplars or to lack of interest in or patience with the long *Parson's Tale*. All of these instances, however, occur relatively late and are isolated in the textual tradition, in manuscripts related to others which do contain the *Parson's Tale* and *Retraction*.[32] Here too it is hypothetically possible, but on balance most unlikely, that these manuscripts derive independently from some Chaucerian original which did not contain Fragment X.

In two manuscripts of greater textual significance, Vaughan sees possible evidence that scribes, their supervisors, or readers have engaged in some editorial tidying-up of the conclusion to the *Parson's Tale* by suppressing the *Retraction*.[33] In neither case, however, does the overall evidence of these two manuscripts support his inferences about why we do not find the *Retraction* in them. First, in Gg the end of the *Parson's Tale* is followed by 'Heere taketh the makere of this book his leve' – which in Ellesmere serves as Incipit to the *Retraction* – at the bottom of the verso of a leaf. The following leaf is missing, and Vaughan suggests it may have been removed because of discomfort with the *Retraction* that presumably followed. In Gg, however, leaves are missing at many transitions in the *Tales*, evidently because someone (or a number of people) removed leaves with borders, illuminated initials, or illustrations. While we cannot be sure exactly what elements the leaf containing the *Retraction* would have included, most likely it would have contained at least an illuminated initial. Thus the widespread pilfering of especially attractive and valuable leaves from Gg, rather than editorial excision directed specifically at the *Retraction*, seems the best explanation for this leaf's absence.[34] In the second important manuscript Vaughan cites as a case of possible excision, Ll^2, the *Parson's Tale* is the only work by Chaucer in a devotional anthology. As Vaughan acknowledges, including any mention of the pilgrimage framework or of Chaucer's career would have been inconsistent with the scribe's purposes in creating Ll^2.[35] Although Vaughan suggests that the *Retraction* may once have been present and was excised because it was deemed 'unacceptable,' the physical structure of Ll^2 shows that in fact the *Retraction* was never included.[36]

The *Retraction* appears to have been lost from a total of twenty-five manuscripts of the *Tales*. Unfortunately this number includes, in addition to Gg, three others of the early manuscripts transcribed by the Chaucer Society – Hg, Cp, and Dd.[37] The lack of evidence from Hg is especially to be regretted, and to compound it the *Retraction* is also absent from Ch and Py, two manuscripts which might have given us the best idea of how Hg treated the *Retraction*. Moreover, the end of the *Parson's Tale* and the *Retraction* have been lost from Ad^3, which while not among those transcribed by the Chaucer Society, is valuable for its relationship to El and perhaps to other very early manuscripts.[38] Thus

we have thirty copies – manuscripts together with early prints having manuscript authority – that include the *Retraction*, and another, Gg,
which preserves an Incipit for the *Retraction*.

Because the *Retraction* is brief and the following discussion will refer
to details of its language and structure, I will reproduce it here as it appears in the 'Ellesmere Chaucer' (El), the most accurate manuscript of
the *Canterbury Tales* that preserves the 'Retraction.'

> ¶ heere taketh the makere of this book his leue
> Now preye I to hem alle that herkne this litel tretys or rede that if ther be
> any thyng in it that liketh hem that ther of they thanken oure lord Ihesu
> Crist/. of whom procedeth al wit and al goodnesse. and if ther be any
> thyng that displese hem. I preye hem also that they arrette it to the defaute
> of myn vnkonnynge and nat to my wyl. that wolde ful fayn haue seyd
> bettre/ if I hadde had konnynge. ffor oure book seith/ al that is writen/ is
> writen for oure doctrine. and that is myn entente ¶ Wherfore I biseke yow
> mekely for the mercy of god/ that ye preye for me that crist haue mercy
> on me and foryeue me my giltes. and namely of my translacions and en-
> ditynges of worldly vanitees/ the whiche I reuoke in my retracciouns ¶as
> is the book of Troilus ¶The book also of ffame/ The book of the .xxv. la-
> dies ¶The book of the duchesse ¶The book of seint valentynes day of the
> parlement of briddes/. The tales of Caunterbury thilke that sownen in to
> synne ¶The book of the leoun and many another book if they were in my
> remembrance/ and many a song and many a leccherous lay. that crist for
> his grete mercy foryeue me the synne ¶But of the translacioun of Boece de
> consolacione/ and othere bookes of legendes of seintes/ and Omelies and
> moralitee and deuocioun/ that thanke I oure lord Ihesu crist and his bliss-
> ful mooder/ and all the seintes of heuene/ bisekynge hem/ þat they from
> hennesforth vn to my lyues ende sende me grace to biwayle my giltes/
> and to studie to the saluacioun of my soule/ and graunte me grace of
> verray penitence confessioun and satisfaccioun to doon in this present lyf
> thurgh the benigne grace/ of hym þat is kyng of kynges and preest ouer
> alle preestes/ that boghte vs with the precious blood of his herte/ so þat I
> may been oon of hem at the day of doome that shulle be saued Qui cum
> patre *et cetera*
> ¶ heere is ended the book/ of the tales of Caunterbury compiled by Gef-
> frey Chaucer of whos soule Ihesu crist haue mercy amen

Let us first survey the various forms the Incipit to the *Retraction*
takes in the manuscripts and early printings. To understand the

relationships among these, it is essential that we compare them in light of the textual relationships determined by Manly and Rickert in their comprehensive study of the fifteenth-century history of the *Tales*. Manly and Rickert outline two large textual groups for the *Parson's Tale*, and assert that the limited evidence for the brief *Retraction* indicates 'the continuance of the groups as in the Parson's Tale.'[39] In each of these large groups we find several different forms of the initial rubric for the *Retraction*; I will consider the two large groups in turn.[40]

As many as eleven members of the first textual group derive from a hypothesized common ancestor for Manly and Rickert's well-defined constant group *c* and their larger and diverse group *d**. The sole manuscript of group *c* that contains the *Retraction* is La, which dates from the first quarter of the fifteenth century and is one of the eight transcribed by the Chaucer Society.[41] It separates the *Parson's Tale* and the *Retraction* with a Latin rubric, 'Explicit Fabula Rectoris / Composito huius libri hic capit licenciam suam.' Another of the Chaucer Society manuscripts is Pw, also dating from the first quarter of the fifteenth century; along with the related later manuscript Mm, it has the rubric 'Explicit Fabula Rectoris / Here taketh the maker of this booke his leue.' Ha², a *d** manuscript from the second quarter of the fifteenth century, reads 'Finis. Here taketh the Maker of this boke his Leue,' and the related Lc, also s. xv 2/4, has simply 'Here taketh the maker his leue.' Another second-quarter manuscript is Ry², which reads 'Thus endeth the parsones tale / And here taketh the Auctour of this book his leue.' The remaining *d** manuscripts appear to be later, from the third quarter of the fifteenth century. Fi has the rubric, 'Here endeth the Parsouns Tale: Here taketh the maker his leue,' and Se reads 'Here enden the talis of Caunturbury / And next thautour taketh leve.' Finally, in Dl and Ra² there is no rubric at all, as only a large initial marks the beginning of the *Retraction*; there is a blank line, or part of a line, between the end of the *Parson's Tale* and this initial.[42]

Four members of this first large group belong to Manly and Rickert's constant group *b*, and in the *Retraction* these are related to another manuscript; this expanded version of the *b* group is indicated by *b**. Between the *Parson's Tale* and the *Retraction*, two *b** manuscripts from the first half of the fifteenth century (Ii and Ne) read 'Explicit Tractatus Galfridi Chawcer de septem peccatis mortalibus vt dicitur pro fabula rectoris et cetera.' The three remaining *b** copies, Caxton's two printings (Cx¹ and Cx²) and the manuscript Tc², are closely related and date from the final quarter of the fifteenth century. Their rubric varies from that of Ii Ne only in substituting 'penitencia' for 'septem peccatis mortalibus.'[43]

A few manuscripts remain in this first large textual group for Fragment X. The very early Ha[4], another of the Chaucer Society manuscripts, contains the unique rubric 'Preces de Chaucer.' In two manuscripts of s. xv 3/4 with mixed affiliations, Bo[1] and Ht, the text runs continuously with no break at all between the *Parson's Tale* and the *Retraction*. In another mixed manuscript completed in 1476/7, Gl, only a large initial marks the beginning of the *Retraction*.

Before going on to consider information from more manuscripts, we might make some preliminary observations about this large group. First, we can see continuity among these copies, which shows that a generalization like 'scribes always provided their own rubrics' inadequately describes their behaviour. Clearly, scribes operated in various ways, sometimes simply copying what was in their exemplar, but elsewhere emending slightly what they copied and occasionally revising rubrics more thoroughly. Within the *b** group, for example, we find nearly identical rubrics, with disagreement only about whether the *Parson's Tale* concerns penitence or the Seven Deadly Sins (in fact, it treats both topics). Within the larger *cd** group, we find more variation, but most of these manuscripts are clearly related, and much of the variation consists of shifts between English and Latin and limited, specific emendations. On the basis of a broader survey of the rubrics in these manuscripts, I would judge that the hypothesized *cd** ancestor read something like, 'Here endeth the Parsons Tale / Here taketh the maker of this book his leue,' although scribes have introduced so many minor variants that none of the surviving manuscripts preserves the rubric in exactly this form. The second thing suggested by this canvass is that we have to consider in each instance whether the readings of these rubrics reveal that these manuscripts derive from one another or from a common exemplar – or if similar variants arose in other ways. Some similarities in variants do seem to be explained by textual relationships; for instance, Mm and Pw, which identically combine a Latin Explicit for the *Parson's Tale* with an English Incipit for the *Retraction*, belong to a well-defined textual 'small group' throughout the *Tales*. On the other hand, there is some evidence of convergent variation – that is, scribes have produced similar readings because they are responding to their exemplars in similar ways, rather than because they are copying from one another. Thus, for example, Fi and Lc have identical variant forms of the Incipit for the *Retraction*, 'Here taketh the maker his leue,' but their textual relationship does not appear to be any closer than their shared membership in the loose d^* group.

The rubrics in Manly and Rickert's second, smaller textual group may be described more briefly.[44] In addition to El, 'Heere taketh the makere of this book his leue' appears in another of the Chaucer Society manuscripts of s. xv 1/4, Gg, and in a closely related manuscript of the third quarter, Ph[1]. In Wynkyn de Worde's printing of 1498 (Wn), an Explicit follows the *Parson's Tale*, 'Here endyth the Person his tale,' and then a woodcut of a pilgrim appears, before the El Incipit for the *Retraction* is printed near the bottom of a folio.[45]

Also among the second large group for Fragment X are three manuscripts of Manly and Rickert's constant group a, Cn Ds[1] Ma, and the related En[3], which read 'Here takith the maker his leve.'[46] Ad[1], related to a and especially close to En[3], contains a very similar Latin rubric, 'Hic capit Autor licenciam.' Cn dates from around the middle of the fifteenth century, the others from the latter half. The earliest surviving a manuscript to preserve the *Retraction*, En[1], of the second quarter of the fifteenth century, slightly varies the word order of the English rubric, 'Here the makre taketh his leue.'[47] Pp, discussed above, is generally related to the a group, but Manly and Rickert seem to express some uncertainty about its affiliation in the latter part of the *Parson's Tale*. Pp contains the rubric of the a manuscripts, 'Here taketh the maker his lyeue,' but this is preceded by 'Explicit de Satisfaccione' and followed by 'Omne promissum [?] est debitum.' Finally, To marks the beginning of the *Retraction* only by a large initial, though a blank line falls between the end of the *Parson's Tale* and this initial.[48]

Interpreting the Manuscript Evidence of the *Retraction*

In what follows I will refer frequently to the 'El form' of the Incipit to the *Retraction*. I should therefore begin my analysis of the information just presented by emphasizing that the El Incipit is by no means isolated in the textual tradition. Of the thirty-one copies containing the Incipit for the *Retraction* (or clearly lacking an Incipit at this point), the nineteen referring to the maker's or author's 'taking his leave' are certainly related. Moreover, this 'leave-taking formula' is the only rubric to appear in both of the Manly/Rickert textual groups for Fragment X.[49] (If we consider 'lack of rubric' a reading, it also has a claim to be represented in both large textual groups.) It is therefore hard to argue that editors are misrepresenting the manuscripts by printing the El rubric in their editions of the *Tales*.[50] While it is worth noticing that a clear majority of copies support the 'leave-taking formula,' it is perhaps more significant that these witnesses include the hypothesized ancestors of three of Manly and Rickert's four major textual groups (or two of three, if we count *cd** as one), along with three major codices outside those groups – El, Gg, and Wn. This dissemination through most of the constant groups and the important manuscripts where the *Retraction* survives creates a *prima facie* case that some version of this formula was the earliest marker of the transition, from which others arose.[51] This conclusion is affirmed by the nature of the witnesses that contain other transitions. As will be discussed in more detail below, these tend to be of relatively late date (not necessarily in itself decisive), are generally less reliable copies, and perhaps most important, often contain evidence in other rubrics of scribal interference or omission.

Let us now resume examining scribes' treatment of this transition, about which I have already made some preliminary observations. Some rubrics, especially those in later or derivative copies, confirm that scribes endeavoured to create what Vaughan calls 'comfortable boundaries.' In a significant number of manuscripts, the nature of the transition from the *Parson's Tale* to the *Retraction* remains somewhat ambiguous. In most witnesses of the second textual group, along with Lc and Ha[4] from the first, we find only an Incipit for the *Retraction*, without any clear indication that the *Parson's Tale* has concluded. In the *b** witnesses, on the other hand, there appears only an Explicit for the *Parson's Tale*, with no title for the *Retraction*. In several of these *b** copies, the *Retraction* begins on a new page or after some blank space, as if the scribes and Caxton wanted to indicate it was a distinct part of the work without making any definite commitment about what kind of part it was. In still other instances – most of the *cd** manuscripts, Pp, and Wn – the scribes have allowed less ambiguity, as we find both an Explicit for the *Parson's Tale* (or in Se, for the *Tales*) and an Incipit for what follows. The scribe of Pp, for example, appears to have worked from an exemplar that contained only an Incipit, and has added an Explicit to make clear that (as he sees it) one part of the *Tales* is ending before another begins. Similarly, those who devised the ancestor of the *cd** manuscripts seem to have added an Explicit for the *Parson's Tale* to an Incipit for the *Retraction* like El's.[52] And Wn preserves what was most likely another, independent attempt to make this boundary more 'comfortable' by adding an Explicit for the *Parson's Tale*.[53]

Across the manuscript tradition of the *Tales*, we can observe a similar scribal tendency to homogenize the rubrics into this form – an Explicit followed by an Incipit. In addition to the *Retraction*, there are other points where it appears that the earliest scribes did not inherit a rubric of this kind, but as the textual tradition evolved, they provided Explicits to delineate more clearly boundaries between parts of the work. This is the case, for example, with the final extant lines of the unfinished Cook's and Squire's tales, where we see some scribes disguising their unfinished states either by suppressing Chaucerian lines that expose the tales' incompleteness, or by supplying additional lines. These scribes – along with others who did not intervene in the text – also added Explicits that declared these tales 'ended.'[54] Further instances of this scribal revision of rubrics can be found at the points where the Host interrupts Chaucer's tale of *Sir Thopas* and where Chaucer begins the *Melibee*. The manuscripts seem to preserve several independent scribal attempts to articulate more fully the relationships among these pieces of the text.[55] They reflect two related expectations that appear to have influenced – with varying consistency – the scribes' adjustment of rubrics throughout the *Tales*: first, one part of the work must end before another can begin; and second, prologues should alternate regularly with tales. The first of these scribal principles has motivated the scribes of Pp and of the *cd* archetype, and the printer de Worde, to add Explicits for the *Parson's Tale* to the Incipits for the *Retraction* they inherited from their exemplars.[56]

The second of these two scribal tendencies – to organize the collection as a series of prologues and tales in regular alternation – probably helps to explain what we find at the *Retraction* in several remaining manuscripts of Manly and Rickert's larger, first textual group as well as in To, which in my view belongs to the second group.[57] Recall that in two manuscripts (Bo[1] Ht) there is no break at all between the *Parson's Tale* and the *Retraction*, and in four others (Dl Gl Ra[2] To), this transition is marked only by a large initial at X.1081 – though in three of these, this initial is preceded by a blank line or part of a line. All of these manuscripts date from the second half of the fifteenth century, and about most of them Manly and Rickert state explicitly that they are of little or no value for determining the Chaucerian text of the *Tales*.[58] In all of them we can observe a general pattern that recurs elsewhere in the manuscript tradition. Alongside the scribal supplementing of inherited rubrics we have just considered, we also find some loss of rubrics as the work passes through several generations of copying. Occasionally, most or all derived rubrics might have been lost at once, perhaps through some disruption in the manuscript's production.[59] In other instances, losses seem to have been more gradual and random, as the text was repeatedly copied by scribes who inevitably made omissions and changes.

Most subject to loss or radical revision, it appears, were the idiosyncratic rubrics that in earlier manuscripts marked pieces of the text as something other than a prologue or a tale. Whether through scribal uncertainty, inattention, or conscious desire to homogenize, the process of transmission wore away, at varying rates, rubrics identifying a piece of the text as, for example, the 'words of the Host' which intervene between several tales and prologues. An instance of such a passage (and rubric) occurs when the Host, at the conclusion of the *Shipman's Tale*, praises it and then calls on the Prioress with elaborate politeness before she begins her *Prologue* and then her *Tale*. These passages came to be marked by no rubric at all, or else scribes transformed the rubrics so that the 'Host's words' became the beginning of a 'Prologue.' The latter scribal solution led to situations where tales had two prologues, or else had two beginnings, which could be marked by different words such as 'tale' and 'narracio.' In all six of these manuscripts which fail to mark the transition from the *Parson's Tale* to the *Retraction*, the rubrics elsewhere in the *Tales* are limited, almost without exception, to those marking the beginnings and endings of either prologues or tales.[60] In this context it is entirely unsurprising and unremarkable to find no rubric at the *Retraction*. Since it is clearly neither prologue nor tale, and thus could not be incorporated into the scribes' rubric systems, they provided no label at all for it.[61] The blank lines, or parts of lines, preceding the *Retraction* in three of these six manuscripts probably attest to the existence of rubrics in their exemplars. Otherwise, these manuscripts offer little specific information about what might have been contained even in their immediate exemplars at this point, and thus cannot be relied on for evidence of Chaucer's intentions where they disagree with more trustworthy copies.

The manuscripts we have examined so far, then, suggest that scribes responded to the leave-taking rubric for the *Retraction* either by expanding it – to include an Explicit for the *Parson's Tale* – or by omitting it. This study of scribal behaviour, therefore, has discovered variation away from rather than toward the leave-taking Incipit – a pattern of

variation which supports the authority of that Incipit as the reading
from which others derive. Because the remaining witnesses that do not
contain this Incipit are relatively isolated, in terms of their textual affiliations, it is harder to be certain that this Incipit was in their exemplars
(either immediate or remote) than we can be for some of the 'unrubri-
cated' manuscripts already considered, such as the d^* manuscripts Dl
Ra^2 or the a^* manuscript To. They do not, however, present any challenge to the authority of the leave-taking Incipit, because they cannot
be trusted to reproduce transparently what was in their exemplars at
this point. First, we may consider Ha^4, which though it is very early,
has been subjected in its text to considerable sophistication.[62] In addition, some of its rubrics appear to be provisional, as if the scribe was
working with an exemplar that was missing some rubrics, or as if he
no longer had access to that exemplar when it came time to provide the
rubrics.[63] It is hard to determine what was the basis for Ha^4's unique
Incipit of 'Preces de Chaucer'; perhaps the scribe devised it *ex nihilo*,
or perhaps it reflects a response to rubrics like those in El (a possibility
to which I will return below). Whatever the case, there is no reason to
suppose that Ha^4 uniquely preserves an 'original' reading from which
other versions of the transition to the *Retraction* derive.

It is likewise difficult to know what those preparing the ancestor of
the b^* witnesses might have been working from when they devised
their idiosyncratic rubric, 'Explicit Tractatus Galfridi Chawcer de septem peccatis mortalibus vt dicitur pro fabula rectoris et cetera.'[64] In
this treatment of the transition we can observe the scribal tendency
to add an Explicit, in order to mark clearly the conclusion of the *Parson's Tale*. By contrast to the modified rubric of the cd^* manuscripts,
however, the b^* rubric contains no Incipit for what follows, an absence
that perhaps suggests the makers of the b^* ancestor did not have a version of the 'leave-taking' Incipit in their exemplars.[65] Or, it may simply
be a matter of scribes suppressing an unfamiliar or irregular kind of
text-division, like the instances we have already observed. The b^* rubric is certainly intriguing, as it reflects an apparent (scribal?) intuition
that Chaucer may have taken existing works and incorporated them
into the pilgrimage framework of the *Tales*. It is even possible that this
rubric reflects knowledge of some independent circulation history for
the *Parson's Tale*. The b^* textual group seems to have originated quite
late compared to others, however, so we cannot regard this rubric
as an authoritative reading or as a reliable guide to how Chaucer himself understood the relationship (or, as some have argued, the lack

thereof) between the 'Treatise on Penitence' and the pilgrimage tale-collection.[66]

Aside from the 'leave-taking' formula, then, none of the other forms of the transition from the *Parson's Tale* to the *Retraction* can offer any claim to Chaucer's authority or to be a post-Chaucerian 'original' from which others derive. The remaining questions therefore are, first, which specific form of the 'leave-taking' formula gave rise to the other; and second, could either of these derive from Chaucer himself? The numbers of copies containing the two versions of this Incipit are virtually equal, as nine include the phrase 'of this book' and ten do not. Both versions are fairly widespread in the tradition. Each appears in both of Manly and Rickert's large textual groups. The form with 'of this book' appears in several 'independent' manuscripts and in the majority of the *cd** manuscripts, while the form without that phrase appears in the *a* manuscripts and the related Ad[1]-En[3] but also in some *cd** manuscripts.[67]

We can find persuasive evidence for the direction of variation between these two forms of the 'leave-taking' Incipit by returning to the *cd** manuscripts, which offer crucial information about how the scribes were responding to what they found in their exemplars. As discussed above, Vaughan proposes (and I agree) that the form we find in these manuscripts, with an Explicit for the *Parson's Tale* added to the 'leave-taking' formula, is derived from the form that survives in El Gg Ph[1]. This would suggest that the *cd** ancestor contained the longer, Ellesmere form of the *Retraction* Incipit, 'Here taketh the makere of this boke his leue,' and that the variant forms we find in *cd* manuscripts are scribal. There are two kinds of variants. Three manuscripts omit 'of this book'; these are not especially closely related, so it seems likely that three different scribes introduced this variant independently.[68] In fact we find the two different forms of the rubric in two closely related manuscripts, Ha[2] and Lc, and so the scribe of Lc probably introduced the variant independently in that manuscript by omitting 'of this book.' The scribe of Se seems to have taken a fairly active role in ordering his manuscript and devising glosses and rubrics, so probably he also suppressed 'of this book' from the longer form he found in his exemplar. The second kind of variant substitutes 'Auctour' for 'maker.' We find this variation in Ry[2] and in Se (which also suppressed 'of this book') and probably also in La's 'Composito.'[69]

These two kinds of variants are motivated by the same scribal impulse to remove an ambiguity present in the Ellesmere rubric. The 'maker of a book' could refer to either an author or a scribe, whereas 'the maker' by itself most often referred to an 'author,' and 'the author of this book' was completely unambiguous.[70] The *Middle English Dictionary* (*MED*) cites a 'Will. le Bokmakere,' along with an 'Alan. Bokeman,' 'Rog. Bukeman,' and 'Joh. Bocman' (see 'bok' 7(c); such terms may have superseded an earlier Middle English 'boker,' q.v.).[71] On the other hand, 'making a book' could also refer to composition, i.e., authorship. The *MED* cites the translator of Vegetius, 'Here þis nede driueþ me to ouertourne auctors, þat is, techeris and makeris of bookys,' and Capgrave's *St. Augustine*, 'He happed to fynde a book þat Tullius Cicero mad' ('maker(e)' 3(a). This entry also shows clearly, however, that 'maker' by itself most often referred to an author. We can see the scribe of a sixteenth-century manuscript negotiate this distinction between makers and those who make books in his colophon: 'And now if ony man or woman or child be holpyn her-by, and haue remedy, first love our lord Ihesu, and thonke the gret goodnes of god. And affter, of your charite, pray for the first maker her-off, and alsoo for me, synner, the writter her-of. For in that intent I toke the labour to make this booke affter my copy.'[72]

Once we perceive, in the *cd** manuscripts, this scribal tendency to reduce the ambiguity in the longer form of the Incipit by suppressing 'of this book' or substituting 'author' for 'maker' (or making both changes), we can understand the variation between El and the *a** manuscripts as resulting from the same impulse: the scribe of the *a* archetype suppressed 'of this book' to remove the ambiguity inherent in the El rubric's 'makere of this book.' Thus the shorter form of the Incipit is derived from the longer form, rather than vice versa (as Vaughan proposed), and the longer form of the leave-taking formula therefore appears to be the reading that gave rise to all other readings we find in the manuscripts and early prints. Observing this pattern, of scribes resolving ambiguities, also enables us now to explain the Incipit of Ha[4], 'Preces de Chaucer,' as a probable response to the Incipit found in El and other copies. By naming the author responsible for the *Retraction*, the Incipit supplied in Ha[4] removes the ambiguity of 'maker of this book' even more definitively than the emendations to 'maker' or 'author.'

Considering the position and language of the *Retraction* only makes clearer why several scribes perceived this ambiguity in the Incipit and took pains to remove it. The *Retraction* appears at the end of the *Tales*, which is also, except in a very few copies, the end of a book, and it includes several kinds of language often found in a genre of scribal writing that has its place at a manuscript's close: the scribal colophon. The *Retraction* includes apology and request for forgiveness, declaration of good intentions, request for the reader's prayer, the writer's prayer, and self-identification. The scribal colophon does not follow a fixed form, but surviving colophons virtually always include at least one of these elements, and many include more than one, in varying combinations.[73] (The sixteenth-century colophon quoted above, for example, includes a request for the reader's prayer and a declaration of good intentions.)[74] Scribes of the *Canterbury Tales*, apparently seeing this similarity between the *Retraction* and scribal colophons, thus felt it necessary to emend the rubric to make clear that what followed was not theirs but rather originated with the author.

There is some additional evidence that scribes perceived similarities between the *Retraction* and what they themselves might write at the end of a manuscript. In two manuscripts, an added line appears in which a scribe has asked to be included in the *Retraction*'s closing prayer, 'so that I may been oon of hem at the day of doom that shulle be saved' (X.1092): 'and he that wrote this book also.'[75] It is as if the scribe found that the *Retraction* he inherited from his exemplar said what he might have added to his copy, and so he has simply written himself into the closing passage's penitential sentiments and prayer.

As far as I am aware, no one has previously drawn this comparison between the *Retraction* and the scribal colophon. The list of Chaucer's works in the *Retraction* seems an obvious difference from a scribal colophon, and scholarship's emphasis on what Chaucer might have meant when he 'revoked' most of the works in his canon may have led us to neglect the lines of the *Retraction* that precede and follow that list. The scribes' response to the *Retraction*, reflected in the variants they introduce, helps us see that the *Retraction* does a good deal more than list Chaucer's works and 'revoke' most of them. My argument that a 'genre' of the scribal colophon is present in the *Retraction* places much emphasis on the ambiguity of the phrase 'the makere of this book,' but clearly the several scribes who emended this phrase heard this ambiguity, and thus we should likewise listen for it.

As is true of most manuscripts of the *Tales* and Chaucer's other works, the majority of medieval manuscripts do not contain scribal colophons, but such colophons did become more frequent in the later Middle Ages. A selective survey of manuscript colophons suggests two additional reasons scribes might have perceived the potential for confusion, on the part of readers encountering a reference to 'the makere of this boke,' about who was responsible for the *Retraction*. First, in manuscripts copied by members of the mendicant orders for their own use, in particular, 'we often find notes on the biography of the scribes and the circumstances in which they worked.'[76] We might compare such notes to Chaucer's list of his writings, which amounts to a biobibliography – perhaps that list is not, after all, such a pronounced departure from some scribal colophons. Second, when sorting manuscripts according to the kinds of texts they contain, surveyors found many colophons in a large group of books they classify as '[o]ther theology,' which includes (among other specific topics) '[t]reatises on the vices and the virtues' – that is, the very genre to which the *Parson's Tale* belongs.[77] The *Retraction* sits exactly where the scribes and their readers might, for a number of reasons, have expected to find a scribal colophon. Several scribes therefore perceived a need to adjust the Incipit so it was clear that this was not, in fact, what their readers were about to encounter.

This repeated scribal response to the Incipit preserved in El and other manuscripts may help us address the second question I posed about that rubric – whether it could derive from Chaucer himself. If scribes were so ready to emend 'Here taketh the makere of this boke his leve' in order to make it less ambiguous – if, to borrow Vaughan's term again, they were uncomfortable with this vague and idiosyncratic boundary – then perhaps we should be wary of assuming that a scribe would have composed this rubric in the first place.[78] Scribal writing seems much more often intended to reduce ambiguities present in the work being copied, rather than to introduce new ones. On the other hand, the resemblances the *Retraction* bears to scribal language, specifically to language that a scribe often added at the end of a manuscript he had copied, may well have been part of Chaucer's purpose. If, as Carter Revard and Derek Brewer have suggested, one of Chaucer's models for the *Canterbury Tales* was the manuscript miscellany or anthology assembled by one or more scribes, then it would have been fitting to conclude the collection with a short text modelled on the scribal colophon.[79] The scribal colophon is not the only model for the *Retraction*, just as the manuscript miscellany is not the only model for the *Canterbury Tales*, but it is a model we might add to the sources and analogues Obermeier has assembled.

In asserting that Chaucer provided the manuscripts' leave-taking Incipit and intended the *Retraction* to conclude the *Tales*, I am arguing in part on the basis of aesthetic coherence, as Huot argues for Machaut's and Froissart's ordering and design of the manuscripts of their collected works. Placing the *Retraction* at the conclusion of the *Canterbury Tales* accords with Chaucer's design for the work, and considering that conjunction as part of Chaucer's intentions helps us see new facets both of the collection and of the *Retraction* itself. We can extend this argument, and understand the function of the *Retraction* more fully, if we also consider certain language in the *Retraction* and the El Explicit that follows it. The language of the Explicit echoes and extends that of the Incipit, as Chaucer is now said to have 'compiled' the book. 'Compiled,' like 'makere,' could refer both to scribal activity and to authorial composition in the later Middle Ages, and that ambiguity is made more visible by the reference to the 'book of the tales of Caunterbury.' M.B. Parkes's influential essay on *ordinatio* and *compilatio* has led to a widespread reading of the term 'compiled' in this Explicit as referring to Chaucer's production of a text or work – his compilation from various sources, whether these are understood as the pilgrims who told the tales he records, or the Latin sources identified by marginal glosses in El and other manuscripts.[80] As I will argue further below, however, in this context 'compiled' more likely refers to book production (as opposed to 'text production'), specifically to Chaucer's bringing together and arranging his own works in the Canterbury collection.

It is also widely assumed that the Explicit stating that Chaucer 'compiled' the *Tales* was devised for the (posthumous) production of El, and is therefore scribal, but there is strong evidence that the El Explicit originated earlier in the textual tradition.[81] Although the Explicit does not survive in as many copies as does the 'leave-taking' Incipit (in its various forms), it appears in de Worde's edition; in a manuscript closely related to the early and important (but damaged) Gg; and in so many *d** manuscripts that it must have been present in the lost *cd** ancestor.[82] Furthermore, other manuscripts, from additional textual groups, contain in their rubrics for the *Retraction* language which suggests that the El Explicit was present in their exemplars.[83] Less obviously, but significantly, two manuscripts which omitted the *Retraction* include at other points in the *Tales* rubrics with language so similar to that of the El Explicit that I would surmise they are based on it, rather than being coincidentally similar but independent scribal productions.[84] Even Hg, at the opening of the *General Prologue*, presents a title for the work – 'the book of the tales of Caunterbury' – which makes clear that the production of El did not mark the first time the *Tales* were conceived of as a 'book.'[85] Finally, although the word 'compile' was not necessarily unusual in the late fourteenth century, I will argue below that in the Explicit it is used in an unusual, somewhat specialized sense, which would make it less likely that it was supplied by a scribe.

Chaucer's Making and Book-Making

The language of the rubrics referring to 'the makere of this boke' and Chaucer's compiling the 'book' works in concert with that of the *Retraction* itself, which insistently repeats the word 'book' in the titles of Chaucer's works, to emphasize that Chaucer is the kind of author – the clerk-poet – for whom 'making' is inextricable from book-making. The rubrics make this repetition of 'book' within the *Retraction* more resonant, and more clearly strategic, than it might be without them. This model for Chaucer's authorship, and indeed this very language, is consistent with what Chaucer says about himself elsewhere in his poetry. Glending Olson has written perceptively about Chaucer's referring to himself (as he does to his French contemporaries) as a 'maker,' as opposed to the 'poets' of the classical world and trecento Italy, but in the present context we should add and emphasize that in several of the passages concerning Chaucer's 'making,' the word 'book' is close at hand.[86] Consider, for example, the well-known stanza near the end of *Troilus and Criseyde* (V.1786–92):

> Go, litel bok, go, litel myn tragedye,
> Ther God thi makere yet, er that he dye,
> So sende myght to make in some comedye!
> But litel book, no makyng thow n'envie,
> But subgit be to alle poesye;
> And kis the steppes where as thow seest pace
> Virgile, Ovide, Omer, Lucan, and Stace.

As in the Incipit to the *Retraction*, Chaucer is the 'makere' of a 'bok.' He uses these words together from the beginning of his career: in the *Book of the Duchess*, the narrator refers to himself as the one 'that made this book' (96), and in the *House of Fame*, the eagle asserts that the narrator 'hast set thy wit . . . To make bookys, songes, dytees' (620, 622). And Chaucer continues to use the same language in both versions of the *Prologue* to the *Legend of Good Women*.[87] Beyond these specific collocations of 'maken' and 'bok,' of course, Chaucer often reminds his readers that he creates by reading books and by writing.

We might compare this language to the many medieval portraits which show an author at his desk, surrounded by books, and which place at their centre the author's hands holding pen and knife, along with the book in which he or she writes.[88] To a modern reader – perhaps especially to a modern scholar – this model of authorship might seem only natural or inevitable. Some portraits, however, did employ different iconography, showing an author on horseback (if he was a knight), or performing as a musician, or receiving the inspiration for his or her work through a mystical experience.[89] Recalling these other possible ways of representing an author can make clear that there was a specific agenda in Chaucer's consistent, even insistent references to himself as a maker of books.

In addition to serving this general project of integrating Chaucer into book culture, however, the *Retraction* also functions in a more specific way. The position of the *Retraction* at the book's conclusion, where we might expect a scribal colophon, and the language of its rubrics imply that Chaucer is not just a maker of books, but the maker of *this* book – the book a reader holds in his or her hands. When the Incipit identifies the speaker of the *Retraction* with the 'maker of this book,' it creates the illusion that the manuscript book in a reader's hands can be identified with the book Chaucer himself prepared. As John Burrow has pointed out, because in manuscript culture the distinction between an author's draft and subsequent copies was less clear than in the age of printed books, it was 'possible to suggest, albeit playfully, that the reader had before him . . . the very pages upon which the poet describes himself as writing.' These suggestions had 'the effect of momentarily collapsing the distinction' between the book in which a poet composed and the present copy a reader held; 'a poet's book [i.e., the one in which he composed and wrote] might figure as a present physical reality to a reader of manuscript.'[90]

To put it another way, the *Retraction* elides the scribe(s) and their production of the intermediary copies through which the work has in fact reached a reader. The *Retraction* with its rubrics asserts the author over the scribe, and creates a fiction of Chaucer's direct supervision and control over the transmission of his text.[91] This is a point where, to adopt Burrow's argument about several non-Chaucerian 'books,' we feel contact with Chaucer's original, with the actual book that Chaucer made, even when we read the copies which are all that

remain. One reason that readers are especially interested in the question of whether Chaucer 'meant' what he said here, and are likely to
invoke the issue of sincerity, is that the *Retraction* so strongly creates a
sense of presence – as if Chaucer is dropping his 'masks' and is 'speaking' more directly to the reader than he does elsewhere in his work.
That illusion of presence is often discussed as a matter of voice – for
example, in the arguments about who is 'speaking' as the text moves
from the *Parson's Tale* into the *Retraction*. Careful attention to the words
of the rubrics, however, argues that the illusion of presence is actually
created by the object we hold in our hands, because the trope of Chaucer's direct involvement in the physical production of 'this' book col-
lapses that distance between the book Chaucer 'made' and our copy.
One sign of this strategy's power is that we have this illusion of 'presence' even when reading a modern edition that includes this rubric. The
omission from the *Retraction* and its rubrics of certain information we
might expect to find in a scribal colophon – a specific date or place of
the book's production – actually adds to this effect, since if it were provided this information might distance Chaucer's book from a reader's
copy.

Chaucer's poem to 'Adam Scriveyn' is the other place where he
most fully develops this author-mythology of a writer exercising control over the production of his works. There, Chaucer chastises Adam
for his 'negligence and rape' and remarks that he must labour 'to cor-
recte and eke to rubbe and scrape' Adam's copies of his works (7, 6).
This suggests that readers can trust their copies of Chaucer's writing
because the author has undertaken a kind of quality control, repair-
ing Adam's errors. In 'Adam Scriveyn,' the scribe has a name distinct
from Chaucer's (which appears in the title the poem bears in the sole
manuscript preserving it), and a distinct identity constituted by his
lesser care for the integrity of the author's texts. In the *Retraction*, by
contrast, Chaucer seems to submerge his voice in the scribe's, or to
impersonate the scribe, thus raising the possibility of confusion that
some actual scribes strove to eliminate by emending the Incipit for
this passage.[92] At the same time they create this confusion, of course,
the *Retraction* and its rubrics also expose it as illusory, as the passage
lists the author's works and the Explicit provides his full name. Ultimately, there can be no doubt about who was the 'maker of this book.'
This strategy might remind us of the paradoxical effect of Chaucer's
framing the collection as he does. Through the fiction of the Canterbury pilgrimage, and his pose as the faithful recorder of the pilgrims'

stories, Chaucer seems to disperse his authority among those narrators, but the collection's ultimate effect is to enlarge our notion of Chaucer the author, as he proves himself the master of so many genres, themes, linguistic registers, and styles.

If the *Retraction* and its rubrics make a claim for Chaucer's status as a clerk-poet, that claim is mixed with expressions of humility. The assertion of Chaucer's authority and control over his text, and the attachment of his name to his canon, are qualified by his surrender to divine judgment. In this mixed tone, the *Retraction* may be compared with Chaucer's acknowledgment, in 'Adam Scriveyn,' that his work in the future will be copied in his absence, in circumstances where he can exercise control, if at all, only by means of the curse he lays on Adam. Similarly, in *Troilus and Criseyde* the stanza quoted above, in which Chaucer directs his 'litel bok' to join those of the classical *auctores*, is followed immediately by lines in which he expresses fears about the vulnerability of his vernacular poem to mishandling by scribes and to the historical phenomenon of linguistic variation (V.1793–8).

Compiling and Authorship in Late-Medieval France and England

It would be a mistake, however, to suppose that the Explicit's characterization of Chaucer as the compiler of the book was meant as an expression of modesty or humility. It is sometimes assumed that calling Chaucer a 'compiler' in this context is incompatible with claiming for him the status of author, an assumption which has influenced judgments about whether Chaucer might be responsible for the Explicit. Stephanie Trigg, for example, asserts that 'the final colophon . . . stresses the book, the content, and the act of *compilation*, rather than authorship.'[93] Chaucer does use the word 'compilator' in this disclamatory sense in the Prologue to *A Treatise on the Astrolabe* (59–64): 'But considre wel that I ne usurpe not to have founden this werk of my labour or of myn engyn. I n'am but a lewd compilator of the labour of olde astrologiens, and have it translatid in myn Englissh oonly for thy doctrine.' Moreover, in an influential discussion of vernacular references to compilation, Alastair Minnis has compared Chaucer's account of himself in the *General Prologue* as a mere reporter of his fellow pilgrims' tales and words to the late-medieval 'compiler's stock disavowal of responsibility.'[94]

As Minnis goes on to observe, however, the *Retraction* differs in significant ways from that *apologia* near the beginning of the *Tales*, and from other Chaucerian disclaimers in works such as the *Astrolabe* and *Troilus and Criseyde*:

> Although Chaucer had exploited several aspects of the theory of *compilatio* in several works, in his 'retracciouns' he was not prepared to assume the role of the 'lewd compilator' to whom no blame could accrue. On the contrary, he takes the blame for the sinful material that he wrote . . . The 'shield and defence' of the compiler has slipped, and for once we see Chaucer as a writer who holds himself morally responsible for his writings.[95]

The question that arises is how we might account for the use of the word 'compiled' in this context, where Chaucer seems not to be evading responsibility or disclaiming the status of author. Minnis tentatively suggests that this colophon was supplied by an editor or 'literary executor' who perceived connections between Chaucer's apologetic stance as compiler in the *General Prologue* and the apologetic tone of the *Retraction*: 'it may have been realised that Chaucer's *apologia* for his 'complete works' served admirably as an *apologia* for the diverse *materiae* which he had brought together in the *Canterbury Tales*.'[96]

I would propose a different way to reconcile the Explicit's use of 'compiled' with Chaucer's discarding, in the *Retraction*, the stance of the compiler who merely assembles and records others' material and words. In the French culture which had done so much to form Chaucer's literary identity, the verb 'compiler' could be used to refer not only to the act of assembling material from existing writings, but also to a writer's ordering his own works and directing their disposition on the page. Whereas Chaucer uses 'compilator' in the former sense in the *Astrolabe*, I would argue that he uses 'compiled' in the latter sense in the Explicit to the *Retraction* and the *Tales*.[97] In the context of the *Retraction*, then, Chaucer's reference to his compiling constitutes a claim rather than an apology, because for his French contemporaries acting as a compiler in this second sense of the word was not an alternative to authorship but an essential aspect of it. Sylvia Huot makes clear how associating himself with the physical act of writing and with the production of compilations of his own works became a way for Machaut to achieve the status of vernacular *auctor*: 'Machaut went further than any previous French poet in establishing his identity as a writer, author, and compiler and in exploring the poetic implications of this stance; it is no doubt partly for this reason that Eustache Deschamps honored him as "noble poet" in the first known application of the term *poete* to a vernacular author.'[98] Ardis Butterfield, commenting on similar trends, draws specific connections between roles traditionally assigned to scribes (as distinct from authors) and authorial status: 'Froissart's appropriation of the medium of the scribal rubric for both the content and presentation of his writing shows how far the scribe was usurping the author's position. It is as if the author can only truly emerge by in turn usurping the scribe's space and borrowing his mantle.'[99]

I have been arguing that Chaucer, in the specific context of the *Retraction*, usurps the scribe's space in two ways. First, he includes at the close of his book-sized work, where a scribe might have placed a colophon, his own colophon-like passage, as if he is crowding the scribe(s) out of a part of the book they might have expected to oversee. Second, Chaucer appears to have provided rubrics for the *Retraction* we find in some manuscripts, as Butterfield has suggested he may have devised some of the rubrics preserved in manuscripts of *Troïlus and Criseyde*. Yet I believe those rubrics to the *Retraction* may assert a more far-reaching claim: that Chaucer, in 'compiling' the *Tales*, has usurped the scribe's role throughout the work by taking responsibility for its arrangement and design. To support this view, I would like to compare the language of these rubrics with that in several closely contemporary manuscripts containing the works of Christine de Pizan. I take Christine here as a product and representative of the French literary culture which also shaped Chaucer; Christine began to write just too late to have been a source for Chaucer's use of 'compiled' in the sense for which I am arguing.[100] Moreover, I do not mean to imply that Chaucer is unique in employing the strategies I have outlined here, or unique in his probable debts to French models. Gower, for example, seems to have similarly appropriated the closing space of his book-length *Confessio Amantis*, and to have looked to his French contemporaries for models of how to articulate his authorship through *ordinatio*.[101] This is not surprising, since Gower is writing within the same Anglo-French culture as is Chaucer. It is possible that in their incorporation of book-making into authorship, as in other aspects of their poetic practice, Chaucer and Gower are influencing each other.[102] But it is in French usage that I have found the clearest evidence that to 'compile,' in late medieval vernacular writing, could mean to 'format' or 'arrange' one's own writing.

The earliest collection of Christine's works, for example, uses the word 'compilé' in this sense. Chantilly, Musée Condé 492–93 is one of two copies of the *Livre de Cristine*. Like the other surviving copy, it has a careful though not luxurious *ordinatio*, including a layout (of Christine's writings) in two columns, a program of miniatures and flourished initials, and in the *Epistre Othea*, Glosses and Allegories arranged to follow the Texts to which they relate. While neither of these appears to be an 'autograph' manuscript, Christine most likely designed the ordering and *ordinatio* which survives so consistently in these two copies.[103] The Chantilly manuscript also includes a table of contents, which it introduces in this way:

> Cy commencent les rebriches de la table de ce present volume, fait et compilé par Cristine de Pizan, demoiselle. Commencié l'an de grace mil.ccc. iiij[xx].xix. Eschevé et escript en l'an mil.Quatrecens et deux, la veille la nativité Saint Jehan Baptiste.

> [Here begin the rubrics of the table of contents of this present volume, made and compiled by Christine de Pizan, a noble lady. Begun in the year of grace 1399 [o.s.]. Completed and copied in the year 1402, on the eve of the nativity of St. John the Baptist [23 June].][104]

Several elements of the context in which 'compilé' is used argue that it refers to aspects of book production, rather than to the act of creating a text, which is the more familiar sense of 'compile.' First, the word 'volume' makes clear that this incipit refers to a material object; it does not share the ambiguity of either 'livre' or the English 'book,' which could signify a work or composition as an intellectual construct, as well as the physical medium in which it was recorded or realized. Second, what we might regard as the academic sense of 'compile' – to gather, select, and arrange material from the authoritative writings of others – does not seem to be appropriate either in the immediate context of this incipit and the table of contents, or in the more general context of the *Livre de Christine*; in only a few, at most, of the nineteen works collected could Christine be supposed to be acting as an academic compiler. A related point is that this incipit contains none of the modesty *topoi* often found in passages where writers refer to themselves as academic compilers. Finally, the incipit's reference to rubrication supports the idea that Christine's compiling included page design. One does not have to exert too much force on the incipit's syntax to read 'compilé' as referring to the 'rebriches' of the 'table' as well as to the 'volume.' The incipit suggests that in this 'volume' Christine has collected the works she has written to date, arranged them in order, and provided various extratextual features to augment their presentation.

Christine also uses various forms of this word in the more common deprecatory or academic sense – for example, in *Le Livre des Fais et Bonnes Meurs du Sage Roy Charles V*, which, she explains, she composed by drawing on chronicles and other written sources and the reminiscences of those who knew and admired the king. Modesty is often an element in these descriptions of her work; she refers, for instance, to 'ceste petite compillacion par moy traittee,' and calls it a 'compilacion' in another passage that expresses elaborate deference to her patron, Duke Philip of Burgundy.[105] In the manuscript on which the modern edition is based, however, appears an incipit very similar to that of the *Livre de Christine*. Its immediate context, like that for the incipit discussed above, suggests that 'compile' again refers to the design and production of the manuscript rather than to Christine's method of composition. Moreover, its close similarity to the incipit of the *Livre de Christine* argues, to my mind, that Christine herself devised both incipits:

Cy commence la table des rubriches de cest present volume appelle le Livre des fais et bonnes meurs du sage roy Charles, V^e roy d'ycellui nom, fait et compile par Cristine de Pizan, demoiselle, acompli le desrenier jour de novembre, l'an de grace mille.IIII^c. et quatre, et est parti le dit livre en troys parties.

[Here begins the table of contents of the rubrics of this present volume, called the book of the deeds and good conduct of the wise king Charles, the fifth king of that name, made and compiled by Christine de Pizan, a noble lady, completed on the last day of November, in the year of grace 1404, and the said book is divided into three parts.]

If we accept the traditional date for Chaucer's death of 1400, it would have been impossible for him to have seen a copy of either this work or the *Livre de Christine*. But Christine's use of 'compilé' to refer specifically to aspects of book production makes clear that such a sense for the word was present in the Anglo-French literary culture of which Chaucer was a part. The best way to explain the presence of 'compiled' in the Explicit to the *Tales*, therefore, is to suppose that it is being used much as Christine used 'compilé' in these two incipits. The word is attributing aspects of arrangement and manuscript design to Chaucer, rather than identifying the work as a *compilatio* in the more established sense. True, Chaucer had implied he was the *compilator* of the pilgrims' tales in the *General Prologue*, but that pretence has been dropped in the *Retraction*, where he takes responsibility for 'the tales of Caunterbury, thilke that sownen into synne.' Furthermore, although El and other manuscripts draw attention to Chaucer's Latin sources in some parts of the work, and highlight his use of *auctores* by including their names as glosses in the two prose tales, this apparatus is quite intermittent. This extratextual material is not extensive enough to support the idea that the collection as a whole is being presented, in El or in other manuscripts, as a *compilatio* from other sources. The presence of this apparatus therefore does not appear to have determined the use of 'compiled' in the Explicit. Instead, as in some of Christine's usage, the word seems to be attributing the manuscripts' arrangement and design to the author. Whereas in the *General Prologue*, Chaucer's compiling activity has the status of fiction, in the *Retraction*, where the 'I' of the *Canterbury Tales* is identified as the author who exists and has written outside that fiction, the description of him as one who has 'compiled' seems intended to describe his activity in the 'real world' – his engagement with the material details of book production.

For this shift from within to outside the fiction, exemplified by the shifting implications of Chaucer's characterization as a compiler, he may also have drawn on French models. Barbara Altmann's remarks on the ending of *Le Livre des Cent Balades*, another French work contemporary with Chaucer, cannot help but remind one of the *Retraction*. According to Altmann, as it nears its close the penultimate *balade*

> redefines the narrator and blurs the lines between the diegetic and the extradiegetic, the fictional and the real. With this self-referential gesture the narrator breaks the frame, as it were . . . In late medieval narrative, including the love debate and the broadly defined *dit*, the narrator often makes a bridge in the closing lines between the clerkly aspect of his role as a character in the story and the author in the world of readership and patronage. It is a moment of slippage or articulation between the imaginative and the material worlds of textual production.[106]

Chaucer too makes a similar move in the *Retraction*, shifting from the 'actor' on the Canterbury pilgrimage to the 'auctor' who has invented the pilgrims, composed their tales, and arranged this collection of his narratives in a book. This 'auctor,' moreover, identifies himself as the author of other works with which the reader of 'this book' is presumably familiar, and by commenting on those works together with the 'tales of Canterbury,' integrates the latter into his canon and finally attaches his name to the entire *corpus*.[107]

Exactly how far Chaucer's enterprise extended from the imaginative into the material world of textual production will no doubt be a subject of ongoing debate. All surviving manuscripts surely include some scribal writing, including in the *ordinatio* to which 'compiled' seems to refer, and even the most trustworthy manuscripts can differ significantly in the ways they are 'compiled.'[108] My purpose here has been mainly to argue that one of the effects of the *Retraction* as we find it in El and other witnesses is to help develop an 'author-mythology' of Chaucer's involvement in book production. The rubrics of the *Retraction* are, however, one crucial element in the creation of that effect, and the manuscript evidence encourages us to conclude that these rubrics can be attributed to Chaucer himself. This suggests that Chaucer's involvement in at least some aspects of book production was not merely a matter of 'mythology.' I have argued that Chaucer, somewhat like Christine, developed a system of self-reference in which textual allusions to his works' status as books worked together with the language of his rubrics to identify him with a specific literary culture. The parallels with Chaucer's French contemporaries are not perfect, but some of the differences may result simply from differing levels of material support for vernacular writing and differing systems of patronage. Observing Christine's self-references, including in her rubrics, helps us perceive more clearly what Chaucer is doing when he doubly usurps the scribal spaces in his book – by offering his authorial version of the scribal colophon in the *Retraction* and by providing his own rubrics. If the practice of his French contemporaries is any guide, Chaucer may well have asserted his own authorship most actively through precisely those extratextual elements of his book that were traditionally the province of scribes. According to Butterfield, 'For Froissart, the art of *ordinatio* is part of the process of creative composition. The art of exerting control over the *ordinatio* of one's own poetry stimulates and indeed begins to define for Froissart and for Machaut the public role of authorship.'[109] I believe that we can see this integration of *ordinatio* and authorship elsewhere in the *Canterbury Tales*, such as in the manuscripts' presentation of the tales told by Chaucer the pilgrim. The *Retraction*, however, is one of the points where

Chaucer has most fully elaborated this integration. Critical focus on Chaucer's assertion that he is 'revoking' his secular works has led readers to assume that in the *Retraction* Chaucer was withdrawing from vernacular or lay literary culture. Fuller attention to the entire *Retraction*, to its appearance in the manuscripts, and to the conventions of authorship among Chaucer's contemporaries shows that, on the contrary, Chaucer's inclusion of the *Retraction* in the *Canterbury Tales* served as a crucial means to identify his own work with that culture.[110]

NOTES

1 Benson, *The Riverside Chaucer, Canterbury Tales* X.1081–1092, 328. Unless otherwise noted, all citations from Chaucer's works are from this edition. For the standard abbreviations of the titles of Chaucer's works, used in this essay, see *The Riverside Chaucer*, 779.

2 Obermeier, *The History and Anatomy of Auctorial Self-Criticism* and 'Chaucer's "Retraction."' Obermeier's rhetorical approach to the *Retraction* is intelligently extended by Jamie C. Fumo in 'The God of Love and Love of God.' Míceál Vaughan offers a compelling challenge to biographical readings of the *Retraction* as Chaucer's 'deathbed repentance' in 'Personal Politics and Thomas Gascoigne's Account of Chaucer's Death.' In the notes to *Auctorial Self-Criticism*, 210–20, Obermeier provides an overview of scholarship on the *Retraction*; see also Fumo, 'The God of Love and Love of God,' 163–6.

3 Obermeier, *Auctorial Self-Criticism*, 210 and 212. Obermeier's essay in the present volume extends to the *Manciple's Tale* her examination of Chaucer's self-reference.

4 Sebastian Coxon, 'Wit, Laughter, and Authority in Walter Map's *De nugis curialium* (Courtiers' Trifles),' 38.

5 Deborah McGrady, 'Reading for Authority,' 172. More generally, as McGrady discusses, Christine makes persistent references to writing, copying, and reading.

6 Ibid., 164.

7 Ibid., 169–70. McGrady does not firmly commit herself to the idea that Christine 'authored' the rubric she is discussing (171).

8 For instance, McGrady attributes two distinct formats, including layout, rubrics, and illustration, for her *Epistre Othea*, to Christine herself, with one format succeeding another during the first decade of the fifteenth century; ibid., 169.

9 For an overview of the manuscripts of Christine's works, with a focus on those produced in Christine's 'scriptorium' and with many references to specific studies, see Laidlaw, 'Christine and the Manuscript Tradition.'

10 We might even go so far as to call this self-promotion or self-advertisement in the case of the passage in *Advision Christine* where she claims that readers clamoured for copies of her works; this passage is discussed by McGrady, 'Reading for Authority,' 159.

11 Cerquiglini-Toulet, 'Christine de Pizan and the Book,' 114.

12 Huot, *From Song to Book*. McGrady has reconsidered the extent of Machaut's involvement in book production and assigns a greater role to scribes and illustrators in *Controlling Readers*.

13 Cerquiglini-Toulet, *The Color of Melancholy*, 40.

14 Huot, *From Song to Book*, 277.

15 Ibid., 275 and 277.

16 Ibid., 277.

17 For explorations of such possibilities, see, for example, Hardman, 'Chaucer's Articulation of the Narrative in *Troilus*'; Partridge, 'Minding the Gaps'; Caie, 'The Significance of the Early Chaucer Manuscript Glosses'; and several subsequent essays by Caie. For a canvassing of arguments about the glosses to the *Canterbury Tales*, see Partridge, 'The Manuscript Glosses to the *Wife of Bath's Prologue*.'

18 Butterfield, '*Mise-en-page* in the *Troilus* Manuscripts'; and Kendrick, 'The *Canterbury Tales* in the Context of Contemporary Vernacular Translations and Compilations.' For more speculative suggestions that lost 'early elaborate court manuscripts of Chaucer's works' might have resembled extant Machaut manuscripts, see Guillaume de Machaut, *Le Jugement du roy de Behaigne* and *Remede de Fortune*, 53.

19 Arch reviews the scholarship on this question in 'A Case against Chaucer's Authorship of the *Equatorie of the Planetis*.'

20 Hypotheses that Chaucer may have overseen a few of the earliest surviving manuscripts of some works have yet to be laid out in detail or to gain general acceptance; for one such proposal, see Blake, 'Geoffrey Chaucer and the Manuscripts of *The Canterbury Tales*.' The earliest surviving copies of many works, such as the dream visions, the *Legend of Good Women*, and most of the lyrics, are so certainly dated to the fifteenth century (sometimes well into it), that there can be no question of Chaucer's direct supervision of these copies.

21 Huot, *From Song to Book*, 240–1. Croenen, Figg, and Taylor, in 'Authorship, Patronage, and Literary Gifts,' propose that Froissart presented f. fr. 831 to Thomas of Woodstock, Duke of Gloucester, and that it was therefore

not the manuscript presented to Richard II on the occasion Froissart recounts.

22 Manly and Rickert also fail to provide full and consistent answers to these questions in the various parts of *The Text of The Canterbury Tales* (hereafter cited as 'Manly and Rickert'), though their analyses of the textual relationships among manuscripts are generally reliable. A survey of the following, all based on aspects of the manuscripts and all exerting some influence, will reveal how sharply divergent are hypotheses about how the *Tales* came into circulation: Benson, 'The Order of *The Canterbury Tales*'; Blake, *The Textual Tradition of the Canterbury Tales*; Pearsall, *The Canterbury Tales*, ch. 1, 'Date and Manuscripts,' 1–23; Owen, *The Manuscripts of The Canterbury Tales*; and Hanna, 'The Hengwrt Manuscript and the Canon of *The Canterbury Tales*' and '(The) Editing (of) the Ellesmere Text.'

23 Mooney, 'Chaucer's Scribe.' Mooney identifies Pinkhurst, the copyist of the Hengwrt and Ellesmere *Canterbury Tales* as well as other manuscripts of Chaucer's works, with the scribe Chaucer addresses in his short poem, 'Chaucers Wordes unto Adam, His Owne Scriveyn.' She argues therefore that Chaucer and Pinkhurst enjoyed a professional relationship of long duration, with Chaucer commissioning and overseeing Pinkhurst's production of his works. Although she is sometimes forced, due to the nature of her evidence, to build one conjecture upon another, I consider the evidence generally to support the inferences Mooney draws about Chaucer's relationship with Pinkhurst. Gillespie expresses salutary caution about drawing highly specific inferences from the poem to Adam scriveyn in 'Reading Chaucer's Words to Adam.'

24 Owen, 'What the Manuscripts Tell Us.'

25 Vaughan, 'Creating Comfortable Boundaries.'

26 This idea is hinted at in Pearsall, *The Canterbury Tales*, 22–3, and developed in Pearsall, 'The Uses of Manuscripts,' 31–2, and in Pearsall, 'Pre-empting Closure in "The Canterbury Tales,"' 24–7. The idea that the rubric which appears at the end of El reflects a particular scribal or editorial interpretation of the *Tales* appears with some frequency in the critical commentary.

27 This may be especially true for rubrics; it is hard to imagine that Chaucer could have progressed as far as he had in composing the tales, prologues, and links without indicating major divisions in and thus making navigable a work that had come to occupy hundreds of folios.

28 The most convenient source of full shelfmarks and sigla for the manuscripts discussed in this essay is the Textual Notes to the *Canterbury Tales* in Benson, *The Riverside Chaucer*, 1118–19.

29 It is not clear, however, that even Owen and Vaughan wish to claim that these manuscripts preserve a more authorial form of the *Tales* because they derive independently from a Chaucerian exemplar that did not include the *ParsT* and *Retraction*. Owen, in 'What the Manuscripts Tell Us,' 239–40 and 244, cites these omissions as part of an 'undercurrent of scribal discomfort with the Parson's Tale and with the Retraction.' But scribal discomfort is not necessarily a reason to doubt that these works, and their position in the collection, are Chaucer's; in fact, as I argue below, scribal discomfort may sometimes argue in favour of a specific reading's authorial quality.

30 Powell offers a persuasive exploration of these connections in 'Game Over.' Chaucerians have traditionally regarded the *Parson's Prologue*, *Parson's Tale*, and *Retraction* as constituting Fragment X, one of a series of discrete textual 'fragments' collected as the *Canterbury Tales*. Powell argues that the traditional division between Fragment IX, consisting of the *Manciple's Prologue* and *Tale*, and Fragment X is unfounded.

31 Bo^2 and Ps are two of the *Tales* manuscripts where the tastes of the patrons (or compilers) most clearly influenced their contents, so we need to be especially careful about supposing that either provides a straightforward reflection of its exemplars. More specifically, while each of these manuscripts omits at least one verse tale, both omit the two prose tales, which suggests that form as well as content was influencing the preferences of those shaping Bo^2 and Ps. Compare Pp, which, although it includes other verse by Chaucer, includes from the *CT only* the prose. The Ps Incipit for the *MLTIntr*, which (confusedly) calls it 'verba Galfridi Chauncers compilatoris libri,' may well derive from an Explicit to the *Retraction* found in nine manuscripts and de Worde's 1498 printing (this Explicit is discussed below), and thus implies that Fragment X was in the exemplars used for Ps. The presence of an Incipit for *Mel* suggests that at least part of that tale was also present in the Ps exemplars. For a recent study of Ps, see Crane, 'Duxworth Redux.' For some views that conflict with Crane's, see Partridge, 'Minding the Gaps,' 54 and 78, n. 23, and my remarks below on the Explicit to the *Tales* that attributes their compiling to Chaucer.

32 Manuscripts omitting Fragment X are Sl^2, a *c* MS, and Bw, which is at least in part a d^* MS. In Ha^3, often a b^* MS but related to Gg in Fragment X (Manly and Rickert, 1:211), the scribe simply stopped copying at X.253, left the remainder of the leaf blank, and also left blank the following leaf, the last of a quire. For the 'constant groups' of Manly and Rickert's analysis of the textual tradition, see Ralph Hanna's outline in

the Textual Notes to the *Canterbury Tales* in Benson, *The Riverside Chaucer*, 1119–21, and my remarks below on the textual groups for the *Retraction*.

33 Vaughan, 'Creating Comfortable Boundaries,' 69–70 and 84–5, note 19.

34 Vaughan, 'Creating Comfortable Boundaries,' 85, note 19, interprets Gg as suggesting that 'at an early stage of transmission . . . excision offered as attractive an alternative as inserting categorical rubrics,' but presents no evidence that the excision occurred 'early' or at any time in the fifteenth century. If, as I have proposed here, the leaf was pilfered for its initial or border, the excision may well have occurred in a later century.

35 Vaughan, 'Creating Comfortable Boundaries,' 69–70.

36 Ibid., 84–5, note 19. The *ParsT* ends on fol. 128 of Ll², the fifth leaf in what was originally a quire of eight (fols 124–30). The following blank fol. 129 is clearly the sixth of this quire, so nothing has been excised between the end of the *ParsT* and this blank leaf. The quire instead is missing either its seventh or eighth leaf; I see no reason to suppose that the scribe would have written the *Retraction* on this leaf after one or two blank leaves following the *ParsT*. For confirmation of my collation and of my conjecture that Ll² never contained the *Retraction*, I am most grateful to Dr Kate Harris (personal correspondence, 14 January 2000).

37 From all of these manuscripts the *ParsT* has been lost entirely or in part: Hg breaks off near the beginning of X.551, and Cp at X.290; Dd breaks off at VIII.855 and thus has lost all of Fragment X.

38 Ad³ breaks off at X.472; loss of leaves has also carried away X.178–210 and X.382–441.

39 Manly and Rickert, 8:176.

40 I have edited their lists of the manuscripts in each of these two groups, to include only those that contain the *Retraction*. Manly and Rickert classify Cp and Hg with the first large textual group for Fragment X.

41 In the two other manuscripts of group *c*, the *Retraction* is absent due either to loss of leaves (Cp; see note 37, above) or failure to copy (Sl²; see note 32, above).

42 In the immediate context with which we are concerned, the transition from the *ParsT* to the *Retraction*, manuscripts of groups *b** and *cd** share a textual variant, an added sentence at the very conclusion of the *ParsT*. In La, for example, this reads 'To þilke lif he vs bringe þat bouht vs wiþ his precious blode AmeN.' See Vaughan's record of variants in 'Creating Comfortable Boundaries,' 77–81.

43 From other manuscripts usually or sometimes part of or related to the *b* group, the *Retraction* is missing due to loss of leaves (He, Ra¹, Mc) or because the scribe stopped copying (Ha³; see note 32, above).

44 To this second group I have added Wynkyn de Worde's 1498 edition
   (Wn), which was not collated for Manly and Rickert's Corpus of Variants.
   More recent studies have shown that although de Worde relied on
   Caxton's second printing for the text in most tales, for the prose tales
   and some other parts of the text he drew on a lost manuscript of high
   authority. Thus Wn is of considerable value in analysing the variants
   at the conclusion of Fragment X. Two studies of the affiliations of de
   Worde's manuscript are Ransom, 'Prolegomenon to a Print History of The
   Parson's Tale'; and Tokunaga, 'Representing Caxton's Chaucer.' Ransom
   concludes that of the surviving manuscripts, Gg is closest to Wn for
   the first half of the *ParsT*, which is his basis for collation. Earlier studies
   of other portions of the *Tales* have also mentioned Gg, along with the
   closely related Ph[1], and Hg. Partridge, 'Wynkyn de Worde's Manuscript
   Source' demonstrates the relationship of Wn's glosses to El's, while
   acknowledging that this is not necessarily inconsistent with the kinship of
   Wn's text to Gg.

45 See Vaughan, 'Creating Comfortable Boundaries,' 86, note 26.

46 Dl and Ds[1] are now owned by Toshiyuki Takamiya, and Vaughan
   proposes new sigla for them (Tk[1] and Tk[2]). I use the traditional sigla.

47 The *Retraction* has been lost from Dd, the earliest surviving relatively
   complete *a* manuscript; see note 37, above.

48 I have followed Vaughan ('Creating Comfortable Boundaries,' 63–5 and
   74–5) in grouping To with the *a** manuscripts. The comments by Manly
   and Rickert on To's textual affiliations do not carry much conviction
   (1:536–7).

49 The evidence does not support Vaughan's implication that the rubrics of
   El are isolated in the textual tradition. In 'Creating Comfortable Boundaries,' 49, he refers to 'rubrics that appear in Ellesmere and a few other
   manuscripts.'

50 El is one of only three copies, along with Gg and Ph[1], containing its exact
   form of the *Retraction* Incipit. But even its exact form is not *unusually* isolated in the tradition. If we make no allowances for variants, then no single
   form of the transition from the *Parson's Tale* to the *Retraction* recurs in more
   than five manuscripts – 'here taketh the maker his leue' in Cn Ds[1] En[3]
   Lc Ma.

51 Vaughan's argument that two other forms of the transition – no rubric
   (i.e., a continuous text) and Ha[4]'s 'Preces de Chaucer' – preceded (and
   gave rise to) the briefer, *a*-group form of the leave-taking formula,
   and that the longer form of this rubric originated in El, contradicts
   the hypotheses underlying Manly and Rickert's classification of the
   manuscripts – hypotheses derived from comprehensive collation. Their

classification implies that El exerted limited influence on the textual tradition. In light of this conclusion, it is hard to credit the notion that the El rubrics were devised specifically for the production of El and thence found their way into the many *cd** manuscripts, as well as Gg and Wn.

52 This Explicit for the *ParsT* seems to have been abbreviated in the exemplar shared by Ha^2 (which reads simply 'Finis') and Lc, and then omitted in Lc, perhaps because the 'Amen' that concludes the *ParsT* in the *cd** manuscripts was thought sufficient to mark the end of that part of the work. Both the *ParsT* Explicit and the *Retraction* Incipit seem to have been suppressed from two other *d** manuscripts, Dl and Ra^2, a situation that will be discussed further below.

53 That is, although the Wn Explicit for the *ParsT* closely resembles those in some *cd** manuscripts, it appears that convergent variation explains this similarity. In general, there is no evidence that the *cd** manuscripts exerted any influence on Wn or the (lost) manuscript(s) behind it. It is impossible to know for certain whether de Worde or the scribe of his manuscript added this Explicit; since de Worde appears to have modified rubrics he took over from his manuscript, the Explicit to the *ParsT* may be his. In 'Representing Caxton's Chaucer,' Tokunaga shows that de Worde's rubrics contain both distinctive similarities to those in major manuscripts (such as El) and unique variants.

54 For details see Partridge, 'Minding the Gaps.'

55 Among manuscripts of groups *b**, *c*, and *d**, some include an Explicit for *Thopas* at VII.919, others only an Incipit for the 'Prologue of Melibee'; two include both rubrics. At VII.967, Explicits for *Thopas* appear in several manuscripts, while others instead include an Explicit for the 'Prologue.'

56 The scribes seem to have regarded clarifying the structure of the work as a service to their readers. Compare their tendency to remove ambiguity from the language of Chaucer's text, as discussed by Windeatt in 'The Scribes as Chaucer's Early Critics.'

57 This scribal enthusiasm for the prologue/tale structure established in Fragment I also helps account for their provision of prologues for tales which Chaucer had left without prologues. These scribal prologues usually appear in the manuscripts of group *d**, where we also find the homogenization of Incipits and Explicits I discuss in these paragraphs. For texts of these scribal links and prologues, see Bowers, *The 'Canterbury Tales': Fifteenth-Century Continuations and Additions*.

58 See Manly and Rickert, 1:60 (Bo^1), 1:185 (Gl), 1:253 (Ht), and 1:458 (Ra^2). In Fragment X, Dl and Ra^2 are affiliated with the *d** manuscripts, which are generally less reliable than some other groups and manuscripts. Vaughan

acknowledges that the manuscripts are late and of little value for establishing Chaucer's text ('Creating Comfortable Boundaries,' 51 and 58), but nevertheless argues that their lack of rubrication best preserves Chaucer's own intentions for the unity of the *ParsT* and the *Retraction*.

59 This appears to have been what happened in Mc, where the scribe has left spaces of one line or more between prologues and tales, but for whatever reason, never inserted rubrics.

60 This pattern is readily apparent from the accounts of these manuscripts in McCormick, *The Manuscripts of Chaucer's Canterbury Tales*.

61 Thus I disagree with Vaughan when he judges it unlikely that scribes ignored or omitted the rubrics and other markers of this transition they found in their exemplars ('Creating Comfortable Boundaries,' 58–9). For support, I would point (for example) to Dl and Ra^2. Both contain the added sentence at the end of the *ParsT* that connects them to the b^*cd^* manuscripts, and Vaughan includes them with the cd^* manuscripts in his chart on 79. Their lack of the *ParsT* Explicit and *Retraction* Incipit found in other cd^* manuscripts must be due to omission or conscious suppression, rather than their reaching back to an earlier, 'unedited' form of the transition. Vaughan in fact discusses at some length the possibility that the scribe of To omitted some form of the leave-taking formula that was present in his exemplars, and acknowledges that the scribe's general practice with rubrics (which includes occasional omissions elsewhere) constitutes evidence for this possibility. He also speculates that the scribe may have decided that the 'Amen' which concludes his copy of the *ParsT*, along with the large initial that begins the *Retraction*, sufficed to indicate a break in the text, and may have simply omitted the leave-taking formula 'to avoid added complications' (63–5). I consider Vaughan's explanation in this particular instance sound, but would propose extending it to the other manuscripts which contain no rubric between the *ParsT* and *Retraction*. Vaughan places particular emphasis on Ht, on account of its apparent textual relationship to Hg (55–8 and 87–8, notes 35–7). But distinctive similarities between the rubrics of Hg and those of Ht are only intermittent. If the scribe of Ht was sometimes working from Hg or its exemplars (which I accept as quite possible), he edited the rubrics to emphasize the collection's structure as a series of prologues and tales. For example, his opening rubric, 'Here beginneth the prolog of the tales of Caunterbury,' seems to modify Hg's 'Here bygynneth the book of the tales of Caunterbury,' and the Ht scribe is generally careful to provide both Explicit and Incipit at each transition and to describe the subject matter of each tale. On the other hand, the Ht scribe downplays the anomalous transition from the unfinished *CkT* to *Gamelyn*. Ht contains

at least one instance of the tendency to label every part of the work as either prologue or tale, even when this creates duplication, for rubrics describe both VI.287 and VI.329 as beginning the 'prolog of the Pardoner.' It is a mistake to suppose that a scribe who developed rubrics at some transitions would not have omitted those at others; scribes did not always treat all kinds of transitions the same way.

62 That Ha[4] has been subjected to 'editing' and is consequently untrustworthy was demonstrated at length by Tatlock in *The Harleian Manuscript 7334* and confirmed by Manly and Rickert, 1:222. Vaughan cites proposals that Ha[4] predates El ('Creating Comfortable Boundaries,' 61), but Scott, comparing their borders in 'An Hours and Psalter,' seems to imply that Ha[4] was produced later than El; see 104 and 117, note 44.

63 The beginnings of a significant number of prologues and tales, in various parts of the collection, are marked only by a marginal 'Narrat' or by no rubric at all. The one other French rubric in Ha[4] (besides the widespread 'Lenuoye de Chaucer' at IV.1177) is the unique Incipit or direction about where the inserted *Gamelyn* is to begin, at I.4414: 'Ici comencera le fable de Gamelyn.' This is a point where the scribe, or his supervisor, is clearly interfering in his exemplar (Partridge, 'Minding the Gaps,' 58–60). The linguistic similarity supports the idea that 'Preces de Chaucer' likewise was devised specifically for Ha[4] rather than derived from its exemplars.

64 But see my remarks on Ii and Ne below, in my discussion of the rubrics that conclude the *Retraction* and the *Canterbury Tales*. Gg and Ha[3] share an Incipit to the *ParsPro* describing it (mistakenly) as 'the wordys of Chaucer to the Host,' but this does not appear to be directly related to the *b** manuscripts' identification of the *ParsT* with Chaucer.

65 Vaughan reports that it appears the 'leave-taking' Incipit has been erased in Ii, but he does not draw out the implication that Ii therefore provides yet another witness to this Incipit ('Creating Comfortable Boundaries,' 67). What Vaughan reports as an erased 'Inc' I might read instead as 'hic,' which might have been the opening of a Latin form of the El rubric. This would be especially significant if, as Owen implies, the other *b** copies derive their Latin Explicit for the *ParsT* from Ii ('What the Manuscripts Tell Us,' 240–2). If Owen is correct, that might complicate our notion of a *b** archetype.

66 The rubric may in fact constitute a response to an independent circulation of the *ParsT* that followed from, rather than antedated, its inclusion in the *Canterbury Tales*. The evidence of Ll[2] shows that the treatise had been selected from the collection by the end of the first quarter of the fifteenth century, perhaps before the *b** ancestor had been prepared. This can only be conjecture, of course, but the antecedence of the Parson's 'treatise'

as an independent one may be a phenomenon of its reception at some point in the fifteenth century, rather than of its authorship in the fourteenth.

67 Thus several of the ten manuscripts containing the shorter form of the rubric really constitute one witness, the lost archetype of the *a* group, but that is a witness of very high authority.

68 Vaughan tentatively suggests that lack of space led to the omission of this phrase in Fi Lc Se ('Creating Comfortable Boundaries,' 78–9). In Fi there is space for the words 'of this book'; another explanation must be sought for their omission. In Lc and Se this Incipit does fit snugly into the space provided, but both of these are *de luxe* manuscripts and their layout presumably was well planned, so the variant in the rubric cannot be explained as a spontaneous, offhand scribal strategem for fitting the Incipit into limited space. Moreover, it is striking, and demanding of explanation, that all these scribes should emend the *Retraction* Incipit the same way, by omitting 'of this book.'

69 There is also some evidence for this variation in Ad[1], where the 'makre' of the English rubric preserved in En[3] became 'Autor' when the rubric was translated into Latin.

70. Trigg notices the ambiguity of the El Incipit but discusses its implications only briefly, in *Congenial Souls*, 66–7. I would emphasize, as Trigg does not, that 'maker of this book' was more ambiguous than 'maker' alone. I do not find persuasive Vaughan's proposal that 'maker' could refer either to the Parson or Chaucer, and that adding 'of this book' was a scribal means of removing that ambiguity to make the rubric refer clearly to Chaucer ('Creating Comfortable Boundaries,' 65).

71 *Middle English Dictionary.* Compare an instance cited in Rust, *Imaginary Worlds in Medieval Books*, 27: 'John Lacy, a fifteenth-century scribe and anchorite, refers to himself as the "maker" of Oxford, St. John's College MS 94 – as "hym þᵗ maad þis book" (fol. 153r).'

72 Oxford, Bodleian Lib., MS Rawlinson A.393 (1528–9), fol. 99a, quoted from Keiser, 'MS. Rawlinson A.393,' 447. Bryan offers a survey of the early Middle English vocabulary of writing in *Collaborative Meaning in Medieval Scribal Culture*, 27–46. This account demonstrates there was some overlap in the terms used for copying and composition, but Bryan does not propose that any of her instances exploits this overlap for artistic ends, as I suggest occurs with 'makere of this boke.'

73 For transcriptions of many scribal colophons, see Bénédictins du Bouveret, *Colophons de manuscrits occidentaux*. Sayce, 'Chaucer's "Retractions,"' has also identified the elements of the *Retraction* in many other *authorial* apologies. I do not mean to propose the scribal colophon as a closer

analogue of the *Retraction* than those authorial apologies canvassed by Sayce and Obermeier, but rather as an additional and previously unnoticed analogue, to which scribes seem to have been especially sensitive.

74 We can also find prayers, requests for prayers, and self-identification in what scribes of the *Tales* add to or substitute for the El colophon which identifies Chaucer as the writer or compiler of the book: 'of your charite praieth for the writer of this book' (Ds[1]); the names of scribes, prayers, requests that others pray for them (Gl); 'quod cornhyll' (Ha[2]); 'Iste liber constat Iohanni Brode Iuniori etc' (Ma); 'scripta per William Stevenus' (Ra[2]). Moreover, Wynkyn de Worde, after the El colophon, adds information about when and where he printed the book.

75 The variant appears in Ht Ra[3]. It is unclear if this represents two scribes' identical emendations of the *Retraction*; the two manuscripts do not otherwise seem to be closely related.

76 Overgaauw, 'Where are the Colophons?' 91. I am grateful to Erik Kwakkel for drawing my attention to this essay.

77 Ibid., 85–6. Overgaauw emphasizes that while he and his colleagues found many colophons in such manuscripts, such writing 'was produced abundantly in all parts of Latin Christendom,' so 'we are unable to say whether . . . by the middle of the 15th century, datings in this sort of manuscripts were frequent or not' (86).

78 Patterns of scribal behaviour likewise cast doubt on conjectures that the *Retraction* is either inauthentic or posthumously imported from some other (Chaucerian) context. As has been discussed, scribes tended to respond most strongly to the work's alternation of prologues and tales, and to reinforce it, not only by their treatment of rubrics but also through their occasional interpolation of prologues for tales that lacked them and (less often) tales such as *Gamelyn* or *Beryn*. It is not impossible that scribes would bring into the *Tales* an anomalous piece of prose such as the *Retraction*, but it is not what the overall evidence of the manuscripts would lead us to expect.

79 Revard, 'From French "Fabliau Manuscripts"'; Brewer, *English Gothic Literature*, 116: 'It is like one of the great Gothic anthologies, the Auchinleck or Thornton manuscripts, not only copied but composed by one man.'

80 Parkes, 'The Influence of the Concepts of *Ordinatio* and *Compilatio*,' 65. Cf. Doyle and Parkes, 'The Production of Copies,' 190.

81 The comment on El in Parkes, 'The Influence of the Concepts of *Ordinatio* and *Compilatio*' and in Doyle and Parkes, 'The Production of Copies' appears to be most influential in shaping this assumption. One measure of

this influence is that even while arguing at length that El in important respects reflects Chaucer's intentions, Astell accepts the attribution of the El Explicit to the El scribe or 'editor'; see *Chaucer and the Universe of Learning*, 1–3, 9–10. In 'The Order of *The Canterbury Tales*,' 112, Benson attributes the El Explicit to 'the scribe of O^1,' the scribal copy he understands as antedating and giving rise to the surviving manuscripts of the *Tales*.

82 Eight other manuscripts and de Worde's edition include the El Explicit. Seven of those manuscripts are members of the d^* group; although the Explicit is not in La, their testimony suggests that it was present in the cd^* archetype. Gg lacks the leaf that contained the *Retraction*, but the closely related Ph^1 is the final manuscript to include the El Explicit.

83 No a^* manuscript preserves the Explicit in the El form, but Ad^1 echoes it so closely as to suggest that it was present in the scribe's exemplars: 'Explicit narracio Rectoris et ultima inter narraciones huius libri de quibus composuit Chauucer, cuius anime propicietur deus AMEN.' In both Ad^1 and En^3, which has 'here endith the Persounys Tale' at this point, the rubrics have been adjusted because these 'books' continue past the end of Chaucer's *Tales* to Lydgate's tale, the *Siege of Thebes*; they cannot be regarded as evidence for Vaughan's hypothesis that the *ParsT* and *Retraction* once were an integral work in a single voice ('Creating Comfortable Boundaries,' 65). Other manuscripts also contain hints that the El Explicit may have been in their exemplars or archetypes. Chaucer's full name appears in the Explicits of Ii and Ne, and the word 'liber' in that of Ii. The Ha^4 Incipit for the *Retraction*, 'Preces de Chaucer,' might suggest its exemplar included the El Explicit containing Chaucer's name.

84 In Ps, the Incipit for the *MLTIntro* refers to 'verba Galfridi Chauncers compilatoris libri,' which may well have been drawn from the El Explicit (cf. n. 31 above). Because Ps omits the *ParsT* and the *Retraction*, this Incipit to the *MLIntro* may have provided an opportunity to record in Ps the name and role of the author. John Shirley's long initial rubric to the *Canterbury Tales*, preserved in Ha^3, refers to 'the tales of Caunterburye wiche beon compilid in this boke filowing first foundid ymageind and made . . . by the laureal and moste famous poete . . . clepid Chaucyer a Gaufrede of who soule god for his mercy have pitee of his grace Amen.' That Shirley's exemplars included the El Explicit for the *Retraction* is perhaps made more plausible by the fact that in Fragment X Ha^3 is closely related to Gg and to Ph^1, which includes the El Explicit. In 'Duxworth Redux,' 28–9, Crane compares these rubrics in El, Ps, and Ha^3, but seems to assume that they preserve independent scribal characterizations of the work as a *compilatio*.

85 The presence of this title in Hg usually receives little or no notice in discussions of the El Explicit.

86 Olson, 'Making and Poetry in the Age of Chaucer.' In 'The God of Love and Love of God,'170–1, Fumo argues that the 'leavetaking' Incipit to the *Retraction* departs from Chaucer's pattern of using 'makere' to refer to God, but if we take into account cognate words such as the verb 'make(n)' – as Fumo does in discussing Chaucer's references to God's making – then the El Incipit appears to be consistent with Chaucer's references to his own activity.

87 In the F Prologue, Alceste attempts to assuage the God of Love's anger at the narrator by explaining that 'He made the book that hight the Hous of Fame' (417). When she commissions the stories of good women that will follow the Prologue, Alceste directs the narrator, 'whan this book ys maad, yive it the quene,/ On my byhalf, at Eltham or at Sheene' (496–7). In the G Prologue, which I accept as the revised version, the God of Love asks, 'Hast thow nat mad in Englysh ek the bok/ How that Crisseyde Troylus forsok' (264–5), and Alceste defends him by suggesting he rather mindlessly multiplies books: 'He may translate a thyng in no malyce,/ But for he useth bokes for to make,/ And taketh non hed of what matere he take' (341–3).

88 The iconographic overlap between scribe and author is suggested by the fact that many of the medieval illustrations of 'scribes' in de Hamel, *Scribes and Illuminators* are actually portraits of named authors such as the Evangelists. Kendrick offers a broad survey of the associations of authorship with writing in *Animating the Letter*.

89 Huot discusses the range of ways manuscript portraits represent the *trouvères* in *From Song to Book*, 53–64. Luongo considers a fascinating instance in which those portraying a woman mystic progressively reduced her association with the act of writing, in 'Saintly Authorship in the Italian Renaissance.'

90 Burrow, 'The Poet and the Book,' 241 (both passages).

91 Kendrick argues that portraits showing an author producing or presenting a manuscript of his works achieve a similar effect; *Animating the Letter*, 194–206.

92 There is a connection between the scribes' disambiguation of the 'leavetaking' Incipit and persistent scholarly speculation that Chaucer did not write the *Retraction*, or wrote it under some kind of pressure, or did not intend it to appear at the end of *Tales*, or did not provide it with the rubrics preserved in El and other manuscripts. In their various ways, these hypotheses assert that the *Retraction* does not 'sound like Chaucer' – in

other words, that it sounds scribal, which is exactly what several
of the fifteenth-century scribes understood. Indeed it does 'sound scribal,'
but I am proposing here that Chaucer meant it to.

93 Trigg, *Congenial Souls*, 81. At 253, note 16 she cites in support of this
    idea Strohm's argument that *'compilator* has a lower status than *auctor*
    or even *maker*' in 'Jean of Angoulême,' 71. Compare Crane's remarks in
    'Duxworth Redux,' 28–9.

94 Minnis, *Medieval Theory of Authorship*, 199.

95 Ibid., 208. In 'The God of Love and Love of God,' Fumo argues that
    Chaucer's submission to God in the *Retraction* enables him to assert a
    claim to authorship.

96 Minnis, *Medieval Theory of Authorship*, 209.

97 The *Retraction* reverses the disclamatory stance of *GenPro* and *MillPro*,
    and this sense of 'compiled' is likewise inverted from what it had meant
    at the work's beginning for Chaucer to be acting as compiler. 'Compiled'
    therefore enlarges, rather than diminishes, the scope of what Chaucer
    is responsible for; he is responsible for not only contents but also
    arrangement.

98 Huot, *From Song to Book*, 238.

99 Butterfield, *'Mise-en-page* in the *Troilus* Manuscripts,' 78.

100 For an overdue general comparison of the two writers in these terms, see
    Coletti, ' "Paths of Long Study." '

101 Echard, 'Last Words'; Butterfield, 'Articulating the Author.'

102 Gower asserts that he wishes to 'make/ A bok for Engelondes sake' and
    the 'Prologue' repeatedly refers to books and writing; Gower, *Confessio
    Amantis* (selections), 'Prologue,' 23–4. The revised, 'Henrician' Explicit to
    the *Confessio* repeats the word 'liber' three times in the space of six lines
    (Echard, 'Last Words,' 103). Both passages might be compared to the
    ending of *TC*, including the stanza discussed above, and to the *Retraction*
    and its rubrics.

103 I am indebted here to the account of these manuscripts in Laidlaw,
    'Christine and the Manuscript Tradition,' 234–5.

104 Quoted and translated in Laidlaw, 'Christine and the Manuscript Tra-
    dition,' 234. It is entirely possible that Christine was modelling her rubrics
    on those in manuscripts of works by Machaut and Froissart, perhaps
    including those studied by Huot in *From Song to Book*. The *Livre de
    Christine* also bears some interesting similarities to a manuscript ap-
    parently overseen by Deschamps, who acted as a kind of mentor to
    Christine. I am undertaking a separate study of possible models for
    Christine's use of 'compile' in the sense I am arguing for here, and of
    related vocabulary in the French and English traditions.

105 Christine de Pisan, *Le Livre des fais et bonnes meurs du sage roy Charles V,* 193 and 5.

106 Altmann, 'Notions of Collaborative Authorship,' 56. Altmann read this paper at the workshop from which most papers in the present volume are drawn.

107 Obermeier comments perceptively on the self-canonizing functions of the *Retraction* in *The History and Anatomy of Auctorial Self-Criticism,* 216–20.

108 There are of course well-known differences in order. Other differences, I would suggest, are more often a matter of degree than of kind. For example, discussion of the El Explicit, including the word 'compiled,' has tended to treat it as if it is confined to El, but as demonstrated here, it is not. Nor are many of the elements that writers have supposed reflect the work's nature as a compilation. For example, while some glosses seem to have been devised for El, about half of its glosses on the verse tales are also found in Hg and seem to have been in the *a* ancestor, and three quarters or more of the prose glosses appear also to have been in a related lost manuscript very near the head of the textual tradition. That is, although 'compiled' forms part of an integrated effect of El, it is an oversimplification to suppose that this effect was created entirely in the production of El itself. I have tended to emphasize the *aesthetic* effect of the 'compiled' Explicit – together with the *Retraction* Incipit it creates the illusion that Chaucer has overseen whatever copy a reader holds. But we might reconsider the *evidentiary* value of the El Explicit – that Chaucer may be affirming that he is responsible for elements of design of 'the book' of the *Tales,* and that arrangement of its contents was one of his responsibilities as author. A less controversial implication of the arguments I have developed here might be that we should discard the accepted title of *Retraction* for the conclusion of the *Canterbury Tales,* which seems to have been devised in the early eighteenth century (Vaughan, 'Creating Comfortable Boundaries,' 85–6, note 24), in favour of the *Leave-taking,* for which there is strong manuscript support.

109 Butterfield, '*Mise-en-page* in the *Troilus* Manuscripts,' 71.

110 I am grateful to the University of British Columbia for an HSS grant which enabled me to conduct research on the manuscripts' treatment of the *Retraction.*

6 Reading for Authority: Portraits of Christine de Pizan and Her Readers

DEBORAH MCGRADY

The fifteenth-century debate on the *Romance of the Rose* initiated an animated discussion among Parisian *literati* regarding the qualities that set an author apart from a common *jongleur*.[1] As is to be expected, debaters contended that wisdom, wit, and talent were essential in determining aesthetic value, but their assertions also reveal that reading contributed in important and complex ways to the establishment of literary authority. For Jean de Meun's supporters, Jean de Montreuil and the Col brothers, the generations of admiring *Rose* readers confirmed the poet's status as an *auctor*.[2] On the opposing side, Christine de Pizan and the university chancellor Jean Gerson contended that because several scathing passages in the latter half of the *Rose* could have a profoundly deleterious effect on naive readers, one must conclude that Jean de Meun lacked the moral fiber to be considered even an *acteur*.[3] For Christine Jean de Meun's writings provoked unhealthy behaviour; the text so enraged some men that their anger erupted in domestic violence, while women submitted to a reading would be filled with shame and horror. Gerson went even further, expressing concern for the spiritual welfare of *Rose* enthusiasts. According to Christine and Gerson, the *Rose* was unworthy and dangerous reading. The debaters concurred that the skills and practices of *Rose* readers were also of extreme importance. Nowhere is the value placed on reading methods in determining literary authority more apparent than in the treatment of Christine's own interpretative strategies by herself and her opponents. As we shall see, Christine's reading of the *Rose* not only served to challenge Jean de Meun's authoritative status, but it set the stage for her use of her own reading abilities over the course of her literary career as a means of establishing herself as an author in her own right.

Christine Reading the *Rose*

It appears that in large part, concerns regarding the authority of both authors and readers spurred Christine de Pizan to comment on the *Rose* debate. In the summer of 1401, she composed an unsolicited response to Jean de Montreuil's now lost *Traité sur* le Roman de la Rose. Where the *Traité* celebrated Jean de Meun as a modern *auctor*, Christine's response countered that a brief examination of the text revealed it to be unworthy of serious study:

> ... le leu et consideray au long et au lé le mieulx que le sceu comprendre. Vray est que pour la matiere qui en aucunes pars n'estoit a ma plaisance m'en passoye oultre comme coc sur brese: si ne l'ay planté veu ...[4]

> [I read [the *Roman de la Rose*] and considered it at length as best as I knew how. It is true that the material in some parts was not to my liking and I passed over it quickly for I did not plant my sight there ...]

If Christine first appears here to assume a self-deprecating role as an ignorant reader, her account of skimming some passages while skipping over others testifies to her mastery of the advanced rapid reading skills that Paul Saenger has associated with late-medieval highly literate communities.[5] Yet in securing her authority as an experienced reader trained in these advanced skills, Christine simultaneously demotes the *Roman de la Rose*, by suggesting that it is unworthy of more careful study.[6] The complex manipulations on display here were not ignored by her opponents, whose responses quickly moved beyond defending Jean de Meun to judging the authority of some readers to evaluate the master.

That Christine dared to apply rapid reading techniques to the *Roman de la Rose* inspired some of her opponents' most biting remarks. Jean de Montreuil and Pierre and Gontier Col repeatedly protested that Jean de Meun should not be accused of writing dangerous material; instead untrained readers who possessed neither the skills nor the wisdom to appreciate his writings should be castigated. In this vein, Jean de Montreuil fulminated that Christine and others who would dare criticize the Master Jean de Meun only did so because they 'had poorly read, poorly studied and poorly understood such a complex work' (male visum perscrutatumque et notatum). 'These people,' he continued, 'recognized themselves that they had read [the work] superficially, had depended on excerpts, and had shown little concern for context' (hi qui superficietenus nec eodem contextu, aut ex integro se legisse profitentur).[7] Responding directly to Christine's account of skimming the text, Pierre Col scornfully counselled that she and others refrain from criticizing the master until they had 'read [the work] at least four times – and at a reasonable pace ...' (qu'i le lisent avant quatre fois du moins – et a loisir ...).[8] Clearly, for both Christine and her opponents, reading skills were loaded weapons; they commandeered a text's reception and reflected readers' intellectual abilities.

Rose supporters deliberately contrasted the monkish practices of meditation and rereading with skimming, skipping passages, and reading widely and quickly. Thus those skills that Saenger associates with the highly literate appear here as the shoddy attempts of charlatans to pass as intellectuals. Jean de Montreuil dismisses them as the lazy habits of the unlearned:

> But what irritates me the most is that among our detractors, certain only read this remarkable work ... superficially, or were content to skim it, as they freely admit; others, even if they studied it with care are, believe me, incapable of understanding such an important work and thus are forever closed off from its mysteries.

> [Sed me nimis urit quod tales existunt nostri detractores quorum aliqui romantium huiusmodi ... viderunt summotenus aut legerunt in transitu, ut referunt; alii vero qui tametsi enixe studuerint, minime, credi michi, tante rei sunt capaces aut susceptibilies misterii.][9]

Jean de Montreuil is categorical in his distinction between the learned elite and the ignorant laity, the latter category being the space to which he relegates Christine and all *Rose* opponents.

Although most of these complaints regarding poor reading expressed by Jean de Meun's supporters were adroitly excised from Christine's version of the debate presented to the queen of France, Isabeau de Bavière in 1402, the polarity captured in the distinctions between the learned and the untrained provided Christine with much needed markers to stake out her own authorial territory. Acutely aware of her precarious status as a literate lay woman who challenged conventions both by writing and reading, Christine carved out a new identity for herself in the preface to the queen's version of the debate, where she pitted

herself as the untrained laywoman, a self-described 'simple and ignorant woman of the court,' against 'clerics and others'.[10] These comments are complicated by abundant examples in her letters of her skill
in literary analysis, argumentation, and philosophical reflection. Scholars argue that Christine used this unique twist of self-debasement and
abundant proof to the contrary to cultivate a 'clerkly female persona.'[11]
But Laurel Amtower, commenting on the portrait of the author-figure
as reader in the *Cité des dames*, counters that Christine performs as a
'lay reader' who 'provides a powerful counterexample to the academic
interpretive tradition.'[12] I would argue, however, that Christine's treatment of reading in the debate that is then pursued in her later works
reveals that she played off both a clerical culture and a lay culture to
construct a distinctive authoritative self-portrait that straddled the two
realms. As a self-educated woman of the court, Christine could ally herself fully neither with the learned community of men trained in monas-
teries and universities nor with the court society that rarely engaged in
study. An analysis of textual and visual portraits of Christine produced
from the time of the *Rose* debate to the presentation of her collected
works to the queen of France (British Library, MS Harley 4431 or MS R)
around 1414 reveals her unique strategy for securing authority by
drawing on clerkly and lay reading identities.[13] The queen's collection,
which includes works written from 1399 to 1405, reveals through text
and image a dependence on reading to establish Christine's authority.
In the abundant allusions to reading in this codex, the author and her
book-makers depict Christine the writer as circulating among a large
and diverse community of readers that includes learned and lay members. What sets Christine apart is her unique amalgamation of both
categories to create a unique reading authorial persona. Further cultivation of her distinctive authorial identity hinges on the presentation
of a new type of lay reader imagined for her own writings and detailed
in later productions. Whether bolstering her readerly identity or constructing a unified 'readership,' Christine the author, time and again,
draws on reading to validate her authority.

Christine as Reader

As Jacqueline Cerquiglini-Toulet notes, 'the *mise-en-scène* of Christine's
writing is often anchored in a scene of reading.'[14] Yet these scenes are
more than catalysts for the poet's compositions, for they underwrite a
larger strategy to establish authority. In the months preceding the *Rose*

debate, Christine had already defined herself both as widely read and as capable of exposing the deceptive words of writers and courtiers alike. In the *Epître au dieu d'amours* (1399), a work that outlines her attacks of the *Roman de la Rose* that would be more fully developed in her debate letters, the narrator evokes the breadth of her studies and analytical abilities when she judges as pure lies the innumerable books authored by clerics who malign women in both French and Latin:

> Et ainsi font clers et soir et matin,
> Puis en françois, leurs vers, puis en latin,
> Et se fondent dessus ne sçay quelz livres
> Qui plus dient de mençonges qu'un yvres.

> [And so clerics compose verses day and night, first in French, then in Latin, and they lose themselves in I don't know what books that record more lies than those told by a drunkard.] (ll. 277–80)[15]

Such an overarching statement concerning the breadth of her reading experience and her analytical abilities gives way to greater reflection on the personal and spiritual rewards reaped through study of serious works. In the *Chemin de long estude* (1402), the narrator speaks of her intimate knowledge of Boethius, whose work consoled her during a time of deep sorrow:

> Et lors me vint entre mains
> Un livre que moult amay,
> Car il m'osta hors d'esmay
> Et de desolacion:
> Ce ert De Consolacion
> *Böece*, le prouffitable
> Livre qui tant est notable.
> Lors y commençay a lire,
> Et en lisant passay l'ire
> Et l'anuyeuse pesance
> Dont j'estoie en mesaisance–
> Car bon exemple ayde moult
> A confort, et anuy toult–
> Quant ou livre remiray
> Les tors fais, et m'i miray,
> Qu'on fist a Böece a Romme …

[And then I got hold of a book I loved very much and that pulled me from my worry and anguish: it was the *Consolation* by Boethius, the worthy book that is full of lessons. Thus I began to read it and in reading my anger passed away as well as the heavy concern of which I was consumed – for a good example gives comfort and rids one of sorrow – when I began to study in the book the unfair treatment given to Boethius in Rome and to put myself in his place.] (ll. 202–16, pp. 98–100)[16]

In the *Livre des fais et bonnes meurs du sage roy Charles V* (1404) and the *Advision Cristine* (1405), Christine testifies to her growing reputation among the nobility as a learned writer impassioned with study. According to the narrator of the *Livre des fais et bonnes meurs*, the duke of Burgundy commissioned this new work after receiving a copy of her *Mutacion de Fortune*, an ambitious account of world history that combines knowledge culled from learned books with Christine's own richly allegorized account of widowhood. This combination of book knowledge and lived experience is identified as the duke's reason in selecting Christine to write the biography. As in the *Mutacion*, the narrator profits from her dual status as a learned reader and as a woman of the court with much experience to generate the text. She claims that extensive study of learned works combined with lengthy reflection on her childhood at court and discussions with living servants of Charles V resulted in the present biography (I.1–I.2). The following year, when writing the *Advision Cristine*, the poet again points to her ability to bridge the realms of the learned world and court society as the source of her success. She acknowledges that the nobility clamoured for copies of her books because she mixed study, the occupation of the learned, with the lived experiences unique to a woman of the court (Part III, chap. XI, ll. 8–17, p. 111). By conjoining the two, she gave 'birth to new readings' ('par l'engendrement d'estude et des choses veues nasquissent de moy nouvelles lectures,' *Advision*, Part III, chap. X, ll. 33–4, p. 110). Through this discourse of procreation, Christine compares her personal growth from reader to authoritative writer to the woman who ultimately creates new life.

In these frequent reflections on her status as a learned laywoman in the period following the *Rose* debate, Christine goes beyond advertising her literacy. She bears witness to the formal reading practices she has mastered. References to the wide range of works she consults speak to the breadth of her erudition. Detailed accounts of her reading experiences illustrate her familiarity with learned study practices that demanded seclusion and lengthy reflection. Where she skimmed the *Roman de la Rose*, more respected writings by authors ranging from Boethius to Saint Augustine and Aristotle are subject to intense study, which includes rereading, glossing, and applying new knowledge to her current situation. Echoing the advice of the university chancellor, Jean Gerson, that readers should place themselves in the affective realm of the author to benefit from a work's wisdom,[17] Christine's study of Boethius hinges on the double meaning of *mirer* (l. 215, cited above) – to heal and to reflect, as in a mirror. Through Boethius, Christine emerges as a learned reader capable of reading, studying, meditating, and responding to an authoritative text. By imitating Boethius in her own extensive study (*long estude*), she succeeds in standing in for Boethius, the consummate scholar and reader. One cannot help but see in the *Chemin* a scripted response to *Rose* supporters who questioned her familiarity with the meditative reading skills of the learned.[18] In turn, her own claim to enjoy a substantial and engaging audience who seeks out her books offers further evidence of the success of her reading and subsequent writings.

Christine the reader is best developed, however, at the outset of the *Cité des dames* (1405), where she draws on her vast reading experience to question the praise lavished on yet another misogynistic author. Rather than proceed directly into her attack of Matheolus as she had done with Jean de Meun, Christine first reiterates her status as a respectable and even respected reader. The *Cité* opens with Christine coming to the end of a long day of study. She begins:

> Selonc la maniere que j'ay en usaige, et a quoy est disposé le excercice de ma vie: c'est assavoir en la frequentacion d'estude de lettres, un jour comme je fusse seant en ma celle avironnee de plusieurs volumes de diverses mateires, mon entendement a celle heure aucques travaillié de reccuillir la pesenteur des sentences de divers aucteurs par moy longue piece estudiés, dreçay mon visaige enssus du livre, deliberant pour celle fois laissier em pais choses soubtilles et m'esbatre et regarder aucune joyeuseté des dist de pouettes. Et comme adonc en celle entente je cerchasce entour moy d'aucun petit livret, entre mains me vint d'aventure un livre estrange, nom mie de mes volumes, qui avec autres livres m'avoit esté baillié si comme en garde.

> [According to my habit and my life custom, that is the constant study of the liberal arts, one day when I was in my cell and completely surrounded

by several volumes on various matters, my mind, after many hours of study, desired to leave the profound matter of these authors that I had studied for a long time. I turned my attention to finding a book that would allow me to leave this subtle material and to enjoy myself by looking at some light writings by poets. And while I was in my cell, I looked around me for some little book, and by chance a strange/foreign book fell into my hands, one that was not part of my volumes, but one that was with other books loaned to me.] (I.1.1, p. 616)

Physical evidence of her commitment to reading in private abounds in her cell, where she is 'completely surrounded by several volumes.' It is quickly established that her voracious reading habits are known and supported by others, because some of the books in her possession have been left on loan. Capable of differentiating between serious and entertaining reading materials, Christine decides to push aside learned texts and to seek out some light writing to amuse herself. She will, however, leave this reading unfinished until the next morning because her mother interrupts her study. In her early morning encounter with this book that turns out to be Matheolus's *livret* or small book entitled the *Lamentations*, Christine fortifies her self-portrait as an accomplished reader in large part by challenging Matheolus's position as a respected author. In spite of her mastery of studious reading methods as displayed in the account of the previous day's activities, Christine applies to the *Lamentations* the same set of skills that facilitated a rapid reading of the *Roman de la Rose*. We see her 'visitant un pou ça et la et veue la fin' [reading here and there, and then examining the end ... I.1.1a, p. 617]. Once again, as was the case with Jean de Meun's text, even this casual reading of a faulty work becomes a catalyst for more advanced reading skills. Meditating on her wide study of the literary and philosophical canon of her time, Christine concludes that Matheolus constitutes yet another sad example of 'philosophes, pouettes, tous orateurs' [philosophers, poets, and rhetoricians, I.1.1a, p. 618] known for their attacks on women. This realization pushes Christine into an even deeper level of meditation that makes her appear as a 'personne en etargie' [a troubled person, I.1.1c, p. 619]. This state of profound thought calls to mind *contemplatio* identified by Hugh of Saint Victor as among the highest forms of study and practised by learned clerics and academics throughout the middle ages.

The opening scene of the *Cité des dames*, therefore, vividly details the author's mastery of a full range of reading skills that extend from the new rapid reading techniques associated with late medieval study to the dominant model of reading detailed in Hugh of St. Victor's *Didascalicon*. Written in the 1120s, the *Didascalicon* enjoyed a renaissance in late medieval France.[19] To speak of the reading experience, Hugh developed a multitier program that moved the student to ever higher levels of understanding, beginning with *lectio* and moving on to *meditatio, oratio, operatio*, and finally, *contemplatio*. These stages are deliberately reenacted at the outset of the *Cité*, where Christine moves from the casual reading of a single text (*lectio*) to reflect on its relationship with an entire corpus studied over the years (*meditatio*), before lamenting her fate as a woman (a form of *oratio*), then falling into profound contemplation (*contemplatio*) that sustains her decision to rewrite women's history (*operatio*). In essence the opening scene of the *Cité* offers a self-conscious portrait of the readerly identity Christine adopted in the debate and for which she was berated, but here she provides such a methodical analysis of the stages of discovery that little room for criticism is available.

Christine's reading account at the outset of the *Cité des dames* inspired an elaborate opening illustration that was reproduced in several copies of the work. The dimensions (typically one third of the folio) and the detail of the illustration are all the more surprising given that the *Cité* frequently appears in larger collections of the author's works and commonly falls at the end of the manuscript, where such an expensive illustration might have been missed. The opening illustration in MS R is representative of the *cité* tradition. It groups the reading stages detailed by Christine into two distinct phases demarcated by a central column (figure 6.1).[20] The first phase transpires in the poet's study, where the move from *lectio* and *meditatio* to *oratio* is visually expressed. The *cité des dames* master portrays Christine standing before a desk loaded with books, including an open book that connotes the reading event. The desk functions as a physical barrier distinguishing these first stages of reading and meditation from *oratio* or Christine's call for guidance. Her pleas are answered by the appearance of the three allegorical figures, Ladies Reason, Rectitude, and Justice, standing in the doorway. In the second portion of the miniature, Christine and Lady Reason stand before the wall of the City of Ladies. Here the artist anticipates the association between building and writing developed in the narrative. The scene portrays Lady Reason holding a large stone, which represents the revised account of an individual woman's story, while Christine applies the mortar with her trowel, a metaphor later associated with pen and ink.[21] Having moved between *operatio* and *contemplatio*, Christine's

Figure 6.1. *Le livre de la cité des dames:* Christine in her study and building the walls of the 'city of ladies.' © British Library Board, MS Harley 4431, fol. 290r.

activities in the second portion of this frontispiece insist on the dynamic aspects of reading. Her status as a literary master affords her the authority to challenge respected authors and fellow readers who have misconstrued women's role in society. These gathered reinterpretations constitute 'corrective readings' (or the *nouvelles lectures* of the *Advision*) born of Christine's own meditative study of a wide variety of texts from classical, religious, and light writings to documented and observed historical events.

In the *Cité des dames*, therefore, the scene of reading developed through text and image does not simply serve to justify taking up the pen. Instead, similar to accounts of reading detailed in numerous works she composed between 1399 and 1405, this extraordinary scene establishes Christine as an authoritative figure based on her dealings with a wide range of writings. Her extraordinary intimacy with recognized *auctores* of late medieval culture empowers her first as a learned figure and then as an author, her unique experience as a woman of the court provides a distinct context, and her lengthy years of study endow her with the right to question, refute, and rewrite faulty readings of her clerkly counterparts.

Christine's Authority as Defined by Her Readers

As Christine benefited from her status as a displeased woman reader of the *Rose* and then the *Lamentations* to set herself apart from clerics, so in her didactic writings she turns to her status as a learned reader to set herself apart from the lay culture that formed and educated her. Christine's lay audience often consists of illustrious leaders with whom she shared the same social space of court society. Yet she remains distinct, not because of her inferior social status as one might expect, but because of her 'superior' status as a master of books. In the biography of Charles V, Christine discusses her patrons' passion for books, but she is careful to distinguish their interests from her own. If Christine relishes spending the day locked away studying scholarly works, her patrons prefer collecting 'beautiful books' (chap. XII) and listening to works read aloud (chaps XII and XIV).[22]

Christine's description of her actual patrons in the king's biography complements the visual portraits of her benefactors and designated recipients that decorate numerous copies of her works. In these miniatures, Christine's audience is rarely engaged in independent study of books. Instead patrons and courtiers typically appear as listeners of oral readings or spectators before the written artefact. The queen's manuscript is particularly distinctive because of the quantity of audience 'portraits' that decorate its pages. In MS R, 112 out of 144 illuminations depict court audiences interacting with written texts. Six of these images constitute donation scenes in which the poet presents her work to a patron. Even these conventional scenes in MS R tend to reinforce Christine's intimate familiarity with the written word while maintaining a striking distance between the book and the designated patron. In the well-known frontispiece of MS R (figure 6.2) depicting Christine's presentation of her book to the queen, as well as in the opening miniature to the *Epistre Othea* in the same codex, Christine the author retains exclusive control of the written artefacts held firmly in her hands.[23] Neither the queen nor the duke of Orleans has contact with the closed codex. In both cases, the author-figure, through placement and comparative size, dominates a crowded court space. But it is the richly bound books with their leather binding, heavy clasps, and gold-tipped pages that take up a disproportionate amount of visual space.

Other opening miniatures forego the conventional book donation to favour instead novel settings that bring the book to life. In the *Livre du debat de deux amans* and the *Livre des trois jugemens*, the poet presents

Figure 6.2. Christine offering her collected works to Queen Isabeau de Bavière. © British Library Board, MS Harley 4431, fol. 3r (frontispiece).

the patron with the debaters rather than with the written artefact, thereby visually evoking both the oral qualities of debate literature and the lively court setting of an oral reading that the depicted author orchestrates and oversees.[24] Yet the narrator herself is described in the *Trois jugemens* as having access to written complaints rather than contact with the actual plaintiffs (ll. 661–4).[25] In a similar vein, the opening illuminations heading only the MS R versions of the *Proverbes moraux* and the *Enseignements moraux* place Christine in the position of a learned master. Placed before an all-male audience of clerics, courtiers, and her son, she points to the open book from which she ostensibly reads (figure 6.3).[26] As in earlier scenes of the queen and the duke of Orleans receiving Christine's books, the codex depicted in these impresses the viewer with its size, as would the imposing MS R, which measures 380 x 280 mm and contains 398 folios.

The opening illustration to the *Livre du duc des vrais amans* insists on this divide between Christine the literate laywoman and court society (figure 6.4). Unlike typical scenes in which the poet travels to the patron's realm to deliver a work, the opening image unique to MS R

Figure 6.3. *Proverbes moraux:* Christine seated in a lectern before an open book speaks with an all-male audience. © British Library Board, MS Harley 4431, fol. 259v.

finds the prince invading the poet's study. The miniature reinforces the poet's complaint in the prologue that while she would rather pursue her studies, she must satisfy her patron's command and retell a love story that he has told her: 'je raconte,/ Tout ainsi comme il me conte' [I retell everything as he told it to me, ll. 26–7, p. 68]. The *Cité des dames* miniaturist portrays the duke barging into Christine's study with his entourage. Her simple dress and sparse surroundings contrast sharply with the duke's ostentatious costume. By way of his sweeping gesture that doubles back on him, the patron displays, like a peacock's plumage, his gold jewellery, the emblazoned patterns of his red silk tunic, and especially its rich fur lining. The modestly attired poet, already pushed into the corner, leans slightly backwards, as if to make room for the prince's intrusive presence. The stack of books on a high shelf, the uncommonly large book behind her visitor, the imposing desk, and the sealed windows evoke the intense study that

Figure 6.4. *Livre du duc des vrais amans:* Christine in her study receives the duke who commissions the present work. © British Library Board, MS Harley 4431, fol. 143r.

preoccupies the poet. Yet the duke and his entourage show little interest or respect for the world of study Christine inhabits. Instead, they lean on her desk, block the doorway, and break the silence with their obvious conversation. At the centre, the poet negotiates with the prince, and in the doorway, the prince's entourage engages in its own discussion, as suggested by their lively gestures. The arrival of the duke and his friends vividly illustrates the great divide separating our literate laywoman from an audience that preferred to collect, tell, dictate, listen to, and admire its own stories.

Christine's Reader Expectations

Alongside these striking textual and visual efforts to distinguish Christine from her lay audience through reference to reading, MS R contains occasional invitations to the laity to consider the benefits of reading and studying the poet's works. Once again, early writings register the first expression of what will be developed more intently after the *Rose* debate. In the *Debat de deux amans* (1400), for instance, the narrator places reading and listening on equal footing when addressing her audience, even though the *dit* genre insists on its orality:

> Si n'est nul mal et en lieu et en temps
> Lire *et* ouÿr de choses esbatans

> [There is no wrong at any given time or place to read *and* listen to pleasant things (emphasis added), ll. 41–2].[27]

Anagrams were yet another strategy used by Christine early on to tempt her audience into examining the written word. Her early use of anagrams depends largely on sounding out words. For example in *Le dit de la rose* (1401), the work invites the audience to voice or 'cry out' her name (ll. 646–9).[28] In both the *Livre des trois jugemens* and the *Dit de Poissy*, however, Christine anchors her name more significantly to the actual page on which the text is inscribed. Thus in both instances, the audience is directed to examine the last verse to discover her hidden identity (ll. 1526–31 and ll. 2068–75, respectively).[29]

As Christine's reputation grew, her books reveal efforts to reshape her audience as book-bound students. In the *Epistre Othea*, the push for a literate, text-bound audience becomes especially apparent. The work consists of 100 founding myths expressed in brief poetic verse, which are then twice glossed by the poet. The first gloss develops an allegorical interpretation of the myth (referred to as *glose* in framing rubrics); the second presents an anagogic reading (referred to as *allégorie* in framing rubrics). The collection is then framed with an account of the goddess Othea's presentation of these readings to Hector. Already in the prologue, Christine played on the double meaning of *entendre* (to hear, to understand) to distinguish between the casual listener and the more studious (but still aural) audience when she referred to the work as 'Bel a ouyr et meilleur a entendre' (Nice to listen to but better to hear/understand, l. 59, p. 196). This call for a more intense reading experience would have a dramatic effect on the *mise en page* of its various renditions.[30]

Written in 1401 and surviving in fifty extant copies, the *Epistre Othea* reveals in its paratextual commentary, layout, and redactions the author's progressive privileging of readers over listeners in her corpus.

The work clearly represented a challenge for the many scribes and artists that collaborated in its numerous material renderings.[31] Of the redactions produced during Christine's lifetime and believed to have been produced under her supervision, two distinct versions emerge. In the earliest extant copies of the work, book-makers adopted the traditional layout reserved for the *auctores* that had been glossed over the centuries. Thus each summarized myth was framed with Christine's own glosses, thereby inviting the poet's audience to 'view' the work as another authoritative writing meant for study. But as early as 1405, an alternative format for the work was adopted.[32] In this revised version, a column layout placed the glosses immediately after the myth. Unlike the earlier *mise en page*, this format offered a sequenced approach that would have facilitated any form of reading, whether read in private or performed in public. Yet in spite of facilitating an oral reading rendered difficult by the layout of earlier versions, this new format also afforded space to numerous paratextual additions that encouraged the audience to engage with the material artefact if a complete reading of the work was to be performed. First, inserted rubrics announcing the different parts of each myth guided the reader in navigating the tripartite structure. Second, later renditions of the *Epistre Othea* attributed a greater role to illustration. In comparison to the six-image cycle accompanying the earliest extant copy produced c. 1401 (BnF, MS fr. 848), a 1408 copy owned by the Duke of Berry (BnF, MS fr. 606) and the queen's copy in MS R both contain 101 miniatures. In these heavily illustrated renditions, besides a donation scene opening the work, each mythological story is preceded by an illustration that locates a mythological figure in billowing clouds. Below the celestial character is an ever-changing audience. For example, in the illustration decorating the story of Diane, the artist foregoes the details of the myth to focus instead on the many possible reading experiences made possible by the text. To emphasize the reading experience, Diane is depicted in the heavens with an open book in hand. Below her, the viewer discovers a diverse crowd of readers. Whether gazing on books in small groups, pointing up at the figure in place of written material, or discussing among themselves, the audience in this later *Othea* miniature cycle models a rich array of reception modes that move from the written word, to images, to public readings (figure 6.5).

MS R as well as the duke's earlier copy of the work, as later versions of the *Othea*, insist on a 'material reading' of the text that would entail holding the book, gazing on its images, and studying its

Figure 6.5. *Epistre Othea:* Diane reading from a book while members of her audience consult their copies. © British Library Board, MS Harley 4431, fol. 107r.

text.[33] Rubricated instructions that precede the first illustration in these later versions of the work make clear the preference for a material reading over an aural reception of the text:

> Affin que ceulz qui ne sont mie clers poetes puissent entendre en brief la significacion des histoires de ce livre, est a savoir que, par tout ou les ymages sont en nues, c'est a entendre que ce sont les figures des dieux ou deesses de quoy la letre ensuivant ou livre parle, selon la maniere de parler des ancians poetes. Et pour ce que deÿté est chose espirituelle et eslevee de terre, sont les ymages figurez en nues; et ceste premiere est la deesse de sapience.

> [So that those who are neither clerics nor poets are able to understand quickly the significance of the story in this book, it should be noted

that wherever a figure is surrounded by clouds, it is to be understood that these figures are the gods or goddesses that are discussed in the subsequent passages in a style reminiscent of the ancient poets. It is because these deities are spiritual and not of the earth that they are placed in the clouds. The first image is of the goddess of wisdom.] (1.1–9, p. 197)

This rubric stresses that the images have been incorporated to aid the lay reader or 'those who are not learned poets' so that they can 'quickly' grasp the significance of each story. Whether Christine authored this rubric that links text and image to create a more fluid reading experience matters less than the fact that sharp distinctions between learned and lay readers announced here complement comments elsewhere in Christine's corpus.

Several critics have argued that the *Othea* was intended as an actual reading manual for Christine's audience. These scholars argue that the aggressive interpretive strategies adopted by the poet to reread Ovid were to be adopted by Christine's readers.[34] When we consider the paratextual evidence, however, it appears that rather than inviting imitation, text and image insist on the lesser status of Christine's audience as non-poets and members of the less-learned laity. Rather than encourage the intense study Christine performs, text and image seek to facilitate quick comprehension, spotlight the materiality of the text, and finally, incite group discussion of the work as suggested in the Diane illustration and repeated in the other 100 miniatures in the MS R *Othea* miniature cycle.[35]

In the MS R dedication to the queen dating from c. 1414, Christine anticipates the invitation to her audience to engage in a hybrid form of reading as expressed in the enclosed *Epistre Othea*. Here again she conjoins public and private reading strategies when speaking of the reception of her works. But while conceding that one can learn much in listening to the diverse 'matieres' found in her collection, she asserts that the actual reading of books promises even greater riches:

... les sages tesmoignent
En leurs escrips, les gens qui songnent
De *lire en livres* voulentiers,
Ne peut qu'aucunement n'eslongnent
Ygnorence ...

[Wise men assert in their writings that people who consider *reading books* of their own accord can but only chase away ignorance (emphasis added).]
(ll. 37–41)

In contrast to listeners, readers can become agents of change capable of 'chasing away ignorance.' Christine enhances this invitation to read books with a detailed account of the care she has personally put into the compiling, transcription, and decoration of the very codex she offers the queen (ll. 49–60).[36]

The accompanying frontispiece offers a resounding visual echo of this hybrid reading experience (figure 6.2). Painted most likely between 1410 and 1414, the illustration places Isabeau de Bavière in her private chambers, the new space of private devotion and reading in late medieval society, rather than in the public space occupied by so many male patrons in the same manuscript. The queen's bedchamber, although richly decorated with luxurious fabrics, is as absent of distraction as is Christine's study depicted throughout the codex, including the opening illuminations to the *Duc des vrais amans* and the *Cité des dames*. The large and comfortable space of the queen's private chambers accommodates an intimate community of women who might read and discuss the hefty book Christine offers the queen. Unlike the Duke of True Lovers' entourage who conversed among themselves, the queen's ladies form a respectful circle around the author and her book. Keeping their hands in their laps, there is no indication that they engage in separate conversation. Behind the group, there is the promise of an even more intimate reading experience. Nestled between the window and the bed, a chair and table appear. This furniture would have easily accommodated a reader, whether the queen herself or, more typically, an author willing to read the work to the queen in private, much like Jean Froissart attests to doing for the Count of Foix.[37]

This community of women gathered around the author and her book also calls to mind Christine's numerous earlier admonishments in the *Livre des trois vertus* (1405) that women teach their daughters and female servants to read, study, and discuss works together. After advising mothers to encourage their daughters to read in particular devotional and didactic works, Christine provides a concrete example of the benefits of such a practice by citing her own corpus. But rather than select one of her more obvious examples of such writings, for example the *Epistre Othea* or her *Oraison Nostre Dame*, Christine turns to a courtly example, the *Livre du duc des vrais amans*. Choosing the very work she introduces as a commission that tore her from her own studies, the narrator recopies a letter of warning that the Dame de Sebille sent to the young lady of the romance who was to read and meditate on its advice. The narrator prefaces this auto-citation with an invitation to her female audience to reread the letter and discuss together its ethical value (*Livre des trois vertus*, ch. XVI, p. 109). In case they are bothered by the idea of 'reading' it or if they have already 'seen' the letter, Christine advises them to skip over it and proceed to the next chapter:

> Si la puet passer oultre qui veult, se ou lire lui anuye ou se autre foiz l'a veue, quoy qu'elle soit bonne et prouffitable a ouïr et notter a toutes haultes dames et autres, a qui ce puet et doit apertenir.

> [One can pass over this letter if desired if reading it seems tiresome or if it has been seen before, although it is good and beneficial to hear and comment on the text before all women of high rank as well as others, to whom this work can and should be relevant.] (109)

Referencing her audience's freedom to skip over the letter, Christine appears to downplay the value of her work, as she had previously devalued the *Rose* and the *Lamentations* by adopting this practice. As noted earlier, however, reading skills also speak to a reader's abilities and intentions. In this address to her audience, Christine does not so much devalue her work as she passes judgment on her audience. She indicates that either readers will skip over the letter because they have already read the piece and are therefore familiar with her corpus or because they are not the type of readers who would be interested in or capable of applying serious study methods to the text that would entail reading and then analysing the piece. Thus she does not assume that all of her audience will practise the same advanced study habits that she has mastered and repeatedly displayed in her various works. Nor does she imagine that they will read her works in solitude. Instead, here again, she envisions a hybrid reading experience for her audience, one in which small groups will read the written word together and discuss its significance.

That Christine was successful in cultivating her unique authority as a learned laywoman whose books enjoyed immense popularity is apparent in the sheer quantity of extant copies of her works as well as in the empowering visual portraits not only of a woman writer but as a woman reader that decorate her manuscripts. In the testimonies of her contemporaries, we discover further evidence of her success. Around 1403, Eustache Deschamps composed a verse epistle addressed to Christine. He opens with fulsome praise for Christine as a female lay author:

> Muse eloquent entre les ix, Christine,
> Nompareille que je saiche au jour d'ui:
> En sens acquis et en toute doctrine,
> Tu as de Dieu science et non d'autruy;
> Tes epistres et livres, que je luy
> En pluseurs lieux, de grant philosophie,
> Et ce que tu m'as escript une fie,
> Me font certain de la grant habondance
> De ton scavoir qui tousjours monteplie,
> Seul en tes faiz au royaume de France.

[Of the nine muses you are the most eloquent, Christine. I know of no one who can match you in our days: accomplished both in wisdom and doctrine, you received from God your science, and from no one else; your letters and your books, all filled with great philosophy, which I have read in many places, and also what you once wrote to me, make me certain of the great abundance of your knowledge, which still grows. (You are) unique in your accomplishment in all of France.] (ll. 1–10)[38]

First acknowledging Christine's extraordinary mastery of wisdom and doctrine that places her alongside the most authoritative of female voices – the nine muses – Deschamps marvels over her status as a reader of learned works *and* as a producer of books intended for study. He celebrates the profound thought contained in her writings and attests to his own attentive reading of them. In subsequent stanzas, he praises her for her mastery of the 'vii ars de clergie' [seven arts of the clergy, l. 19], requests that she accept him as her student, and compares her favourably to Boethius.

Deschamps presents a formidable argument in defence of Christine's claims of authorship, and he does so by alluding to the reading strategies that she maximized in the debate on the *Roman de la Rose*. In the debate, Christine's mastery of a full range of reading and interpretive skills forced her opponents to read and respond to her arguments, even if they disguised their engagement with open ridicule. Over the course of her literary career, Christine liberally called on reading to cultivate her authorial identity. In countless verbal and visual portraits, Christine's passion for reading empowered her to straddle both the clerkly and lay worlds of her time. But it was her audience who was called upon to secure her status as a bona fide author through their engagement with her books. Where her opponents in the *Rose* debate attempted to dismiss her because of her status as a laywoman instead of a learned cleric, Christine's authorial persona expresses a unique identity that draws from both traditions to create a distinctive identity for her. Throughout Christine's corpus, text and image work together to set the writer apart both from the learned clerkly figures she repeatedly challenged as poor readers of texts and events as well as from court laity who could not be expected to read in the careful and meditative ways that were mastered by Christine. Indeed, key to Christine's authorial identity was first and foremost her mastery of reading skills; before ever claiming herself an author, Christine shaped her authorial identity around her status as an unparalleled reader.

NOTES

1 The distinction is reflected, for example, in the remarks by Jean de Montreuil in Hicks, *Le Débat*, 34, ll. 49–51. I have cited the texts of the Latin and French documents in the debate from this edition. Whenever provided in this essay, translations into English are mine.

2 Jean de Meun's defenders regularly point to the 'master's' many disciples as proof of the poet's greatness; see e.g. Hicks, *Le Débat*, 23, ll. 23–5; 30, ll. 30–3; 44, ll. 50–8.

3 Ibid., 164, ll. 37–42.

4 Ibid., 13, ll. 47–50.

5 See especially, 'Written Culture at the End of the Middle Ages,' in Saenger, *Space between Words*, 256–76.

6 On the spread of silent reading to the laity, see ibid. Saenger's study emphasizes the scholarly advantages of new reading techniques whereas the Debate reveals the cultural values assigned reading practices at the end of the Middle Ages.

7 Hicks, *Le Débat*, 34, ll. 41–2 and 46–7.

8 Ibid., 110, ll. 740–1. In a similar vein, Montreuil facetiously inquired into the reading practices of a high-placed, unnamed opponent in a later letter,

submitting 'Maybe you skimmed too quickly the work you condemn, or maybe you read it long ago ...' (ibid., 38, ll. 18–21).

9 Ibid., 44, ll. 36–42.

10 Ibid., 5, ll. 20–1 and 6, l. 30.

11 There is an extensive bibliography on the many approaches to establishing authority in Christine de Pizan's work. Key works include Brownlee, 'Discourses of the Self'; Margolis, 'Clerkliness and Courtliness'; and Mcleod and Wilson, 'A Clerk in Name Alone.'

12 Amtower, *Engaging Words*, 2. On the reading practices of the laity, see Parkes, 'The Literacy of the Laity.' My use of learned literacy and lay literacy echoes Parkes's differentiation between the professional and cultivated leader. The new nomenclature is used to emphasize the medieval view that the difference was a direct result of one's education and social class.

13 Millard Meiss offers a detailed codicological description of the manuscript in *French Painting in the Time of Jean of Berry*, 1:293–6. On Christine's involvement in the production of the codex, see Laidlaw, 'Christine de Pizan – A Publisher's Progress.' Open access to the fully digitized codex is available through *Christine de Pizan: The Making of the Queen's Manuscript (London, British Library, Harley 4431)*. Thus while reproductions are provided here together with references to reproductions elsewhere, the best access to these images is provided by this website.

14 Cerquiglini-Toulet, 'Christine de Pizan and the Book,' 118.

15 Christine de Pizan, *Oeuvres poétiques*, 2:10.

16 Reference from Christine de Pizan, *Le chemin de longue etude*.

17 Gerson, *La Montaigne de meditation*.

18 For a complementary reading of the links between these two texts, see Solterer, *The Master and Minerva*, 164–71.

19 Hugh of St Victor, *The Didascalicon of Hugh of St. Victor*; and Hugh of St Victor, *Hugonis de Sancto Victore Didascalicon de studio legendi*. For discussion of the impact of this work on medieval practices, see Illich, *Vineyard of the Text*; and 'Reading Between the Lines' in McGrady, *Controlling Readers*, 21–44.

20 The opening illustration in MS R is not unique. It had already appeared in an earlier collection of Christine's works offered to the Duke of Berry around 1408 (BnF, MSS fr. 835, 606, 836, 605, and 607).

21 Cf. Hindman, 'With Ink and Mortar,' and Blanchard, 'Compilation and Legitimation in the Fifteenth Century.'

22 One important exception is Charles V himself, whom the narrator repeatedly refers to as a passionate and serious student of erudite writings. Of course, Charles V was never Christine's patron, but he ostensibly serves as

a model of the ideal patron who recognizes the ethical and intellectual value of his writers.

23 These illustrations are reproduced and discussed in McGrady, 'What Is a Patron?' figures 27 and 28.

24 Illustrations are reproduced in Altmann, *Love Debate Poems*, plates 2 and 3, following page 54.

25 Altmann, *Love Debate Poems*, 171.

26 The opening illustration to the *Enseignemens moraux* is reproduced in Quilligan, *Allegory of Female Authority*, 30, figure 4.

27 Altmann, *Love Debate Poems*, 85.

28 Christine de Pizan, *Oeuvres Poètiques*, 2:48.

29 Altmann, *Love Debate Poems*, 193 and 257–8.

30 On the influence of layout on reception in the medieval context, see Sylvia Huot's seminal work *From Song to Book*.

31 On book-makers' influence on the *Epistre Othea* copies, see Hindman, *Painting and Politics*. Gilbert Ouy and Christine Reno have argued for Christine's close supervision and possibly transcription of this and other works. See especially their 'Identification des autographes de Christine de Pizan.'

32 Gianni Mombello details the genesis of the different versions in *La Tradizione manoscritta dell' 'Epistre Othea.'*

33 I have explored the concept of material reading that entails drawing audiences into an active engagement with the material artifact in *Controlling Readers*; see especially part 2, 77–146.

34 See Brown-Grant, *Moral Defence of Women*, especially 52–88; Noakes, *Timely Reading*; and Krueger, *Ideology of Gender*.

35 The notion of group discussion as developed in Christine's works suggests a more democratic notion of textual communities than as studied by Brian Stock. Where Stock sees textual communities developing around a single interpreter of texts in the eleventh and twelfth centuries, Christine's treatment of reading communities begins with her as the privileged interpreter but progressively expands to include all discussants. See Stock, *The Implications of Literacy.*

36 Christine de Pizan, *Oeuvres Poètiques*, 1:xv (both passages cited).

37 Jean Froissart, *Chroniques, Livre III*, 1:188–9.

38 Eustache Deschamps, *Oeuvres completes*, 6:251.

7 Vernacular *Auctoritas* in Late Medieval England: Writing after the *Constitutions*

KIRSTY CAMPBELL

This essay examines the challenges that religious writers of late medieval England faced in their tasks of providing guides to salvation for readers of the vernacular. In her essay in this volume, Anita Obermeier explores the way that Chaucer's creation of metaphorical censorship scenarios highlights some of the problems and challenges that secular writers faced in late medieval England. The first part of the present essay also examines connections between censorship and authorship, though in a different context. Writers of religious works in England after 1409 faced a very real threat of censorship in the form of ecclesiastical decrees outlawing certain practices of writing, translating, and reading. The first part of this essay will explore the question of whether this attempt at censorship on the part of the ecclesiastical institution had any significant effect on activities of authorship by examining the corpus of one particularly prolific writer: Bishop Reginald Pecock (c. 1390–1460). The second part of this essay will explore the question of whether inherited views about the inferiority of vernacular texts, as opposed to the Latin texts of the theological *auctores*, influenced the conceptualization and construction of authorship and authority throughout Pecock's work. As a whole, the essay poses the question of what it meant to be an author of treatises of spiritual and devotional instruction in late medieval England; I problematize current approaches to answering that question by examining the case of Reginald Pecock.

The six books that survive from the vast collection of vernacular theological writings that Pecock claims to be preparing for lay readers throughout the 1440s and 1450s constitute an ambitious project of education in Christian belief and practice. As a bishop of the church, Pecock considered it his job to publish works that would provide readers with knowledge of essential truths such as the nature of God, the benefits and punishments meted out by God, the moral law of God, the wretchedness of man, the wickedness of man, and the ways of achieving salvation. As a writer of vernacular theology after 1409, however, Pecock may have found himself subject to ecclesiastical decrees limiting his role as a vernacular author by restricting the kinds of material he could treat in his books.

Arundel's *Constitutions*, the subject of wide scholarly debate for the past two decades, was a set of legislations put in place in 1409 to put an end to Lollardy, the English heresy, which 'began life as a powerful expression of reformist tendencies *inside* the Church' but which evolved into a popular, community-based movement stimulated by preaching and vernacular textual activity.[1] Debate over the impact of this set of legislations is witnessed by the shifting use of the term 'vernacular theology' to categorize the religious literature published and read in the late fourteenth and early fifteenth centuries. First coined by A.I. Doyle in his famous but unfortunately unpublished 1953 thesis, the term was used provocatively by Nicholas Watson in his seminal 1995 article 'Censorship and Cultural Change' to differentiate a body of challenging and intellectually explorative fourteenth-century religious writing from a very different kind of writing produced in a climate of censorship in the fifteenth century.[2] According to this account, the binary relationship between Lollardy and the church determines what sort of books and tracts will be written and read. 'Vernacular theology' faded out, it seemed, as the church tightened its grip on dangerous ideas.

More recently, scholars have challenged the idea that all religious writing of this period must be seen in the context either of a rebellious Wycliffite surge against orthodoxy or an institutional response to the Wycliffite heresy. In their critique of contemporary literary history, Stephen Kelly and Ryan Perry write that scholarly attention to Lollardy has limited our ways of understanding the religious works written in the aftermath of the English heresy:

The scholarly attention paid to the circulation of Wycliffite ideas and of the Wycliffite Bible itself distorts, we contend, the scene of fourteenth and fifteenth century theological speculation in England. Scholarship has presented us with a camera obscura, in which either the influence on religious writing of Wycliffite thought is pictured as all-pervasive or Wy-cliffitism is perceived as an ideological fiction propagated by the authorities in order to legitimate a tightening of secular and/or ecclesiastical control.[3]

Certainly in Pecock's case, as I write elsewhere, Wycliffite thought was indeed influential, galvanizing Pecock's thinking and prodding him to reach for new ideas about lay religiosity, but Wycliffite thought mingles in Pecock's corpus with a diverse array of ideas, notably from Aquinas and Aristotle.[4] The diversity of influences within Pecock's own writings mirrors a broader diversity of thought that scholars have observed in recent studies of the religious and literary scene of late medieval England. Kathryn Kerby-Fulton, for example, has argued that this period can be better understood as achieving a dynamic intellectual culture where diversity of thought was possible and customary, as people of all kinds pressed in different ways against and beyond traditional orthodoxies.[5] In this account, the term 'vernacular theology' is opened up to include challenging and intellectually explorative writing that exists beyond the confines of the binary of Lollardy and institutional church.

Most recently, the term 'vernacular theology' has been used by a wide range of scholars working to 'draw our attention to the richness and variety of vernacular literary production under the umbrella of religion.'[6] In the 2006 journal *English Language Notes* a cluster of articles by Elizabeth Robertson, Daniel Donoghue, Linda Georgianna, Kate Crassons, C. David Benson, Katherine Little, Lynn Staley, James Simpson, and Nicholas Watson suggests new ways of understanding the religious writing of late medieval England and demonstrates 'the insights to be gained' from viewing vernacular theology as a 'capacious category,' even suggesting that thinking in terms of 'plural, vernacular theologies, is surely more apt.'[7] 'Capacious' is just the word for Reginald Pecock's body of work, which can be understood as a strain of 'vernacular theology' produced with an awareness of the constraints of official legislation against dangerous thought but also with a sense of the importance of contributing to this very institutional project (but perhaps in a more creative way) of unifying the church and shoring up orthodoxy.

First, I return to the *Constitutions* to show that Pecock must have been aware of the official church's response to dangerous thought, but that it is not necessarily the case that he felt that the legislation applied to him, a representative of the church. Indeed, I argue that it is more likely that Pecock was shaping his own response – perhaps to supplement, extend, or even replace official legislation – to what worried him so much about religion in fifteenth-century England: the spectre of disunity and the spread of untested, multitudinous opinion.

The fourth article of the *Constitutions* prohibits the teaching and preaching of subjects like the articles of faith and the sacraments in a way that brings into doubt or departs in any manner from the teaching of 'the holy mother church.'[8] The fifth article condemns any open or private dispute among schoolchildren regarding the Catholic faith or the sacraments.[9] The seventh article requires that owners of translated scriptures obtain a licence from ecclesiastical authorities.[10] The eighth article forbids disputation in the schools regarding 'any conclusions or propositions in the catholic faith.'[11] Several aspects of Pecock's work have been cited as signs of his compliance with the *Constitutions*. These include his transition into Latin from the vernacular in the discussion in his *Reule of Crysten Religioun* of complex truths about the Trinity; his avoidance of prolonged discussion of the sacraments; his failure to quote scripture in either Latin or English in his teaching in the *Reule* on articles of the faith regarding the benefits of God, to which 'natural resoun may not atteine by certeinte neither by eny stronge probabilnes';[12] and his reinforcement of the regulation demanding that Bible readers have proper licences in his *Repressor of Over Much Blaming of the Clergy*.[13] This apparent self-censorship seems to indicate that Pecock was one of many writers who restricted themselves 'to the kind of discourse acceptable to the censor,' showing that they 'were acutely sensitive to legislation surrounding the publication of dangerous matter.'[14] Even Pecock's careful prose, or his 'discursive sobriety and caution,' emblematized by his sense that fictions provide 'erroneous paths to divine truths,' provide some scholars with evidence of the 'profound effect of the severity of censorship throughout this period.'[15]

Pecock's compliance with the *Constitutions*, such as his insistence on the need for readers of scripture to have the necessary licences, appears to suggest that his activities as an author of vernacular theology were limited and curtailed by Arundel's decrees. If we look closely at each of these examples, however, we can find other possible explanations for Pecock's apparent self-censorship. First, his use of Latin instead of the vernacular to express complex truths about the Trinity is not a clear instance of self-censorship in accordance with the fourth article, which prohibits the teaching or preaching of the sacraments or articles of faith beyond that delivered by the church. Indeed, in this section of the *Reule*, Pecock distinguishes between his own practice and that of the church in delivering articles of faith, and in particular articles of faith concerning the Trinity. In this oft-cited passage, the article of faith in question is the belief that 'in the oon and the same substaunce and godhede ben thre persoonys, whiche persoonys ben Fadir, Sone and Holy Goost, and of whiche persoonys the Fadir bringith forth, gendrith and bigetith the Sone, the Fadir and the Sone spiren and bringen forth the Holigoost.'[16] Pecock tells us that the church teaches this article of faith in the Trinity 'withoute eny evidence to be takun into resoun fro the thing of the same trouthe in it silf, so that the undirstonding or the resoun of the lay peple hath no thing in the biholding upon the trouthe deliverid, by which thing he may be cheerid or holpen to conceive and perceive the same trouthe.'[17] Pecock teaches this same article first by providing quotations from relevant biblical passages that confirm the plural number of persons in the Trinity, their singular substance, and their manner of proceeding into being. He then goes on to confirm or support the same with arguments that follow from this truth 'to whom we comen at the lest ful likely by discurse and light of natural resoun.'[18] Pecock provides rational proofs or evidences for the article of faith concerning the number, substance, and bringing forth of the persons in the Trinity while the church merely delivers this information 'in his owne nakid forme as articlis of bileeve ben woned [to] be delivered to the lay peple.'[19] Pecock acknowledges here that his manner of teaching articles of faith departs from the customs of the ecclesiastical institution, and therefore is not in line with article 4 of Arundel's *Constitutions*. And though he accepts that some clerics may feel that this teaching should be ultimately excluded from his book, it is important to note that he goes ahead with it nonetheless, citing several arguments in support of his methods. This suggests that Pecock is not modifying his books in line with the expectations of a censor, but merely noting the possibility that some clergy will object, erroneously, to his particular methods. Pecock's use of Latin rather than the vernacular to discuss even subtler truths about the Trinity is provided as evidence that it would be possible for him to discuss much more difficult truths than he already has – to prove that his approach, though unconventional, is not as radical as it could be.

Pecock's practice of expanding the church's teaching on the articles of faith through the provision of rational 'evidence' also can be seen in his discussion of the eucharist and the priesthood, later in the *Reule*, in which he provides rational arguments to stimulate rational thought about articles of faith concerning the sacraments.[20] For example, Pecock provides the authoritative statement on what is to be believed, teaching that it is 'to be seid, feelid and holde that the preesthode into which Crist puttid and settid the seid xij persoons was ordeined by positijf ordinaunce of Crist,' but he also teaches the rational grounds that lead 'lightly and esily' into this same truth.[21] Rather than teaching the basic articles of the faith as outlined by holy mother church, therefore, Pecock extends his teaching in order to root readers' faith more securely: 'fforwhy whanne ever mannis resoun hath eny evidence coming for the thing to be trowid wherby he is holpen to conceive, perceive and trowe the same thing, it is lightir thanne to him forto conceive, perceive and trowe than whanne the resoun lackith al such evidence coming fro the thing and that he schulde trowe is al to gidere above his resoun.'[22]

There are a number of indications that signs of Pecock's apparent compliance with the censor can instead be interpreted as evidence of Pecock's own idiosyncratic teaching methods. First, his treatment of the articles of faith suggests that his authorship of a program in lay theological education was influenced more by his own theories concerning effective teaching than his fear of possible censorship. Second, his frequently stated opinion that lay reading of the Bible should be undertaken only with the interpretive guidance of learned clerics and only after a strong foundation of knowledge has been laid in the moral philosophy, or what he calls the 'doom of resoun,' is a more obvious reason for his comment that lay Bible readers need to have licences. On this issue, Pecock is in full agreement with Arundel about the potential dangers of lay Bible reading. Third, Pecock's failure to provide extensive treatment of controversial topics such as the sacraments is probably directly related to the fact that he was writing an entire book on the sacraments and wanted to locate extensive discussion there. I would suggest that the minimal discussion that he does provide on subjects like the nature of the priest's power in celebrating the eucharist, and the comparison between this power and the power of a man in the gendering of a child, is not obviously written with possible censorship in mind, but instead makes free use of arguments from reason to extend the church's teaching of the articles of faith.[23]

Pecock's decision to omit certain matters from his works and to keep the scriptures at arm's length from his readers therefore may not be an indication that he crafted his program of theological instruction with Arundel's restrictive legislation in mind, but that he too was searching for just as powerful a solution to problems, like Lollardy, that still threatened the health and vitality of the Christian community. I think it more likely that Pecock is proposing an alternative solution to that of Arundel with his corpus of theological materials, and that his bold confidence in the value of his project – the subject of the second part of this essay – supports this notion. Indeed, perhaps it was even the failure of this draconian legislation that prompted Pecock to come up with a better solution: a project of lay education that would do a more systematic job of getting people thinking in more uniform, orthodox ways. As Kathryn Kerby-Fulton writes, 'censorship in a manuscript culture is especially difficult to enforce, and that the authorities would be so unrealistic about what they could enforce is also no surprise given the failure of other would-be draconian legislation in this period.'[24] Any study of the authorship of vernacular religious texts in fifteenth-century England is complicated by the question of the actual effects of the *Constitutions* and depends upon our development of a clearer picture of the climate for writing religious works in the vernacular during the period following this legislation. Pecock's example indicates that writers going about their business of providing religious writings to lay readers may have seen the *Constitutions* simply as an outdated attempt to deal with heresy that could be adapted and modified as conditions within the Christian community changed and as new pedagogical imperatives presented themselves.

Though authors of religious writings in late medieval England may not have been hampered to the degree that we have previously assumed by ecclesiastical legislation limiting what could be taught or preached to the laity, they did face the challenge of providing religious instruction in a language that was not as authoritative as that used by their theological predecessors. The theoretical preoccupations of writers working in the vernacular during a period when Latin was still the language of literary authority considerably complicate the study of the vernacular authority of religious writings. During this period, 'the languages of cultural prestige were Latin and, for much of the later Middle Ages, French, and the role of the English writers had to be justified and defined.'[25] Writers intent on producing religious works in the vernacular during the fifteenth century had to contend with the fact that 'official positions' on literary authority in Latin literary criticism 'institutionally and theoretically excluded vernacular writing.'[26] Vernacular works were accorded an 'inferior and non-authoritative status' and considered 'insubstantial and ephemeral' in comparison with the works of Latin *auctores* such as Augustine.[27] A study of the vernacular authority of religious works dating from the fifteenth century is therefore made more complex by the 'persistent engagement of Middle English writers with Latin notions of authorship and authority.'[28]

However, despite these inherited views about the inferiority of the vernacular and despite general awareness of the cultural prestige of Latin writings, we should not be too quick to assume that writers working in late medieval England thought about the literary authority of Latin and vernacular writings in terms of a strict binary relationship: 'despite the powerful claims, which continued to be made by some clerics, for Latin as the only language possessing true authority . . . the Latin-vernacular divide was far from monolithic.'[29] As they translated works from Latin and other European vernaculars into English, and as they produced their own works in their mother tongue, 'Middle English writers' awareness of Latin and French authority was complex, by no means simply subservient, and fully capable of producing distinctive ideas of vernacular authorship.'[30] The degree to which Middle English writers recognized and accommodated official positions on literary authority differed. While some may have accepted the theoretical inferiority of their own literary works, others may have seen Latin and vernacular writings on more of a continuum rather than in a binary relationship.

In this part of the essay, I address this issue by examining the way that Pecock constructs and conceptualizes the authority of his vernacular religious writings in light of theoretical questions of authorship and authority. I argue that an awareness of official positions on literary authority does not necessarily result in an acceptance of the inferiority of vernacular writings.[31] Indeed, Pecock seems most concerned about going about his business to provide expectant readers with a supply of reading material that suited their tastes, their concerns, and their particular situations.

Pecock's works are full of confident claims to authority, a strong sense of authorial identity, and claims to originality. He is continually at work on establishing his own works as the most authoritative religious writings available to all members of society, boldly asserting that his theological works are the best choice of reading material for lay readers. For example, Pecock suggests in his *Reule of Crysten Religioun* that he has not seen 'eny book by him silf or with his purtenauncis' that resembles his, and that the knowledge provided by his book 'can not so esily be leerned in other bokes, neither in sermouns or prechingis, neither by mennys spekingis.'[32] In his *Repressor of Over Much Blaming of the Clergy*, Pecock suggests that his works present the most important doctrinal truths 'more pleinly and more fully and sooner' than the Bible itself.[33] His entire corpus is saturated with assertions of his works' value not just for ordinary Christians but also for religious authorities such as monks and priests. Furthermore, Pecock does not defer to the *auctores*. Rather than directing readers to Latin texts for clarification, he often directs readers to other works in his own corpus, suggesting that his corpus forms a self-sufficient and self-sustaining system of theology. According to Bonaventure's definition of an *auctor*, as one who 'writes the words of another as well as his own, but his own words are primary while the other's are used for clarification,' Pecock appears to have reached a new stage of authorship in which his words are always primary, and clarify each other.[34] Readers can therefore approach Pecock's texts in the same way they would approach an authoritative book like the Bible, finding interpretive aid internally. Finally, Pecock envisions his own work as a source for compilers; he states that his book is a source of 'greet habundaunce' from which readers can make 'summe extractis or out draughtis' into 'smaler bokis and treticis.'[35]

The authoritative tone of Pecock's works reflects the aggressive, orthodox, and indeed authoritative role Pecock played as a bishop, teacher, and defender of the faith. It also reflects his belief that his theological systems, and his approach to didactic and catechetical material, were superior to other available models. His authoritative tone also characterizes his opening to the *Donet*, in which he likens the detraction of his opponents to the criticism faced by *auctors* such as Jerome:

> Sithen seint Jerom had manye detractouris and inpugners of hise writingis, as he him silf witnessith, what merveyle is if I so have? And sithen ful manye famose doctouris writingis ben had in greet deinte and in greet profite in the chirche of God, and ben wel and profitably suffrid to be red and occupied, not withstanding that, here and there among, they fallen fro it that might be bettir seid, and whiche they mighten not at the

fulle comprehende, what merveile were it though it so falle by me, whiche entende not forto even me to hem, but forto be a profitable procutoure to lay men, into whoos leerning and edifyng, as to me semeth, over litil writing into this time hath be devisid?[36]

This passage reflects Pecock's complex notions of textual authority. He seems to accept official notions of the inferior status of vernacular writings at the same time as he brings into question the superior status of the writings of the Latin *auctores*. He likens his situation to that of Jerome, aligning his project with more authoritative writings. He defers to 'famose doctouris' and indicates that he is not 'a quartir so good' as authors like Jerome and Gregory.[37] Pecock calls himself a mere *procutoure* and claims no desire to even himself with an *auctor* like Jerome, but he also carefully criticizes those writings which show that even the fathers did not always comprehend and give proper expression to the timeless, universal truths for which they were supposed to be searching. At the same time as Pecock claims to recognize and accept the inferior and non-authoritative status accorded to vernacular writing, he brings into question the very definition of an authoritative writing as one produced by a famous doctor like Jerome.

Pecock's complicated view of the authority of his own text, the authority of other texts contemporary with his own, and the authority of his revered theological predecessors is illuminated by his prologue to the *Reule of Crysten Religioun*, where he draws a distinction between his vernacular theology and the religious writings of others, saying that he intends his book to 'rebuke, drive doun and converte the fonnednes and the presumpcioun' of people who spend their time reading 'unsavery bokis' which treat matters of Christian doctrine 'unsufficiently, suspectly . . . and perilosely.'[38] These books are held by the people as 'riche jewelis to be dertheworthly biclippid, loved and multiplied abrood of alle cristen peple.'[39] Pecock intends his *Reule* to compete with these unsavoury books, by treating Christian doctrine in a more profitable, fruitful way. The way he defines his own texts as authoritative, as opposed to those other inferior, non-authoritative vernacular texts, can help us understand Pecock's views on literary authority.

This distinction between authoritative vernacular works and non-authoritative vernacular works is at the heart of the dream vision that he describes as the impetus to the creation of his text. In a waking vision, Pecock is approached by a multitude of beautiful ladies who call themselves the daughters of God and describe themselves as 'treuthis of universal philosophie comprehending lawe of kinde and lawe of feith.'[40] These ladies inform Pecock that they have been banished from their rightful place as the spouses of clerks – the sons of God – in the land of reasonable souls. Instead of paying attention to their rightful spouses, clerks have been distracted by reading texts that are barren of spiritual truths. The daughters of men, mere 'worldly trouthis, oolde rehercellis, strange stories, fablis of poetis, newe invenciouns,' have attracted the attention of the clerks by their deceptive, sophisticated language and fancy apparel, but on the inside, they have no real spiritual value.[41]

The result of this adulterous liaison between clerks and worldly truths, or the result of the clerk's reading of fictional, poetic, allegorical books, is the creation of a monstrous offspring: a multitude of heretical books 'that housis schulde rather to tere than contene hem, wittis schulde be encumbrid eer than they schulde rede hem and remembre hem.'[42] These dangerous books have infiltrated every level of society through preaching, social gatherings, and family discussion. The result is that false opinions, including erroneous interpretations of the Bible, are held up as religious truths. The daughters of God hope to solve this problem by taking Pecock as their rightful spouse so that together, they may create a spiritual progeny that will spread key doctrinal truths. By inspiring Pecock's pen, the daughters of God will entice Christians back to orthodox belief.

The dream vision is the key for understanding Pecock's conceptualization of literary authority because it defines the legitimacy of Pecock's text in terms of its grounding of divine truths in 'the profis and witnesse maad for hem by resoun and by plente of holy scripture' at the same time as it defines the illegitimacy of other texts in terms of the lack of this grounding.[43] Pecock distinguishes his own works from those written by clerks who have been seduced by their reading of texts that claim, but only seem to contain, religious truths. Such works take fictions and allegories as their basis for their treatment of religious truths. In so doing, they distort and misrepresent these religious truths.[44] These clerks have engendered a race of monstrous texts by becoming fixated on allegories and fictions rather than the universal truths of philosophy – their theological works have become so invested in fanciful ways of depicting religious matters that they have lost their basis in reason and faith. Pecock's works, on the other hand, will have at their core the truths of universal philosophy that God has communicated to man through reason and through the Bible; he will only use allegory and other fictional devices to serve the expression of these truths.

Pecock's dream vision suggests that he envisions his vernacular corpus as a group of texts firmly rooted in God's truths, as opposed to those that have their grounding in imaginative descriptions.[45] In the *Donet* he discusses in greater detail certain kinds of illegitimate works, which do not treat religious truths properly, as he explains how they differ from his own works. Pecock complains that popular catechetical and didactic treatments of familiar subjects such as the Ten Commandments, the Seven Gifts of the Holy Ghost, and the Seven Deadly Sins are not properly grounded in the truths of reason and faith:

> It might seeme that moche of her such seid bisynes aboute the seid vij yiftis of God is not but vanite and feinid curiosite; fforwhy what ever treting, affermyng, or holding, not being historial or cronical, which is not groundid in resoun or revelacioun maad to us by scripture, or in othire surely and certeinly or probabily had revelacioun from God, is not but feined thing and vanite. . . . Wherfore it might seeme that suche teching is forgid, feinid and vein curiosite, difficulting, harding and derking Goddis lawe more than it is derke in it silf, and traveiling and troubling mennis wittis with birthen which is not necessarie, and therby letting mennis wittis to attende into profitable and necessary thingis.[46]

For example, Pecock argues that certain writers or preachers are so intent on making their teaching on the Seven Deadly Sins fit with their allegorical interpretation of the Seven-headed Beast of the Apocalypse that they refuse to consider rational arguments about the complex nature of Sloth. Pecock explains that Sloth can be considered, at times, as a 'specialist moral vice' but at other times as a general moral vice; this point is overlooked by those preachers who are more interested in aligning their explanation of the Seven Sins with 'a moral undirstonding or an allegorie or an anagogie of holy scripture.'[47] Pecock states, 'if in divinite were no strenger groundis forto holde therby thingis to be trewe than ben mystik conceitis takun by holy scripture, as ben tropologies, allegories and anagogies, divinite were a simple and an unsure faculte.'[48] Questions about the nature of sin must be resolved through rational thought as well as creative exegesis. The important point about Pecock's criticism of other vernacular approaches to theological education is his fundamental distinction between those teachers who ground their teachings in 'resoun or revelacioun maad to us by scripture, or in othire surely and certeinly or probabily had revelacioun from God,' and those whose teachings which may be well-intended, and may stimulate the emotions of readers, but are based on 'forgid, feinid and vein curiosite.'[49]

Pecock therefore establishes important criteria for differentiating between an authoritative vernacular work and an insubstantial, ephemeral vernacular work. Interestingly, the standards for discerning authority in a vernacular work are the same as those that readers must use in treating the work of the Latin *auctores*. In the *Reule of Crysten Religioun*, Pecock criticizes the common practice of slavish dependence on and cleaving to the works of the theological *auctores* 'without the resolving of tho writingis into the groundis and principlis of the faculte to which they perteinen.'[50] He indicates that the doctors' treatment of religious truths must only be adhered to if they are grounded in truths of reason and faith: 'And sothely sithen alle laboren for noon other entent and alle they pretenden hem silf in noon other auctorite but as ministris and enserchers of treuthe of resoun, and as pupplischers and schewers forth therof to othere, it folewith that as fer as they schewen of resoun in her expowning, so fer they oughte to be allowid, bileeved and received, and ferther not.'[51] For Pecock, any work (whether in Latin or the vernacular) that is grounded in the truths of reason and faith is authoritative; any work (whether by the doctors or contemporary writers) that cannot be shown to accord with these truths is illegitimate. Having indicated that the works of the *auctores* are to be approached with this in mind, he exclaims to God,

> the ruyde and simple leving to thy scripture and to doctouris seyingis, without resolving of it into ferther groundis out of whom her writingis and seyingis comen forth, hath holde men, and dooth holde so yit, into greet derkenes and blindnes where and whanne they wenen to se broode, and so to be ful bonde, boistose and thral, unmanly unnaturaly unclerkely unleernedly, where it were more convenient and more good to be in other wise governed. And this same seid simple leving to scripture and to doctouris schendith our verry scole leerning and clergie and kunning.[52]

Pecock indicates that the true source of authority in theological writings is the ground from which they arise: the book of reason. The writings of the *auctores* merely witness and rehearse the timeless truths that exist outside of all texts, in 'the largist book of autorite that ever

God made, which is the doom of resoun.'[53] Pecock defines the role of the doctors as searchers and labourers rather than creators of truths: 'no doctour of divinite which ever was, was auctor or maker of divinite or of eny trouth of divinite; but eche of hem was oonly a scoler and a lerner and a laborer in divinite forto finde and knowe of divinitees treuthis.'[54] Pecock suggests that readers must be careful in ascribing authority to that famous tradition of authoritative writing by the doctors of the church, and argues that the definition of an authoritative work is one which witnesses truths rationally perceived by the writer.

For Pecock, the basis for determining a work's authority is the same for both vernacular and Latin texts: an authoritative text is grounded in the truths of reason and faith. Throughout his corpus, he defines the role of a theological writer not as an *auctor* or 'maker' of divine truths – this is God's role – but as a searcher, labourer, and witness to God's truths.[55] Whether this witnessing is done in the vernacular or Latin does not seem to matter. By establishing that a truly authoritative *auctor* is a searcher and gatherer of truths, Pecock levels the playing field between himself and his theological predecessors. The ultimate authority is God, who has inscribed his truths for mankind to find in the inner book of reason and in the outer book of scripture. The job of the theological author is to find these truths and throw light on them for all others to see. This conception of authorship lies behind Pecock's presentation of himself, variously, as a forester hewing down and bringing to the townspeople branches from the 'forest of lawe of kinde which God plauntith in mannis soule whanne he makith him to his image and likenes';[56] a merchant who brings to the people of England 'chaffre' that he has found and 'fett fer from othire cuntrees biyonde the see' for their 'profite and eese';[57] a gardener who labours to cultivate God's truths in the field of the 'lawe of kinde';[58] a messenger preaching truth and conversion like the apostle Paul;[59] and a compiler-figure who writes down the truths that he sees before him in a dream vision as women standing in his study, first seeing them and then giving them form in his texts. In all of these depictions of Pecock's authorial identity, his text is not so much his own creation as it is a reliable collection of truths whose most important function is to provide lay readers with access to a source of truths that are primary, revealed by God himself. The definition of an *auctor* is he who accesses the pure source of God's truths of faith and reason; the authoritative text is written by a figure like Pecock, who is a compiler of sorts. He traces his authority to God himself rather than to revered forefathers. According to this definition, it does not matter whether this authoritative text is written in Latin or the vernacular; Pecock's understanding of the nature of authorship helps to establish an authoritative role for vernacular texts to play, blurring the distinction between honoured predecessors like Jerome and industrious moderns like Pecock. In a way, this authorial stance resembles that of Christine de Pizan, as suggested in Deborah McGrady's essay in this volume on the way that Christine bases her claims for authority on her reading abilities. Pecock's ability to read the book of reason, as well as the Bible, secures him a place as a theological authority while it distinguishes him from other writers of the vernacular who lack this reading ability.

Pecock's critical appraisal of contemporary and authoritative theological texts consistently reveals his belief that any language is suitable for a discussion of theological matters, as long as the discussion is grounded in reason and faith. The ways in which Pecock justifies and authorizes his vernacular works seem above all to be determined by his particular situation and rooted in the specificities of his task, intended audience, and circumstances: Pecock is determined to provide the laity with the kind of reading material that will utterly convince them of the truths of the orthodox faith. His notion of what is the best reading material for lay Christians – texts that offer insight into truths of reason and faith – informs his presentation of himself as an author and his conception of what gives a theological text authority. His particular approach to religious education therefore influences the way he positions himself as an authoritative author, while providing a precedent for a kind of vernacular theology based on a critical reading not of the inherited tomes of commentary but of the primary texts of the book of reason and the Bible. Pecock shows confidence in the ability of his vernacular works to stand beside Latin sources and Latin materials as worthy reading material, as well as their ability to constitute a worthy addition to a growing supply of vernacular reading material.

This notion of vernacular authority may also be influenced by Pecock's awareness of a burgeoning tradition of vernacular works available to readers and his sense of the need to set his works apart in some way, not so much from Latin works but from other spiritual fare in English. He claims that his praise for his own works is not boasting but a kind of advertising of his goods to the 'peple of Englonde' who are now fortunate enough to choose from a wide variety of spiritual goods.[60] In order to get them to buy his books rather than books full of errors and useless matters, Pecock must convince readers of the 'profite and eese' of his books – of the 'preciosite and the profitablenes' of his 'chaffre.'[61] Claims to a weighty authority for his texts may grow out of a desire to distinguish his works from a mass of other material available in the mother tongue. Such a desire seems to indicate that writers were not scared away by the *Constitutions* or by inherited views about the inferiority of the vernacular. Indeed, the case of Reginald Pecock suggests that we must revise our view of the production of religious writing in fifteenth-century England by considering what his works can tell us about a growing sense of possibility and flexibility in creating texts in the vernacular that would revitalize the Christian community.

NOTES

1 Watson, 'Censorship and Cultural Change,' 826. For Lollardy, see Somerset et al., *Lollards and Their Influence*; Hudson, *The Premature Reformation*; and Aston, *Lollards and Reformers*.
2 Doyle, 'Survey of the Origins,' 1. For the early debate over the questions raised by Watson, see Somerset, 'Professionalizing Translation,' 147. Somerset draws attention to the role played by Nicholas Watson's 1995 article 'Censorship and Cultural Change' in establishing a consensus of scholarly opinion on the impact of Arundel's *Constitutions* on the religio-literary landscape of late medieval England. In this article, Watson translated the various articles of the *Constitutions* and interpreted their significance as follows: 'The legislation as a whole constitutes one of the most draconian pieces of censorship in English history, going far beyond its ostensible aim of destroying the Lollard heresy and effectively attempting to curtail all sorts of theological thinking and writing in the vernacular that did not belong within the pragmatic bounds set by earlier legislation like Pecham's Syllabus of 1281' ('Censorship and Cultural Change,' 826).
3 Kelly and Perry, 'Hospitable Reading,' 1.
4 See Campbell, *The Call to Read*.
5 See Kerby-Fulton, *Books under Suspicion*.
6 Robertson, 'Introduction,' 78.
7 Georgianna, 'Vernacular Theologies,' 87. Kate Crassons also discusses the 'capaciousness' of vernacular theology. See Crassons, 'Performance Anxiety,' 95.

8 For the Latin text of the *Constitutions*, see Wilkins, *Concilia magnae Britanniae et Hiberniae*, 3:314–19. For Foxe's English translation, provided in these notes, see Foxe, *Acts and Monuments*, 3:242–9. Article 4: 'Forasmuch as the part is vile, that agreeth not with the whole, we do decree and ordain, that no preacher aforesaid, or any other person whatsoever, shall otherwise teach or preach concerning the sacrament of the altar, matrimony, confession of sins, or any other sacrament of the church, or article of the faith, than what already is discussed by the holy mother church; nor shall bring any thing in doubt that is determined by the church, nor shall, to his knowledge, privily or apertly pronounce blasphemous words concerning the same' (3:244–5).

9 Article 5: 'Forasmuch as a new vessel, being long used, savoureth after the head, we decree and ordain, that no schoolmasters and teachers whatsoever, that instruct children in grammar, or others whosoever, in primitive sciences, shall, in teaching them, intermingle any thing concerning the catholic faith, the sacrament of the altar, or other sacraments of the church, contrary to the determination of the church; nor shall suffer their scholars to expound the holy Scriptures (except the text, as hath been used in ancient time); nor shall permit them to dispute openly or privily concerning the catholic faith, or sacraments of the church' (3:245).

10 Article 7: 'It is a dangerous thing, as witnesseth blessed St. Jerome, to translate the text of the holy Scripture out of the tongue into another; for in the translation the same sense is not always easily kept, as the same St. Jerome confesseth, that although he were inspired, yet oftentimes in this he erred: we therefore decree and ordain, that no man, hereafter, by his own authority translate any text of the Scripture into English or any other tongue, by way of a book, libel, or treatise; and that no man read any such book, libel or treatise, now lately set forth in the time of John Wickliff, or since, or hereafter to be set forth, in part or in whole, privily or apertly, upon pain of greater excommunication, until the said translation be allowed by the ordinary of the place, or, if the case so require, by the council provincial' (3:245).

11 Article 8: 'For that Almighty God cannot be expressed by any philosophical terms, or otherwise invented of man . . . we do ordain and specially forbid, that any manner of person, of what state, degree, or condition soever he be, do allege or propone any conclusions or propositions in the catholic faith, or repugnant to good manners (except necessary doctrine pertaining to their faculty of teaching or disputing in their schools or otherwise), although they defend the same with ever such curious terms and words' (3:245–6).

12 See Pecock, *Reule*, 202. To make the language of the editions of Pecock's
    works from which I quote more accessible, I have generally brought the
    use of the letters i, y, u, and v into conformity with modern practice;
    substituted gh and y, as appropriate, for the yogh; substituted th for the
    thorn; modified capitalization in accordance with modern practice; and
    eliminated the italics Pecock's editors have used to mark abbreviations in
    the manuscripts.

13 Pecock, *Repressor*, 37: 'This what I have now seid of and to Bible men I
    have not seid undir this entent and meening, as that I schulde feele to
    be unleeful laymen forto reede in the Bible and forto studie and leerne
    ther in, with help and counseil of wise and weel leerned clerkis and with
    licence of her governour the bischop; but forto rebuke and adaunte the
    presumpcioun of tho lay persoones.' Also note Pecock's omission of 'wijs
    and discrete and weel avisid undirminingis' by the laity of their clerical
    superiors in relation to the third article of the *Constitutions*, which forbids
    preachers from discussing the vices of the clergy among the laity. See
    Pecock, *Repressor*, 4: 'though alle othere governauncis of the clergie, for
    whiche the clergy is worthy to be blamed in brotherly and neighbourly
    correpcioun, I schal not be aboute to excuse neither defende; but preie,
    speke, and write in al pacience and doctrine, that the clergie forsake hem,
    leve, and amende.' Though Pecock does acknowledge that there is a place
    for 'wijs and discrete and weel avisid undirnimingis, whiche they in
    other times maken or mowe make to the clergie,' he does not provide any
    examples of well-founded lay criticism of the clergy (3).

14 Simpson, *Reform and Cultural Revolution*, 340.

15 Ibid., 343.

16 Pecock, *Reule*, 72.

17 Ibid., 91.

18 Ibid., 76.

19 Ibid., 91.

20 This section begins on page 308.

21 Pecock, *Reule*, 319.

22 Ibid., 91.

23 See Pecock, *Reule*, 313.

24 Kerby-Fulton, *Books under Suspicion*, 397.

25 Wogan-Browne et al., *The Idea of the Vernacular*, 3.

26 Machan, *Textual Criticism*, 97.

27 Ibid., 98 and 118. The editors of Wogan-Browne et al,, *The Idea of the
    Vernacular*, write that what conferred authority on texts and authors was
    'age, authenticity, and conformity with truth' (6). An authoritative writer

or poet was a kind of 'iconic figure, removed from the world of everyday contingencies as he admonishes his readers to conform to the timeless truths his verses are implied to contain' (6). Intellectually removed from the mundane world, and dedicated to the pursuit of truth, an *auctor* created works whose value and relevance would endure, benefiting future civilizations. Machan writes that the *auctores* were 'those Latin writers whose compositions were made venerable by their antiquity and enduring by their language' – their writings were privileged because their works were thought to convey universal, timeless truths (*Textual Criticism*, 96). Machan continues: 'What enabled indisputable identification of auctores were the literary qualities and the culturally and institutionally sanctioned ethical truths (*auctoritates*) of their works' (97).

28 Wogan-Browne et al., *The Idea of the Vernacular*, 3.

29 Ibid., 3.

30 Ibid., 4.

31 The refusal to accept and accommodate official positions on literary authority, and the strategic manipulation of these official positions and notions has, of course, been treated in the discussions of figures like Chaucer and Gower by scholars such as Alastair Minnis.

32 Pecock, *Reule*, 13 and 9.

33 Pecock, *Repressor*, 58. Pecock is worried about the potential confusion that can result from lay reading of the Bible; reading the Bible requires much learning and scholarly preparation. He views his own works as prerequisite to the intellectual labour of reading the Bible, and intends his works to provide clarification of difficult biblical passages. Pecock's hesitance in allowing lay readers to approach the Bible directly reflects ecclesiastical concerns about lay Bible reading; his goal is not, however, to forbid the production or possession of biblical translations but to better prepare readers for the intellectual difficulties that this activity presents.

34 This translation of Bonaventure's well-known definition of the *auctor* is cited from Wogan-Browne et al., *The Idea of the Vernacular*, 3.

35 Pecock, *Reule*, 22.

36 Pecock, *Donet*, 7–8.

37 Ibid., 7.

38 Pecock, *Reule*, 17–18.

39 Ibid., 18.

40 Ibid., 32.

41 Ibid., 32.

42 Ibid., 33.

43 Ibid., 35.

44 Perhaps we could speculate that Pecock is thinking here about works like *Jacob's Well*, which bases its treatment of the catechetical basics like the Seven Deadly Sins on the extended allegory of a pit oozing with filth that represents man's sinful body. While the figure of the pit may move readers emotionally, motivating them to detest sin and desire the cleansing waters of virtue, such a basis for a treatment of religious truths is figurative and fictional, rather than rooted in rational truths.

45 See Mishtooni Bose's articles for her interpretation of Pecock's dream vision, 'Reginald Pecock's Vernacular Voice' and 'The Annunciation to Pecock.'

46 Pecock, *Donet*, 115.

47 Ibid., 106–7.

48 Ibid., 107.

49 Ibid., 115.

50 Pecock, *Folewer*, 68.

51 Pecock, *Reule*, 464.

52 Ibid., 465.

53 Pecock, *Folewer*, 9–10.

54 Ibid., 65.

55 Pecock, *Reule*, 465.

56 Pecock, *Repressor*, 29.

57 Pecock, *Donet*, 83.

58 Pecock, *Repressor*, 29: 'maters and conclusiouns and trouthis of lawe of kinde . . . leggith ful fair abrood sprad growing in his owne space, the feeld of mannys soule, and there oon treuthe cometh out of an other treuthe, and he of the iij^e., and the iij^e. out of the iiij^e., and into time it bicome unto openest treuthis of alle othere in thilk faculte of moral philsophie, and to the principlis and groundis of alle othere trouthis in the same faculte, (even as the spray cometh out of the braunche, the braunche out of the bough, the bough out of the schaft, and the schaft out of the roote).'

59 Pecock, *Donet*, 83.

60 Ibid., 83.

61 Ibid., 83.

8 Master Henryson and Father Aesop

IAIN MACLEOD HIGGINS

If Dante's encounter with Virgil is the most famous example of a medieval Christian poet paying corrective homage to a classical master, Robert Henryson's meeting with Aesop is likely the least well known.[1] Why these two imagined encounters with literary authority have had such different fates is not hard to explain. The most important reason is the diminished reputation of the Aesopic fable, with Aesop himself having been reduced in recent centuries to little more than a name holding together a disparate body of (mere) children's stories. To be sure, Aesopic fables were already regarded as children's stories as early as Quintilian (35–c. 96 CE), who recommended that boys about to learn oratory 'should learn to paraphrase Aesop's fables, which follow right after the nursemaids' fables.'[2] From the postclassical period to about the early eighteenth century, though, fables were also regarded as capable of being adapted to serious moral, social, and political ends, such that Martin Luther could rank them with the prophets and the psalter. Henryson, as we shall see, does not go quite so far as Luther, but he nevertheless uses his gravely decorous encounter with Aesop to weigh the merits of fabulation against preaching, leaving his readers with an ambivalent answer as to which they should prefer.

Another important reason why this imagined meeting is less well known is that it takes place in Middle Scots, a language whose distinctive orthography and vocabulary can discomfit the eye used to southern ('Chaucerian') English forms. Compounding the linguistic challenge is the fact that Henryson's *Morall Fabillis* has never benefited from a popularizing edition or translation. Indeed, the first readily accessible translation did not appear until 1987 and is now long out of print, while

Douglas Gray's 1998 Penguin Classics edition of the *Selected Poems of Robert Henryson and William Dunbar* went out of print almost as soon as it was issued.[3] This clearly is quite a different situation from Dante's, not to mention that of the linguistically demanding *Gawain*-poet, who has enjoyed many popularizing editions and translations since the early decades of the twentieth century, including ones by J.R.R. Tolkien.

A third reason for the meeting's neglect – a reason whose effect is magnified by the surface difficulty of the Middle Scots – has to do with the placement of the encounter in the *Fabillis* as compared to the *Commedia*. Dante, as is well known, meets Virgil at the very start of the *Commedia*, some sixty lines into the first canto of the *Inferno*, and his classical master then accompanies him for nearly two thirds of the entire work; in contrast, Henryson embeds his brief encounter with Aesop right in the middle of his collection of *Morall Fabillis*, some 1300 lines after the opening. To get to that meeting, which lasts some seventy lines (not including the 200 or so lines of Aesop's own fable and its moral), the reader has to pass through a prologue and six separate fables with their accompanying, often lengthy *moralitates*. This latter feature, too, has been a decided impediment to the work's post-medieval reception, and has no doubt prevented the collection from being taken up even as a children's book.

How, in the centuries since the *Commedia* and the *Morall Fabillis* were first composed, could Henryson's Middle Scots collection of heavily allegorized animal stories ever have held its own against Dante's visionary journey through the cosmos toward God, a journey recounted in one of Latin's very own medieval vernacular offshoots and during which the laurels of Western literary culture effectively changed linguistic brows, passing from Virgil's Latin to Dante's Italian? The question is rhetorical, of course, which is not to say that it is not worth pondering, since to take it seriously would require considering larger questions of literary reception, canon formation, and cultural as well as linguistic politics.[4] The question is rhetorical because my focus here is not the reasons for Dante's and Henryson's very different textual afterlives or even with those afterlives themselves. Rather, my concern is with the uses of a single literary forefather (Aesop) in a too-little-known, minor masterpiece of the later Middle Ages, Henryson's *Morall Fabillis*. For just as Henryson's work represents the high point of medieval Aesopic fabling – possibly even the high point of the Western Aesopic tradition generally, on a par with Jean de la Fontaine's achievement – so his imagined meeting with

Aesop is as complex and fascinating an instance of late medieval attitudes toward literary authorship and authority as any that has come down to us, Dante's not excepted.

One sign of this scene's complexity and significance is the paradoxical fact that scholars have almost entirely ignored it in their editions of *The Morall Fabillis*. This is the last thing one would expect given both the meeting's uniqueness in the Aesopic corpus since antiquity and its centrality to the structure and meaning of Henryson's own work. Indeed, in another paradox, it has been the meeting's very structural centrality that has kept its thematic centrality hidden, proving the truth of a point that Denton Fox made nearly half a century ago: 'Henryson has been underrated, I think, because his readers have not always extended the parallel with Chaucer far enough to notice that he shares Chaucer's art of concealing his art.'[5] Like Chaucer, he sometimes conceals his art, as he does in this case, by drawing explicit attention to it. The difference – and this remains true despite the rise in the Scottish poet's reputation since Fox wrote – is that Henryson's concealments have largely been left unexplored in editorial commentary, as if such moments need little or no discussion precisely because their author drew attention to them. With the partial exception of Fox and George Gopen, editors since Henryson's first scholarly editor, David Laing, have added little to Laing's brief comment in 1865 that 'the *description* of Aesop . . . is very much opposed to the ordinary representation of this perhaps imaginary personage.'[6]

More surprising than the relative editorial neglect of Henryson's encounter with Aesop has been the paucity of critical response to it. Only four critics, writing at roughly ten-year intervals since the early 1970s, have given Henryson's meeting with Aesop sustained consideration.[7] Clearly, the time is ripe for a synthesis and development of their work in the form of a detailed reading of that central encounter and its concealed art. The reading that follows considers this crucial episode in the context of the *Morall Fabillis* as a whole, and accordingly is organized not analytically, but sequentially, in keeping with the experience of moving through the collection from the title-page on. Such an approach means that the discussion's central points will typically appear stepwise across the entire discussion, rather than concentrated in one place at a time, but this sequential-experiential manner of proceeding seems to me necessary if we are to appreciate Henryson's achievement here as a writer who is as capable as Dante or Chaucer of seeing the rich thematic implications of form and structure –

in this case, for matters of moral as well as literary authority in the vernacular. In the words of Tim William Machan, one of the few recent critics to give Henryson's authorial insights more than passing attention, the meeting with Aesop is distinguished even from Dante's with Virgil by its 'thematic complexity.'[8] One does have to acknowledge, certainly, that Henryson works with smaller structures and lesser genres than Dante or Chaucer, and that he uses his literary insights in the service of another literary agenda altogether, but even granting that Henryson falls short of Dante as a visionary poet and appears more ideologically conservative than the morally elusive Chaucer, it is clear that he can be as literarily bold as either of them in pursuit of his own particular aims.

Aesop the Phrygian and Aesop the Roman

The surviving witnesses to the original text of Henryson's mid- to late fifteenth-century (?)[9] collection of edifying beast fables are few, but it is worth noting that all four of the prints used by modern editors to establish the text call the work *The Morall Fabillis of Esope the Phrygian*.[10] Henryson himself is relegated by the title-page of these prints and that of the Harley manuscript to the role of 'compiler' (though at least an 'eloquent and ornate' one), and three of the prints as well as the Harley manuscript refer to him as 'Maister.'[11] Setting aside these references for now, I would note that the distinctive phrase 'Aesop the Phrygian' is almost certainly meant to recall the legendary figure memorialized as a canny trickster in the anonymous Greek *Life of Aesop*, often known nowadays as *The Aesop Romance* (probably second century CE).[12] This comic biography made its way into circulation in Western Christendom in 1448, when it was translated into Latin by the Italian humanist, Rinuccio da Castiglione of Arezzo.[13] Rinuccio's version was given its first vernacular circulation by Heinrich Steinhöwel, whose bilingual Latin-German Aesop was published in 1476–7. The Latin text was subsequently hived off from this edition and reprinted only twice, but the German text became in the 1480s the direct and indirect source of translations into Czech, Dutch, English, French, and Spanish (Catalan and Danish renderings were made in the middle of the next century).[14]

According to this entertaining, picaresque life, Aesop was a grotesquely ugly slave who for his piety and goodwill toward a priestess of Isis received the gift of speech, a gift that he put to good use, above all in his instructive fables. Here is William Caxton's English rendering

Figure 8.1. Steinhöwel's Aesop. Aesopus, *Fabulae*, trans. Heinrich Steinhöwel ([Augsburg], [Günther Zainer], [ca. 1477/8]), frontispiece. Bayerische Staatsbibliothek München, 2º Inc.s.a. 9, frontispiece. By permission.

(first printed in 1483–4) of the 'dyfformed and euylle shapen' Aesop's initial appearance in his life story: 'he had a grete hede / large vysage / longe Iowes [jaws] / sharp eyen / a shorte necke / corbe backed [hunchbacked] / grete bely / grete legges / and large feet.'[15] That the titles of the Henryson prints allude to this legendary ugly Aesop is confirmed by the 1571 Bassandyne edition, whose title-page includes a large woodcut depicting the ancient fabulist according to the recent Rinuccian tradition. For comparison, two earlier Aesops are also reproduced here, and a brief look at the set of images reveals the ancient fabulist getting handsomer (or at least less ugly) the farther north he travels; the Scottish edition has perhaps been deliberately revised so as to soften the contrast between the publisher's pictorial image and the author's verbal portrait (figures 8.1, 8.2, 8.3).

Figure 8.2. Caxton's Aesop. . . . [T]he book of . . . fables of Esope . . . translated . . . by wylham Caxton ([Westminster: William Caxton, 1484]), fol. 1v. By permission of the British Library.

The misshapen figure depicted here is decidedly *not* the one we meet in Henryson's work. His presence on the same title-page that calls him 'Esope the Phrygian,' though, clearly indicates the publisher's desire to associate the Scottish book with the ugly Aesop resurrected over a century earlier by Rinuccio – and no wonder, given the figure's pan-European success.

In contrast to his later publisher(s), whose first concern was successful marketing, Henryson made his Aesop not Phrygian, but Roman, and he also made him handsome rather than ugly. Whether he did so in response to the grotesque image put into circulation by Rinuccio and Steinhöwel is impossible to say, given the uncertain dating of the *Fabillis*, but it is within the realm of possibility. Henryson, after all, is thought to have died by 1505, which means that he could have known

Figure 8.3. Bassandyne's Aesop. *The morall fabillis of Esope the Phrygia[n]* (Edinburgh: Thomas Bassandyne, 1571), from the title-page (A1r). By permission of The Trustees of the National Library of Scotland.

(of) the new Aesop while working on his collection, and indeed there is some scholarly dispute over the matter, particularly regarding his possible indebtedness to Caxton.[16] To my mind, the image of the handsome Roman Aesop that Henryson creates gains extra resonance if it can be read as a counterimage, although nothing in my argument for its significance depends on its being so. The central scene does its thematic work, regardless of what Henryson knew.

That he may well have invented his image independently is supported by the one other medieval depiction of a handsome Aesop known to me – the portrait found in an anonymous Latin/German school miscellany of about 1440–60 (Munich, Bayerische Staatsbibliothek MS Clm 3974, fol. 213r). Placed at the close of Ulrich Boner's *Der Edelstein*, the oldest extant fable collection in German, partly framed by Latin commentary, and entitled 'Magister Esopus et poeta,' this portrait depicts Aesop as an ancient philosopher – elderly, bearded, robed, turbaned or hooded, and holding a copious scroll in his left hand. Commenting on this image of 'the lone, robed authority figure of the ancient sage,' Michael Curschmann has perceptively suggested that its 'Aesop is entirely a creature of the imagination, designed to embody the *function* of the text.' When this manuscript was made, Aesop had 'no biographical identity, and so, reflecting the role of the fable in the medieval school and the desire to integrate this new vernacular rendering into that tradition, the artist drew an ancient philosopher whose teaching unfolds before him.'[17] Something similar can be argued for Henryson's depiction of Aesop, as I will do in due course, for whether or not it represents a counterimage, the portrait emerges as a function of the text, doing local thematic work, although also with a temporal dimension that comes of its distinctive narrative embodiment.

Still, whether or not Henryson knew of any other depictions of Aesop prior to making his own, his attempt to create an idealized (counter-?) image for the ancient fabulist turned out to be a complete failure; the ugly Phrygian won the day, enjoying a long afterlife.[18] One obvious reason for the ugly Aesop's triumph, in addition to the image's being supported by an entertainingly picaresque *Life*, is that it effectively embodies the paradox of the Aesopic fable: a paltry thing, almost subliterary, that nevertheless contains something as grand as wisdom (compare in this respect the discrepancy between the physical and the intellectual or moral Socrates). Since Henryson's goal, I believe, was to elevate the Aesopic fable both literarily and morally, he needed also to elevate its 'original' author. It might be interesting to speculate whether the reputation of the Aesopic fable would not have fallen off as it did, had a very different portrait of its originator dominated the popular as well as the learned imagination.

Whatever the nature of Henryson's knowledge of the ugly Phrygian Aesop of the Rinuccian tradition, only two fabulists before him had ever made the ancient figure a Roman: Marie de France and John Lydgate. Marie's twelfth-century Aesop, moreover, is Roman merely by implication, since, according to her, he translated the fables from Greek into Latin.[19] Lydgate's early fifteenth-century figure, however, is explicitly Roman, being presented in the headnote to the first two tales as 'Isopus, the phylosopher of Rome' and in the first tale itself as 'the poete laureate' who 'Whylom in Rome to plese the senate, / Fonde out fables.'[20] It may be that Lydgate (a more likely source than

Marie)[21] was Henryson's inspiration for the Roman Aesop, but if so, it was as grit is inspiration for a pearl; indeed, the difference between the two authorial portraits is as great as the difference between Lydgate's passing mention and Henryson's memorable set piece. What makes Henryson's portrait of Aesop so memorable is not just what Derek Pearsall calls the Scottish poet's 'realising imagination' as a storyteller, a gift seen clearly against Lydgate's lead-footed lurches in his fables from narrative to moral platitudes;[22] it is also, and more significantly, Henryson's delayed dramatic deployment of the portrait to serve his own complex ends as a moral fabulist – and this is why his narrative depiction is inevitably richer than that of the static portrait appended to Boner's *Edelstein*. Both the delay and the dramatization are crucial to the Scottish poet's use of Aesop, as we shall see. In respect of the dramatization, moreover, he resembles Dante – who likewise brings Virgil onstage as a guide, and does so at a moment of crisis for the narrator – far more than he does his two Insular predecessors. The force and originality of Henryson's delayed dramatic encounter with Aesop can be seen most easily if we start by looking at the Aesop whom readers meet at the outset of the *Moral Fables*, first in the Prologue, then in the tales prior to the ancient fabulist's onstage appearance.

Aesop the Nominal Authority, Henryson the Canny Intermediary

This initial Aesop is not so much a person as a name and a brief Latin citation – a received authority, in other words – and thus very much akin to the authorizing figure temporarily trotted out by Marie and Lydgate. The crucial difference is that in Henryson's rich sixty-three-line Prologue Aesop is also used to defend the very genre associated with his authoritative name. The details of Henryson's apology for Aesopic fabulation, though, fascinating and even potentially contradictory as they are, cannot detain us here. Suffice it to say that after some twenty-seven lines in defence of 'feinȝeit [made-up] fabils of ald poetre' (1) – largely according to the traditional doctrine that an invented story can be *utile* as well as *dulce*[23] – Henryson rests his case by quoting his ancient predecessor. The Aesop he draws on, though, is of more recent vintage than antiquity, borrowed from the widely circulated twelfth-century Latin version of Walter of England: 'thus Esope said, I wis [know], / *Dulcius arrident seria picta iocis* [serious things adorned with humour please more sweetly]' (27–8).[24] The Scottish poet's authorizing strategy here is familiar enough – indeed, it is no different from that of any modern literary critic who a short way into the requisite methodological preface turns for support to the appropriate reigning theorist by quoting a well-known talismanic phrase (e.g., as Barthes reminds us, 'the birth of the reader must be at the cost of the death of the Author').

Thus introduced halfway through the Prologue as a well-known defender of serious pleasantries, Aesop in the remaining thirty-odd lines of Henryson's Prologue emerges through three further references as a conventionally medievalized classical model. He is called 'this poete,' 'my author,' 'this nobill clerk' (29, 43, and 57), and described as a figure whose rhetorical skills the contemporary Scottish fabulist cannot hope to equal, even as he borrows his stories and his moral authority. At first glance, these three references may suggest that Henryson is simply setting himself up as a medieval mouthpiece for a received classical authority, much as Lydgate typically does.[25] A closer look, though, reveals that already here he has subtly begun the Chaucerian work of making that authority his own, of modernizing him. 'This poete,' he calls him in the line immediately following the Latin quotation, invoking Aesop as a *literary* precursor and specifying his relationship to him:

Of this poete,[26] my maisteris, with ȝour leif [leave/permission],
Submitting me to ȝour correctioun,
In mother toung, of Latyng [from Latin], I wald preif [attempt]
To mak ane maner of translatioun.   (29–32)

In proposing to make *a sort* of translation, Henryson may seem merely to be fulfilling the rhetorical demands of the opening modesty topos, but his metre and syntax reveal this to be a complex, almost Chaucerian humility, asserting through apparent deference, revealing by apparent concealment. Giving his mother tongue pride of metrical place by mentioning it first in a line with two caesuras, and showing it capable of Latin-like periodic syntax, Henryson allows an alert reader to anticipate the possibility that his 'maner' of translation might be wilfully free rather than woefully inadequate.

And wilfully free is precisely what Henryson's Aesopic fables are. Indeed, six of the thirteen are not even Aesopic at all, but Reynardian, arranged so as to make the classical tales frame the medieval ones as if they had always been part of the corpus: two Aesopic, three

Reynardian, two Aesopic, three Reynardian, two Aesopic.[27] This wilful freedom is claimed in the very first fable, 'The Cock and the Jasp,' in which Walter's eight-line sketch is brilliantly expanded to a fifty-six-line story and the closing moral distich swells to forty-two homiletic lines that end by urging readers to seek 'science' (154, 158), or wisdom – presumably by reading further in Henryson's own collection. Aesopic fables, it is true, were transmitted in part precisely to be rewritten, since shrinking or expanding them was standard classroom practice since antiquity, but acknowledging this should not blind us to Henryson's genuine originality as a 'translating' fabulist. His is not a one-off display of virtuosity, like Chaucer's *Nun's Priest's Tale* – whose very different context is a fractious storytelling contest open to all genres – but the most sustained engagement with the Aesopic tradition and its corpus in its entire history. Indeed, if Chaucer's tale can be read as a parody of the moralized beast fable that almost explodes the form altogether, Henryson's collection, including his own answering tale of 'The Cock and the Fox,' may well be understood as a brilliant salvage operation designed to recover the post-Chaucerian tatters and reassemble them into a coherent and authoritative body. Despite his deference in the Prologue to the unnamed 'maisteris,' then – a deferential gesture that places the 'Scolmaister of Dunferling' in the role of pupil pleasing his schoolteachers – Henryson is up to more here than just the repetition of a common classroom exercise. What he is instead doing is analogous to the practice of medieval Latin exegesis as described by Rita Copeland; such exegesis 'works,' she says 'to displace the original text' both materially and conceptually to the extent that it ultimately becomes the *auctoritas* it sought to comment on, or, in this case, to translate into a 'mother toung.'[28]

While Henryson largely does displace his fabular sources both materially and conceptually, he does something more subtle with Aesop himself, not so much displacing as relocating him, and in the process seating himself (Henryson) at the right hand of his literary father. Indeed, when he eventually brings Aesop onstage, he uses the ancient author's appearance to transform himself, the modern poet, into a new *auctoritas*. Before he does so, though, he uses the Prologue to redefine Aesop to suit his local needs. He calls him not just 'this poete,' but 'my author,' the possessive pronoun reconfirming the apparent submission already implied by Henryson's claim to be *sort of* translating – or perhaps, if read retrospectively from after his meeting with Aesop, quietly announcing Henryson's appropriation of the ancient authority: '*my* author.' As an author, Aesop's authority stems, Henryson suggests, from his exemplary animal tales with their insight into the beastly nature of human beings who are governed above all by their appetites. The language Henryson uses here makes Aesop a kind of scholastic figure; his fictional beasts dispute, argue, propound syllogisms, and conclude (44–6), but not to parodic effect like Chaucer's Chauntecleer and Pertelote, but rather so as to reveal through 'similitude / How many men in operatioun [action] / Ar like to beistis in conditioun' (47–9). By this point, then, the classical authority has become a full-fledged medieval figure, a transformation Henryson himself announces when he calls his predecessor 'this nobill clerk, Esope' (57). This concluding honorific title, moreover, implicitly raises the Scottish poet's own stature as a scholar-poet bidding to become a contemporary authority, hoping to emulate the Aesop who has reached a universal audience (high *and* low) through the power of his 'gay metir,' his 'facound purpurate [empurpled eloquence],' and his mode of *writing* 'be figure' (58–60).

'First of ane cok he *wrate*' (61; emphasis added), says Henryson, implicitly presenting himself (falsely) as no more than an intermediary of the inaugural fable. Note too that he stresses again Aesop's literacy, as if to raise the stature of the fable by removing it from the domain of orality (this is no old wives' tale, he implies, no medieval version of pub chatter: 'so there's this chicken comes into a midden, eh, and . . . '). The inaugural tale told, Henryson invokes the literate Aesop to supply the required moral: 'Bot of the inward sentence and intent / Of this fabill, as myne author dois write, / I sall reheirs in rude and hamelie dite [homespun style]' (117–19).[29] In the two Aesopic tales that follow – the first ('The Two Mice') immediately, the second ('The Sheep and the Dog') after three intervening Reynardian fables – further passing references to the ostensible ancient source serve to confirm Aesop's original authority and Henryson's intermediary role. 'The Two Mice,' for instance, begins deferentially by citing 'Esope, myne authour' (162), while 'The Sheep and the Dog,' opens by asserting that it is 'ane taill' that 'Esope . . . puttis in memorie' (1146).

These two passing references to Aesop do not, however, prevent Henryson's narrator from occasionally stepping forward as the immediate local authority. Absent entirely in the first tale, Henryson's narrator emerges briefly in the first *moralitas* with a priestly flourish that is anything but 'rude and hamelie.' It ends thus: 'Quha [who] can gouerne ane realme, cietie, or hous, / Without science? No man, I ȝow assure' (136–7). Just three stanzas later, the 'I' and 'ȝow' have been neatly bundled into a 'we' who fail to seek knowledge and wisdom, leading the narrator to break off in apparent frustration, almost provocatively: 'Of this mater to speik, I wair bot wind [I would be wasting my breath], / Thairfore I ceis and will na forther say. / Ga seik the iasp, quha will, for thair it lay' (159–61). Since the next lines, which also begin the next tale, assert that 'Esope, myne authour, makis mentioun / Of twa myis [mice]' (162–3), readers are shown precisely where to seek the precious jewel of wisdom and who will lead them there. Having briefly asserted his presence and maybe even his solidarity with his readers, Henryson here steps aside for Aesop. When this fable ends, though, it is Henryson who returns, first to tell his readers what he has 'hard say' (358) about the fate of the country mouse, and then to address them as 'freindis' with a kind of homily on the tale's 'gude moralitie' (365–6).

Quietly confirming this displacement – or rather relocation – of Aesop as the collection's presiding authority is the fact that the first two Aesopic tales are now followed by three Reynardian stories for which Aesop rightly is given no credit and during which he gets no mention even as Henryson occasionally makes his own presence felt. The shift to Reynardian tales is thus a large-scale structural change assimilating the ancient corpus of fables to the medieval tales, as well as vice versa; what Henryson calls Aesop's 'buke' (59) has now been transformed into a thoroughly medieval – that is, contemporary – work. That Henryson was well aware of his subtle intermediary role here is suggested by the excellent insight of Edward Bradburn, who considers the first two stanzas (lines 397–410) of the first Reynardian tale, 'The Cock and the Fox,' as a 'mini-"prologue" to the rest of the fable'; 'at the point when he is beginning . . . [his] "Reynardian" (and thus "non-Aesopic") fables,' Bradburn asserts, 'Henryson chooses to refer clearly to Aesop.'[30] To my ear, the reference is implicit rather than clear, since it depends on verbal echoes of the opening Prologue (Aesop is unnamed), but Bradburn is right to single out these two stanzas, since they are in effect the visible seam where Henryson first splices the medieval Reynardian fable into the Aesopic, creating a new hybrid composition by appropriation, wherein the classical and the medieval each redefine each other. It is probably no accident either that this seam appears right where Henryson is about to answer Chaucer directly. In any case, the crucial point is that the direction of appropriation is necessarily two-way, even somewhat ambiguous, like Henryson's own relation to Aesop, his nominal authority.

A Dramatic Break with Tradition

These interpolated Reynardian tales turn the collection's thematic focus toward problems of achieving earthly justice and are followed by an appropriate Aesopic fable, 'The Sheep and the Dog.' As Henryson tells it, this is a dark tale about the dire consequences of injustice and the corruption of courts both ecclesiastical and civil, and the narrator makes himself present even more than usual in this tale. He moralizes in the narrative proper, condemning the unjust judgment at least twice (see 1220–9 and 1248–50), and appealing for agreement to the audience in general ('trow ȝe'; 1220) as well as to 'clerkis' in particular (1229). In addition, and more significantly, Henryson has his narrator turn more than half the *moralitas* over to the wronged sheep.[31] Glossed at the start of the *moralitas* as 'the figure / Of pure [poor] commounis . . . daylie . . . opprest / Be tirrane [tyrannical] men' (1258–60), the sheep does not remain a mere signifier, but suddenly turns once again into a narrative character, making a David-like lament about injustice: 'O lord, quhy [why] sleipis thow sa lang?' (1295; cf. Ps. 44(43): 23). Not only does this lament occur in the wrong place, as it were, interrupting the rational clarity of the *moralitas*, but the narrator also takes care to say that he has personally seen and heard it: 'Bot of this scheip and of his cairfull cry / I sall reheirs, for as I passit by / Quhair that he lay, on cais I lukit doun [I happened to look down], / And hard him mak sair lamentatioun' (1282–5).

Henryson was far more circumspect in the previous Aesopic fable, 'The Two Mice,' where he claims only to have 'hard say' about both the country mouse's dwelling and her fate after the story ends (197 and 357–8). Such circumspection occurs also in the second of the three following Reynardian tales, 'The Fox and the Wolf,' but there the narrator is more actively involved in being prudent, and in a way that begins to draw attention to him. For in 'The Fox and the Wolf,' he explicitly declines to report on the fox's confession to the friar wolf so as not to violate a Christian sacrament: 'Quhen I this saw, I drew ane lytill by [I stepped back a little], / For it effeiris [is proper] nouther to heir nor spy / Nor to reueill [reveal] thing said vnder that seill [seal]' (694–6).

The narrator's increasingly prominent role as 'ear-witness' in these three tales ('Two Mice,' 'Fox and Wolf,' 'Sheep and Dog') is striking, given his insistence on the written nature of the Aesopic inheritance. One might argue, of course, that it is merely characteristic of the several boundaries that are blurred throughout the *Morall Fabillis*: most obviously, the line between animal and human, which shifts to suit local needs. The most memorable of such boundary-scumbling moments is surely the hen Pertok's comic comment in 'The Cock and the Fox' about replacing the abducted Chantecleir with 'ane berne [that] suld better claw oure breik' (529; a man who ought to claw our breeches better). In my view, though, the narrator's references to actual (over)hearing also resemble other such medieval moments where attention is productively directed to the fact that the typical transmission of stories is at once written and oral, so that the reader or hearer cannot overlook their compound mediation: recall, for instance, Chaucer's insistence in the Miller's Prologue that 'whoso list . . . [the coming cherl's tale] nat yheere, / Turne over the leefe and chese another tale' (CT.I.3176–7), a gesture that calls the audience to attention. Above all, this role as 'ear-witness' to a written inheritance makes implicitly clear that Henryson – not Aesop – is each tale's nearest intermediary; it is the contemporary poet who is giving the old written stories their new living voice by deciding what to tell and what to withhold. The storyteller conceals as well as reveals, such moments collectively suggest, and there is 'ernest' in the 'game,' so be alert. Reading the Fabillis from a somewhat different angle, Machan insightfully points to the narrator's increasing prominence and independence as a rhetorical presence by the time we reach this sixth tale, 'The Sheep and the Dog,' and he sees this emergence as paralleling a thematic shift from individual folly to 'the issue of God's presence in this world.'[32] It is worth noting here that this increasing rhetorical prominence in the form of ear-witnessing has occurred in every other tale after the opening 'Cock and Jasp.' By this structural logic, the narrator should emerge even more fully two tales after 'The Sheep and the Dog,' which, as we shall see, is exactly what happens.

Yet no sooner has Henryson established this pattern than he partly breaks it, splicing the third and the fourth accounts of ear-witnessing together with a strikingly unexpected and dramatic vision, namely, the scene in which the narrator meets his writing master and gets him to tell in 'his own voice' a tale ('The Lion and the Mouse') of earthly justice served. That this encounter with Aesop comes as a break with the manner of proceeding so far is signalled by the explicitly marked Prologue in which it occurs. Yet even as the Prologue to 'The Lion and the Mouse' marks a formal break, it also dovetails neatly with the preceding moralitas, in which a mere five stanzas earlier Henryson appeared alongside his plaintive sheep on the unexpectedly reappearing narrative stage. The almost total breakdown of the boundary between tale and *moralitas* – a breakdown that occurs immediately following the breakdown of earthly justice explored in the tale – signals that Henryson has seemingly come to a moment of crisis in his work as a fabulist. His tales so far have shown only an increasingly desperate human/animal world in which few mend their sinful ways and which God apparently allows to persist unchanged. 'This warld ouerturnit is,' says the sheep (1307), speaking allegorically as the long-suffering good Christian. The interruption of the usual sequence of tales by an explicit Prologue confirms the crisis. Instead of merely moving forward with the now well-established discontinuous continuity of the fable collection, Henryson has here arranged things so as to draw conscious attention to both the gaps and the links; the seams thus created are even more visible than the one at the start of 'The Cock and the Fox,' a symptom of the need to reconsider where an Aesopic anatomy of 'misleuing' (6), or ill-living, has led the poet. This slightly protracted moment of hesitation, crisis, and recommencement may not be quite the continuous, radical beginning-again that William Langland undertakes throughout *Piers Plowman*, a work whose surface is covered with seams, but it is nevertheless analogous. Here, as in *Piers Plowman*, we see a medieval Christian writer reach an impasse in his literary confrontation with contemporary problems and then attempt to get round it by shifting the very ground on which he stands, preferring to find a way to keep going whatever the formal cost.

Leaping far from the wintry cave in which the fleeced sheep of the previous tale laments the injustice he has suffered while God apparently sleeps, Henryson begins the Prologue to 'The Lion and the Mouse' on a mid-morning in June, readjusting the conventional Maytime opening of earlier French and English poems to suit the northern location. 'Put[ting] all sleuth [sloth] and sleip asyde,' the narrator rises to wander Dante-like alone in the woods: 'to ane wod I went alone *but gyde* [without guide]' (1326–7, emphasis added). Guideless though he is, the narrator finds himself at ease in the *locus amoenus* to which his walk quite expectedly takes him: 'my mirth wes mair [greater] for thy [therefore]' (1334). Soon, though, the sun's heat prompts him to take shelter by lying down among the flowers in the shade of a 'hawthorne grene' (1343),[33] and that brief narrative hiatus serves its conventional function as a transition to a dream.

The dream that follows, though, is not the expected allegorical love vision, but before turning to examine the unexpected vision itself, it is worth pausing for a moment to insist on Henryson's audacity here in embedding a dream vision of any sort at the centre of a collection of beast fables. The conventional procedure, as in Chaucer's otherwise highly unconventional *Parliament of Fowls*, is to embed the beast fable in the vision. Henryson's audacity here is all the more remarkable when we recognize that he has linked the central dream not only to the previous tale, as I have argued, but, as we shall see, to the following one as well, 'The Preaching of the Swallow,' where a waking vision serves to comment on the sleeping one. Only one critic to date has thought to remark on Henryson's boldness here, although in his view it is the central vision and tale alone that stand out in the *Morall Fabillis*,[34] not the pairing of 'The Lion and the Mouse' with 'The Preaching' or indeed the triple centre created by the flanking of 'The Lion' by 'The Sheep and the Dog' and 'The Preaching.' That this complex inter-linking of the three central tales is no mere accident follows, I think, from the fact that Henryson has already inter-linked the three immediately previous tales through their focus on the fox and his increasingly difficult adventures. In contrast to von Kreisler, A.C. Spearing merely considers 'Henryson conscious of the importance of the centre,' and he does so despite his study's having been the first to show clearly how Henryson's placement of 'The Lion and the Mouse' could be understood as both structurally and thematically significant and thus having helped settle the question of the order of the *Morall Fabillis*.[35]

Most puzzling of all are Dieter Mehl's claims that the two visionary episodes and their tales 'do not depend for their effect on any other poems in the collection,' and indeed that 'they would have to undergo extensive revision if they were meant to be incorporated into a series of fables.' 'The originality of the frame,' he insists, 'makes it very unlikely that the poet wrote the fable as part of a collection.'[36] While it is true that the two framed tales could stand alone, they clearly gain in significance from their careful placement in a larger context; the carefully shaped work that the insights of Fox, von Kreisler, Spearing, Machan, and Wheatley have helped us see is almost certainly not 'the afterthought of some ingenious compiler,' as Mehl would have it.[37] The concatenation of evidence both structural and thematic strikes me as too strong to accept Mehl's countercase against the Bassandyne order of the *Morall Fabillis*, and I would add an observation not yet advanced by any of the pro-Bassandyne critics I have cited: namely, that this multiply significant centre, whether conceived of as 'The Lion and

the Mouse' only or – in my view – as that tale and its two immediate neighbours, fits very neatly indeed with Henryson's insistence on
the shell-and-kernel theory of reading fables; if a single fable can
be thought of as a hard 'nuttis schell' holding an instructive 'kirnell'
(15–16), so by extension can a unified collection be regarded as a shell
with a kernel, the macrocosm of the book (to use a different medieval
metaphor) mirroring the microcosm of each tale.[38]

Before he falls asleep, to return now to the Prologue to 'The Lion
and the Mouse,' the narrator makes the sign of the cross – an unusual
gesture in such contexts – and the dream that comes is accordingly
just as unusual. No allegorical female figure or classical goddess appears to him from out of the blue; instead, the narrator sees another
lone *male* walker in the woods: 'in my dreme, me thocht come throw
the schaw [wood] / The fairest man that euer befoir I saw' (1347–8).
Reinforcing the impact of this startling vision is its placement as a
couplet closing the stanza in which it occurs. Having led his audience to expect something deriving ultimately from Guillaume de Lorris's *Roman de la Rose*, Henryson instead gives them an encounter that
harks back to the beginning of Dante's *Inferno*. To put it another way,
having led his audience to anticipate a scene of instruction in the trials
of eros – and only one of the tales so far, 'The Cock and the Fox,' has
even alluded to eros as a possible subject for the beast fable – Henryson gives them what will turn out to be an almost Dantesque passing on of the patriarchal line in moral fabulation, a kind of *translatio
studii* focused on the literary genre most closely associated with the
classroom. Not only that, but the fable that is told within the dream
vision concerns the social 'vertew of pietie [pity/natural piety/justice]'
(1595) – public *caritas*, in other words, and not private eros.

If we suppose that Henryson's original audience would either
have had no clear image of Aesop at all or have imagined him to be
the deformed slave of recently revived fame, we can assume that they
would not yet have known for sure who this 'fairest man' might be.
Readers familiar with Dante, to be sure, might have had their suspi-
cions, but they would still have to wait a bit to have them confirmed.
For deliberately, no doubt, Henryson withholds Aesop's name for
another twenty-seven lines – long enough for a fourteen-line portrait
and the first part of the larger fifty-two-line encounter designed either
to invent an Aesop appropriate to his new circumstances or possibly
to overturn the recently popular image of the ancient author. According to the portrait, this fair and as yet unknown Aesop is dressed in a

white gown with a 'chymmeris . . . off chambelate purpour broun' (1349–50): that is, a sleeveless upper robe of a costly dark purple eastern fabric. Confirming the academic connotations of the 'chymmeris' are Aesop's hood 'off scarlet' (presumably the rich cloth as well as the colour) with its hackled silk border stretching to his 'girdill' (1351–2). Topping off this initial sketch of embodied intellectual power appropriately adorned are details that locate Aesop in time and remind the audience that his task will be to instruct the dreamer: a 'bonat [hat] round . . . off the auld fassoun [old fashion]' (1353), under which we see, expectedly, white hair and, less expectedly, large grey eyes and curly hair reaching to his shoulders (1354–5).[39] Having introduced the still-unnamed figure as a revered and handsome elder, Henryson now takes care to establish him as a writer. He carries a roll of paper, we learn, has a quill pen behind his ear, and wears at his belt an inkhorn, a fine gilt 'pennair,' or pen-case, and a silken bag (1356–9).

Henryson's distinguished editor, Denton Fox, after noting that the 'traditional description of Aesop' depicts him as ugly, asserts that this portrait is composed entirely of 'traditional iconographic details.'[40] To support his claim, though, he offers a quotation from Robert Greene's *Vision*, a work published in the early 1590s, that is, a century or more after the *Morall Fabillis* were composed. Still, the claim is true enough, as such historically recent portraits as the Latin/German Aesop and the Ellesmere Chaucer suggest, and Greene's later 'description of Sir Geffrey Chawcer' does share several details with Henryson's picture of Aesop, including the sleeveless robe of 'Chamlet,' the bonnet, and the 'Inckhorne.'[41] But surely the point here is that Henryson is using tradition to remake tradition to his own ends. His Aesop has no precedent except perhaps the Latin/German illustration, and if it actually was a response to the recently established tradition of the ugly Phrygian, it would be hard not to think of it as explicitly, deliberately untraditional. Unlike Greene's Chaucer, moreover, who is short, lean, small-legged, and 'blithe and merry' in countenance, Henryson's Aesop is 'Off stature large, and with ane feirfull face' (1361). The ancient poet is, in other words, far more a powerful patriarch than a jolly uncle as he comes striding toward his still-recumbent Scottish heir. To recall Curschmann's claim about the Latin/German Aesop, this is a figure who visually embodies the function of the text, something we can see even more clearly if we pursue the link with Greene's *Vision*. Machan's excellent discussion of Henryson's relation to Aesop notes how both Henryson's and Greene's scenes enact 'the transference of authorship from "auctores" to vernacular writers,' but misses Henryson's distinctive use of the 'traditional iconography' to renovate the tradition of Aesopic moral fabulation.[42] Neither does Machan note that Aesop's more fearsome features are given by Greene to Gower, since Greene's purpose is to have the two medieval poets debate for him – worried as he is about his own works and reputation – the uses and value of literature; Greene's 'blithe' Chaucer defends literary freedom ('Poets wits are free, and their words ought to be without checke'), while his Gower sourly censures literary lightness ('the lightnesse of the conceit cracks halfe the credite, and the vanitie of the pen breeds the lesse beleefe').[43] Henryson, as we shall see, has framed the debate in entirely different terms: not those of levity versus gravity, for instance, or freedom versus responsibility, but those of moral fabulation versus holy preaching, and Henryson's narrator himself takes part in the implicit debate.

'God speid, my sone' (1363) are this 'feirfull'-faced Aesop's first words, and Henryson responds to them 'with reuerence.' 'Welcome, father,' he answers, as Aesop sits down beside him (1365–6). Machan rightly notes the significance of Aesop's speaking first here, but seems to me to miss part of the point of Aesop's sitting down so quickly beside Henryson; this is a gesture, Machan claims, 'both imaging his superiority once again and also implying a certain familiarity with the Scots writer.'[44] Familiarity in the context of hierarchy is indeed the point, since the exchange implies that the two authors know (or know of) each other already, but what is therefore striking about the scene is the lack of any reverencing gesture (as opposed to words) on Henryson's part. Henryson does not first rise, as a literary son should before his ceremonially attired father, nor does he bow, or even offer Aesop a place beside him; if this is an image of superiority, it is at best an ambivalent one, the superior signalling a kind of equality in the face of inaction by the inferior. The ancient author has stooped to conquer, as it were, bringing himself down to the contemporary poet's earthly level. No less bold than his embedding a dream vision in a collection of beast fables is this moment in which the ancient fabulist in effect places the contemporary poet beside him, although its boldness is perhaps most fully appreciated in retrospect, after Aesop names himself. Henryson does not say on which side of him Aesop sits, but after reading 'The Preaching of the Swallow,' one is tempted to imagine it as the left; this after all would leave the modern poet seated at the right hand of his pagan father. That this is a plausible arrangement follows from the substance of their dialogue and the contrast between the tales they tell. In any case, even the apparent familiarity between the two men turns out to be ambivalent, more that of teacher and pupil than of ancient and contemporary authors – and the thing about gifted pupils is that they can eventually displace their teachers.

Taking advantage of the freedom that the dream vision allows an author from the trammels of logic and custom that constrain words and actions in the waking world, Henryson now behaves like a deferential yet decisive immigration officer. Having greeted his 'father,' he asks this ancient figure to identify himself and explain the purpose of his visit: 'Displeis ȝow not, my gude maister, thocht [although] I / Demand ȝour birth, ȝour facultye, and name; / Quhy ȝe come heir, or quhair ȝe dwell at hame' (1367–9). Henryson's questions certainly derive from the tradition of the naive dreamer and they may also draw on the *accessus* tradition, with its focus on introducing authority,[45] but to call the narrator an immigration officer is to do more than make a small joke; in the guise of the naive interlocutor, he is, it seems to me, ensuring here that this fair unknown – and how foreign he actually is we will see in a moment – is legitimately present in the fabular dreamscape.

What Aesop says in response, addressing Henryson once again as 'my sone' (1370), may well have been designed to make him a Dantesque guide and perhaps also to demolish the image of him as a deformed slave from Asia Minor, but even if it was not, the response remains unexpected: 'I am off gentill blude; / My natall land is Rome, withoutin nay' (1370–1). If this is a counterportrait, it already anticipates and answers its objectors, since in it the phrase 'withoutin nay' (there is no denying), a stock collocation normally used to fill out a line and buy a rhyme, actually pulls its semantic weight. Whatever the case, Henryson has supplemented Lydgate's description of the Roman Aesop by making him of noble blood, and he now goes on to specify further the English monk's definition of him as 'the phylosopher of Rome'[46] by having him schooled there and making him expert in civil law (1372–3). Not only that but – and here is the real surprise – this noble, educated Aesop is visiting Henryson from heaven: 'now my winning [dwelling] is in heuin for ay [ever]' (1374). Before the reader even has time to feel the shock of that claim, Henryson finally has the ancient author name himself, insisting yet again on Aesop's literacy: 'Esope I hecht [am called]; my writing and my werk / Is couth and kend to mony cunning clerk' (1375–6). Whether the result is by design or by accident, it is hard to imagine a more thorough, more cunningly dramatized refutation than this of *The Life*'s comic portrait of Aesop as a misshapen trickster.

Several critics claim that Henryson is here 'converting Aesop to a Christian now residing in heaven,' and one even calls the conversion 'one of Henryson's most radical appropriations of Aesopic authority,' since it creates an Aesop 'deserving an authority different from that belonging to pagans.'[47] This, however, is precisely what Henryson does *not* do. Fox, in claiming that Henryson makes Aesop 'an authority on *ciuile law* because this ['The Lion and the Mouse'] is a fable about justice,'[48] gets closer to the point, namely, that the radical transformation of Aesop here involves making the lowly fabulist into the highest pagan authority on secular matters – his metier is *civil*, not canon, law – by asserting that the prudent moral teaching of his fables has been such as to place him, like Langland's Trajan, among the saved pagans.[49] Underscoring this point is not just the subsequent exchange between Aesop and Henryson, but also the contrast between the two tales that immediately follow this encounter: Aesop's comic fable of justice whose moral is entirely secular in its aim and Henryson's tragic tale of the swallow's failed preaching whose moral is explicitly Christian.

Indeed, the rhetorical force of Aesop's subsequent words to Henryson would be diminished, were they to come from a Christian. He functions narratively rather like the Sultan and other non-Christians in *Mandeville's Travels*, whose critiques of the failings of Christian society are more, not less, powerful because they come from the mouths of morally upright outsiders.[50] 'O maister Esope, poet lawriate, / God wait [knows] ȝe ar full deir welcum to me' (1377–8), the narrator says now that this fairest visitor from heaven has finally identified himself. This is a highly emotional response from the narrator, and it is so presumably because Aesop has neatly arrived just after he has reached a major impasse. Confirming one's sense that Aesop has arrived as a kind of answer to the poet's problem is the narrator's immediately following question, which deliberately recalls the defence of fabulation articulated in the opening Prologue: 'Ar ȝe not he that all thir [these] fabillis wrate, / Quhilk [which] in effect, suppois [although] thay fenȝeit be, / Ar full off prudence and moralitie?' (1379–81). Prudence and morality – not Christian teachings – are the shared ground of the good pagan and the baffled Christian, and that shared ground is what ought to justify storytelling. Accordingly, the narrator beseeches 'Esope, [his] maister venerabill' to do him a charitable deed: to deign to tell 'ane prettie fabill / Concludand with ane gude moralitie' (1384, 1386–7). Aesop's answer is entirely unexpected: 'My sone, lat be, / For quhat is it worth to tell ane fenȝeit taill, / Quhen haly preiching may na thing avail?' (1388–90). In support of his assertion that made-up tales are worthless where holy preaching is no use, Aesop offers a sharp, if conventional critique of contemporary Christian society. Nowadays, he asserts, hardly anyone is devoted to 'Goddis word'; 'the eir is deif, the hart is hard as stane'; sin flourishes openly 'without correctioun'; 'the e [eye] inclynand to the eirth ay doun'; and the world is so 'roustit' (rusted) with 'canker blak / That now my taillis may lytill succour mak [can provide little help]' (1392–7). In short, where the revealed truth has been useless, a veiled truth is pointless.

Henryson's narrator accepts Aesop's response without argument, thereby implicitly endorsing its critique of Christian society, but he does not drop his request. Undeferential again, he appeals to his master's nobility ('ȝit, gentill schir') and his 'fatherheid' (1398–9)[51] in asking yet again to be told a moral fable, this time because 'Quha wait nor I may leir [who knows whether I might not learn] and beir away / Sum thing thairby heirefter may auaill?' (1402–3). The narrator has shifted, that is, from attempting to instruct his audience to asking for instruction himself. One might contrast here the tone of the echoing passage in The Testament of Cresseid: 'Quhat wait gif [who knows whether] all that Chauceir wrait [wrote] was trew?' (64). This altered request is a crucial move because not only does it implicitly confirm the crisis that generated the vision – the narrator himself needs help – but it also places this new almost-equal of Aesop on the same level as his audience. Just as Aesop wrote symbolically so as not to have to take criticism from high or low (59–60), wanting to reach both, so Henryson has cannily positioned himself beside, below, and eventually even above Aesop and his audience alike. He may aspire to be a didactic literary author like Aesop, and Aesop in this encounter may even be confirming him in that aspiration, but he too has something to learn from his classical master. Just before the narrator's rhetorical presence reaches its fullest point in the work, then, he allows implicitly that the fabular physician must also heal himself – a useful gesture for achieving the recommended captatio benevolentiae in this later Prologue.

Acceding to the narrator's second request, Aesop tells an extended, Henrysonian version of the famous fable of a lion saved from entrapment by a tiny mouse – or rather here, by a tiny mouse and a community of rodent helpers – because the great beast once 'had pietie' (1569) on the small. These, the fable's concluding words, could well have sufficed for the moral, but the importunate narrator wants more: '"Maister, is thair ane moralitie / In this fabill?" "ȝea sone," he said, "richt gude." / "I pray ȝow, schir," quod I, "ȝe wald conclude"' (1570–2). Aesop's moral is entirely political: the lion represents 'ane potestate' who neglects justice (1575); the forest is the unstable 'warld' (1582); and the mice, the 'commountie' that has become disobedient under an indifferent sovereign (1587). More notable than the moral itself are its addressees: Aesop's explanation is directed not to a generalized 'ȝe' or to clerics, as the narrator's fables so far have been, but to 'ȝe lordis of prudence,' and they are exhorted to 'considder the vertew of pietie' (1594–5). Advice on how to do this follows, and then the tone suddenly shifts as Aesop glosses darkly, almost threateningly, the 'rurall men' (1608) who had trapped the lion in their net. He suggests that they represent those who patiently nurse their hurts until the time for revenge comes, cutting off his comment cryptically: 'For hurt men wrytis in the marbill stane [i.e., have long memories]. / Mair till expound, as now, I lett allane, / Bot king and lord may weill wit quhat I mene: / Figure heirof oftymis hes bene sene' (1611–14). This is no doubt deliberately obscure, but the general political point seems clear enough: that injustice will out, possibly violently, and from the bottom up, if it is not addressed at the top. As Spearing has shown, here at the poem's 'sovereign midpoint,' in a neat conjunction of form and theme, we see, darkly hinted at, the possible consequences of sovereignty misused.[52]

Having declined to speak further on this matter, Aesop implicitly acknowledges the limits of his pagan wisdom, addressing the narrator now not as a literary heir but as a kind of (Christian) innocent: 'My fair child, / Perswaid the kirkmen ythandly [diligently] to pray / That tressoun of this cuntrie be exyld, / And iustice regne, and lordis keip thair fay [faith] / Vnto thair souerane lord baith nycht and day' (1615–19). With these words Aesop disappears and the narrator awakes, taking but a single line to return from the paradise of dreams and fiction to the fallen world, symbolized as before by the wood: 'Syne [then] throw the schaw [wood] my iourney hamewart [I] tuke' (1621).

Father Aesop, I Presume?

The next tale, 'The Preaching of the Swallow,' turns to 'the kirkmen' mentioned by Aesop, taking a tragic turn as the characters fail to follow the preacher's prudent advice. Before the story, though, comes another (a third) lengthy Prologue, this one not explicitly named as such. It opens by shifting the ground from the disoriented and troubled 'schaw' (wood) to the hierarchically ordered cosmos, starting with God, whose 'hie prudence' far exceeds 'mannis iugement' (1622–5). What follows is the theological explanation for the absence of the earthly utopia envisioned by Aesop, contrasting the all-knowing, all-seeing, all-powerful Christian God with his limited human creation trapped in a body that blinds the soul (1622–49). Faith not knowledge is what matters – and yet, Henryson insists, using the standard medieval trope of Nature as God's other book, God can be known through his creatures (1650–77). Implicitly this account, which concludes with a tour of the four seasons (1678–1712), stands as a rebuke to Aesop, whose moralizing was entirely secular. As if to confirm that point, the narrator once again appears on the stage, this time in spring, not wandering in the woods alone, but now happily surveying the orderly human labour by which the dominion granted in Genesis is asserted (1713–26). This time, in other words, his pleasure results not from Nature itself, but from having seen the wood in a new light: that of the Christian notion of the divine order inherent in natural beauty.

To make the link between Aesop's and his own tale unmistakeable, the once again well-pleased narrator takes shelter 'vnder ane hawthorn grene' (1729; cf. 1343). This time, however, like the narrator in Richard Holland's *Buke of the Howlat*, he remains wide awake. If Aesop's potentially just classical world belongs to dream time and dream space, the narrator's disturbed Christian one belongs to the waking present – a present in which he witnesses the very story he tells, 'swa ferliand [thus marvelling] as [he] had sene ane farie [wonder]' (1775). The fact that this second vision is a waking one blurs the distinction between prologue and tale in much the same fashion as Henryson blurred the distinction between tale and *moralitas* at the end of 'The Sheep and the Dog.' The prologue-cum-tale's present, moreover, is one in which time passes, unlike the endless summer of the previous dream and utopian tale. Henryson carefully makes one aware here of both the seasonal time in which the tale as a whole unfolds and the real time of the narrator's separate occasions of witnessing.

To begin, the narrator recounts the action that occurs above and around him in spring. A wondrous flock of birds suddenly alights in the hawthorn, and from the top the swallow preaches: be prudent and think of 'the fynall end' (1760), or the churl will use the flax he is planting to net and kill you. Right away, then, the fable is contrasted with Aesop's, whose concern was the temporal and not the eternal. As one might expect, the birds led by the lark respond with scorn to the preaching. The narrator then departs, returns to the very same spot in summer, and recounts the action that occurs (much as before), before departing a second time, 'for it drew neir the none [noon]' (1824). Confounding our expectation that the narrator will return a third time, Henryson alters the narrative here, recounting the action that occurs in fall and winter – almost as if this were a prospective vision within an actual one, the narrator seeing in the present the likely outcome in the final end. This accelerated, as-if-prospective action culminates in the slaughter of all the birds that fail yet again to heed the swallow's preaching, but the narrator is now here only by implication, explaining that 'it wes grit hart sair [a great heart-sore] for to se / . . . / And for till [to] heir' the churl finally killing the birds (1874–6). Left alone in the end, the swallow offers her predictable reading of events, slightly adapted from Walter of England's moral: this is what often happens 'On thame [to those] that will not tak counsall nor reid [advice] / Off prudent men or clerkis that ar wyis [wise]' (1883–4). So predictable is this conclusion that one might overlook the fact that it is actually applied to both Aesop's and the narrator's stories: one has to take advice from the prudent (the righteous pagan Aesop) as well as the preacher. To put it another way, the Christian needs but also supplements the noble pagan, just as Henryson has done with his father Aesop.

The story is not quite over, though, for the swallow still has to have her last word: 'This grit perrell I tauld thame mair than thryis; / Now ar thay deid, and wo is me thairfoir' (1885–6). To make clear that this is a moment of displaced personal anguish, the swallow is allowed to depart and the narrator is left alone with the fatal aftermath: 'Scho tuke hir flicht, bot I hir saw no moir' (1887). The swallow gone, the narrator turns to the *moralitas* and with it to Aesop, 'that nobill clerk, / Ane poet worthie to be lawreate' (1888–9), who is puzzlingly said to have written, as a break from 'mair autentik werk' (1890), the very tale in which the narrator has just participated as a witness. If Aesop gets credit for the tale, though, the narrator quietly steps forward to claim the coming *moralitas*: Aesop 'this foirsaid fabill wrate, / Quhilk at this tyme may weill be applicate / To gude morall edificatioun, / Haifand ane sentence according to ressoun' (1891–4). What follows according to reason is a thoroughly and explicitly Christian reading of the tale.

The unstable world of Aesop's moral to 'The Lion and the Mouse' is placed here in a Christian cosmos: the churl is the 'feind' (1897), for example, while the birds are sinfully 'Greddie [greedy] to gadder gudis temporall' (1918), which are useless in hell. In addition, the narrator's address to 'worthie folk' (1888) ends with a communal prayer: 'Pray we thairfoir quhill we ar in this lyfe' for freedom from sin, the cessation of war and strife, for perfect charity and love, and to be the angels' companions in bliss (1944–9) – for not only Aesop's visionary earthly utopia, that is, but for the fruits of the Kingdom of Heaven as well.

Conclusion

By this point, Aesop has been thoroughly appropriated, confirmed, and corrected by Henryson, who turns now to three blackly comic Reynardian tales ('The Fox, the Wolf, and the Cadger'; 'The Fox, the Wolf, and the Husbandman'; and 'The Wolf and the Wether') before finishing his collection with a pair of dark Aesopic fables ('The Wolf and the Lamb' and 'The Paddock and the Mouse'). Elaborating at length the moral of 'The Preaching,' this increasingly bleaker sequence of tales shows again and again how naked force wins the day over both ignorance and innocence. The audience is returned to the 'overturnit' world of 'The Sheep and the Dog,' except that now that world is even harsher: the fleeced unfortunates often end up dead as well. Indeed, in the collection's final story, both the innocently deceived and the cunning deceiver share a brutal and unexpected death, no doubt because each is so focused on his worldly concerns that they cannot see the transcendental view from the top of the hawthorn as the Swallow has described it. It is even possible that this final story alludes once more to the erotic world that the visionary centre of the poem obliquely conjures up only in order to ignore it. For in this final tale, the female mouse and the female paddock are bound together in the flesh – literally, by a cord – as they attempt to cross the water so as to satisfy the mouse's desire for tastier food than 'hard nuttis' (2796); their grotesque 'dance' as the paddock tries to drown her en route is perhaps a kind of parody of the 'olde daunce' of love and it leads to their death by forces from without (personified here as a 'gled,' or kite; 2896) that use their self-absorption as cover for a fatal attack. If so, then the close of the collection harks allusively back to its complex centre.

In any case, what is remarkable about Henryson's versions of 'The Lion and the Mouse' and 'The Preaching of the Swallow,' as indeed of the whole collection, is their complex critical homage to Aesop. Appearing first as a nominal authority and the source of both the fables and their morals, Aesop suddenly materializes in the noble flesh at the exact halfway point of the collection, and is there thoroughly incorporated into the collection. Henryson allows him to offer a good pagan's vision of earthly justice before himself telling an adapted tale of failed preaching. Independent though he is shown to be, then, this visionary visitor is also very much Henryson's Aesop, the source that needs to be supplemented. This latter gesture, the homiletic supplement, is especially complex in that it confirms Aesop's remark about the uselessness of tale-telling when holy preaching fails, and yet it uses an Aesopic fable to enact both preaching and its failure. Not only that, but when the fable is over, Henryson uses the *moralitas* to preach once again and then, as an apparent last resort, to pray. Both fiction and sermons may be ineffective, Henryson seems to admit, and if so, prayer is all that remains, but such a dire situation is the fault of readers and hearers, not of poets and preachers; in any case, the Christian poet has no choice but to be a preacher as well, as the prayer suggests, for truth and the possibility of eternal damnation or salvation require it.

Having no Beatrice to turn to – only the centre of his poetic world is visionary, not the whole of it – Henryson cannot quite abandon Aesop in the way that Dante abandons Virgil. Instead, he has to incorporate him into his own moral world, both depending on him and surpassing him: transforming him, in other words. That Henryson might have had his doubts about this necessary transformation may be signalled by his using Aesop's utopian moment of earthly harmony to turn the overall movement of his collection from comedy to tragedy, from laughter to tears. Earthbound as Dante is not, Henryson can only despair over the fact of earthly injustice and pray for a Christian end, not once but several times throughout the work, including in its very last words. As a literary and moral father, Aesop is in Henryson's eyes worthy enough to be considered a Roman noble educated in civil law and wise enough in his works to be saved along with other just pagans – a portrait that may be a deliberate counterimage to that of him as a Phyrgian slave. But even such a fine father has something to learn from his son, and in the end it is Henryson who paradoxically masters Aesop, freeing the slave and appropriating his work, mixed with more recent Reynardian fables, into the contemporary Christian literary cosmos. Father Aesop, the collection implicitly says, make way for Master Henryson, who is anything but the mere compiler of the early title-pages.

NOTES

1 Gavin Douglas offers a witty variation on this sort of scene in the Prologue to the thirteenth book of his *Eneados*, where Virgil's fifteenth-century Christian continuator, Maffeo Vegio, has to beat the translator into agreeing to add the modern supplement.

2 'Aesopi fabellas, quae fabulis nutricularum proxime succedunt, narrare . . . condiscant' (*Institutio oratoria*, 1.9.2). On the fable's status, see Marianne Powell, *Fabula Docet*, 59–65; see also Wheatley, *Mastering Aesop*, 3. Gray, *Robert Henryson*, 31–69, remains an excellent overview of the traditions of the beast fable.

3 Henryson, *Moral Fables*. Gopen, who edited and translated the text, notes that his highly inaccessible predecessors numbered but three: Smith, *The Fabulous Tales of Esope the Phrygian* (1577); Ross, *The Book of Scottish Poems* (1878), which includes only part of the work; and Fratus, *Robert Henryson's Moral Fables* (1971). Since this essay was written, Seamus Heaney has published a translation of Henryson, *The Testament of Cresseid & Seven Fables*, which may bring the latter to a wider readership.

4 Bloomfield, 'Rediscovering Henryson,' insists, without offering evidence, that Henryson was 'vastly popular with his public in his own and the following century,' but that he has been 'left out of the canon in the twentieth century for reasons that actually sprang up in his own time': namely, that he had no discernible influence on his contemporaries or later writers (43), possibly because his being 'old-fashioned' caused them 'embarrassment' (44). This not very coherent study's main purpose is to generate interest in Henryson, particularly among students of animal stories, through a modern English translation by Marijane Osborne of 'The Fox and the Wolf' (this rendering can be added to the list in note 3 above). The question of Henryson's reception remains to be investigated more fully.

5 Fox, 'The Scottish Chaucerians,' 172.

6 Laing, *Poems and Fables*, 292 (emphasis added). Laing's three-volume successor, edited by G. Gregory Smith (*Poems*, 1906–14), anticipates subsequent editions in saying nothing about the meeting in the introduction or the textual notes. The next scholarly edition, by Woods (*Poems and Fables*, 1933; slightly revised in 1958), refers to the encounter only in passing, as if it were of no special significance: 'And, when the poet

is visited in a dream by his master Aesop, listen to their conversation' (xviii, in both editions). Two later editors give the passage somewhat more notice, starting with Fox, whose excellent 1981 edition remains the standard text and commentary. In his commentary, Fox notes explicitly that 'Aesop suddenly appears at this midpoint of the collection,' considers the scene 'effectively' handled, and makes a few brief interpretive suggestions in response to specific words or images (*Poems*, quoting 263 and 264). Yet having drawn attention to the scene, Fox does not pursue the implications of his observations. In a 1987 student edition and translation, Gopen follows Fox in insisting on the importance of the fable in which Aesop appears to Henryson, but says only that it is 'a scene between the narrator and Aesop, in which the sense of omniscience is transfered to his mentor,' likewise leaving its larger significance unexplored (Henryson, *Moral Fables*, 12). Other student or popular editions all but ignore the encounter in their editorial matter: see, for instance, those of MacDiarmid (1973); Elliot (1974); Barron (1981); Bawcutt and Riddy (1992); and Kindrick (1997).

7 MacQueen, *Complete and Full with Numbers*, came to my attention only after this essay was essentially complete. MacQueen's insightful reading of the *Moral Fables* focuses on numerology, and discusses the fables schematically rather than sequentially; for example, he describes *The Lion and the Mouse* as 'a companion piece and *sequel* to *The Preaching of the Swallow*' (172; emphasis added). His emphases and claims are thus quite different from those made here, and might be regarded as complementary rather than opposed to mine.

8 Machan, 'Robert Henryson,' 204.

9 Little is known about Henryson's life and even less about the likely dates of his major works; see Fox, *Poems*, xiii–xxii, for a review of the evidence and some tentative conclusions, namely, 'that Henryson was a man of some age in 1462,' 'that he was active in 1477–8' (xxi), and that the individual fables may have been written at various times (xx).

10 The title as given here is from the Bassandyne print (Edinburgh, 1571), the most important witness; the other three prints are Charteris (Edinburgh, 1569–70), Hart (Edinburgh, 1621 [date conjectural]), and Smith (London, 1577), an 'Englished' text whose title varies slightly: *The Fabulous tales of Esope the Phrygian* (see Fox *Poems*, l–lv, for further details). The other four witnesses are manuscripts, only the first two of which are textually important (see Fox, *Poems*, xxxiv–xli, liii–liv, for further details): Bannatyne (1560s; 'Heir followis the fyift pairt of this buik contenyng the fabillis of Esop with diuers vthir fabillis . . . '; it contains ten of the thirteen fables, some possibly copied from prints, in a unique order intercalated with

works by other authors); Harley (1571; considered a copy of a print; its title is *The Morall fabillis of Esope*); Asloan (early sixteenth century, now incomplete, some of it copied from prints; contains 'The Two Mice' only, six other tales now lost); Makculloch (c. 1500? for Henryson text, which consists of only the Prologue and 'The Cock and the Fox').

11 Only the Hart print lacks the title 'Maister,' although like all but the Smith print it calls Henryson 'Schoole-master of Dumfermeling,' supplying the missing title by inference, as it were.

12 See Daly, *The Aesop Romance*, with a useful brief introduction and an up-to-date bibliography.

13 Rinuccio's translation, one of two surviving Latin renderings, was made from the shorter of the two surviving early recensions of the Greek original (Daly, *The Aesop Romance*, 110); Daly's translation is based on the longer text. Current scholarly opinion considers the shorter version 'merely an epitome which was probably not written before the Byzantine era'; see Holzberg, 'Fable: Aesop. Life of Aesop,' 634.

14 On Steinhöwel's Aesop and its remarkable popularity, see Wheatley, 'The Aesopic Corpus,' esp. 49. Although Steinhöwel considerably broadened the canon of available Aesopic tales, he made his lasting mark on the later tradition with *The Life*. For a visual representation of the collection's wide circulation, see Lyall, 'Henryson's *Morall Fabillis* and the Steinhöwel Tradition,' esp. the table, 'Versions and Editions of the Steinhöwel Collection,' 378–81.

15 Lenaghan, *Caxton's Aesop*, 27; cf. Daly, *The Aesop Romance*, 111. See Holzberg, 'Fable,' for a brief account of *The Life*'s literary qualities.

16 See Fox, *Poems*, xv and xix, for the date of death. Fox has argued against Henryson's 'supposed indebtedness to Caxton's translations' of Reynardian and Aesopic material (*Poems*, xx; see especially his 'Henryson and Caxton'), but his case, though persuasive, is not decisive; and Lyall has recently argued – also persuasively, but not decisively – that 'Henryson knew and used the Steinhöwel collection in some form,' indeed most likely in 'one or more versions' ('Henryson's *Morall Fabillis*,' 363, 375). The 'fundamental methodological difficulty' facing both of these arguments, as Lyall notes (365), is that Henryson was a translator in the best medieval sense, rewriting his sources to such an extent that one can never be sure whether some apparent borrowing is not an independent invention.

17 Curschmann, 'Marcolf or Aesop?' 11; see 10, fig. 5 for the manuscript image (also reproduced in Wheatley, 'Aesopic Corpus,' 62, fig. 1).

18 Wheatley, 'Aesopic Corpus,' 50–3, briefly examines the image of the ugly Aesop on the title-pages of the early prints deriving from Steinhöwel; on their afterlife, see Müller, 'Picturing Aesops'; and Smith, 'Aesop, A

Decayed Celebrity.' On Aesop's ugliness in relation to the ancient evidence, textual and pictorial, see Baker, 'A Portrait.'

19 Marie de France, *Les Fables*: 'Esop[es] escrist ... / ... / Unes fables ke ot trouvees, / De grui en latin translatees' (Aesop wrote some fables that he had found, translated [them] from Greek into Latin; Prol. 17–20; my translation); 'Esope apel'um cest livre, /Qu'il translata et fit escrire, / Del griu en latin le turna' (This book is called Aesop which he translated and had written; he rendered it into Latin from the Greek; Epil. 13–15; my translation).

20 Lydgate, *Isopes Fabules*, line 11 ('poete'); cf. 827 ('Isophus, the famous olde poyete'). The dating of Lydgate's fables is uncertain; on the evidence of the scribe's rubric in a very late manuscript, scholars tend to regard them as early works, but Pearsall (who agrees with the scholarly consensus) plausibly suggests that 'the *Fabules* were a task that Lydgate returned to at odd times' (*John Lydgate*, 192–3).

21 On Henryson's possible knowledge of Lydgate, see Fox, *Poems*, xlviii–xlix.

22 Pearsall, *John Lydgate*, 195. Pearsall does not discuss the portraits of Aesop.

23 Unless otherwise stated, all quotations of the *Morall Fabillis* are taken from Fox, *Poems*. For good discussions of the Prologue's defence of fabulation, see Powell, *Fabula*, 66–74; Machan, 'Robert Henryson,' 195–200; and Wheatley, *Mastering Aesop*, 151–5. The most recent study is Bradburn, '"Prolog" and "Moralitie,"' who makes a persuasive case for considering this opening to be not *the* Prologue as such, but rather the first of three (possibly four).

24 Walter's Prologue opens thus: 'Ut iuuet et prosit conatur pagina presens. / Dulcius arrident seria picta iocis' (The present work tries to please and be useful. / Serious things adorned with humour please more sweetly); see Wright, *The Fables of 'Walter of England,'* I.2 (my translation). This 'was by far the most widely transmitted of all fable collections ... in the fourteenth and fifteenth centuries,' as some two hundred manuscripts and thirty-four incunabular editions now testify (2–3).

25 For a comparative discussion of Lydgate's and Henryson's use of references to their authorities, see Machan, 'Textual Authority.'

26 The textual witnesses are divided on this term: the Bannatyne and Makculloch MSS read 'poete,' whereas the Bassandyne and Charteris prints and the Harley MS read 'Authour.' I follow Fox in preferring the Bannatyne reading (its readings are often superior, despite its almost certainly unauthorial ordering of the fables themselves: see note 26 below). Even if 'authour' were Henryson's term, though, it would scarcely affect my argument, since Henryson calls Aesop a 'poete' three more times in the *Fabillis*

(1337, 1889 and 2588), the first two times in association with the weighty adjective 'lawriate/lawreate.'

27 Gopen calls this arrangement the work's 'synthetic symmetry' (Henryson, *Moral Fables*, 17). Since not all of the surviving witnesses present the tales in the same order, one has to face the question whether this (the Bassan-dyne and traditionally accepted) arrangement is the correct one; Fox answers this question persuasively in the affirmative (*Poems*, lxxv–lxxxi), and Gopen's study of the various levels of coherence in this order would seem to me to clinch the argument. On this point, see also Machan, 'Robert Henryson,' 200.

28 Copeland, *Rhetoric, Hermeneutics, and Translation,* 103.

29 'Dite' here is not necessarily pejorative; it echoes line 13, 'the subtell dyte of poetry,' where it also paired with 'sentence'; hence my rendering as 'style.'

30 Bradburn, ' "Prolog" and "Moralitie," ' 129 and 130.

31 For a different, but complementary reading of this tale and its notable elements, see Wheatley, *Mastering Aesop*, 159–61. On the sheep's speaking as a character in the *moralitas*, for instance, Wheatley notes that such direct address by characters also occurs in the morals appended to seven fables in the *Auctores octo*, but adds that 'these examples do not represent exactly the technique employed by Henryson' (249, note 15). To put this positively, I would argue that here precisely we see how gifted Henryson was as a pupil of Chaucer, from whom he learned to exploit 'technique' to much larger ends.

32 Machan, 'Robert Henryson,' 201–2 (quoting 202).

33 On the hawthorn's significance in such a context, see Eberly, 'A Thorn,' who stresses the tree's ambivalent, even ironic potential, but that is true of all such symbols or motifs; their use in context is crucial.

34 Von Kreisler, 'Henryson's Visionary Fable'; see 397 and 401–2, respectively. Machan calls the scene 'unprecedented' ('Robert Henryson,' 204), and leaves it at that, although in a subsequent comparative study he refers to the entire *Morall Fabillis* as a 'strikingly original composition' ('Textual Authority,' 191).

35 Spearing, 'Central and Displaced Sovereignty,' quoting 253. Spearing's understated and underappreciated insight here was to marry the principle of 'numerical and spatial constructivism' (made possible by Fowler's *Triumphal Forms*) to the evidence provided by Fox in his case for the fables' ordering in *Poems*.

36 Mehl, 'Robert Henryson's *Moral Fables,*' quoting 85 and 87, respectively. Wheatley, *Mastering Aesop,* 162, points out that at least two fables in the elegiac Romulus have framing narratives.

37 Mehl, 'Robert Henryson's *Moral Fables*,' 87. To be sure, Mehl stresses Henryson's own 'ambition and experimental originality' (87), but he seems to want these to have a partly Chaucerian result: the impossibility of finishing. He is apparently persuaded by MacQueen's earlier claim that 'no convincing explanation of the Prologue has . . . ever been given' except that of composition for separate publication; see MacQueen, *Robert Henryson*, 168.

38 L. Ebin, though, has referred to the central tale as 'the sentence which underlies the shell of the two outer tales'; see 'Henryson's "Fenyeit Fabils,"' 230.

39 This is uncannily like the image of the Aesop in the mid-fifteenth-century Latin/German school miscellany (see note 16 above). A few details, though, recall the depiction of Mercury in *The Testament of Cresseid* (239–45): see Bawcutt, 'Henryson's "Poeit."'

40 Fox, *Poems*, 265 (notes to 1348 and 1349–60, respectively).

41 Greene, *Greenes Vision*, 209.

42 Machan, 'Robert Henryson,' 205.

43 Greene, *Greenes Vision*, 215 and 220, respectively.

44 Machan, 'Robert Henryson,' 206.

45 Bradburn, '"Prolog" and "Moralitie,"' 135.

46 Lydgate, *Isopes Fabules*, headnote to Prologue and Fable 1.

47 Machan, 'Robert Henryson,' 206 ('converting'); and Wheatley, *Mastering Aesop*, 163 ('radical appropriations'). See also Patterson, *Fables of Power*, 32.

48 Fox, *Poems*, 267 (note to 1371–3).

49 Gray, however, recognizes that Aesop's account of his dwelling places him 'apparently' amongst 'the righteous heathen' (*Robert Henryson*, 40).

50 Higgins, *Writing East*, 115–17.

51 This latter term, Fox suggests (*Poems*, 267, note to 1399), was 'used especially in addressing ecclesiastics of high rank.' It is this suggestion, presumably, that has led to the recent reading of Aesop as Christian. If so, it seems to me not strong enough evidence, since at most it places Aesop among the great pre-Christian patriarchs who were saved by their good living; in any case, and more important, it reaffirms Henryson's relation to Aesop in the patriarchal line of descent that here defines moral fabling. This Latin father speaks here in the mother tongue.

52 Spearing, 'Central and Displaced Sovereignty,' 254–67; see also von Kreisler, 'Henryson's Visionary Fable,' 397–402.

9 Erasmus's *Lucubrationes*: Genesis of a Literary Oeuvre

MARK VESSEY

Frontispiece

The spring of 1515 was a busy time for Erasmus and his associates.[1] His printer in Basel, Johann Froben, was about to publish his edition of Seneca. Preparations were in hand for editions of Saint Jerome and the New Testament, works whose publication in the following year would raise Erasmus to the height of fame. An expanded edition of his collection of Latin and Greek proverbs, the *Adagia*, was forthcoming. A new printing of the satirical *Praise of Folly* was also expected. Erasmus, now in his late forties, was making a trip to England. On 17 April 1515 his friend and editorial assistant Beatus Rhenanus wrote to him from Froben's shop with a report on various works in progress. Toward the end of his letter he broached the topic of our study. 'And indeed,' Beatus writes, 'Froben is ready forthwith to print your *Lucubrationes* (for that is the title displayed on the frontispiece of the book), as soon as he knows there is no longer any chance of your adding or removing anything.'[2] The modern editor of Erasmus's correspondence points out that Froben did not in fact publish the *Lucubrationes* that year, perhaps because another of his printers, Matthias Schürer of Strasbourg, a city just seventy-five miles away, was also getting ready to issue them. The Strasbourg edition, a modest quarto, appeared in September 1515 and was reprinted in each of the next two years.[3]

Many stories could be told about this book, the *Lucubrationes* of Erasmus. One of them would take as its focus Erasmus's 'poniard' or 'handbook' of a Christian soldier, the *Enchiridion militis christiani*, the longest piece in the volume and a text which, within a few years, would be counted among the most influential literary expressions of reformist

Christian piety in Europe; it is commonly held to embody the essence of Erasmus's ideal of the spiritual life, the *philosophia Christi*.[4] Another story would concentrate on the prayers in the book, which made it into a kind of primer or manual of lay devotion, in keeping with Erasmus's larger sense of his role as a Christian teacher and preacher whose pulpit was the press.[5] Yet other accounts would pick out elements in the book that document the author's career as a Latin poet, as an expositor of holy scripture, and as a theological controversialist. These are all good stories, and have already been partly told in other contexts. That is to say, they have been told outside the context of the *Lucubrationes*, considered as a physical and bibliographic entity – outside 'the book.' So far as the book itself has held the gaze of modern historians, it has usually been as the source of an illustration. The woodcut border of the frontispiece (figure 9.1) depicts eight exemplary figures of biblical and Christian learning: the poet-king David, the prophet Isaiah, the apostle Paul, the evangelist John, and the four great Latin 'Doctors' of the Church – Jerome, Ambrose, Augustine, and Gregory the Great. Another of the stories that could be told of the *Lucubrationes* would highlight this portrait gallery and its relation to the ideals of Christian learning and eloquence now being set forth by Erasmus. Although that is not our subject today either, we can still make use of the frame provided by the pictorial border, to draw attention to the centre of the page and the main description of the book itself.

There we read:

D. ERASMI. RO
TERODAMI VIR
Ivndecunq[ue] doctissimi Lucu=
brationes, quarum Index
positus est facie
sequenti.

[Works (literally, 'Wakes' or 'Exertions by Lamplight') of D. Erasmus of Rotterdam, a man most learned in all respects, an Index of which has been placed over the page.]

Then comes a Greek tag, which can be translated 'Take heart, for humans come of divine stock,'[6] and publishing information.

By the second decade of the sixteenth century, it was already possible to judge a book by its title-page.[7] Before opening this one, we

Figure 9.1. Title-page of the *Lucubrationes* (Strasbourg: Matthias Schürer, 1515). The Bodleian Libraries, University of Oxford, Mar. 864.

should pause long enough to notice the terms in which it announced itself in the title.

After the author's name, 'Erasmus of Rotterdam,' preceded by an honorific (D. for *Dominus*, 'Lord') due him as the member of a religious order (unless the 'D.' was now familiarly taken for his first name, 'Desiderius'),[8] the title comprises three elements:

a. The author's qualifications
He is a man of universal learning – literally, 'most learned on all sides,' 'in all directions' – 'vir undecunque doctissimus,' like the ancient Roman polymath Marcus Terentius Varro, to whom this epithet was normally attached. We shall come back to Varro and the many-sided erudition that he represents.

b. The book in hand: *Lucubrationes*
We have seen Beatus stress this element in his letter to Erasmus: 'your *Lucubrations* (for that is the title displayed on the frontispiece of the book).' Why was he so explicit on the point? Had there been discussion of other possible title-words for the volume? Was he tactfully querying Erasmus's preference? Or simply checking that this was not one of the things he might still want to change? The question of the precise significance of the title *Lucubrationes* will be one of our concerns below.

c. The index (with a capital I) or table of contents, to be found overleaf
Merely practical as it may seem, this pointer to an appended list of works is in close relation to the other elements above. The title *Lucubrationes* by itself would give little hint of the actual contents of the book. Even Beatus and Froben might still be unsure of what a volume with this title could include, as they waited for Erasmus to finalize his plan for it. The author's name on the cover-page would raise certain expectations. By 1515, however, the name of Erasmus raised too many. He had already published across a range of different genres and in several different bibliographical formats. He was widely known as a poet, as a compiler of proverbs, as a moralist, as a classicizing teacher of Latin, and as a satirist. He had edited and translated ancient texts. He was thought to have ambitions in the field of biblical exegesis. Some of his letters had appeared in print. Cheaply as such praise was bestowed by humanist publishers of the time, the billing of

Erasmus as 'vir undecunque doctissimus' was more than ordinary puffery. A man of such proven versatility might send almost anything to press under a title like *Lucubrationes*. To get even a preliminary sense of what was in this book, the reader would indeed have to turn the page.

For the sake of our story, I propose that we leave the page unturned for a little longer. For if the historical interest of this book as a book is to appear, we need to step back far enough to see the longer trajectories of three narratives that cross in it. Those narratives are lexicographical, bibliographical, and biographical, having to do respectively with the lives of individual words, the lives of particular books, and the life of an unusual man, Erasmus of Rotterdam. In due course, the three kinds of life story will merge again into one, centred on the book.

A Hard Day's Night, or: Talking about My Lucubration

Beginning with words, we begin naturally with 'lucubration.' However refined or Latinate one's English, this word no longer comes trippingly off the tongue. It is strictly an 'inkhorn' term, one of those words transposed into English by men trained in the Latin grammar schools of the sixteenth century and then typically, if not always, mocked into early disuse by other, less pretentious speakers of the vernacular. The schoolmaster in Shakespeare's *Love's Labour's Lost* is a connoisseur of such terms; it is his companion, Costard, who brings forth that mother of all anagrams, the monstrous but perfectly formed Latin word *honorificabilitudinitatibus*. From the Latin noun *lucubratio*, which declines in oblique cases of the plural to *lucubrationibus*, we have the English word 'lucubration,' which enters the language exactly on cue toward the end of the sixteenth century and is defined in the dictionary as (1) 'nocturnal study or meditation' and so (2) 'literary work, esp. of a pedantic or elaborate character' (*OED*). *Lucubrum* in Latin apparently meant a small lamp, though the word itself is not attested outside lexica. There is a corresponding verb, 'to lucubrate,' in Latin *lucubrare*, meaning to burn the midnight oil or stay up late, presumably for the purpose of producing literary works.

The English words have a distinctly archaic sound. No one admits any more to 'lucubrating' and anyone who now ventured with a straight face to publish his or her *Lucubrations* would be asking for trouble. It is a long time since such works were in vogue. A scan of the library catalogue at my university yielded two Latin-titled items,

Lucubrationes Thucydidiae and *Lucubrationes Lucretianae*, both by classical scholars now long dead. In English there were *The Lucubrations of Humphrey Ravelin, Esq.* (1824); *The Lucubrations of Isaac Bickerstaff, Esq.*, otherwise known as *The Tatler*, composed in the 1720s by Richard Addison and Joseph Steele; and my personal favourite from this company, *A Hymn to the Chair, or, Lucubrations serious and comical, on the use of chairs, benches, forms, joint-stools, three-legged stools, and ducking-stools* [...] *to which are added the beauties and advantages of other necessary utensils to rest the bum upon, and ease the mind, the body and the breeches* (1732). Already by the early eighteenth century, it appears, the genre and title of English 'Lucubrations' were alike irredeemably debased.

In Latin, by contrast, the language and ideology of *lucubratio* are perfectly classical and largely untainted by the imputation of pedantry that we find almost from the start in the English tradition. The link between night-wakefulness (in Greek, *agrypnia*) and literary labour is a commonplace of Hellenistic poets and their Latin imitators; Horace is notably fond of it.[9] The words *lucubrare* and *lucubratio* themselves belong to Latin prose. In the *Thesaurus Linguae Latinae*, citations of these words as applied to reading, writing, and related forms of intellectual activity follow the main axis of literary-rhetorical tradition from Varro and Cicero to the Elder Seneca, Quintilian, the Younger Pliny and Suetonius, Aulus Gellius, Lactantius, Jerome and Augustine, Martianus Capella, and Boethius – a list that already includes the authors of most of the standard texts of Renaissance humanism. It is reasonable to assume, therefore, that the idea of burning the midnight oil was part of the stock-in-trade of Latin writerly self-presentation that European literati of the fifteenth and early sixteenth centuries took over from their classical forebears and recycled for their own purposes. The *Lucubrationes* of Erasmus, as it was titled, would then be one more sign of a fashion for language that glamorized the labour of new-style literary professionals and freelances. To be sure of these assumptions, we would need to make a study of the use of 'lucubratory' terms in Latin literature, say from Petrarch onward. To the best of my knowledge, that has still to be done.[10] Without attempting to anticipate the results of such further inquiry, I shall argue here that, solid as the classical Greek and ancient Latin, medieval Christian, and Renaissance humanist precedents may have been for Erasmus's talk of lucubration, that talk – as and when we begin to hear it – has a distinctly, originally Erasmian accent. These are the nightworks of a certain time and milieu, and of a particular authorial project.

Three kinds of textual data converge in support of the hypothesis. First of all, the one undeniably classical precedent for the use of *Lucubrationes* as the title for a book can be shown to have had a particular incidence on Erasmus. Secondly, a chronological survey of Erasmus's writings between the mid-1490s, when his public literary career began, and the late 'teens of the sixteenth century, by which time he was the most famous living humanist scholar in Europe, reveals the stages of a personal discovery and deliberate deployment of the idiom of literary lucubration. Thirdly, if there was an ancient Latin Christian author who could have provided a model for such a proceeding, it was the one that Erasmus himself most zealously cultivated, Jerome. We shall take the last of these arguments first.

Jerome has already been mentioned as one of the ancient authors who used the term *lucubratio*. More than most Latin writers before him, he laboured the word in descriptions of his own activity, where it serves both as an ostensible device of modesty and for self-advertisement. Jerome likes to claim that he has dashed off one of his treatises or longer letters in a single burst of night work – 'unius noctis lucubratione,' 'una et brevi lucubratione.' The implication is that his readers should be ready to forgive any faults in the work but also to marvel at his powers of rhetorical invention and expression. The *Thesaurus Linguae Latinae* lists three instances of *lucubratio* used by Jerome in this disclamatory-declamatory sense, which seems to have been peculiar to him among the Christian authors of late antiquity. Immediately below the dictionary's entry for *lucubratio* is another for the diminutive form *lucubratiuncula*, 'a little nightlight work.' Here the note of false modesty dominates. Single instances are provided by Marcus Aurelius in a letter to his tutor Fronto and by the fourth-century Gallo-Roman poet Ausonius, a master of such feints. Twelve more citations follow, all from the works of Jerome, the majority of them either from his letters or from his polemical treatise *Against Vigilantius*.[11] On quantitative grounds, Jerome appears to have had no rival among ancient authors in the profession of lucubratiuncularity.

There is just one more instance of *lucubratiuncula* in the *Thesaurus*, this time used in the plural form *lucubratiunculae* and for a finished literary product rather than the process of literary composition. It occurs in the preface to the *Noctes Atticae* or 'Attic Nocturns' of the late second-century author Aulus Gellius. Introducing this work of a thousand and one nights of affable erudition, Gellius gently disparages it as 'these trimmings of a late-burning lamp' (*lucubratiunculas istas*).[12] Though not actually a book title, *lucubratiunculae* as he uses it thus stands for a book of almost the same name. (A few pages earlier, Gellius has included the Greek title *Nychnous*, meaning 'Lamps,' in a list of possible titles for works like his own.)

Having reached this point in our lexicographical inquiry, we can close the dictionary and turn back to the evidence of sixteenth-century Latin books.

It is almost as if we never looked away. That nonce usage of the plural *lucubratiunculae* by Aulus Gellius points us to one of the earliest books published in the name of Erasmus. Among grounds that we could conjecture for Beatus Rhenanus's harping on the title *Lucubrationes* in his 1515 letter to Erasmus would be his knowledge that a similar collection of this author's writings had already been circulating for some years, in more than one edition, under the title of *Lucubratiunculae*. Indeed, in a letter to Erasmus written barely two weeks after the other, Beatus seems to slip up, asking him for the final corrections to his *'Lucubratiunculae.'*[13] To appreciate the character and historical significance of the later publication, we must briefly consider the contents and circumstances of this predecessor volume. From lexicography we pass to bibliography.

The Book Speaks

The original *Lucubratiunculae* of Erasmus was published by Dirk Martens in Antwerp in February 1503 (or just possibly 1504, depending on which style of dating he used), the first of several works of his to be issued by this printer. Martens had a line in devotional books, and the list of contents on the title-page of the *Lucubratiunculae* declared this to be a work of the same type, 'especially useful for young adults.' Here are the contents as given on the title-page of a copy of the 1509 reprint, now in the Bodleian Library in Oxford:

Erasmus, Lucubratiunculae aliquot
(Antwerp: Dirk Martens, 1503 [1509])
[Items numbered in square brackets are not listed on the title-page]

[1] Ai^v	Libellus loquitur ('The book speaks'): 'Nil moror . . .'	
	Poem 16 Reedijk; CWE 85: no. 36	
2 Aii–Avii^v	Epistula exhortatoria ad capessendam virtutem ad generosissimum puerum Adolphum principem	

Veriensem
Ep. 93 Allen (excerpts only); CWE 29:4–13'Oration
on the Pursuit of Virtue'

3   Avii^v–Biiii   Precatio cum erudita tum pietatis plena ad Iesum
dei virginisque filium
CWE 69:4–16
'Prayer to Jesus, Son of the Virgin'

4   Biv–Ciii^v   Paean in genere demonstrativo virgini matri
dicendus
CWE 69:20–38
'Paean in Praise of the Virgin Mother'

5   Ciii^v–Cviii   Obsecratio ad eandem semper gloriosam
CWE 69 42–54
'A Prayer of Supplication to Mary, the Virgin
Mother, in Time of Trouble'

6   Cviii–Cviii^v   Oda de casa natalicia pueri Iesu
Poem 33 Reedijk; CWE 85: no. 42
'Ode on the Shed Where the Boy Jesus Was
Born'

7   Di–Niv   Enchiridion militis christiani
CWE 66:24–127
'Handbook of the Christian Soldier'

[8] Niv–Nvi   *Ep.* 108 Allen; CWE 70:9–13
Letter of Erasmus to John Colet

9   Nvi–Riiii   Disputatiuncula de pavore, taedio, moestitia Iesu
quam habuit instante passionis hora
CWE 70:14–67
'A Short Debate concerning the Distress, Alarm,
and Sorrow of Jesus as the Hour of His Crucifixion
Drew Nigh'

10 Riiii^v–Rviii   . . . cum non nullis aliis.
Poem(s) 34–7 Reedijk; CWE 85, no. 50
'In Praise of Michael and All Angels'

By far the longest single item in the volume, filling more than half
of its 200-odd pages, was the *Enchiridion militis christiani* or 'Handbook

of the Christian Soldier' (7), a set of rules for a lifestyle based on
prayer and Bible study. The rest of the book's contents cover a range
of edifying genres. There is a letter of moral exhortation addressed to
a young nobleman named Adolph of Burgundy (2); several prayers
that Erasmus had composed at the request of the latter's mother,
Anna van Borssele (3–5); an ode on the site of Jesus's nativity (6); a
partial transcript of a theological debate that had taken place a
few years earlier between Erasmus and the Oxford divine, John Colet
(8–9); and finally a suite of poems apparently designed as decoration
for a church (10). While all the prose pieces, including the *Enchiridion*,
were printed for the first time in 1503, the poems had already been
published together in Paris in or around 1496, in a little collection of
Erasmus's verses issued under the title of one of them, the *Carmen de
casa natalicia Iesu* ('Poem on the Shed Where Jesus Was Born'). The difference in the respective publication histories of prose and verse elements of the *Lucubratiunculae* will turn out to be of some importance
for our story.

The *Lucubratiunculae* of 1503 bears no preface or commendation,
apart from the lines printed on the verso of the title-page and ascribed
to the book itself as a speaking subject (figure 9.2):

> Libellus loquitur:
> Nil moror aut laudes levis aut convicia vulgi:
> Pulchrum est vel doctis vel placuisse piis.
> Spe quoque maius erit mihi si contingat utrunque;
> Cui CHRISTUS sapit, huic si placeo, bene habet.
> Unicus ille mihi venae largitor Apollo,
> Sunt Helicon huius mystica verba meus.

> [The book speaks: I do not care about the praise or the insults of the su-
> perficial mob. The fine thing is to please either the learned or the pious.
> If I happen to do either of these, it is more than I hoped for. If I please
> someone who relishes the wisdom of Christ, it is well. Christ alone is my
> Apollo, the source of my vein; his mystic words are my Helicon.] (CWE
> 85:75)

In the collection of Erasmus's poems published by Froben in 1518, this
one is preceded by the notation 'In fronte Enchiridii,' indicating that
it served as an epigraph for the *Enchiridion*. The description reflects
the reordering of contents in a new, expanded edition of Erasmus's

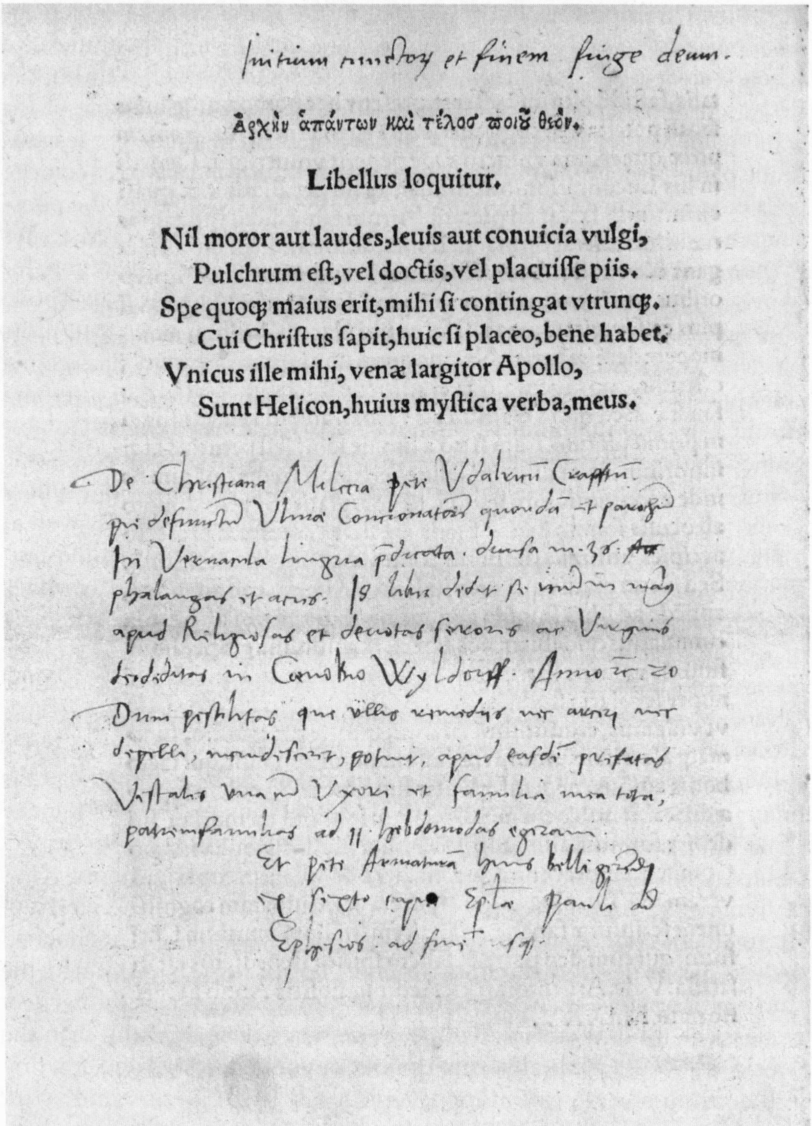

initium omniboy et finem finge deum.

Ἀρχὴν ἁπάντων καὶ τέλος ποιῶ θεόν.

Libellus loquitur.

Nil moror aut laudes, leuis aut conuicia vulgi,
Pulchrum eſt, vel doctis, vel placuiſſe piis.
Spe quoqᵽ maius erit, mihi ſi contingat vtrunqᵽ.
Cui Chriſtus ſapit, huic ſi placeo, bene habet.
Vnicus ille mihi, venæ largitor Apollo,
Sunt Helicon, huius myſtica verba, meus.

[handwritten note, several lines, largely illegible]

Figure 9.2. Sig. 4v of the *Lucubrationes* (Strasbourg: Matthias Schürer, 1515), facing the first page of the *Enchiridon militis christiani*. The Bodleian Libraries, University of Oxford, Mar. 864.

devotional writings issued by Froben in the same year, in which the *Enchiridion* appeared in first place and gave its title to the volume as a whole, replacing '*Lucubrationes*.' As we can see, however, it did not at first occupy that position but 'spoke' instead for the ensemble of the texts that made up the *Lucubratiunculae*. The wish to please the learned or the pious rather than the undiscerning multitude is, or would come to be, a characteristically Erasmian refrain. The last two lines of the poem stand a little apart in their literary-mythological colouring. Christ, says Erasmus (or rather his book), is the source of my poetic inspiration, his words are the sacred spring at which I drink. The references to Apollo and Helicon are genre-specific. This is the profession of a poet, more precisely of a Christian poet in a classical landscape. Such classicizing Christian poetic professions had been normal since late antiquity and would have been familiar to Erasmus's early readers. What is notable about this one is its appearance at the threshold of a book consisting mainly, though not exclusively, of texts in prose. The slight but salient generic incongruity can be seen to have a biographical basis, as well as bibliographical implications. To account for it, we need to remind ourselves who and what kind of a person it was that first decided, in 1503, to offer these nocturnal meditations to a reading public. The title-page of the *Lucubratiunculae* calls him Erasmus 'of the canonical order of the blessed Augustine,' an Augustinian canon or monk, but that is not the whole story. For neither in life nor in literature was Erasmus ever just canonical.

In retrospect, partly no doubt because he was such an odd case at the time, Erasmus is frequently held up as the defining example of Renaissance Christian humanism. If that phrase means anything with respect to him, it must be understood to denote a set of choices about ways of living with literary texts.[14] First as a young monk in the house of Augustinian canons at Steyn near Gouda and then as an unattached ecclesiastic in Paris in the mid- to late 1490s, Erasmus combined the study of Christian theology with a passionate interest in the writers of classical antiquity – first mainly those who wrote in Latin, then the Greeks as well. Gradually, this double devotion crystallized for him in the vision of a revival of the 'classical' Christian literary and scriptural culture of the age of the church fathers, from Irenaeus, Tertullian, and Origen in the second and third centuries to Jerome, Augustine, John Chrysostom and their contemporaries in the fourth and fifth. The Latin coordinates of this patristic ideal were signalled by the four lower figures on the title-page of the *Lucubrationes* (figure 9.1) – albeit somewhat approximately, since Erasmus held no brief for Gregory the Great.[15] Meanwhile, the figures in the upper register stood for the biblical, Christ-centred wisdom and eloquence that it was the duty of the Christian teacher in all ages to transmit. Thus schematized, Erasmus's intellectual commitments were clear. The scheme, however, was neither conceived not promulgated overnight, as it were 'unius noctis lucubratione.' Its realization was a lifetime's work, the cumulative effect of the 'lives' of all the works that Erasmus published between the mid-1490s and his death in 1536, whose generational bio-bibliography we as historians now reconstruct.

The 'life' of a writer, as readers of Western literature have come to understand it, is constituted in an important sense by the chronological series of his or her works, each seen as standing in a formal and generic relationship to all previous works by him- or herself and other writers, living and dead. Erasmus is one of the exceptions who help establish this rule. In the early 1490s, having obtained permission from his superiors to leave the monastery at Steyn and, without renouncing his religious vows, to pursue a studious life outside the cloister, he began improvising a career of scholarship and teaching based on the latest humanist models. He also began experimenting with ways of presenting himself as a writer, first by circulating manuscript copies of his compositions among his friends and then, and thereafter increasingly, by committing his works to the new medium of print.[16] His printed debut seems to have been the 1496 (?) volume of poems on Christ's birthplace and other sacred subjects, to which reference has already been made. In 1497 he contributed two poems and a commendatory letter to a collection published by his friend Willem Hermans, the *Sylva odarum*. Through the rest of the 1490s and into the early years of the new century he continued writing poems for friends and patrons, most of which later appeared in print. He also tried his hand at verse translations from Greek. In 1506–7, a collection of nearly fifty of his poems was published in Paris under the title of *Varia epigrammata*, annexed to an edition of the *Adagia*. In his introduction to the Toronto (CWE) edition of Erasmus's poetry, Harry Vredeveld suggests that this volume 'marks the end of the first half of [his] career.' He explains:

> For the last time poetry receives, so to speak, equal billing with his prose. Hitherto Erasmus' verse had always balanced out his prose in importance, if not necessarily in length . . . But after the publication of the *Adagia* and *Epigrammata* in the winter of 1506–7 the earlier balance between poetry

and prose in Erasmus' writing shifts suddenly and dramatically in favour of prose. Henceforth, whether he was inserting metrical translations from Greek into the *Adagia*, writing complimentary poems or epitaphs, or recording his reaction to one event or another, poetry would be mostly reduced to a pastime for himself, a service to his friends, a handmaiden to his prose. (CWE 85:xxiii)

Vredeveld's argument about the shift from verse to prose can be supported by a statement of Erasmus himself in the account he gave of his literary works in a letter of 1523 to Johann von Botzheim. 'First,' he says, 'I will recount what I have written in verse, for in boyhood my predilection for verse was such that it was with reluctance that I turned to prose composition. And in that field [i.e., prose] I strove for some time before succeeding, if one may use the word success. Nor is there any form of poetry which I did not attempt' (CWE 9:294).

If the young Erasmus had any non-monastic vocation in view, it was evidently that of *poeta*, a role conceived by him as the purest embodiment of the New Learning that had begun to spread from Italy to the Low Countries while he was a boy.[17] Acting on this hint, some of the best modern scholars have represented Erasmus's career as a conversion from poetry to theology. 'Erasmus ex poeta theologus' is the title of one justly influential article.[18] The formula is good, provided it is treated as no more than a formula, and a potentially deceptive one at that. For poetry and theology, as Erasmus came to understand them, could never have been so opposed as to make it likely that a person would come to one by departing from the other. If any single text announced Erasmus's maturing sense of Christian, literary, and theological vocation, it was the *Enchiridion* of 1503, or rather – to speak bibliographically again – the *Lucubratiunculae* of that date, with its liminary invocation of Christ as the infuser of a rich vein . . . of what? Poetry? Theology? Or both at once?[19]

In his survey of Erasmus's literary production in the early years of the sixteenth century, Vredeveld mentions the *Adagia* (published in its primitive form in 1500, in Paris), the *Panegyric* for Archduke Philip of Austria (printed by Martens in Antwerp in February 1504), and the *Enchiridion* (of 1503). Like many scholars, he speaks already of the *Enchiridion* as if it were a book unto itself, although it would not appear in a separate volume until 1515.[20] By 1518, when Froben issued Erasmus's *Epigrammata*, the verses invoking Christ instead of Apollo could fairly be said to stand 'in fronte Enchiridii,' at the beginning of

the *Enchiridion*, meaning either this work alone or the ensemble of devotional pieces which it introduces in the Basel editions of 1518 and
after. But that was not their first printed location. Nor is there any reason to think that they were originally composed as an accompaniment
to the *Enchiridion* rather than for the *Lucubratiunculae* as a whole. In any
case, it is in their bibliographical context in the *Lucubratiunculae aliquot*,
on the other side of the page bearing that title, speaking for the *libellus*,
that they first acquired a public meaning.

Immediately above those verses in the 1503 volume (and repeated
in the same place in the 1515 and later *Lucubrationes*, figure 9.2) stands
a line of verse in Greek, which can be translated 'Make God the beginning and the end of everything,'[21] a preliminary injunction that is also
already postliminary, preemptively circumscribing the entire contents
of this formally and generically miscellaneous volume. The imperative
'make' (i.e., 'consider,' 'reckon') is of the middle voice of the verb *poiein*;
God (*theos*) has become the means and measure of a new kind of *poiesis*.
Then follows (in the verses already quoted) a Christ-centred meditation
on the double life of the literary work – its reception by the public and
its (prior) conception in the mind of the author – spoken by the work
itself in its physical guise as book: on the one hand, creative inspiration; on the other, critical reaction. Of both of these, as we have seen,
the language of *lucubratio* also directly speaks, expressing as it does
an author's awareness that, for a work of his to please the discerning,
it must first have cost him pains, however divine his inspiration. Unless it is a fluke of the press, the appearance of a bilingual profession of
theology-as-poetry at the beginning of a volume whose title-page (in
1515) would assert the utility of an Augustinian canon's extramonas-
tic vigils looks like an act of Erasmian policy. Can we be sure of this?
Having heard the book speak, we now turn again to the biographical
record.

Catching the Light of Print

It is clear from his earliest extant correspondence, dating from his
time at the monastery of Steyn, that Erasmus had imbibed the elements of a classical and classicizing theory of literary production at an
early age, and in milieux where literary exercise and ascetic spirituality were closely associated, as they had been in the main monastic
tradition of Latin Christianity since late antiquity.[22] In the letters he
exchanged with another young monk, Cornelis Gerard, in the late

1480s, he already cuts the figure of a tireless votary of the Muses – in the latest Italian style and with the best patristic licence. For the reasons already stated, we can be sure that he encountered the Latin term *lucubratio* and its cognates at an early stage in his studies; the word was to be found in the most accredited humanist sources, including Quintilian. We have also seen that the diminutive *lucubratiuncula* was a special favourite of Jerome, if not a virtual 'Hieronymism,' and no texts were dearer to the young Erasmus than those of that Latin father, especially his letters, in which the term appears most often. Given these facts, it is remarkable that neither *lucubratio* nor *lucubratiuncula* seems to have belonged to Erasmus's active vocabulary before 1500. Neither word, so far as I can see, occurs in any positive sense in his correspondence of the 1480s and 1490s as presented by Allen's edition.[23] Then, as if overnight, the situation changes.[24] All but absent hitherto, the word *lucubratio* suddenly becomes a leitmotif of Erasmus's literary enterprise. What does it betoken? It may be no more or less than this: Erasmus was going into print, *in prose*.

By the year 1499, during the latter part of which he made his first visit to England, Erasmus had several major projects in hand, all of them essentially works of prose and in some way contributory to the ideal of a revived Latin literary culture that would be the vector of a Christian morality and spirituality based on the Gospels. One of them was the dialogue, 'Against the Barbarians' (*Antibarbarorum libri*), containing a full statement of this cultural program, which was many times rewritten and not finally published until 1520. There was a draft treatise on letter writing (*De conscribendis epistolis*), the printed version of which would likewise be more than twenty years coming. There were sketches for what would emerge in 1512 as the *De copia*, a guide to the cultivation of rhetorical abundance. There were the models of Latin conversation, the *Colloquia*, to be published in a greatly expanded form in 1518. There was a paraphrase of Lorenzo Valla's disquisition on Latin style, the *Elegantiae*, which would appear in 1529.

As the long intervals between the genesis and printing of these works suggest, Erasmus did not at first find ready commercial outlets for his productions. The difficulty of finding printers to publish his work is a minor theme of his correspondence at the turn of the century. Of the friends in whom he confided, apparently one of the most sympathetic was Jacob Batt, tutor to the young nobleman for whom Erasmus had written the 'Oration on the Pursuit of Virtue,' which would appear a few years later as the first item in the *Lucubratiunculae*.

After leaving England in late January of 1500, Erasmus visited Batt in Flanders on his way to Paris. He seems to have left some of his working papers behind at the end of his stay, which Batt then sent on to him. In the first line of a letter from Paris, Erasmus refers to these materials as 'vigilias meas, hoc est opes' (my waking nights – that is, riches).[25] In the opening of another, he speaks of 'meas lucubrationes.'[26] For the first time in Erasmus's oeuvre, we actually read the smell of midnight oil. The smell grows sharper. Writing to the same Batt a few days later, Erasmus describes his arrival in Paris as a return to ceaseless work, 'assidua lucubratio.' Heaviest on his hands was his treasury of proverbs, the *Adagia*, a work 'not short and of endless toil' (opus . . . neque breve et infiniti laboris), and one that was about to appear in print, the first major prose text of Erasmus to do so.[27] When it came out in the summer of 1500, in Paris, this *opus novum* bore the note of lucubration prominently before it.

Prefacing the *Adagiorum collectanea* to his English friend and patron, William Blount, Lord Mountjoy, Erasmus disingenuously describes it as a recreational work, carried out when a severe fever made it impossible for him to pursue weightier tasks, 'intermissis gravioris operae lucubrationibus.'[28] The preface contains a catalogue of ancient writers who delighted in the proverbial style, both classical and Christian. Among pagan writers, Erasmus mentions that man of universal learning Marcus Varro, 'vir undecunque doctissimus,' and his fellow Roman polymath the elder Pliny, 'vir multiiuga doctrina.'[29] The *Adages* was designed as a shortcut to the encyclopedic culture of the classical world.[30] With good reason, Erasmus lingers over the preface to Pliny's *Natural History*, in which the author claimed that he had been obliged to treat all matters comprised in the Greek *enkyklios paideia*.[31] A few pages later in his address to the emperor Vespasian, Pliny ran through a list of the titles Greek and Latin authors had given to works of compilation like his own.[32] It includes the title *Lucubrationes* chosen for a (lost) work by a certain Bibaculus – a tippler by name as well as by nature, Pliny jokes, implying that this man's nocturnal meditations relished more of the wine jar than of the lamp. This is our sole reference to a work of ancient literature entitled *Lucubrationes*, and it occurs in a passage that was demonstrably under Erasmus's eye during his preparation of the *Adagia*. Pliny's list of titles had been imitated by Aulus Gellius, who, as we have seen, spoke of his own *Noctes Atticae* as *lucubratiunculae*.[33] Gellius too, like the elder Pliny, was a major source for the *Adagia*, and his name appears prominently a few lines later in Erasmus's preface to Mountjoy.[34]

After Gellius and his kind, Erasmus turns to Christian authors, or to the ancient Christian author who in his estimation stood head and shoulders above the rest for variety and rarity of erudition: Jerome.[35] The origins of Erasmus's plan for a new edition of Jerome lie in his appreciation of the range of proverbial and other types of allusion contained in this writer's work, and of the difficulties thereby created for later readers.[36] Apart from its more strictly theological qualities, it was the assimilative power of Jerome's literary learning, its copiousness and pungency of expression, that impressed Erasmus and made this Latin father a model for the Christian Latin culture that he was intent on promulgating in his own age. Although the term *lucubratio* is not explicitly linked to the name of Jerome in the preface to the *Adagia*, there is no missing his presence as chief cantor of the literary night office there advertised. Soon afterwards, Erasmus would begin referring to the works of Jerome as 'Hieronymi lucubrationes.'[37]

In his own mind, the *Adagia* marked Erasmus's debut as a publishing author. He took pains to ensure that the first edition, a slim but attractively printed quarto volume of 152 pages, was well noticed. For the verso of the title-page he had secured a letter of commendation from the distinguished Latin poet Fausto Andrelini, who may have seen a draft of the preface as well as an advance copy of the main text, since he obligingly echoes the terms of Erasmus's own self-presentation, urging him to make all speed to publish the delectable fruits of his hard work ('tam iucundas tamque frugiferas lucubrationes').[38] In the months immediately following publication, Erasmus wrote around to his friends in England and on the continent, apologizing for deficiencies in the first edition, promising revisions, and urging them to promote the book in whatever ways they could. To Jacob Batt, meanwhile, he spoke impatiently of his desire to complete the larger program of works on which he had embarked, 'omnes nostras lucubratiunculas ad umbilicum ducere.'[39] If we assume that Allen's reconstruction of the original sequence of the letters is broadly reliable, this is the first instance of the application of the formerly Gellian and Hieronymian diminutive *lucubratiunculae* to Erasmus's own works. Around the same time, in a letter dedicating some annotations on a work of Cicero's to Jacob de Voecht of Antwerp, Erasmus jokes that he owes Jacob not only his *lucubrationes*, the fruits of study, but also his *cessationes*, the fruits of idleness, a play on words that can perhaps be interpreted as a further sign of the recent 'discovery' of *lucubrationes* as a suitable term by which to designate and dignify the sum of his works in various (mainly prose) genres of erudition.[40]

Let me be plainer. I am suggesting that the breakthrough represented by the 1500 *Adagiorum collectanea*, the first of Erasmus's printed publications to catch the eye of a northern humanist public, is also the advent of a new, more eclectic conception of humanist literary oeuvre.

The best evidence for this claim is the volume of *Lucubratiunculae aliquot* published in Antwerp in 1503 by Dirk Martens. The importance of that collection should not be exaggerated. Erasmus himself seems not to have been fully convinced of the value of all its pieces, and there are signs that the book was assembled in some haste, perhaps to test the marketability in moral and theological genres of an author whose disciplinary versatility, even if not hitherto proclaimed on title-pages, was beginning to be measured in print. As a volume pointing toward the more specifically Christian and biblical projects that Erasmus was already meditating, the *Lucubratiunculae* has a significance in retrospect that it can scarcely have had at the time, when it does not seem to have attracted any special attention. That said, the terms of the title-page and of the poem ascribed to the book on the verso fit well enough with the lucubratory scenario that we have seen developing in Erasmus's writings around 1500 for it to appear most likely that they too were calculated.

In the *Lucubratiunculae* Erasmus presents himself as a humanist poet for whom poetry and humanism now represent a multigeneric, ultimately theological enterprise of textual instruction, conducted chiefly through print and largely in prose. As we noted in an earlier section, the classical ideology of literary night work was originally identified with poetic inspiration, while the Latin word *lucubratio* and its cognates were attached from the start to prose genres of erudition. As if profiting from this ambiguity, with Jerome as his sponsor, the author of the *Lucubratiunculae* trusts in Christ to infuse his book with an eloquence already shared by the biblical poets, prophets, and evangelists, and their patristic successors. Partly implicit in the argument of the *Enchiridion*, this theory of scriptural poetics would be inscribed both verbally and pictorially on the frontispiece of the 1515 *Lucubrationes*. Now let us turn the page.

Index

As with its ancestor, the *Lucubratiunculae*, we may begin by detailing the contents of the *Lucubrationes*, after the fashion of the (incomplete) list that appears in the book itself (figure 9.3), this time on the verso of the title-leaf. Again, our copy is one in the Bodleian Library in Oxford.

Erasmus, *Lucubrationes*
(Strasbourg: Matthias Schürer, 1515)
[Items numbered in square brackets are not listed on the verso of the title-page]
Additions with respect to *Lucubratiunculae* [= *Ll*] numbered in bold

[1]	sig.2–4	Preface to the Reader by Nikolaus Gerbel	
[2]	sig.4ᵛ	Libellus loquitur ('The book speaks'): 'Nil moror . . .' (figure 9.2)	= *Ll* 1
3	1–119	Enchiridion militis christiani 'Handbook of the Christian Soldier'	= *Ll* 7
[4]	120–3	Letter of Erasmus to John Colet = *Ll* 8	
5	123–75	Disputatio de tedio et pavore Christi 'A Short Debate concerning the Distress, etc.'	= *Ll* 9
6	175–87	Exhortatio ad virtutem . . . 'Oration on the Pursuit of Virtue'	= *Ll* 2
7	187–97	Precatio ad virginis filium Iesum 'Prayer to Jesus, Son of the Virgin'	= *Ll* 3
8	197–208	Paean virgini matri canendus ... 'Paean in Praise of the Virgin Mother'	= *Ll* 4
9	208–18	Obsecratio ad Mariam in rebus adversis 'A Prayer of Supplication to Mary'	= *Ll* 5
10	218–35	Oratio in laudem pueri Iesu 'A Speech in Praise of the Boy Jesus'	
11	235–6	Letter of Erasmus to Beatus Rhenanus *Ep.* 327 Allen; ASD V-2:31–2; CWE 63:6–7	
12	237–85	Enarratio allegorica in primum psalmum: 'Beatus vir [. . .]' ASD V-2:34–80; CWE 63:8–63 'An Allegorical Interpretation of Psalm 1'	

285	Peroration to Beatus Rhenanus ASD V-2:80; CWE 63:63

[pagination ends]

13	Aaiii^v–Aaiiii^v	Carmen de casa natalicia pueri Iesu 'Ode on the Shed Where the Boy Jesus Was Born' = *Ll* 6
14	Aaiiii^v–Bbi^v	Carmen Iesu ad mortales Poem 85 Reedijk; CWE 85: no. 43 'The Expostulation of Jesus with Mankind'
15	Bbii–Bbii^v	Carmina complura de puero Iesu Poems 88, 90, 86, 87 and 89 Reedijk; CWE 85: nos. 44–8 'Several Poems on the Boy Jesus'
16	Bbiii–Bbvi^v	Carmina de angelis 'Poems on the Angels' = *Ll* 10
17	Bbvii	Carmen graecanicum virgini sacrum Mariae Poem 92 Reedijk; CWE 85: no. 51 'An Iambic Poem . . . to the Virgin of Walsingham in Britain'
[18]	Bbvii	Commendatory Poem by Nikolaus Gerbel
[19]	Bbvii^v	Recommendation to the Reader, by N.G.

As can be quickly verified by running an eye down the right-hand margin, all the contents of the earlier *Lucubratiunculae* are reprinted here, but they have been redistributed. In first place, after the prefatory verses spoken by the book itself, comes the *Enchiridion*, which as before gives way to the discussion with Colet on Christ's emotions on the Mount of Olives (2–5 = *Ll* 1, 7–9). Next come the other prose pieces from the *Lucubratiunculae* – the exhortation to virtue and the prayers – in the same sequence in which they appeared previously (6–9 = *Ll* 2–5). The following item, the first Erasmian addition to the present volume (10), is a speech 'On the Boy Jesus' composed for recitation by boys in John Colet's new school at St Paul's in London. At first glance, this piece could seem oddly separated from the poem 'On the Shed Where the Boy Jesus Was Born' (13 = *Ll* 6) and its sequels from the verse collection of the same title (16 = *Ll* 10), and no less oddly parted

¶LVCVBRATIONVM
Index.

¶Enchiridion Militis Chriſtiani. *Carta . prima*

¶Diſputatio de Tedio & pauore Chriſti. 123

Exhortatio ad virtutē, ad Adolphū principē Verienſem. 145

Precatio ad Virginis filium Ieſum. 181.

Pæan Virgini Matri canendus, compoſitus in gratiam do-
minæ Verienſis. 191

Obſecratio ad Mariam in rebus aduerſis. 208

Oratio in laudem pueri Ieſu. 218

꜄ Enarratio allegorica in primū pſalmum Beatus vir. 231.

Carmen de caſa natalicia pueri Ieſu. 286

Carmen Ieſu ad mortales. 288

Carmina complura de puero Ieſu. 291

Carmina de Angelis. 293

Carmen græcanicum Virgini ſacrum Mariæ. 301

Figure 9.3. Verso of the title-page *Lucubrationes* (Strasbourg: Matthias Schürer, 1515). The Bodleian Libraries, University of Oxford, Mar. 864.

from the cluster of poems (here 14–15) that Erasmus had written for Colet's boys and first published a few years earlier in a volume for which the oration 'On the Boy Jesus' formed the title-text.[41] On thematic and pedagogical grounds, one might have expected these *puerilia* or 'Boy's Own' Jesus texts to form a single continuous sequence in the latter part of the volume, instead of being interrupted, as they are here, by a lengthy exegesis of Psalm 1 ('Beatus vir') punningly dedicated to Erasmus's colleague Beatus Rhenanus (11–12). However, the seeming disruption may conceal a more important compositional logic. As the volume now unfolds, the transition from prose pieces numbered 2–10 to the verse items numbered 13–17 is mediated by a prose commentary on a biblical poem, the first piece of formal biblical commentary to appear in print from Erasmus's pen.[42] We also observe that the pagination of the volume ends at the point where prose yields to verse.

We may assume, without being able to prove, that Erasmus himself determined the plan of the collection, which was seen through the press in Strasbourg by Nikolaus Gerbel of Pforzheim. Exactly what the division of labour was, and how it came about that Schürer's edition preempted the one contemplated by Froben and Beatus Rhenanus in Basel, cannot now be known. Although Gerbel takes a lot upon himself in his prefatory and final addresses to the reader (1, 18–19), he nowhere claims to have done more than prepare printer's copy and read proof. Unlike Beatus, he does not give any hint of concern about the title *Lucubrationes*.

Yet in 1515, far more so than in 1503, this literary language of the lamp should have struck the initiated reader as an Erasmian signature. It was not only Erasmus's own writings that were now being touted under such titles. For some time, he had been promising Matthias Schürer an edition of certain works of the Dutch scholar, Rudolph Agricola (1444–85), a teacher whom he consistently represented as the prime mover of northern humanism. The *Lucubrationes* of Agricola, as Erasmus and his collaborators called it, was to remain strangely elusive.[43] In August 1515, however, shortly before the appearance of Erasmus's own *Lucubrationes* in Strasbourg, Froben published a much weightier book with that title in Basel, the *Lucubrationes* or 'complete works' of Seneca. We can be fairly certain that this title, never previously attached to Seneca's writings, was Erasmus's choice.

With Erasmus's Seneca, the term *lucubrationes* comes to stand for the totality of a multigeneric oeuvre, as now critically edited and issued in print. Erasmus uses the same capacious model for his edition of Jerome, published by Froben in 1516, albeit initially without the term *lucubrationes* on the title-page.[44] Seneca and Jerome are the first ancient writers produced by Erasmus in collected editions and the two to which he devoted most care. Appearing in quick succession and in similar formats from Froben's printing-shop, they together established the profile of a learned, eloquent, and morally persuasive author-in-print to which Erasmus was now conforming his own output. This style of self-presentation extended but at the same time overtook the more specialized models that we have traced in connection with the *Lucubratiunculae* of 1503 and the *Lucubrationes* of 1515. The *Lucubrationes* as such seems to have gone out of print after 1520.[45] Henceforth the *Enchiridion* would appear variously with and without the other devotional pieces appended, while some of the latter, such as the poems and prayers, were taken up in more formally homogeneous collections.

The titular disappearance of the original *Lucubrationes* is coordinated with a change in Erasmus's general discourse about his works. Although still capable of referring vaguely to a subset of his writings as 'meae aliquot lucubrationes' in a letter to Thomas More of mid-1517,[46] by the end of the decade he was using the word in a more ambitious sense.

On 1 January 1519, Martens (now at Louvain) published a volume entitled *Lucubrationum Erasmi Roterodami index*, a comprehensive list of Erasmus's works to date. It was reprinted a few months later by Froben in Basel, with additions. In 1523, Erasmus sent Johann von Botzheim a fuller catalogue of his works, together with a plan for a collected edition, in which his works would be divided into nine sections or volumes (ten if he ever completed his commentary on Paul's Epistle to the Romans).[47] Seven years later he addressed an updated version of this 'table of contents' to another of his correspondents, Hector Boece.[48] These lists provide the basis for the organization of Erasmus's works in the posthumous *Opera omnia* (Basel, 1538–40) and later collected editions, down to and including the current Amsterdam edition (1969–).[49] In the plan of his complete works, Erasmus assigned the 'Oration on the Pursuit of Virtue,' originally the first substantial item in the *Lucubratiunculae*, to the fourth section or volume, designed for works of moral instruction. The fifth volume, reserved for works of religious instruction ('pertinentium ad pietatem'), would open with the *Enchiridion* and accommodate the rest of the *Lucubrationes*, apart from the debate with Colet. These items were thus subsumed in a larger series of edifying texts, itself contained within the total body of Erasmus's literary oeuvre. To put things in the simplest and at the same time most pregnantly bibliographical terms: what was formerly indexed on the title-page of 1503 or the verso of the title-page of 1515 had now found its place in the all but definitive 'index lucubrationum Erasmi.'

To conclude: by 1523 at the latest, 'the *Lucubrationes* of Erasmus' had ceased to be a particular collection in one small-format volume, to become instead the ensemble of Erasmus's published work in all genres. We have reached the end of the story we set out to tell. The relationship between the lesser *Lucubrationes* or *Lucubratiunculae* and the greater *Lucubrationes Erasmi*, between a modest work of devotion with its origins near the beginning of an author's publishing career and the totality of his literary-religious output as he was able to articulate it two decades later, would be worth lingering over another day. For the time being, it may be enough to have caught the smoke of Erasmus's lamp as it began to rise.[50]

Abbreviations:

Allen   Erasmus, Desiderius. *Opus epistolarum Desiderii Erasmi*. Ed. P.S. Allen et al.

ASD   Erasmus, Desiderius. Opera omnia Desiderii Erasmi Roterodami.

CWE   Erasmus, Desiderius. *Collected Works of Erasmus*.

Reedijk Erasmus, Desiderius. *The Poems of Desiderius Erasmus*. Ed. Cornelis Reedijk.Latin texts of Erasmus's letters (*Ep.*) are referred to by the number in Allen's edition, followed by line numbers where necessary. Where no reference is given for an English translation, it is my own.

NOTES

1 The main source for this narrative is *Epp.* 325–35. For a fuller biographical introduction, see Augustijn, *Erasmus*, ch. 7. For notices on the associates of Erasmus mentioned below, consult the entries in Bietenholz and Deutscher, *Contemporaries of Erasmus*.

2 *Ep.* 328, 50–3: 'Porro Lucubrationes tuas (hunc enim titulum libellus in frontispicio praefert) evestigio Frobennius excudet, simulac intellexerit non esse tibi integrum ei libello quicquam adiicere demereve.'

3 For the publication history of the *Lucubrationes* see CWE 66:2; ASD V-2:23.

4 Expert epitomes by Augustijn, *Erasmus*, ch. 5; and McConica, *Erasmus* ch. 4. Although there are earlier signs of its favourable reception, including separate editions (i.e., apart from the other contents of the *Lucubrationes*) at Louvain in 1515 and at Leipzig in 1515 and 1516, the great success of the *Enchiridion* dates from its republication by Froben at Basel in 1518 with a new introduction addressed by Erasmus to the Benedictine monk Paul Volz. In this and subsequent Basel printings, the *Enchiridion* is the title-piece in a volume containing the former contents of the *Lucubrationes* and additional matter. See the fascicle for the *Enchiridion* (Gand, 1912) in the *Bibliotheca Erasmiana: Bibliographie des oeuvres d'Érasme*. My thanks to Hans Trapman for guidance on this point.

5 See Pabel, *Conversing with God*, and CWE 69 (in the subseries devoted to 'Spiritualia et Pastoralia').

6 The Greek hexameter is line 63 of the pseudo-Pythagorean *Carmina aurea*, a collection of moral maxims thought to have originated in a Neoplatonic milieu in late antiquity, which enjoyed wide currency in the Renaissance when its contents were freely assimilated to the teaching of the Christian gospels: Heninger, *Touches of Sweet Harmony*, 259–62. Erasmus's taste for Pythagorean morality appears already in the *Adagiorum collectanea* of 1500, where a series of sayings attributed to the Greek sage (nos. 93–107) is copied from Jerome, *Adversus Rufinum* 3.39: CWE 31:31, note on line 24. On the centrality of 'Pythagorean' thinking to the *Adagia* and to Erasmus's general theory of the Christian appropriation of pagan wisdom, see Eden, *Friends Hold All Things in Common*. For the tracing of this and another Greek epigraph in the *Lucubrationes* (see below, note 21), I am indebted to my colleague David Creese.

7 Smith, *Title-Page*; and Gilmont and Vanautgaerden, *Page de titre.*

8 Bodenmann, *L'auteur et son nom de plume*, 17 and 36–40.

9 *Thesaurus Linguae Latinae*, s.v. *lucubratio*; Janson, *Latin Prose Prefaces*, 97–8 and 147–8; Ziolkowski, 'Classical Influences,' 19–20; Ker, 'Nocturnal Writers.'

10 Steppich, *Numine afflatur*, provides collateral data, without touching the subject directly.

11 Hence most of these texts fall within the body of Jerome's 'epistolae sive libri epistolares,' which made up Erasmus's personal province in the 1516 Froben edition of the *Opera Hieronymi*. Not surprisingly, Jerome is less prone to use this kind of mock-deprecatory language when speaking of his

biblical commentaries and translations. For Erasmus's edition of Jerome, see now Clausi, *Ridar voce all' antico Padre*; Pabel, *Herculean Labours*.

12 Aulus Gellius, *Attic Nights*, pref. 14 (I: xxxii); the translation is mine. On the character of Gellius's own lucubrations, see Gunderson, *Nox Philologiae*. See also below, note 33.

13 Beatus Rhenanus = Erasmus, *Ep.* 330, 1 Allen.

14 See, on this point, the luminous summaries of Dresden, 'Présence d'Érasme'; and 'Érasme et les belles-lettres.'

15 Vessey, 'Cities of the Mind,' 54–6, with further references.

16 Carlson, *English Humanist Books*, 82–101; Trapp, *Erasmus, Colet and More*; and Jardine, *Erasmus, Man of Letters*.

17 As shown by Jardine, *Erasmus, Man of Letters*, 55–7 and 83–98, the narrative of a northward *translatio studii*, tirelessly prosecuted by Erasmus and his associates, was to some extent a retrospective fiction.

18 IJsewijn, 'Erasmus ex poeta theologus'; the formula is adapted, with acknowledgment, by Rummel for the subtitle of her study, *Erasmus' 'Annotations' on the New Testament: From Philologist to Theologian*.

19 Erasmus's implicit elision of the precarious distinction between poetry and theology that had been maintained in medieval Latin Christianity (see Minnis in the present volume) is a key aspect of his radicalism both as a theologian and as a literary theorist.

20 CWE 85:xxiv; for the early publication history of the *Enchiridion*, see note 4 above.

21 The Greek tag is an iambic trimeter, the first line of a twenty-four-line acrostic poem by the fourth-century Christian writer Gregory of Nazianzus (Poem 30 of his *Carmina moralia*; PG 37, col. 908), each line of which makes a complete sentence. The acrostic spells the alphabet, from alpha to omega, and the title of the poem explains its purpose as paraenetic or exhortatory. The combination of this verse quotation from a father of the church with another attributable to the Greek sage Pythagoras that appears on the title-page of the *Lucubrationes* (above, note 6) would have provided a further clue – for those initiated in the Greek studies that Erasmus's *Adagiorum chiliades* were designed to encourage – to the moral-aesthetic program of these and other works of his.

22 Leclercq, *Love of Learning*; Kantorowicz, 'Wiederkehr.'

23 At *Ep.* 56, 55 he goes so far as to advise a pupil against nighttime study: 'Nocturnas lucubrationes . . . fugito.'

24 Fuller discussion in Vessey, 'Erasmus' Lucubrations and the Renaissance Life of Texts,' esp. 40–9; and in ' "Nothing if Not Critical," ' *sub fine*, where I propose the monastic humanist bibliographer Johannes Trithemius, author of the first printed catalogue of Christian writers and their works,

the *Liber de scriptoribus ecclesiasticis* (Basel: Amerbach, 1494), as a possible
exemplar for Erasmus's new lucubrology.

25 *Ep.* 119, 1.

26 *Ep.* 123, 1.

27 *Ep.* 124, 4; 44. In the same place, Erasmus refers to his best attempts in
writing as 'elucubratissimis litteris' (line 38). This and the two letters
previously cited first appeared in print in the *Farrago nova epistolarum,* a
collection of Erasmus's letters published by Johann Froben at Basel in 1519.

28 *Ep.* 126, 14.

29 *Ep.* 126, 71–3 (CWE 1:258, lines 83–6): 'Did not that consummate scholar,
Marcus Varro, derive such pleasure from proverbial witticisms that he
made them the sole source of subjects as well as titles for his Satires? Some
of them are still quoted nowadays.' Erasmus continues with Latin poets.
'Passing over Martial and Ausonius, and coming to a different kind
of literature (*ad aliud auctorum genus,* i.e. prose authors): that man of
multifarious learning, the elder Pliny, reveals how enthusiastic he was
about this kind of stylistic ornament; for example, in the celebrated preface
to his [natural] history of the world . . .'

30 Mann Phillips, '*Adages*'; and Eden, *Friends Hold All Things in Common.*

31 Pliny, *Nat. hist.,* pref. 15. Pliny goes on (18) to describe his book as the work
of nights: 'Homines enim sumus et occupati officiis *subsicivisque temporibus*
ista curamus, *id est nocturnis*' (For we, like other mortals, being burdened
with business, attend to these matters in our spare time, meaning night
time). In this context, lucubration is the mark of the literary amateur, one
for whom composition is an activity of leisure (*otium*), albeit leisure now
stolen from sleep. The set phrase *subsiciva tempora* (left-over hours) is
precise. The younger Pliny develops the theme of his uncle's nocturnal
study in his biographical tribute to him (*Ep.* 3.5.9). Cf. Erasmus, *Ep.* 145, 77:
'Plinianas lucubrationes.'

32 Pliny, *Nat. hist.,* pref. 24: 'Nostri grossiores Antiquitatum, Exemplorum
Artiumque, facetissimi Lucubrationum, puto quia Bibaculus erat et
vocabatur' (Among us Romans, the more stolid have chosen titles like
Antiquities, Examples, Arts, while the wittier ones have gone for
Lucubrationes, in that case I think because the author was Bibaculous by
name and nature).

33 Aulus Gellius, *Attic Nights,* pref. 4–10 (I: xxvi–xxx), 14 (I: xxxii). Gellius's
list of Greek titles includes one chosen by Erasmus shortly after 1500:
Encheiridion.

34 Mann Phillips, '*Adages,*' 393–403, provides a tabulation of Erasmus's
sources in successive editions of the *Adagia;* see also 41–61 on the
conception of the *Adagiorum collectanea* of 1500.

35 *Ep.* 126, 113 (CWE 1:260): 'If, again, as Christians we feel more drawn
to an instance taken from a Christian writer, then I should not hesitate
to put forward Jerome to represent this numerous class, for his
scholarship is so profound and so various that, compared with him, the
others appear able neither to swim, as the saying goes, nor to read and
write.'

36 Clausi, *Ridar voce all' antico Padre,* 29–31, underlines the close relationship
between the *Adagia* and Erasmus's project for a 'restoration' (*restitutio*) of
Jerome, as it began to take shape around 1500. He also notes that it was
in this period, while living in Paris, that Erasmus set about the study
of Greek. As suggested by the bilingual lists of book titles in Pliny and
Gellius, and by Jerome's exhibition of his Greek learning (including Greek
proverbs), an essential element of classical Latin *lucubratio* was the study
of Greek literature. Horace had laid down the law in the *Ars poetica*: 'vos
exemplaria Graeca / nocturna versate manu, versate diurna' (lines 268–9).
See further Goldhill, *Who Needs Greek?* ch. 1, on Erasmus. /

37 *Ep.* 138, 40, to James Batt, another programmatic letter from the *Farrago* of
1519, dated 1500 by Allen. *Lucubrationes* would be Erasmus's habitual term
for the 'works' of Jerome in the publicity for his 1516 edition. From 1526
onward Froben used the title *Lucubrationes omnes* for reprintings of the
Erasmian *opera omnia* of this church father. A pair of scissors for trimming
the wick of a lamp is a feature of the iconography of both Jerome and
Erasmus: Jardine, *Erasmus, Man of Letters,* 75.

38 *Ep.* 127, 4.

39 *Ep.* 138, 45, combined with an expression of his desire to master Greek.
Literally translated, the metaphor 'ad umbilicum ducere' means to read to
the end of a book-roll. Literary production – writing and publishing – is
thus figured as literary consumption, an idea readily assimilable to that of
lucubratio as studious composition or production-as-reception.

40 *Ep.* 152, 4. In the very first line of this preface Erasmus evokes the practice
of dedicating one's works (*lucubrationes*) to eminent men, in the hope of
reward for one's exertions (*vigiliarum praemium*). Despite the generality
claimed for the precedent, the obvious classical instance for Erasmus
would still have been the elder Pliny's dedication of his *Natural History* to
the emperor Vespasian.

41 For these and other details of provenance for the poems, see the notes in
CWE 85–6.

42 Analysis of the commentary on Psalm 1 might demonstrate its role in the
revised, handbook-length articulation of the author's theological poetics
represented by the 1515 *Lucubrationes*. A context in his larger oeuvre is

already suggested by the lines from a letter to Guillaume Budé (*Ep.* 421, 112) cited by modern editors of this text: 'In Psalmum Beatus Vir praelusi. Paulum aggrediar. Hieronymus prodibit totus renatus' (I have tried my hand at Psalm 1. I am about to tackle Paul. Jerome will come forth entirely reborn).

43 *Ep.* 311, 25 (addressed to M. Schürer as publisher of the *De copia* in October 1514): 'Lucubrationes Rodolphi Agricolae, hominis vere divini, iamdudum expectamus'; *Ep.* 342, 43 (Nikolaus Gerbel to Erasmus in August 1515, from Schürer's printing-house in Strasbourg); cf. *Epp.* 606, 612, and 676–7. On the edition of Agricola, finally realized by Alaard of Amsterdam in 1539, see Jardine, *Erasmus, Man of Letters*, 89–95. Similarly, in the preface to a 1503 edition of the poems of his and Erasmus's former teacher at Deventer, Alexander Hegius, James Faber refers to the latter's writings as *lucubratiunculas* (=Erasmus, *Ep.* 174, 1 Allen).

44 The phrase 'Hieronymianis lucubrationibus' appears already in the headnote to the index of works appearing in the preliminaries to the *tomus primus*.

45 Allen 1: 29 refers to 'editions by Marten in 1520 and by Froben in August 1535, which I have not been able to examine.' André's Godin's list of editions of the commentary on Psalm 1 in ASD V-2:23 contains no mention of the *Lucubrationes* after a Basel edition of October 1519.

46 *Ep.* 584, 16: another letter first printed in the *Farrago* of October 1519. This text, along with the other, ostensibly earlier ones from the *Farrago* by which I have tried to document the emergence of an Erasmian lucubrology around 1500, would thus have been promulgated in the very period at which the author's use of these terms altered significantly.

47 Edited by Allen vol. 1 and beginning: 'Non pateris . . . quicquam mearum lucubrationum deesse tuae bibliothecae' (You can't bear to have any of my nightworks missing from your library). For the earlier *Lucubrationum* [. . .] *index* see Allen's headnote.

48 *Ep.* 2283. English translations of the catalogues from the letters to Botzheim and Boece appear in CWE 24:694–702, the complete letter to Botzheim at CWE 9:291ff.

49 See the editors' prolegomena in ASD I-1:vii–xviii; CWE 24: i–xviii, and especially Reedijk, *Tandem bona causa triumphat*.

50 My particular interest in the *Lucubrationes* dates from an invitation I received in 2002 to speak about the collection of early editions of Erasmus's works now held by the library of Keio University, Tokyo. An earlier version of the present study appeared in *Codices Keionenses: Essays*

on Western Manuscripts and Early Printed Books in Keio University Library, ed. Takami Matsuda (Tokyo: Keio University Press, 2005), 87–117. I am grateful to Professor Matsuda and his colleagues in the Faculty of Letters at Keio University for their generous hospitality and for allowing me to use previously published material here.

Bibliography

Allen, Judson. B. *The Ethical Poetic of the Later Middle Ages*. Toronto: University of Toronto Press, 1980.

Allen, Mark. 'Penitential Sermons, the Manciple, and the End of *The Canterbury Tales*.' *Studies in the Age of Chaucer* 9 (1987): 77–96.

Allen, Peter L. *The Art of Love: Amatory Fiction from Ovid to the Romance of the Rose*. Philadelphia: University of Pennsylvania Press, 1992.

Althoff, Gerd. 'Zur Bedeutung symbolischer Kommunikation für das Verständnis des Mittelalters.' *Frühmittelalterliche Studien* 31 (1997): 370–89.

Altmann, Barbara K. *The Love Debate Poems of Christine de Pizan*. Gainesville: University Press of Florida, 1998.

– 'Notions of Collaborative Authorship: *Les Cent Ballades* Attributed to Jean le Seneschal.' *Journal of the Early Book Society* 8 (2005): 47–70.

Amtower, Laurel. *Engaging Words: The Culture of Reading in the Later Middle Ages*. New York: Palgrave, 2000.

Andersen, Elizabeth, et al., eds. *Autor und Autorschaft im Mittelalter*. Tübingen: Max Niemeyer Verlag, 1998.

Arch, Jennifer. 'A Case against Chaucer's Authorship of the *Equatorie of the Planetis*.' *Chaucer Review* 40 (2005): 59–79.

Ascoli, Albert Russell. *Dante and the Making of a Modern Author*. Cambridge: Cambridge University Press, 2008.

Astell, Ann. *Chaucer and the Universe of Learning*. Ithaca, NY: Cornell University Press, 1996.

– 'Nietzsche, Chaucer, and the Sacrifice of Art.' *Chaucer Review* 39 (2005): 323–40.

Aston, Margaret. *Lollards and Reformers: Images and Literacy in Late Medieval Religion*. London: Hambledon, 1984.

Augustijn, Cornelis. *Erasmus: His Life, Works, and Influence*. Trans. J.C. Grayson. Toronto: University of Toronto Press, 1991.

Aulus Gellius. *The Attic Nights of Aulus Gellius*. With an English translation by John C. Rolfe. Loeb Classical Library. 3 vols. London: W. Heinemann; New York: Putnams Sons, 1927–8.

Axton, Richard. 'Gower – Chaucer's Heir.' In *Chaucer Traditions: In Honour of Derek Brewer*, ed. Ruth Morse and Barry Windeatt, 21–38. Cambridge: Cambridge University Press, 1990.

Bacon, Roger. *Moralis philosophia*, pars VI, 4. Ed. E. Mazza. Zurich: In Aed. Thesauri Mundi, 1953.

Baker, Donald C., ed. *A Variorum Edition of the Works of Geoffrey Chaucer: The Canterbury Tales*, Part 10: The Manciple's Tale. Norman: University of Oklahoma Press, 1984.

Baker, Howard. 'A Portrait of Aesop.' *Sewanee Review* 77 (1969): 557–90.

Barchiesi, Alessandro. *The Poet and the Prince: Ovid and Augustan Discourse*. Berkeley: University of California Press, 1997.

Barron, W.R.J., ed. *Robert Henryson: Selected Poems*. Manchester: Fyfield, 1981.

Bawcutt, Priscilla. 'Henryson's "Poeit of the Auld Fassoun."' *Review of English Studies* ns 32 (1981): 429–34.

Bawcutt, Priscilla, and Felicity Riddy, eds. *Selected Poems of Henryson and Dunbar*. Scottish Classics Series 16. Edinburgh: Scottish Academic Press, 1992.

Bein, Thomas. '*Mit fremden Pegasusen pflügen.*' *Untersuchungen zu Authentizitätsproblemen in mittelhochdeutscher Lyrik und Lyrikphilologie*. Philologische Studien und Quellen 150. Berlin: E. Schmidt, 1998.

Bénédictins du Bouveret. *Colophons de manuscripts occidentaux des origines au XVIe siècle*. 6 vols. Freibourg: Éditions universitaires, 1965–82.

Bennett, Michael J. 'The Court of Richard II and the Promotion of Literature.' In *Chaucer's England: Literature in Historical Context*, ed. Barbara A. Hanawalt, 3–20. Minneapolis: University of Minnesota Press, 1992.

Benson, Larry D., ed. *The Canterbury Tales: Complete*. Boston: Houghton Mifflin, 2000.

Benson, Larry D. 'The Order of *The Canterbury Tales*.' *Studies in the Age of Chaucer* 3 (1981): 77–120.

– ed. *The Riverside Chaucer*. Boston: Houghton Mifflin, 1987.

Bergson, Henri. *Le Rire: Essai sur la signification du comique*, 90th ed. Paris: PUF, 1950.

Biemans, J.A.A.M. 'Het Gronings-Zutphense Maerlant-handschrift: Over de noodzakelijkheid der handschriftenkunde.' *Queeste: Journal of Medieval Literature in the Low Countries* 3 (1996): 197–219.

Bietenholz, Peter G., and Thomas B. Deutscher, eds. *Contemporaries of Erasmus: A Biographical Register of the Renaissance and Reformation*. 3 vols. Toronto: University of Toronto Press, 1985–7.

Bischoff, B. *Die südostdeutschen Schreibschulen und Bibliotheken in der Karolinger-zeit: Teil II Die vorwiegend österreichischen Diözesen.* Wiesbaden: Harrassowitz, 1980.

Blanchard, Joël. 'Compilation and Legitimation in the Fifteenth Century: *Le Livre de la Cité des Dames'* (trans. Earl Jeffrey Richards). In *Reinterpreting Christine de Pizan*, ed. Earl Jeffrey Richards et al., 228–49. Athens: University of Georgia Press, 1992.

Blake, N.F. 'Geoffrey Chaucer and the Manuscripts of *The Canterbury Tales*.' *Journal of the Early Book Society* 1 (1997): 95–122.

– *The Textual Tradition of the Canterbury Tales.* London: Arnold, 1985.

Block, Elizabeth. 'Poetics in Exile: An Analysis of *Epistulae ex Ponto* 3.9.' *Classical Antiquity* 1 (1982): 18–27.

Bloomfield, Josephine. 'Rediscovering Henryson: An Exploration of the Obstacles in Canon Reformation.' *Bestia* 1 (1989): 42–52.

Bodenmann, Reinhard. *L'auteur et son nom de plume: Autopsie du'un choix: Le cas des des pays francophones et germanophones du XVIe siècle.* Brussels: Maison d'Érasme, 2006.

Boffey, J., and J.J. Thompson. 'Anthologies and Miscellanies: Production and Choice of Texts.' In *Book Production and Publishing in Britain, 1375–1475*, ed. J. Griffiths and D. Pearsall, 279–315. Cambridge: Cambridge University Press, 1989.

Børch, Marianne. 'Chaucer's Poetics and *The Manciple's Tale*.' *Studies in the Age of Chaucer* 25 (2003): 287–97.

Bose, Mishtooni. 'The Annunciation to Pecock: Clerical *Imitatio* in the Fifteenth Century.' *Notes and Queries* 47 (2000): 172–6.

– 'Reginald Pecock's Vernacular Voice.' In *Lollards and Their Influence in Late Medieval England*, ed. Fiona Somerset et al., 217–36. Woodbridge, Suffolk: Boydell, 2003.

Bowen, Barbara C. 'Renaissance Collections of *Facetiae*, 1344–1490: A New Listing.' *Renaissance Quarterly* 39 (1986): 1–15.

– 'Renaissance Collections of *Facetiae*, 1499–1528: A New Listing.' *Renaissance Quarterly* 39 (1986): 263–75.

Bowers, John M., ed. *The 'Canterbury Tales': Fifteenth-Century Continuations and Additions.* Kalamazoo, MI.: Medieval Institute, 1992.

– *Chaucer and Langland: The Antagonistic Tradition.* Notre Dame, IN.: University of Notre Dame Press, 2007.

Bracciolini, Poggio. *Facezie.* Ed. Stefano Pittaluga. I grandi libri Garzanti 570. Milan: Garzanti, 1995.

Bradburn, Edward W. ' "Prolog" and "Moralitie": Authorial Apostrophe in Robert Henryson's *Fables*.' In *Older Scots Literature*, ed. Sally Mapston, 126–38. Edinburgh: John Donald, 2005.

Brewer, Derek. *English Gothic Literature*. London: Macmillan, 1983.

Brown-Grant, Rosalind. *Christine de Pizan and the Moral Defence of Women: Reading Beyond Gender*. Cambridge: Cambridge University Press, 1999.

Brownlee, Kevin. 'Discourses of the Self: Christine de Pizan and the Rose.' *Romanic Review* 79 (1988): 199–221.

– *Poetic Identity in Guillaume de Machaut*. Madison: University of Wisconsin Press, 1984.

Bryan, Elizabeth. *Collaborative Meaning in Medieval Scribal Culture: The Otho La3amon*. Ann Arbor: University of Michigan Press, 1999.

Burrow, John. 'The Poet and the Book.' In *Genres, Themes, and Images in English Literature from the Fourteenth to the Fifteenth Century*, ed. Piero Boitani and Anni Torti, 230–45. Tübinger Beiträge zur Anglistik 11. Tübingen: Gunter Narr, 1988.

– *Ricardian Poetry*. New Haven, CT: Yale University Press, 1971.

Butterfield, Ardis. 'Articulating the Author: Gower and the French Vernacular Codex.' *Yearbook of English Studies* 33 (2003): 80–96.

– '*Mise-en-page* in the *Troilus* Manuscripts: Chaucer and French Manuscript Culture.' In *Reading from the Margins*, ed. Seth Lerer, 49–80. San Marino, CA: Huntington Library, 1996.

Caie, Graham D. 'The Significance of the Early Chaucer Manuscript Glosses (with Special Reference to the *Wife of Bath's Prologue*).' *Chaucer Review* 10 (1976): 350–60.

Calabrese, Michael A. *Chaucer's Ovidian Arts of Love*. Gainesville: University Press of Florida, 1994.

Campbell, Kirsty. *The Call to Read: Reginald Pecock's Books and Textual Communities*. Notre Dame, IN: Notre Dame University Press, 2010.

Careri, M., et al. *Album de manuscrits français du XIIIᵉ siècle: Mise en page et mise en texte*. Rome: Viella, 2001.

Carlson, David R. *English Humanist Books: Writers and Patrons, Manuscripts and Print, 1475–1525*. Toronto: University of Toronto Press, 1993.

Cerquiglini-Toulet, Jacqueline. 'Christine de Pizan and the Book: Programs and Modes of Reading, Strategies for Publication.' *Journal of the Early Book Society* 4 (2001): 112–26.

– *The Color of Melancholy*. Trans. Lydia G. Cochrane. Baltimore, MD and London: Johns Hopkins University Press, 1997.

Chaucer Concordance at eChaucer. http://www.umm.maine.edu/faculty/necastro/chaucer/concordance. Accessed 10 June 2008.

Chenu, M.-D. *La Théologie comme science au XIIIe siècle*, 3rd ed. Bibliothèque Thomiste 33. Paris: Vrin, 1969.

Christine de Pizan. *Le chemin de longue etude*. Trans. and ed. Andrea Tarnowski. Paris: Librairie générale française, 2000.

– *Epistre Othea*. Ed. Gabriella Parussa. Geneva: Droz, 1999.
– *Le Livre de l'advision Cristine*. Ed. Christine Reno and Liliane Dulac. Paris: Honoré Champion, 2001.
– 'The *Livre de la cité des dames* of Christine de Pisan: A Critical Edition.' Ed. Maureen Curnow. 3 vols. PhD diss., Vanderbilt University, 1975.
– *Le Livre des fais et bonnes meurs du sage roy Charles V*. Ed. Suzanne Solente. 2 vols. Paris: Champion, 1936–40.
– *Le Livre des faits et bonnes moeurs du roi Charles V le Sage*. Trans. Eric Hicks and Thérèse Moreau. Paris: Stock, 1997.
– *Le Livre des trois vertus*. Ed. Charity Cannon Willard and Eric Hicks. Paris: Honoré Champion, 1989.
– *Le Livre du duc des vrais amans*. Ed. Thelma S. Fenster. Binghamton, NY: Medieval and Renaissance Texts and Studies, 1995.
– *Oeuvres poétiques de Christine de Pisan*. Ed. Maurice Roy. Paris: Firmin Didot, 1886–96.
Christine de Pizan: The Making of the Queen's Manuscript (London, British Library, Harley 4431). www.pizan.lib.ed.ac.uk. Accessed 15 June 2010.
Cicero, Marcus Tullius. *De oratore*. Ed. and trans. E.W. Sutton and H. Rackham. Loeb Classical Library. Cambridge, MA and London: Harvard University Press, 1948, repr. 1959.
Claassen, Jo-Marie. *Displaced Persons: The Literature of Exile from Cicero to Boethius*. Madison: University of Wisconsin Press, 1999.
Clark, James G. 'Thomas Walsingham Reconsidered: Books and Learning at Late-Medieval St. Albans.' *Speculum* 77 (2002): 854–82.
Clausi, Benedetto. *Ridar voce all' antico Padre: L'edizione erasmiana delle 'Lettere' di Gerolamo*. Soveria Mannelli: Rubbettino, 2000.
Coffman, George R. 'John Gower, Mentor for Royalty: Richard II.' *PMLA* 69 (1954): 953–64.
Coleman, Joyce. ' "A Bok for King Richardes Sake": Royal Patronage, the *Confessio*, and the *Legend of Good Women*.' In *On John Gower: Essays at the Millenium*, ed. R.F. Yeager, 104–23. Kalamazoo, MI: Medieval Institute, 2007.
Coletti, Theresa. ' "Paths of Long Study": Reading Chaucer and Christine de Pizan in Tandem.' *Studies in the Age of Chaucer* 28 (2006): 1–40.
Cooper, Helen. 'Chaucer and Ovid: A Question of Authority.' In *Ovid Renewed*, ed. Charles Martindale, 71–81. Cambridge: Cambridge University Press, 1988.
Copeland, Rita. *Rhetoric, Hermeneutics, and Translation in the Middle Ages: Academic Traditions and Vernacular Texts*. Cambridge: Cambridge University Press, 1991.
Cox, Catherine S. *Gender and Language in Chaucer*. Gainesville: University Press of Florida, 1997.

Coxon, Sebastian. *The Presentation of Authorship in Medieval German Narrative Literature 1220–1290*. Oxford: Oxford University Press, 2001.

Crane, Susan. 'Duxworth Redux: The Paris Manuscript of the *Canterbury Tales*.' In *Manuscript, Narrative, Lexicon: Essays on Literary and Cultural Transmission in Honor of Whitney F. Bolton*, ed. Robert Boenig and Kathleen Davis, 17–44. Lewisburg, PA: Bucknell University Press, 2000.

Crassons, Kate. 'Performance Anxiety and Watson's Vernacular Theology.' *English Language Notes* 44 (2006): 95–102.

Croenen, Godfried, Kristen M. Figg, and Andrew Taylor. 'Authorship, Patronage, and Literary Gifts: The Books Froissart Brought to England in 1395.' *Journal of the Early Book Society* 11 (2008): 1–42.

Curschmann, Michael. 'Marcolf or Aesop? The Question of Identity in Visio-Verbal Contexts.' *Studies in Iconography* 21 (2000): 1–45.

Daly, Lloyd W., trans. *The Aesop Romance*. In *Anthology of Ancient Greek Popular Literature*, ed. William Hansen, 106–62. Bloomington and Indianapolis: Indiana University Press, 1998.

De Hamel, Christopher. *Scribes and Illuminators*. Toronto: University of Toronto Press, 1992.

De Vreese, W. *De handschriften van Jan van Ruusbroec's werken*. 2 vols. Ghent: Siffer, 1900–2.

Dean, James. 'Chaucer's Repentance: A Likely Story.' *Chaucer Review* 24 (1989): 64–76.

– 'Dismantling the Canterbury Book.' *PMLA* 100 (1985): 746–62.

– 'The Ending of the *Canterbury Tales*, 1952–1976.' *Texas Studies in Literature and Language* 21 (1979): 17–33.

Derolez, A. *Corpus Catalogorum Belgii. The Medieval Booklists of the Southern Low Countries I: Province of West Flanders*. 2nd ed. Brussels: Koninklijke Vlaamse Academie voor Wetenschappen, Letteren en Schone Kunsten van België, 1997.

Deschamps, Eustache. *Oeuvres complètes d'Eustache Deschamps*. Ed. G. Raynaud et le marquis de Queux de Saint-Hilaire. 11 vols. SATF. Paris: Firmin Didot, 1878–1903.

Deschamps, J. *Middelnederlandse handschriften uit Europese en Amerikaanse bibliotheken*. 2nd ed. Leiden: Brill, 1972.

Doyle, A.I. 'Survey of the Origins and Circulation of Theological Writings in English in the 14th, 15th, and Early 16th Centuries with Special Consideration of the Part of the Clergy Therein.' PhD diss. University of Cambridge, 1953.

Doyle, A.I., and M.B. Parkes. 'The Production of Copies of the *Canterbury Tales* and the *Confessio Amantis* in the Early Fifteenth Century.' In *Medieval Scribes,*

Manuscripts and Libraries: Essays Presented to N.R. Ker, ed. M.B. Parkes and Andrew G. Watson, 168–210. London: Scolar Press, 1978.

Douai-Rheims Bible. http://www-rohan.sdsu.edu/%7Eamtower/matthew. htm. Accessed 10 June 2008.

Dresden, Sem. 'Érasme et les belles-lettres.' In *Colloque érasmien de Liège*, ed. Jean-Pierre Massaut, 3–16. Paris: Les Belles Lettres, 1987.

– 'Présence d'Érasme.'In *Actes du congrès Érasme, Rotterdam 27–29 octobre 1969*, ed. Cornelis Reedijk, 1–13. Amsterdam: North-Holland Publishing Company, 1971.

Eberle, Patricia J. 'Richard II and the Literary Arts.' In *Richard II: The Art of Kingship*, ed. Anthony Goodman and James Gillespie, 231–53. Oxford: Clarendon Press, 1999.

Eberly, Susan S. 'A Thorn among the Lilies: The Hawthorn in Medieval Love Allegory.' *Folklore* 100.1 (1989): 41–52.

Ebin, L. 'Henryson's "Fenyeit Fabils": A Defence of Poetry.'In *Actes du 2e colloque de langue et de littérature ecossaises (Moyen Age et Renaissance)*, ed. Jean-Jacques Blanchot and Claude Graf, 222–38. Strasburg: Institut d'études anglaises de Strasbourg, 1979.

Echard, Siân. 'Last Words: Latin at the End of the *Confessio Amantis*.' In *Interstices: Studies in Middle English and Anglo-Latin Texts in Honour of A.G. Rigg*, ed. Richard Firth Green and Linne Mooney, 99–121. Toronto: University of Toronto Press, 2004.

– 'Map's Metafiction: Author, Narrator and Reader in *De nugis curialium*.' *Exemplaria* 8 (1996): 287–314.

Eden, Kathy. *Friends Hold All Things in Common: Tradition, Intellectual Property, and the Adages of Erasmus*. New Haven, CT: Yale University Press, 2001.

Elliott, A.G., trans. '*Accessus ad auctores*: Twelfth-Century Introductions to Ovid.' *Allegorica* 5 (1980): 6–48.

Elliott, Charles, ed. *Robert Henryson: Poems*. 2nd ed. Oxford: Clarendon Press, 1974.

Erasmus, Desiderius. *Collected Works of Erasmus*. Toronto: University of Toronto Press, 1974–.

– *Opera omnia Desiderii Erasmi Roterodami*. Amsterdam: North-Holland Publishing Company, 1969–.

– *Opus epistolarum Desiderii Erasmi*. Ed. P.S. Allen et al. 12 vols. Oxford: Clarendon Press, 1906–58.

– *The Poems of Desiderius Erasmus*. Ed. Cornelis Reedijk. Leiden: Brill, 1956.

– *Precatio ad virginis filium Iesum etc.* Ed. John W. O'Malley and Louis A. Perraud. *Collected Works of Erasmus*, vol. 69; Spiritualia and pastoralia, vol. 4. Toronto: University of Toronto Press, 1999.

Evans, Harry B. *Carmina Publica: Ovid's Books from Exile*. Lincoln: University of Nebraska Press, 1983.

Fletcher, Christopher. *Richard II: Manhood, Youth, and Politics 1377–99*. Oxford: Oxford University Press, 2008.

Fowler, Alastair. *Triumphal Forms: Structural Patterns in Elizabethan Poetry*. Cambridge: Cambridge University Press, 1970.

Fox, Denton. 'Henryson and Caxton.' *Journal of English and Germanic Philology* 67 (1968): 586–93.

– 'The Scottish Chaucerians.' In *Chaucer and Chaucerians: Critical Studies in Middle English Literature*, ed. D.S. Brewer, 164–200. London: Nelson, 1966.

– ed. *The Poems of Robert Henryson*. Oxford: Clarendon Press, 1981.

Foxe, John. *The Acts and Monuments of John Foxe; With a Life of the Martyrologist, and Vindication of the Work, by George Townsend*. 8 vols. Repr. New York: AMS Press, 1965.

Fradenburg, Louise. 'The Manciple's Servant Tongue: Politics and Poetry in *The Canterbury Tales*.' *ELH* 52 (1985): 85–118.

Fratus, David Joseph. 'Robert Henryson's Moral Fables: Tradition, Text, and Translation.' PhD diss., University of Iowa, 1971.

Froissart, Jean. *Chroniques, Livre III, Le manuscrit Saint-Vincent de Besançon, Bibliothèque municipale, ms. 865*. Ed. Peter F. Ainsworth. Geneva; Droz, 2007–.

Fulk, R.D. 'Reinterpreting the *Manciple's Tale*.' *Journal of English and Germanic Philology* 78 (1979): 485–93.

Fumo, Jamie C. 'The God of Love and Love of God: Palinodic Exchange in the Prologue of the *Legend of Good Women* and the "Retraction."' In *The Legend of Good Women: Context and Reception*, ed. Carolyn P. Collette, 157–75. Cambridge: D.S. Brewer, 2006.

– *The Legacy of Apollo: Antiquity, Authority, and Chaucerian Poetics*. Toronto: University of Toronto Press, 2010.

– 'Thinking Upon the Crow: The *Manciple's Tale* and Ovidian Mythography.' *Chaucer Review* 38 (2004): 356–75.

Furrow, Melissa. 'Chaucer, Writing, and Penitence.' *Forum for Modern Language Studies* 33 (1997): 245–57.

Fyler, John. *Chaucer and Ovid*. New Haven, CT: Yale University Press, 1979.

– 'Ovid and Chaucer.' In *Ovid: The Classical Heritage*, ed. William S. Anderson, 143–65. New York: Garland, 1995.

Gameson, R. *The Manuscripts of Early Norman England (1066–1130)*. Oxford: Oxford University Press, 1999.

Georgianna, Linda. 'Vernacular Theologies.' *English Language Notes* 44 (2006): 87–94.

Gerson, Jean. *La Montaigne de meditation*. In vol. 7 of *Oeuvres completes*, ed. Mgr. Glorieux, 10 vols. Paris: Desclele & Cie, 1960–73.

Gillespie, Alexandra. *Print Culture and the Medieval Author: Chaucer, Lydgate, and Their Books 1473–1557*. Oxford: Oxford University Press, 2006.

– 'Reading Chaucer's Words to Adam.' *Chaucer Review* 42 (2008): 269–83.

Gillespie, Vincent. 'The Study of Classical Authors: From the Twelfth Century to *c*. 1450.' In *The Cambridge History of Literary Criticism*, ed. Minnis and Johnson, 145–235.

Gilmont, Jean-François, and Alexandre Vanautgaerden, eds. *La page de titre à la Renaissance: Treize études suivies de cinquante-quatre pages de titre commentées et d'un lexique des termes relatifs à la page de titre*. Turnhout: Brepols, 2008.

Ginsberg, Warren. *Chaucer's Italian Tradition*. Ann Arbor: University of Michigan Press, 2002.

Glaube und Wissen: Die Kölner Dombibliothek. Munich: Hirmer Verlag, 1998.

Goldhill, Simon. *Who Needs Greek? Contests in the Cultural History of Hellenism*. Cambridge: Cambridge University Press, 2002.

Gower, John. *Carmen super multiplici viciorum pestilencia*. In *John Gower: The Minor Latin Works*, ed. and trans. R.F. Yeager, 16–17. Kalamazoo, MI: Medieval Institute, 2005.

– *Confessio Amantis* (selections). Ed. Russell Peck. Repr. Toronto: University of Toronto Press, 1980.

– *Confessio Amantis*. Ed. Russell A. Peck. 3 vols. Kalamazoo, MI: Medieval Institute, 2000.

– *O deus immense*. In *John Gower: The Minor Latin Works*, ed. and trans. R.F. Yeager, 34–9. Kalamazoo, MI: Medieval Institute, 2005.

Gray, Douglas. *Robert Henryson*. Leiden: Brill, 1979.

– ed. *Selected Poems of Robert Henryson and William Dunbar*. London and New York: Penguin, 1998.

Green, Peter. 'Carmen et Error: πρόφασις and αἰτία in the Matter of Ovid's Exile.' *Classical Antiquity* 1 (1982): 202–20.

Green, Richard Firth. *Poets and Princepleasers: Literature and the English Court in the Late Middle Ages*. Toronto: University of Toronto Press, 1980.

Greene, Robert. *Greenes Vision*. In *The Life and Complete Works in Prose and Verse of Robert Greene*, ed. Alexander B. Grosart, 15 vols, 12:189–281. London: Huth Library, 1881–6; repr. New York, 1964.

Greene, Virginie, ed. *The Medieval Author in Medieval French Literature*. New York and Basingstoke: Palgrave Macmillan, 2006.

Greene, Virginie. 'What Happened to Medievalists after the Death of the Author?' In *The Medieval Author in Medieval French Literature*, ed. Virginie Greene, 205–27. New York and Basingstoke: Palgrave Macmillan, 2006.

Griffiths, Jane. *John Skelton and Poetic Authority: Establishing the Liberty to Speak.* Oxford: Oxford University Press, 2006.

Grudin, Michaela Paasche. *Chaucer and the Politics of Discourse.* Columbia: University of South Carolina Press, 1996.

Gumbert, J.P. 'Codicological Units: Towards a Terminology for the Stratigraphy of the Non-Homogeneous Codex.' *Segno e Testo: International Journal of Manuscripts and Text Transmission* 2 (2004): 17–42.

– 'One Book with Many Texts.' In *Codices Miscellanearum: Brussels Van Hulthem Colloquium, 1999,* ed. R. Jansen-Sieben and H. van Dijk, 27–36. Brussels: Archives et bibliothèques de Belgique, 1999.

– 'The Speed of Scribes.' In *Scribi e colofoni: Le Sottoscrizioni di Copisti dalle origini all'Avvento della stampa, atti del seminario di Erice X Colloquio del Comite International de Paleographie Latine (23–28 ottobre 1993),* ed. E. Condello and G. De Gregorio, 57–69. Spoleto: Centro Italiano di Studi Sull'alto Medioevo, 1995.

Gunderson, Erik. *Nox Philologiae: Aulus Gellius and the Fantasy of the Roman Library.* Madison: University of Wisconsin Press, 2009.

Hackett, Jeremiah. 'Roger Bacon on Rhetoric and Poetics.' In *Roger Bacon and the Sciences,* ed. Jeremiah Hackett, 133–49. Leiden and New York: Brill, 1997.

Hanna, Ralph, 'Booklets in Medieval Manuscripts: Further Considerations.' In *Pursuing History: Middle English Manuscripts and Their Texts,* 21–34. Stanford, CA: Stanford University Press, 1996.

– '(The) Editing (of) the Ellesmere Text.' In *The Ellesmere Chaucer: Essays in Interpretation,* ed. Martin Stevens and Daniel Woodward, 225–44. San Marino, CA: Huntington Library; and Tokyo: Yushodo, 1995.

– 'The Hengwrt Manuscript and the Canon of the *Canterbury Tales.' English Manuscript Studies 1100–1700* 1 (1989): 69–89.

Harbert, Bruce. 'Ovid and John Gower.' In *Ovid Renewed,* ed. Charles Martindale, 83–97. Cambridge: Cambridge University Press, 1988.

Hardison, O.B., Jr. *The Enduring Monument: A Study of the Idea of Praise in Renaissance Literary Theory and Practice.* Westport, CT: Greenwood Press, 1962.

– 'Towards a History of Medieval Literary Criticism.' *Mediaevalia et humanistica* 7 (1976): 1–12.

Hardman, Phillipa. 'Chaucer's Articulation of the Narrative in *Troilus*: The Manuscript Evidence.' *Chaucer Review* 30 (1995): 111–33.

Harwood, Britton J. 'Language and the Real: Chaucer's Manciple.' *Chaucer Review* 6 (1972): 268–79.

Hazelton, Richard. 'The *Manciple's Tale*: Parody and Critique.' *Journal of English and Germanic Philology* 62 (1963): 1–31.

Helgerson, Richard. *Self-Crowned Laureates: Spenser, Jonson, Milton, and the Literary System*. Berkeley, Los Angeles, and London: University of California Press, 1983.

Heninger, S.K., Jr. *Touches of Sweet Harmony: Pythgorean Cosmology and Renaissance Poetics*. San Marino, CA: Huntington Library, 1974.

Henryson, Robert. *The Moral Fables of Aesop*. Ed. and trans. George D. Gopen. Notre Dame, IN: University of Notre Dame Press, 1987.

– *The Testament of Cresseid & Seven Fables*. Trans. Seamus Heaney. London: Faber, 2009.

Heriot, Dianne Margaret. '*Prohemia poetarum Fratris Thome de Walsingham*: An Edition with Introduction, Testimonia and Explanatory Essays.' PhD diss., Monash University, Australia, 1992.

Hermans, J.M.M., and A. Lem. *Middeleeuwse handschriften en oude drukken in de collectie Emmanuelshuizen te Zwolle*. Zwolle: Stichting Emmanuelshuizen, 1989.

Hexter, Ralph J. 'The Poetry of Ovid's Exile.' In *Ovid: The Classical Heritage*, ed. William S. Anderson, 41–56. New York: Garland, 1995.

Hicks, Eric, ed. and trans. *Le Débat sur le Roman de la Rose*. Geneva: Slatkine Reprints, 1996.

Higgins, Iain Macleod. *Writing East: The Travels of Sir John Mandeville*. Philadelphia: University of Pennsylvania Press, 1997.

Hill, John M. *Chaucerian Belief: The Poetics of Reverence and Delight*. New Haven, CT: Yale University Press, 1991.

Hindman, Sandra. *Christine de Pizan's 'Epistre Othéa': Painting and Politics at the Court of Charles VI*. Toronto: Pontifical Institute of Mediaeval Studies, 1986.

– 'With Ink and Mortar: Christine de Pizan's *Cité des Dames* (An Art Essay).' *Feminist Studies* 10 (1984): 457–83.

Hines, John. ' "For sorwe of which he brak his mynstralcye": The Demise of the "Sweete Noyse" of Verse in the *Canterbury Tales*.' *Studies in the Age of Chaucer* 25 (2003): 299–308.

Hinton, James. 'Walter Map's *De nugis curialium*: Its Plan and Composition.' *PMLA* 32 (1917): 81–132.

Hobbins, Daniel. *Authorship and Publicity before Print: Jean Gerson and the Transformation of Late Medieval Learning*. Philadelphia: University of Pennsylvania Press, 2009.

Hoffman, Richard L. *Ovid and the Canterbury Tales*. Philadelphia: University of Pennsylvania Press, 1966.

Holmes, Olivia. *Assembling the Lyric Self: Authorship from Troubadour Song to Italian Poetry Book*. Minneapolis and London: University of Minnesota Press, 2000.

Holzberg, Niklas. 'Fable: Aesop. Life of Aesop,' section C of 'Novel-Like Works of Extended Prose Fiction II.' In *The Novel in the Ancient World*, ed. Gareth Schmeling, 633–9. New York: Brill, 1996.

Howard, Donald R. *The Idea of the Canterbury Tales*. Berkeley: University of California Press, 1976.

Hudson, Anne. *The Premature Reformation: Wycliffite Texts and Lollard History*. Oxford: Clarendon Press, 1988.

Hugh of St Victor. *The Didascalicon of Hugh of St. Victor: A Medieval Guide to the Arts*. Trans. and introduction by Jerome Taylor. New York and London: Columbia University Press, 1961; repr. 1991.

– *Hugonis de Sancto Victore Didascalicon de studio legendi: A Critical Text*. Ed. Charles Henry Buttimer. Studies in Medieval and Renaissance Latin 10. Washington, DC: Catholic University of America Press, 1939.

Hunt, R.W. 'The Introduction to the *Artes* in the Twelfth Century.' In *Studia mediaevalia in honorem admodum Reverendi Patris Raymundi Josephi Martin, Ordinis Praedicatorum s. theologiae magistri LXXUM natalem diem agentis*, ed. A. Mansion et al., 85–112. Bruges: De Tempel, 1948.

Huot, S. *From Song to Book: The Poetics of Writing in Old French Lyric and Lyrical Narrative Poetry*. Ithaca, NY and London: Cornell University Press, 1987.

Huygens, R.B.C., ed. *Accessus ad auctores: Bernard d'Utrecht; Conrad d'Hirsau, Dialogus super auctores*. Leiden: Brill, 1970.

IJsewijn, Josef. 'Erasmus ex poeta theologus sive de litterarum instauratarum apud Hollandos incunabulis.' In *Scrinium Erasmianum*, ed. J. Coppens, 1:375–89. Leiden: Brill, 1969.

Illich, Ivan. *In the Vineyard of the Text: A Commentary to Hugh's Didascalicon*. Chicago: University of Chicago Press, 1993.

Jaeger, Stephen C. *The Origins of Courtliness: Civilizing Trends and the Formation of Courtly Ideals 939–1210*. Philadelphia: University of Pennsylvania Press, 1985.

Janson, Tore. *Latin Prose Prefaces: Studies in Literary Conventions*. Studia Latina Stockholmiensia 13. Stockholm: Almqvist & Wiksell, 1964.

– *Latin Prose Prefaces: Studies in Literary Conventions*. Studia Latina Stockholmiensia 13. Stockholm: Almqvist & Wiksell, 1964.

Jardine, Lisa. *Erasmus, Man of Letters: The Construction of Charisma in Print*. Princeton, NJ: Princeton University Press, 1993.

Jeffrey, David L. '*The Manciple's Tale*: The Form of Conclusion.' *English Studies in Canada* 2 (1976): 249–61.

Justice, Steven, and Kathryn Kerby-Fulton, eds. *Written Work: Langland, Labor, and Authorship*. Philadelphia: University of Pennsylvania Press, 1997.

Kantorowicz, Ernst H. 'Die Wiederkehr gelehrter Anachorese im Mittelalter.' In *Selected Studies*, 339–51. Locust Valley, NY: J.J. Augustin, 1965.

Keach, William. 'Ovid and "Ovidian" Poetry.' In *Ovid: The Classical Heritage*, ed. William S. Anderson, 179–217. New York: Garland, 1995.

Keiser, G.R. 'MS Rawlinson A.393: Another Findern Manuscript.' *Transactions of the Cambridge Bibliographical Society* 7 (1980): 445–8.

Keith, A.M. *The Play of Fictions: Studies in Ovid's Metamorphoses Book 2*. Ann Arbor: University of Michigan Press, 1992.

Kelly, Henry Ansgar. *Chaucerian Tragedy*. Cambridge: D.S. Brewer, 1997.

Kelly, Stephen, and Ryan Perry. ' "Hospitable Reading" and Clerical Reform in Fifteenth-Century London.' In *Geographies of Orthodoxy: Mapping English Pseudo-Bonaventuran Lives of Christ, 1350–1550*. http://www.qub.ac.uk/geographies-of-orthodoxy/discuss/2009/04/24/ hospitable-reading-and-clerical-reform-in-fifteenth-century-london/. Accessed April 24, 2009.

Kendrick, Laura. *Animating the Letter: The Figurative Embodiment of Writing from Late Antiquity to the Renaissance*. Columbus: Ohio State University Press, 1999.

– 'The *Canterbury Tales* in the Context of Contemporary Vernacular Translations and Compilations.' In *The Ellesmere Chaucer: Essays in Interpretation*, ed. Martin Stevens and Daniel Woodward, 281–99. San Marino, CA: Huntington Library; and Tokyo: Yushodo, 1995.

Kensak, Michael. 'Apollo *exterminans*: The God of Poetry in Chaucer's *Manciple's Tale*.' *Studies in Philology* 98 (2001): 143–57.

Ker, J. 'Nocturnal Writers in Imperial Rome: The Culture of *Lucubratio*.' *Classical Philology* 99 (2004): 209–42.

Kerby-Fulton, Kathryn. *Books under Suspicion: Censorship and Tolerance of Revelatory Writing in Late Medieval England*. Notre Dame, IN: University of Notre Dame Press, 2006.

Kienhorst, H., and M.M. Kors. 'Codicological Evidence for a Chronological Rearrangement of the Works of Jan van Ruusbroec.' *Quaerendo: A Quarterly Journal from the Low Countries Devoted to Manuscripts and Printed Books* 33 (2003): 135–74.

Kindermann, Udo. *Satyra: Die Theorie der Satire im Mittellateinischen Vorstudie zu einer Gattungsgeschichte*. Erlanger Beiträge zur Sprach und Kunstwissenschaft 58. Nürnberg: Verlag Hans Carl, 1978.

Kindrick, Robert L., ed. *The Poems of Robert Henryson*. TEAMS Middle English Texts Series. Kalamazoo, MI: Medieval Institute, 1997.

Klopsch, Paul. *Einführung in die Dichtungslehren des lateinischen Mittelalters*. Darmstadt: Wissenschaftliche Buchgesellschaft, 1980.

Kolve, V.A. *Chaucer and the Imagery of Narrative: The First Five Canterbury Tales.* Stanford, CA: Stanford University Press, 1984.

Köpf, Ulrich. *Die Anfänge der theologischen Wissenschaftstheorie im 13. Jahrhundert.* Beiträge zur historischen Theologie 49. Tübingen: Mohr, 1974.

Krueger, Roberta. *Women Readers and the Ideology of Gender in Old French Verse Romance.* Cambridge and New York: Cambridge University Press, 1993.

Kwakkel, Erik. 'The Cultural Dynamics of Medieval Book Production.' *Manuscripten en miniaturen: Studies aangeboden aan Anne S. Korteweg bij haar afscheid van de Koninklijke Bibliotheek*, ed. Jos Biemans et al., 243–52. Zutphen: Walburg Pers, 2007.

– *Dit sijn die Dietsche boeke die ons toebehoeren: De kartuizers van Herne en de productie van Middelnederlandse handschriften in de regio Brussel (1350–1400).* Miscellanea Neerlandica 27. Leuven: Peeters, 2002.

– 'Towards a Terminology for the Analysis of Composite Manuscripts.' *Gazette du Livre Médiéval* 41 (autumn 2002): 12–19.

Kwakkel, E., and H. Mulder. 'Quidam sermons: Geestelijk proza van de Ferguut-kopiist (Brussel, Koninklijke Bibliotheek, hs. 3067–73).' *Tijdschrift voor Nederlandse Taal – en Letterkunde* 117 (2001): 151–65.

Laidlaw, James. 'Christine and the Manuscript Tradition.' In *Christine de Pizan: A Casebook*, ed. Barbara K. Altmann and Deborah L. McGrady, 231–49. New York and London: Routledge, 2003.

– 'Christine de Pizan – A Publisher's Progress.' *Modern Language Review* 82 (1987): 35–75.

Laing, David, ed. *The Poems and Fables of Robert Henryson.* Edinburgh: William Paterson, 1865.

Leclercq, Jean. *The Love of Learning and the Desire for God: A Study of Monastic Culture.* Trans. Catharine Misrahi. New York: Fordham University Press, 1961.

Lenaghan, R.T., ed. *Caxton's Aesop.* Cambridge, MA: Harvard University Press, 1967.

Lieftinck, G.I. *De Middelnederlandse Tauler-handschriften.* Groningen: Wolters, 1936.

Loewenstein, Joseph. *Ben Jonson and Possessive Authorship.* Cambridge: Cambridge University Press, 2002.

Luongo, F. Thomas. 'Saintly Authorship in the Italian Renaissance: The Quattrocento Reception of Catherine of Siena's Letters.' *Journal of the Early Book Society* 8 (2005): 1–46.

Lyall, R.J. 'Henryson's *Morall Fabillis* and the Steinhöwel Tradition.' *Forum for Modern Language Studies* 38.4 (2002): 362–81.

Lydgate, John. *Isopes Fabules*. In *The Minor Poems of John Lydgate*, Pt. 2, *Secular Poems*. Ed. Henry Noble MacCracken. EETS os 192. London: Oxford University Press, 1934; repr. London: Oxford University Press, 1961.

MacDiarmid, Hugh, ed. *Henryson*. Harmondsworth: Penguin, 1973.

Machan, Tim William. 'Robert Henryson and Father Aesop: Authority in the *Moral Fables*.' *Studies in the Age of Chaucer* 12 (1990): 193–214.

– 'Textual Authority and Works of Hoccleve, Lydgate, and Henryson.' *Viator* 23 (1992): 281–99.

– *Textual Criticism and Middle English Texts*. Charlottesville and London: University Press of Virginia, 1994.

Machaut, Guillaume de. *Le Jugement du roy de Behaigne* and *Remede de Fortune*. Ed. James I. Wimsatt and William W. Kibler. Athens, GA, and London: University of Georgia Press, 1988.

MacQueen, John. *Complete and Full with Numbers: The Narrative Poetry of Robert Henryson*. Amsterdam and New York: Rodopi, 2006.

– *Robert Henryson: A Study of the Major Narrative Poems*. Oxford: Clarendon Press, 1967.

Mahoney, Dhira B. 'Gower's Two Prologues to *Confessio Amantis*.' In *Re-Visioning Gower*, ed. R.F. Yeager, 17–37. Asheville, NC: Pegasus Press, 1998.

Maidstone, Richard. *Concordia (The Reconciliation of Richard II with London)*. Ed. David R. Carlson. Kalamazoo, MI: Medieval Institute, 2003.

Manly, John M., and Edith Rickert, eds. *The Text of The Canterbury Tales*. 8 vols. Chicago: University of Chicago Press, 1940.

Mann Phillips, Margaret. *The 'Adages' of Erasmus: A Study with Translations*. Cambridge: Cambridge University Press, 1964.

Map, Walter. *'De nugis curialium': Courtiers' Trifles*. Ed. and trans. M.R. James, rev. C.N.L. Brooke and R.A.B. Mynors. Oxford: Oxford University Press, 1983.

Marie de France. *Les Fables*. Ed. Charles Brucker. 2nd ed. Paris: Peeters, 1998.

Margolis, Nadia. 'Clerkliness and Courtliness in the "Complaintes" of Christine de Pizan.' In *Christine de Pizan and Medieval French Lyric*, ed. E.J. Richards, 135–54. Gainesville: University Press of Florida, 1998.

Matthew of Linköping. *Testa nucis* and *Poetria*. Ed. and trans. Birger Bergh. Samlingar utgivna av Svenska fornskriftsällskapet, 2nd ser. Latinska skrifter 9.2. Arlöv: Berlings, 1996.

McCall, John P. *Chaucer among the Gods: The Poetics of Classical Myth*. University Park: Pennsylvania State University Press, 1979.

McConica, James. *Erasmus*. Oxford: Oxford University Press, 1991.

McCormick, William. *The Manuscripts of Chaucer's Canterbury Tales: A Critical Description of Their Contents*. Oxford: Clarendon Press, 1933.

McGrady, Deborah. *Controlling Readers: Guillaume de Machaut and His Late Medieval Audience*. Studies in Book and Print Culture. Toronto: University of Toronto Press, 2006.

– 'What Is a Patron? Benefactors and Authorship in Harley 4431, Christine de Pizan's Collected Works.' In *Christine de Pizan and the Categories of Difference*, ed. M. Desmond, 195–214. Minneapolis: University of Minnesota Press, 1998.

McKinley, Kathryn. 'Lessons for a King: From Gower's *Confessio Amantis* 5.' In *Metamorphosis: The Changing Face of Ovid in Medieval and Early Modern Europe*, ed. Alison Keith and Stephen Rupp, 107–28. Toronto: Centre for Reformation and Renaissance Studies, 2007.

– 'Manuscripts of Ovid in England 1100 to 1500.' *English Manuscript Studies 1100–1700* 7 (1998): 41–85.

Mcleod, Glenda, and Katharina Wilson. 'A Clerk in Name Alone – A Clerk in All But Name.' In *City of Scholars: New Approaches to Christine de Pizan*, ed. Margarete Zimmermann and Diana de Rentiis, 67–78. Berlin and New York: Walter de Gruyter, 1994.

Mehl, Dieter. 'Robert Henryson's *Moral Fables* as Experiments in Didactic Narrative.' In *Functions of Literature: Essays Presented to Erwin Wolff*, ed. Ulrich Broich, Theo Stemmler, and Gerd Stratmann, 81–99. Tübingen: Niemeyer, 1984.

Meiss, Millard. *French Painting in the Time of Jean of Berry: The Limbourgs and Their Contemporaries*. 2 vols. New York: Braziller, 1974.

Middle English Dictionary (2001). http://quod.lib.umich.edu/m/med.

Middle English Dictionary. Ed. Hans Kurath et al. Ann Arbor: University of Michigan Press, 1951–98.

Miller, Jacqueline T. *Poetic License: Authority and Authorship in Medieval and Renaissance Contexts*. Oxford: Oxford University Press, 1986.

Miller, Paul. 'John Gower, Satiric Poet.' In *Gower's 'Confessio Amantis': Responses and Reassessments*, ed. A.J. Minnis, 79–105. Woodbridge: D.S. Brewer, 1983.

Minnis, Alastair. 'Acculturizing Aristotle: Matthew of Linköping's Translation of Poetic Representation.' In *Translation, Interpretation, Meaning*, ed. Anneli Aejmelaeus and Päivi Pahta. Forthcoming (Helsinki).

– 'Fifteenth Century Versions of Literalism: Girolamo Savanarola and Alfonso de Madrigal.' In *Neue Richtungen in der hoch-und spätmittelalterlichen Bibelexegese*, ed. Robert Lerner, 163–80. Schriften des Historischen Kollegs Kolloquien 32. Munich: Oldenbourg, 1996.

– *Magister Amoris: The Roman de la Rose and Vernacular Hermeneutics*. Oxford: Oxford University Press, 2001.

- 'Medieval Imagination and Memory.' In *The Cambridge History of Literary Criticism*, ed. Minnis and Johnson, 239–74.
- *Medieval Theory of Authorship: Scholastic Literary Theory in the Later Middle Ages*. 2nd ed. Aldershot: Scolar, 1988.
Minnis, Alastair, and Ian Johnson, eds. *The Cambridge History of Literary Criticism*. Volume 2, *The Middle Ages*. Cambridge: Cambridge University Press, 2005.
Minnis, Alastair J., and A.B. Scott, eds. *Medieval Literary Theory and Criticism, c. 1100–c. 1375: The Commentary Tradition*. Oxford: Oxford University Press, 1988; rev. ed. 1991, repr. 2001.
Mombello, Gianni. *La Tradizione manoscritta dell' 'Epistre Othea' di Christine de Pizan: Prolegomeni all'edizione del testo*. Turin: Accademia delle Scienze, 1967.
Mooney, Linne R. 'Chaucer's Scribe.' *Speculum* 81 (2006): 97–138.
- 'Scribes and Booklets of Trinity College, Cambridge: Manuscripts R.3.19 and R.3.21.' In *Middle English Poetry: Texts and Traditions; Essays in Honour of Derek Pearsall*, ed. A.J. Minnis, 241–66. York: York Medieval Press, 2001.
Müller, Anja 'Picturing Æsops: Re-Visions of Æsop's Fables from L'Estrange to Richardson.' *1650–1850* 10 (2004): 33–62.
Müller, Jan-Dirk. 'Auctor – Actor – Author: Einige Anmerkungen zum Verständnis vom Autor in lateinischen Schriften des frühen und hohen Mittelalters.' In *Der Autor im Dialog: Beiträge zu Autorität und Autorschaft*, ed. Felix Philipp Ingold and Werner Wunderlich, 17–31. St Gallen: UVK, Fachverlag für Wissenschaft und Studium, 1998.
- 'Lachen – Spiel – Fiktion: Zum Verhältnis von literarischem Diskurs und historischer Realität im *Frauendienst* Ulrichs von Liechtenstein.' *Deutsche Vierteljahresschrift für Literaturwissenschaft und Geistesgeschichte* 58 (1984): 38–73.
Muzerelle, M. *Vocabulaire codicologique: Répertoire méthodique des termes français relatifs aux manuscrits*. Paris: Éditions CEMI, 1985.
Noakes, Susan. *Timely Reading: Between Exegesis and Interpretation*. Ithaca, NY: Cornell University Press, 1988.
Nuttall, Jenni. *The Creation of Lancastrian Kingship: Literature, Language and Politics in Late Medieval England*. Cambridge: Cambridge University Press, 2007.
Obermeier, Anita. 'Chaucer's "Retraction."' In *Sources and Analogues of the Canterbury Tales*, ed. Robert Correale and Mary Hamel, 2:775–808. Cambridge: D.S. Brewer, 2005.
- *The History and Anatomy of Auctorial Self-Criticism in the European Middle Ages*. Amsterdam and Atlanta, GA: Rodopi, 1999.
Olson, Glending. 'Making and Poetry in the Age of Chaucer.' *Comparative Literature* 31 (1979): 272–90.

Ouy, Gilbert, and Christine Reno. 'Identification des autographes de Christine de Pizan.' *Scriptorium* 34 (1980): 221–38.

Overgaauw, Eef. 'Where are the Colophons? On the Frequency of Datings in Late-Medieval Manuscripts.' In *Sources for the History of Medieval Books and Libraries*, ed. Rita Schlusemann, Jos. M M. Hermans, and Margaret Hoogvliet, 81–93. Groningen: Egbert Forsten, 1999.

Ovid. *Fasti*. Tr. James George Frazer. Loeb Classical Library, vol. 5. 2nd ed. rev. G.P. Goold. Cambridge, MA: Harvard University Press, 1989.

– *Metamorphoses Books I–VIII*. Trans. Frank Justus Miller. Loeb Classical Library, vol. 3. 3rd ed. rev. G.P. Goold. Cambridge, MA: Harvard University Press, 1977.

– *Metamorphoses Books IX–XV*. Trans. Frank Justus Miller. Loeb Classical Library, vol. 4. 2nd ed. rev. G.P. Goold. Cambridge, MA: Harvard University Press, 1984.

– *Tristia; Ex Ponto*. Trans. Arthur Leslie Wheeler. Loeb Classical Library, vol. 6. 2nd ed. rev. G.P. Goold. Cambridge, MA: Harvard University Press, 1988.

Owen, Charles A., Jr. *The Manuscripts of The Canterbury Tales*. Cambridge: D.S. Brewer, 1991.

– 'What the Manuscripts Tell Us about the Parson's Tale.' *Medium Aevum* 63 (1994): 239–49.

Pabel, Hilmar M. *Conversing with God: Prayer in Erasmus' Pastoral Writings*. Toronto: University of Toronto Press, 1997.

– *Herculean Labours: Erasmus and the Editing of St. Jerome's Letters in the Renaissance*. Leiden: Brill, 2008.

Parkes, M.B. 'The Influence of the Concepts of *Ordinatio* and *Compilatio* on the Development of the Book.' In *Scribes, Scripts and Readers: Studies in the Communication, Presentation and Dissemination of Medieval Texts*, 35–70. London and Rio Grande: Hambledon, 1991.

– 'The Literacy of the Laity.' In *Scribes, Scripts and Readers: Studies in the Communication, Presentation and Dissemination of Medieval Texts*, 263–97. London and Rio Grande: Hambledon, 1991.

Partridge, Stephen. 'The Manuscript Glosses to the *Wife of Bath's Prologue*.' On *Geoffrey Chaucer: The Wife of Bath's Prologue on CD-ROM*, ed. Peter Robinson. Cambridge: Cambridge University Press, 1996.

– 'Minding the Gaps: Interpreting the Manuscript Evidence of the *Cook's Tale* and the *Squire's Tale*.' In *The English Medieval Book*, ed. A.S.G. Edwards, Vincent Gillespie, and Ralph Hanna, 51–85. London: British Library, 2000.

– 'Wynkyn de Worde's Manuscript Source for the *Canterbury Tales*: Evidence from the Glosses.' *Chaucer Review* 41 (2007): 325–59.

Pask, Kevin. *The Emergence of the English Author: Scripting the Life of the Poet in Early Modern England*. Cambridge: Cambridge University Press, 1996.

Patterson, Annabel. *Fables of Power: Aesopian Writing and Political History.* Durham, NC: Duke University Press, 1991.

Patterson, Lee. *Chaucer and the Subject of History.* Madison: University of Wisconsin Press, 1991.

– 'Court Politics and the Invention of Literature: The Case of Sir John Scattergood.' In *Culture and History, 1350–1600: Essays in English Communities, Identities and Writing,* ed. David Aers, 7–41. Detroit, MI: Wayne State University Press, 1992.

Patton, Celeste A. 'False "Rekenynges": Sharp Practice and the Politics of Language in Chaucer's *Manciple's Tale.' Philological Quarterly* 71 (1991–2): 399–417.

Pearsall, Derek. *The Canterbury Tales.* London: Allen and Unwin, 1985.

– *John Lydgate.* London: Routledge and Kegan Paul, 1970.

– 'Pre-empting Closure in the *Canterbury Tales*: Old Endings, New Beginnings.' In *Essays on Ricardian Literature: In Honour of J.A. Burrow,* ed. A.J. Minnis, Charlotte C. Morse, and Thorlac Turville-Petre, 23–38. Oxford: Clarendon Press, 1997.

– 'The Uses of Manuscripts: Late Medieval English.' *Harvard Library Bulletin* ns 4. 4 (1993–4): 30–6.

Pecock, Reginald. *The Donet.* Ed. Elsie Vaughan Hitchcock. EETS os 156. London: Oxford University Press, 1921; repr. New York: Kraus, 1971.

– *The Folewer to the Donet.* Ed. Elsie Vaughn Hitchcock. EETS os 164. London, Oxford University Press, 1924; repr. New York: Kraus, 1981.

– *The Repressor of Over Much Blaming of the Clergy.* Ed. Churchill Babington. Rerum Brittanicarum Medii Aevi Scriptores. London: Longman, Green, Longman, and Roberts, 1860.

– *The Reule of Crysten Religioun.* Ed. William Cabell Greet. EETS os 171. London: Oxford University Press, 1927; repr. Millwood, NY: Kraus, 1987.

Pelen, Marc C. 'The Manciple's "Cosyn" to the "Dede."' *Chaucer Review* 25 (1991–2): 343–54.

Pitard, Derrick G. 'Sowing Difficulty: *The Parson's Tale,* Vernacular Commentary, and the Nature of Chaucerian Dissent.' *Studies in the Age of Chaucer* 26 (2004): 299–330.

Poor, Sara S. *Mechthild of Magdeburg and Her Book: Gender and the Making of Textual Authority.* Philadelphia: University of Pennsylvania Press, 2004.

Powell, Marianne. *Fabula Docet: Studies in the Background and Interpretation of Henryson's Morall Fabillis.* Odense: Odense University Press, 1983.

Powell, Stephen D. 'Game Over: Defragmenting the End of the *Canterbury Tales.' Chaucer Review* 37 (2002): 40–58.

Preminger, A., O.B. Hardison, Jr, and K. Kerrane, eds. *Classical and Medieval Literary Criticism: Translations and Interpretations.* New York: Ungar, 1974.

Przychocki, G. *'Accessus Ovidiani.'* *Rosprawy Akademii Umijetnos'ci*. 3rd series, 4 (1911): 65–126.

Quain, E.A. 'The Medieval *Accessus ad auctores*.' *Traditio* 3 (1945): 228–42.

Quilligan, Maureen. *The Allegory of Female Authority: Christine de Pizan's* Cité des Dames. Ithaca: Cornell University Press, 1991.

Radulescu, Adrian. *Ovid in Exile*. Trans. Laura Treptow. Iaşi, Romania; Palm Beach, FL: The Center for Romanian Studies, 2002.

Rand, E.K. *Ovid and His Influence*. New York: Longmans, Green and Co., 1928.

Ransom, Daniel. 'Prolegomenon to a Print History of The Parson's Tale: The Novelty and Legacy of Wynkyn de Worde's Text.' In *Closure in* The Canterbury Tales*: The Role of The Parson's Tale*, ed. David Raybin and Linda Tarte Holley, 77–93. Studies in Medieval Culture 41. Kalamazoo, MI: Medieval Institute, 2000.

Raybin, David. 'The Death of a Silent Woman: Voice and Power in Chaucer's "Manciple's Tale."' *Journal of English and Germanic Philology* 95 (1996): 19–37.

Rayner, Samantha J. *Images of Kingship in Chaucer and His Ricardian Contemporaries*. Cambridge: D.S. Brewer, 2008.

Reedijk, Cornelis. *Tandem bona causa triumphat: Zur Geschichte des Gesamtwerkes des Erasmus von Rotterdam*. Vorträge der Aeneas-Silvius-Stiftung an der Universität Basel 16. Basel: Helbing & Lichtenhahn, 1980.

Revard, Carter. 'From French "Fabliau Manuscripts" and MS Harley 2253 to the *Decameron* and the *Canterbury Tales*.' *Medium Aevum* 69 (2000): 261–78.

Reynolds, Suzanne. *Medieval Reading: Grammar, Rhetoric and the Classical Text*. Cambridge: Cambridge University Press, 1996.

Rigg, A. *A History of Anglo-Latin Literature, 1066–1422*. Cambridge: Cambridge University Press, 1992.

Robathan, Dorothy M. 'Ovid in the Middle Ages.' In *Ovid*, ed. J.W. Binns, 191–209. London: Routledge and Kegan Paul, 1973.

Robertson, Elizabeth. 'Introduction.' *English Language Notes* 44 (2006): 77–9.

Robinson, P.R. 'The "Booklet": A Self-Contained Unit in Composite Manuscripts.' In *Codicologica 3: Essais typologiques*, ed. A. Gruys and J.P. Gumbert, 46–69. Leiden: Brill, 1980.

Röcke, Werner. 'Lizenzen des Witzes: Institutionen und Funktionen der Fazetie im Spätmittelalter.' In *Komische Gegenwelten: Lachen und Literatur in Mittelalter und Früher Neuzeit*, ed. Werner Röcke and Helga Neumann, 79–101. Paderborn: Schöningh, 1999.

Ross, J. *The Book of Scottish Poems: Ancient and Modern*. Vol. 1. Edinburgh: Edinburgh Publishing Co., 1878.

Rouse, Mary A., and Richard H. Rouse. 'The Development of Research Tools in the Thirteenth Century.' In *Authentic Witnesses: Approaches to Medieval*

Texts and Manuscripts, 221–55. Publications in Medieval Studies 17. Notre Dame, IN: Notre Dame University Press, 1991.

– '*Statim invenire*: Schools, Preachers and New Attitudes to the Page.' In *Authentic Witnesses: Approaches to Medieval Texts and Manuscripts*, 191–219. Publications in Medieval Studies 17. Notre Dame, IN: Notre Dame University Press, 1991.

Rummel, Erika. *Erasmus' 'Annotations' on the New Testament: From Philologist to Theologian*. Toronto: University of Toronto Press, 1986.

Rust, Martha Dana. *Imaginary Worlds in Medieval Books: Exploring the Manuscript Matrix*. New York: Palgrave Macmillan, 2007.

Saenger, Paul. *Space between Words: The Origins of Silent Reading*. Stanford: Stanford University Press, 1997.

Saul, Nigel. *Richard II*. New Haven, CT: Yale University Press, 1997.

– 'Richard II and the Vocabulary of Kingship.' *English Historical Review* 110 (1995): 854–77.

Sayce, Olive. 'Chaucer's "Retractions": The Conclusion of the *Canterbury Tales* and Its Place in Literary Tradition.' *Medium Aevum* 40 (1971): 230–48.

Scattergood, V.J. 'The Manciple's Manner of Speaking.' *Essays in Criticism* 24 (1974): 124–46.

Scharff, Thomas. 'Lachen über die Ketzer: Religiöse Devianz und Gelächter im Mittelalter.' In *Lachgemeinschaften: Kulturelle Inszenierungen und soziale Wirkungen von Gelächter im Spätmittelalter und in der Frühen Neuzeit*, ed. Werner Röcke and Hans-Rudolf Velten, 17–31. Trends in Medieval Philology 4. Berlin and New York: De Gruyter, 2005.

Schatten van de Koninklijke Bibliotheek: Acht eeuwen verluchte handschriften. The Hague: Koninklijke Bibliotheek, 1980.

Scholla, A. 'Libri sine asseribus: Zur Eindbandtechnik, Form und Inhalt mitteleuropäischer Koperte des 8. bis 14. Jahrhunderts.' PhD diss., Leiden University, The Netherlands, 2002.

Scott, Kathleen. 'An Hours and Psalter by Two Ellesmere Illuminators.' In *The Ellesmere Chaucer: Essays in Interpretation*, ed. Martin Stevens and Daniel Woodward, 87–117. San Marino, CA: Huntington Library; and Tokyo: Yushodo, 1995.

Seibert, Harriet. 'Correspondence: Chaucer and Horace.' *Modern Language Notes* 31 (1916): 304–7.

Simpson, James. 'Breaking the Vacuum: Ricardian and Henrician Ovidianism.' *Journal of Medieval and Early Modern Studies* 29 (1999): 325–55.

– *Reform and Cultural Revolution 1350–1547*. The Oxford English Literary History, vol. 2. Oxford: Oxford University Press, 2002.

Smith, G. Gregory, ed. *The Poems of Robert Henryson*. Scottish Text Society 55, 58, and 64. Edinburgh: Blackwood, 1906–14.

Smith, M. Ellwood. 'Æsop, A Decayed Celebrity: Changing Conceptions as to Æsop's Personality in English Writers before Gay.' *PMLA* 46.1 (1931): 225–36.

Smith, M.M. *The Title-Page: Its Early Development, 1460–1510*. London: The British Library; and New Castle, DE: Oak Knoll Press, 2000.

Smith, Richard. *The Fabulous Tales of Esope the Phrygian*. London, 1577.

Solterer, Helen. *The Master and Minerva: Disputing Women in French Medieval Culture*. Berkeley and Los Angeles: University of California Press, 1995.

Somerset, Fiona. 'Professionalizing Translation at the Turn of the Fifteenth Century: Ullerston's *Determinacio*, Arundel's *Constitutiones*.' In *The Vulgar Tongue: Medieval and Postmedieval Vernacularity*, ed. Fiona Somerset and Nicholas Watson, 145–58. University Park: Pennsylvania State University Press, 2003.

Somerset, Fiona, Jill Havens, and Derrick Pitard, eds. *Lollards and Their Influence in Late Medieval England*. Woodbridge, Suffolk: Boydell, 2003.

Spearing, A.C. 'Central and Displaced Sovereignty in Three Medieval Poems.' *Review of English Studies* ns 33 (1982): 247–61.

– *The Medieval Poet as Voyeur*. Cambridge: Cambridge University Press, 1993.

Steppich, Christoph J. *Numine afflatur: Die Inspiration des Dichters im Denken der Renaissance*. Wiesbaden: Harrassowitz, 2002.

Stock, Brian. *The Implications of Literacy: Written Language and Models of Interpretation in the Eleventh and Twelfth Centuries*. Princeton, NJ: Princeton University Press, 1983.

Storm, Melvin. 'Speech, Circumspection, and Orthodontics in the *Manciple's Prologue* and *Tale* and the Wife of Bath's Portrait.' *Studies in Philology* 96 (1999): 109–26.

Stow, George B. 'Richard II in Thomas Walsingham's Chronicles.' *Speculum* 59 (1984): 68–102.

Striar, Brian. 'The "Manciple's Tale" and Chaucer's Apolline Poetics.' *Criticism* 33 (1991): 173–204.

Strohm, Paul. 'Jean of Angoulême: A Fifteenth Century Reader of Chaucer.' *Neuphilologische Mitteilungen* 72 (1971): 69–76.

– *Social Chaucer*. Cambridge, MA: Harvard University Press, 1989.

Syme, Ronald. *History in Ovid*. Oxford: Clarendon Press, 1978.

Szirmai, J.A. *The Archaeology of Medieval Bookbinding*. Aldershot: Ashgate, 1999.

Tatlock, J.S.P. *The Harleian Manuscript 7334 and Revision of the Canterbury Tales*. London: Chaucer Society, 1909.

Thibault, John C. *The Mystery of Ovid's Exile*. Berkeley: University of California Press, 1964.

Thomas Walsingham. *De archana deorum*. Ed. R.A. van Kluyve. Durham, NC: Duke University Press, 1968.

Tokunaga, Satoko. 'Representing Caxton's Chaucer: Wynkyn de Worde and the *Canterbury Tales*.' *Poetica* 55 (2001): 105–21.

Trapp, J.B. *Erasmus, Colet and More: The Early Tudor Humanists and Their Books*. The Panizzi Lectures 1990. London: The British Library, 1991.

Trigg, Stephanie. *Congenial Souls*. Minneapolis and London: University of Minnesota Press, 2002.

Turner, Denys. *Eros and Allegory: Medieval Exegesis of the Song of Songs*. Kalamazoo, MI: Cistercian Publications, 1995.

Turner, Marion. *Chaucerian Conflict: Languages of Antagonism in Late Fourteenth-Century London*. Oxford: Clarendon Press, 2007.

Vaughan, Míceál F. 'Creating Comfortable Boundaries: Scribes, Editors, and the Invention of the *Parson's Tale*.' In *Rewriting Chaucer: Culture, Authority, and the Idea of the Authentic Text 1400–1602*, ed. Thomas A. Prendergast and Barbara Kline, 45–90. Columbus: Ohio State University Press, 1999.

– 'Personal Politics and Thomas Gascoigne's Account of Chaucer's Death.' *Medium Aevum* 75 (2006): 103–22.

Vessey, Mark. 'Cities of the Mind: Renaissance Views of Early Christian Culture and the End of Antiquity.' In *A Companion to Late Antiquity*, ed. Philip Rousseau, 43–58. Chichester, UK, and Malden, MA: Wiley-Blackwell, 2009.

– 'Erasmus' Lucubrations and the Renaissance Life of Texts.' *Erasmus of Rotterdam Society Yearbook* 24 (2004): 23–51.

Vessey, Mark. ' "Nothing if Not Critical": G.E.B. Saintsbury, Erasmus, and the History of (English) Literature.' In *Erasmus and the Renaissance Republic of Letters: Proceedings of a Conference to Mark the Centenary of the First Volume of 'Erasmi Epistolae' by P.S. Allen, Corpus Christi College, Oxford, 5–7 September 2006*, ed. Stephen Ryle. Disputatio 24. Turnhout: Brepols, forthcoming.

Von Kreisler, Nicolai. 'Henryson's Visionary Fable: Traditon and Craftsmanship in *The Lyoun and the Mous*.' *Texas Studies in Literature and Language* 15 (1973): 391–403.

Wachinger, Burghart. 'Autorschaft und Überlieferung.' In *Autorentypen*, ed. Walter Haug and Burghart Wachinger, 1–28. Fortuna Vitrea: Arbeiten zur literarischen Tradition zwichen dem 13. und 16. Jahrhundert 6. Tübingen: De Gruyter, 1991.

Wallace, David. *Chaucerian Polity: Absolutist Lineages and Associational Forms in England and Italy*. Stanford, CA.: Stanford University Press, 1997.

Watson, Nicholas. 'Censorship and Cultural Change in Late-Medieval England: Vernacular Theology, the Oxford Translation Debate, and Arundel's Constitutions of 1409.' *Speculum* 70 (1995): 822–64.

– *Richard Rolle and the Invention of Authority*. Cambridge: Cambridge University Press, 1991.

Wenzel, S. 'Sermon Collections and Their Taxonomy.' In *The Whole Book: Cultural Perspectives on the Medieval Miscellany*, ed. S.G. Nichols and S. Wenzel, 7–21. Ann Arbor: University of Michigan Press, 1996.

Westervelt, L.A. 'Janglery in *The Manciple's Tale.*' *Southern Review: Literary and Interdisciplinary Essays* 14 (1981): 107–15.

Westphal, Sarah. *Textual Poetics in German Manuscripts, 1300–1500*. Columbia, SC: Camden House, 1993.

– 'The Van Hulthem MS and the Compilation of Medieval German Books.' In *Codices Miscellanearum: Brussels Van Hulthem Colloquium, 1999*, ed. R. Jansen-Sieben and H. van Dijk, 71–89. Brussels: Archives et bibliothèques de Belgique, 1999.

Wheatley, Edward. 'The Aesopic Corpus Divided against Itself: A Literary Body and Its Members.' *Journal of the Early Book Society* 46 (1999): 46–72.

– 'The Manciple's Tale.' In *Sources and Analogues of the Canterbury Tales*, ed. Robert Correale and Mary Hamel, 2:749–75. Cambridge: D.S. Brewer, 2005.

– *Mastering Aesop: Medieval Education, Chaucer, and His Followers*. Gainesville: University Press of Florida, 2000.

Wilkins, David, ed. *Concilia magnae Brittaniae et Hiberniae*. 4 vols. Oxford: Clarendon Press, 1964.

Williams, Gareth D. *Banished Voices: Readings in Ovid's Exile Poetry*. Cambridge: Cambridge University Press, 1994.

– 'Ovid's Exile Poetry: *Tristia, Epistulae ex Ponto*, and *Ibis*.' In *The Cambridge Companion to Ovid*, ed. Philip Hardie, 233–45. Cambridge: Cambridge University Press, 2002.

Windeatt, Barry. 'The Scribes as Chaucer's Early Critics.' *Studies in the Age of Chaucer* 1 (1979): 119–41.

Wogan-Browne, Jocelyn, et al., eds. *The Idea of the Vernacular: An Anthology of Middle English Literary Theory, 1280–1520*. University Park: Pennsylvania State University Press, 1999.

Wood, Chauncey. 'Speech, the Principle of Contraries, and Chaucer's Tales of the Manciple and the Parson.' *Mediaevalia* 6 (1980): 209–22.

Woods, H. Harvey, ed. *The Poems and Fables of Robert Henryson*. Edinburgh: Oliver and Boyd, 1933.

Wright, Aaron E., ed. *The Fables of 'Walter of England.'* Toronto: Pontifical Institute of Mediaeval Studies, 1997.

Wright, Thomas, ed. *The Latin Poems Commonly Attributed to Walter Mapes*. London: Camden Society, 1841.

Wurtele, Douglas. 'The Penitence of Geoffrey Chaucer.' *Viator* 11 (1980): 335–59.

Yeager, R.F., ed. and trans. *John Gower: The Minor Latin Works*. Kalamazoo, MI: Medieval Institute, 2005.

Zimmerman, Michel, ed. *Auctor et auctoritas: Invention et conformisme dans l'écriture médiévale*. Paris: École des chartes, 2001.

Ziolkowski, Jan M. 'Classical Influences on Medieval Latin Views of Poetic Inspiration.' In *Latin Poetry and the Classical Tradition: Essays in Medieval and Renaissance Literature*, ed. Peter Godman and Oswyn Murray, 15–38. Oxford: Clarendon Press, 1990.

Zotz, Thomas. 'Urbanitas: Zur Bedeutung und Funktion einer antiken Wertvorstellung innerhalb der höfischen Kultur des hohen Mittelalters.' In *Curialitas*, ed. Josef Fleckenstein, 392–451. Veröffentlichungen des Max-Planck-Instituts für Geschichte 100. Göttingen: Vandenhoeck & Ruprecht, 1990.

Notes on Contributors

Kirsty Campbell teaches English literature at John Abbott College in Montreal. She is the author of *The Call to Read: Reginald Pecock's Books and Textual Communities* (2010).

Sebastian Coxon is Reader in German at University College London (UCL). His research interests include authorship, late medieval urban literature, and the cultural significance of laughter, wit and ridicule. He published *The Presentation of Authorship in Medieval German Narrative Literature 1220–1290* (2001).

Erik Kwakkel is principle investigator in 'Turning over a New Leaf: Manuscript Innovation in the Twelfth-Century Renaissance,' an NWO-funded research project based at Leiden University, where he also teaches manuscript studies. His publications include a monograph on Carthusian book production (2003) and a co-edited volume, *Medieval Dutch Bible Culture* (2007).

Iain Macleod Higgins teaches at the University of Victoria. His book *Writing East: The 'Travels' of Sir John Mandeville* (1997) received the Medieval Academy of America's John Nicholas Brown Prize in 2001. His translation of *The Book of John Mandeville* is to be published by Hackett.

Deborah McGrady is an Associate Professor of French at the University of Virginia. In addition to her published articles on Christine de Pizan, she is the author of *Controlling Readers: Guillaume de Machaut and His Late Medieval Audience* (2006). She is currently writing a study of alternative avenues of literary circulation in the late Middle Ages, presently entitled 'Beyond Patronage.'

Alastair Minnis is the Douglas Tracy Smith Professor of English at Yale University. His latest monograph is *Translations of Authority in Medieval English Literature: Valuing the Vernacular* (Cambridge University Press, 2009), and a major reference-book which he co-edited with Rosalynn Voaden, *Medieval Holy Women in the Christian Tradition, c.1100–c.1500*, is published by Brepols in 2010.

Anita Obermeier, Professor of English and Director of the Feminist Research Institute at the University of New Mexico, is the author of *The History and Anatomy of Auctorial Self-Criticism in the European Middle Ages* (1999) and the co-editor of *Romance and Rhetoric: In Honour of Dhira B. Mahoney* (2010). Among many other essays, she has also published 'Chaucer's "Retraction"' in *Sources and Analogues of the Canterbury Tales* (2005). She is currently working on a book titled, *Seed, Sex, Superiority: Fertility and Sterility in Medieval Literature*.

Stephen Partridge teaches in the English department at the University of British Columbia. He has published on Chaucerian and other Middle English manuscripts and co-edited *The Book Unbound* (2004).

Mark Vessey is Professor of English (Canada Research Chair) in the Department of English, and Principal of Green College, at the University of British Columbia. He is the co-editor, with Hilmar M. Pabel, of *Holy Scripture Speaks: The Production and Reception of Erasmus' Paraphrases on the New Testament* (2002).

Index

Addison, Richard: *The Lucubrations of Isaac Bickerstaff, Esq. (The Tatler),* 237
Adolf of Burgundy, 241
Aesop, 5, 15–16, 22, 198–202, 205, 209, 215–16, 225
Aesop Romance, The, 201
Agricola, Rudolph, 254
Alcuin, 76n20
Alexander of Hales, 20, 31; *Summa theologica,* 27, 37n46
Al-Farabi, 26
Allen, Judson B., 35n6
Allen, Mark, 101n17, 104nn64–5
Allen, Peter L., 85, 102n23
Althoff, Gerd, 53n24
Altmann, Barbara, 137, 153n106, 177nn24–5, 27, 29
Amtower, Laurel, 157, 176n12
Anderson, Elizabeth, 18n2
Andrelini, Fausto, 249
Aquinas, Thomas, 32, 180
Arator, 22
Arch, Jennifer, 140n19
Aristotle, 6, 12, 24–6, 28–30, 160, 180; *Metaphysics,* 36n39; *Nichomachean Ethics,* 7, 28–9, 36nn33, 37; *Organon,* 7, 28, 33; *Poetics,* 7, 23, 37n46
Arundel, Thomas, archbishop of Canterbury: *Constitutions,* 13–15, 179–84, 193, 193n2, 194nn8–11, 195n13
Ascoli, Albert Russell, 19n2
Astell, Ann W., 80, 100n3, 103n59, 149–50n81
Aston, Margaret, 193n1
Augustijn, Cornelius, 256n1, 257n4
Augustine, 12, 32, 76n20, 78n38, 160, 185, 237, 243
Aulus Gellius, 16, 237, 239, 248–9, 259n33; *Noctes Atticae,* 238, 248, 258n12
Aurelius, Marcus, 238
Ausonius, 238, 259n29
Averroes, 6, 7; *Middle Commentary,* 23–4
Avianus, 22
Avicenna, 26
Axton, Richard, 96, 105n88

Bacon, Roger, 7, 25–6, 30–1, 36nn23, 37

Baker, Donald C., 98, 101nn15, 19, 21, 103n59, 105n96
Baker, Howard, 229n18
Barchiesi, Alessandro, 102n40, 103n45
Barron, W.R.J., 227n6
Barthes, Roland, 207
Batt, Jacob, 247–9, 260n37
Baudry, bishop of Bourgueil, 86
Bawcutt, Priscilla, 227n6, 231n39
Bein, Thomas, 51n6
Bennett, Michael J., 103n47
Benson, C. David, 180
Benson, Larry D., 100n10, 101n15, 139n1, 141nn22, 28, 142–3n32, 149–50n81
Benvenuto da Imola, 24
Bergson, Henri, 53n23
Bernard of Clairvaux, 40–1
Bernardus (Palponista), 22
Beryn, 149n78
Bibaculus: Lucubrationes, 248
Biemans, J.A.A.M., 78n37
Bietenholz, Peter G., 256n1
Bischoff, B., 76n20
Blake, N.F., 140n20, 141n22
Blanchard, Joël, 176n21
Block, Elizabeth, 102n40
Bloomfield, Josephine, 226n4
Blount, William, Lord Mountjoy, 248
Boccaccio, 7, 33; Genealogia deorum gentilium, 31–2; Trattatello in laude di Dante, 31
Bodenmann, Reinhard, 257n8
Boece, Hector, 255, 261n48
Boethius, 12, 158–60, 174, 237
Boffey, J., 73n2, 75n15, 77nn26, 28
Bonaventure, 7, 26–9, 186, 196n34; Breviloquium, 26–7, 30, 34, 36n27
Boner, Ulrich: Der Edelstein, 204, 206

Børch, Marianne, 104n73
Bose, Mishtooni, 197n45
Bowen, Barbara C., 51n7
Bowers, John M., 98, 100n8, 103n48, 105n94, 145n57
Bracciolini, Poggio, 51n8; Liber facetiarum, 39
Bradburn, Edward W., 210, 229n23, 230n30, 231n45
Brewer, Derek, 127, 149n79
Brown-Grant, Rosalind, 177n34
Brownlee, Kevin, 18n2, 176n11
Bryan, Elizabeth, 148n72
Burrow, John, 103n47, 130, 151n90
Butterfield, Ardis, 105n87, 110, 134, 138, 140n18, 152nn99, 101, 153n109

Caie, Graham D., 140n17
Calabrese, Michael A., 85, 102n25
Campbell, Kirsty, 5, 13–14, 99n2, 193n4
Capgrave, John: St. Augustine, 125
Careri, M., 76n23
Carlson, David R., 258n16
Carmina aurea, 257n6
Caxton, William, 117, 120, 144n44, 201, 204
Cerquiglini-Toulet, Jacqueline, 109, 140nn11–12, 157, 176n14
Charles V, king of France, 159, 176n22
Chaucer, Geoffrey, 15, 18, 24, 69, 80–1, 88–9, 110–11, 136, 178, 200–1, 207, 210, 216–17, 230n31; 'Adam Scriveyn,' 131–2, 141n23; Boece, 106; Book of the Duchess, 106, 129; Canterbury Tales, 5, 6, 11–12, 81, 106–7, 111–18, 120–3, 125–9, 132–4, 136–9, 142nn30–1, 144n44, 146–7n61, 147n64, 147–8n66,

149n78, 149–50n81, 150nn83–4,
151–2n92, 153n108; *Complaint of
Mars*, 92; *Cook's Tale*, 121; *Equatorie
of the Planetis*, 111; *Franklin's Tale*,
92; *General Prologue*, 93, 111, 128,
132–3, 137, 152n97; *House of Fame*,
92, 106, 129; *Legend of Good Women*,
11, 81–4, 87, 89, 92–3, 95, 105n86,
106–7, 129, 140n20; *Manciple's
Prologue*, 114, 142n30; *Manciple's
Tale*, 10–11, 80–6, 90–6, 98–9,
101nn15–17, 22, 142n30; *Prologue
of Melibee*, 145n55; *Melibee*, 121;
Miller's Prologue, 93, 152n97;
Miller's Tale, 92; *Monk's Tale*, 92;
Nun's Priest's Tale, 208; *Parliament
of Fowls*, 106, 214; *Parson's Prologue*, 114, 142n30, 147n64; *Parson's
Tale*, 112, 114–15, 117–24, 127,
131, 142nn29–30, 143nn36–7, 42,
144nn44, 50, 145nn52, 53, 145–
6n58, 146–7n61, 147n64, 147–8n66,
150nn83–4; *Prioress's Prologue*,
122; *Prioress's Tale*, 122; *Retraction*,
11–12, 83, 87, 93, 100n14, 106–7,
112–30, 132–4, 137–9, 142nn29–31,
142–3n32, 143nn36, 40–3, 144n50,
145n52, 145–6n58, 146–7n61,
147n64, 148–9n73, 149nn75, 78,
150nn82–4, 86, 151–2n92, 152nn95,
97, 102, 153n108; *Shipman's Tale*,
122; *Sir Thopas*, 121, 145n55;
Squire's Tale, 121; *Treatise on the
Astrolabe*, 81, 107, 132–3; *Troilus
and Criseyde*, 81–2, 92, 106–7, 110,
129, 132–4, 152n102
Chenu, M.-D., 34n3
Chrétien de Troyes, 76n23
Christine de Pizan, 5, 6, 14–15, 18,
108–9, 111, 113, 134, 137–8, 139n7,
152n104, 154–7, 192; *Advision
Cristine*, 159; *Le chemin de longue
etude*, 158, 160–1, 176n16; *Cité des
Dames*, 12–13, 157, 160–3, 166,
172; *Le dit de la rose*, 168; *Dit de
Poissy*, 168; *Enseignements moraux*,
165; *Epistre Othea*, 13, 135, 139n8,
164, 168–9, 171–2; *Epître au dieu
d'amours*, 158; *Livre de Cristine*,
135, 152n104; *Le Livre des Fais et
Bonnes Meurs du Sage Roy Charles
V*, 136, 152n104, 159, 164; *Livre des
trois jugemens*, 164–5, 168; *Livre des
trois vertus*, 172–3; *Livre du debat
de deux amans*, 164, 168; *Livre du
duc des vrais amans*, 165–7, 172;
Mutacion de Fortune, 159; *Oeuvres
poétiques*, 176n15, 177nn28, 36;
Oraison Nostre Dame, 172; *Proverbes
moraux*, 165
Chrysostom, John, 243
Cicero, Marcus Tullius, 237, 249; *De
oratore*, 51n3
Claassen, Jo-Marie, 89, 102nn39–41;
103n47, 105nn98, 100
Clanvowe, John: *Boke of Cupid*, 100n8
Clark, James G., 35n7
Claudian, 22
Clausi, Benedetto, 258n11, 259n36
Coffman, George R., 105n90
Col, Pierre and Gontier, 154–6
Coleman, Joyce, 105n86
Colet, John, 241, 252, 254–5
Coletti, Theresa, 152n100
Cooper, Helen, 100n4
Copeland, Rita, 208, 230n28
Cox, Catherine S., 103n60,
104n63
Coxon, Sebastian, 5, 8–10, 18n2,
19nn3–4, 54n30, 107, 139n4

Crane, Susan, 142n31, 150n84, 152n93
Crassons, Kate, 180, 193n7
Creese, David, 257n6
Croenen, Godfried, 140–1n21
Curschmann, Michael, 205, 228n17

Daly, Lloyd W., 228n12
Dante Alighieri, 39, 198–201, 206, 215, 225; *Commedia*, 24
Dean, James, 91, 93, 100n12, 101n22, 104n63, 105n76
de Cortte, Arnold, 67
de Hamel, Christopher, 151n88
de la Fontaine, Jean, 199
de Lorris, Guillaume: *Roman de la Rose*, 215
de Meun, Jean: *Roman de la Rose*, 12, 82, 89, 154–61, 164, 168, 173–5, 175n2
de Montreuil, Jean, 154; *Traité sur le Roman de la Rose*, 155
Derolez, A., 79n43
Deschamps, Eustache, 13, 78n37, 133, 152n104, 174, 177n38
Deschamps, J., 78n37
Deutscher, Thomas B., 256n1
De Vreese, W., 76nn17–18
de Worde, Wynkyn, 119, 121, 128, 142n31, 144n44, 145n53, 149n74, 150n82
Donoghue, Daniel, 180
Douglas, Gavin: *Eneados*, 226n1
Doyle, A. Ian, 74n3, 149n80, 149–50n81, 179, 193n2
Dresden, Sem, 258n14

Eberle, Patricia, J., 103n47
Eberly, Susan S., 230n33

Ebin, L., 231n38
Echard, Siân, 39–40, 52nn13, 18, 152nn101–2
Eckhart, Meister, 10, 66–7
Eden, Kathy, 257n6, 259n30
Elisha, 41
Elliott, A.G., 35n5
Elliott, Charles, 227n6
Erasmus, Desiderius, 4–6, 16–18, 232, 246, 248; *Adagiorum collectanea*, 17, 232, 244–5, 248–9, 257n6, 258n21, 259n34, 260n36; *Antibarbarorum libri*, 247; *Carmen de casa natalicia Iesu*, 241; *Colloquia*, 247; *De conscribendis epistolis*, 247; *De copia*, 247; *Elegantiae*, 247; *Enchiridion militis christiani*, 232, 240–3, 245–6, 250, 252, 255, 257n4, 258n20; *Epigrammata*, 245; *Lucubrationes Erasmi*, 17, 232–3, 235–9, 243, 250–1, 254–6, 257nn3–4, 6, 258n21, 259n32, 260nn37, 42, 261n45; *Lucubratiunculae*, 16–17, 239, 241, 243, 245–6, 247, 250, 252, 255, 256; *Opera Hieronymi*, 257n11; *Opera omnia*, 17, 255; *Panegyric*, 245; *Praise of Folly*, 232; *Varia epigrammata*, 244
Evans, Harry B., 102n44

Faber, James, 261n43
Figg, Kristen M., 140–1n21
Fletcher, Christopher, 99n2
Foliot, Gilbert, bishop of London, 40, 53n19
Fowler, Alastair, 230n35
Fox, Denton, 200, 214, 216, 226n5, 227nn6, 9, 228n16, 229nn21, 23, 26, 230nn27, 35, 231nn40, 48, 51
Foxe, John, 194n8

Fradenburg, Louise, 104n72
Fratus, David Joseph, 226n3
Froben, Johann, 232, 235, 241, 243,
  245, 254–5, 257nn4, 11, 259n27,
  260n37, 261n45
Froissart, Jean, 109–11, 113, 127, 133,
  138, 140–1n21, 152n104, 172;
  Chronicles, 111, 177n37
Fulk, R.D., 91, 103n60
Fumo, Jamie C., 100n11, 101n20,
  102n24, 139, 151n86, 152n95
Furrow, Melissa, 104n74
Fyler, John, 85, 100n4, 102n26

Gamelyn, 146–7n61, 147n63,
  149n78
Gameson, R., 78nn35, 38
Gascoigne, Thomas, 83
Georgianna, Linda, 180, 193n7
Gerald of Wales, 51n9
Gerard, Cornelis, 246
Gerbel, Nikolaus, 254
Gerson, Jean, 155, 160; *La Montaigne
  de meditation*, 176n17
Giles of Rome: *De regimine princi-
  pum*, 28–9, 36nn33–4, 37
Gillespie, Alexandra, 19n3
Gillespie, Vincent, 19n3, 35n18,
  36nn23–5, 37–8, 141n23
Gilmont, Jean-François, 257n7,
  260n36
Ginsberg, Warren, 102n22
*Glaube und Wissen: Die Kölner Dom-
  bibliothek*, 76n21
Godin, André, 261n45
Goldhill, Simon, 260n36
Gopen, George, 200, 226n3, 227n6,
  230n27
Gower, John, 10–11, 80–2, 84, 86, 92,
  98–9, 217; *Carmen super multiplici*

viciorum pestilencia, 105n90; *Confes-
  sio Amantis*, 95–6, 101n21, 105n86,
  134, 152n102; *O deus immense*,
  96–8, 105n91; *Vox Clamantis*, 96
Gray, Douglas, 199, 226n2, 231n49
Green, Peter, 102n36
Green, Richard Firth, 103n47
Greene, Robert: *Vision*, 216–17,
  231nn41, 43
Greene, Virginie, 18–19nn2–4
Gregory of Nazianzus: *Carmina
  moralia*, 258n21
Gregory the Great, 79n40, 187,
  244
Griffiths, Jane, 19n3
Grudin, Michaela Paasche, 101n22,
  103n57
Gumbert, J.P., 74n9, 76n21, 79n42
Gunderson, Erik, 258n12

Hackett, Jeremiah, 36n23
Hadewijch of Brabant, 10, 68, 78n39
Hanna, Ralph, 74n8, 75n12, 141n22,
  142n32
Harbert, Bruce, 102n34
Hardison, O.B., Jr, 20, 34n2, 35n20,
  36n26, 37n47
Hardman, Phillipa, 140n17
Harris, Kate, 143n36
Harwood, Britton J., 105n78
Havens, Jill, 193n1
Hazelton, Richard, 96, 105nn75,
  89
Heaney, Seamus, 226n3
Hegius, Alexander, 261n43
Helgerson, Richard, 19n3
Heninger, S.K., Jr, 257n6
Henry I, king of England, 53n25
Henry II, king of England, 38–9, 42,
  44–5, 53n19

Henry IV, king of England, 80, 96
Henryson, Robert, 5, 15–16, 18,
   198, 229n25; *Morall Fabillis*, 15,
   198–225, 226n3; *The Testament of*
   Cresseid, 220, 231n39
Heriot, Dianne Margaret, 35nn8, 12,
   14–17
Hermann the German, 6–7, 23–5,
   37n46
Hermans, J.M.M., 76nn18–19
Hermans, Willem: *Sylva odarum*, 244
Hexter, Ralph J., 86, 102nn27–8, 30
Hicks, Eric, 175nn1–4, 7–8,
   176nn9–10
Higgins, Iain Macleod, 5, 15, 18,
   100n7, 231n50
Hildebert, bishop of Tours, 86
Hill, John M., 101n16
Hindman, Sandra, 176n21,
   177n31
Hines, John, 105n77
Hinton, James, 52n12
Hobbins, Daniel, 19n2
Hoffman, Richard L., 100n4
Holkot, Robert: *Moralia super Ovidii*
   Metamorphoses, 102n31
Holland, Richard: *Buke of the Howlat*,
   222
Holmes, Olivia, 18n2
Holzberg, Niklas, 228nn13, 15
Homer, 22
Horace, 22, 95, 237, 260n36; *Ars*
   poetica, 25
Howard, Donald R., 90–1, 101n17,
   103n60
Hudson, Anne, 193n1
Hugh, bishop of Lincoln, 43
Hugh of St Victor, 161; *Didascalicon*
   12–13, 162, 176n19
Hunt, R.W., 34n5

Huot, Sylvia, 18n2, 56–7, 73n2,
   109–11, 127, 133, 140nn12, 14–16,
   21, 151n89, 152nn98, 104, 177n30
Huygens, R.B.C., 34n5

IJsewijn, Josef, 258n18
Illich, Ivan, 176n19
Irenaeus, 243
Isabeau de Bavière, queen of France,
   156–7, 172
Isidore of Seville: *Etymologiae*, 94, 96

Jaeger, Stephen C., 53nn24, 26
Janson, Tore, 257n9
Jardine, Lisa, 258nn16–17, 260n37,
   261n43
Jeffrey, David L., 101n17
Jerome, 5, 14, 16–18, 76n21, 186–7,
   192, 232, 237–8, 243, 247, 249,
   257nn6, 11, 260nn36–7, 261n42;
   Against Vigilantius, 238, 250, 255
John of Hanville, 22–3
John, Saint, 32
Johnson, Ian, 20, 34n1
Justice, Steven, 18n2, 19n4
Juvenal, 22–3

Kantorowicz, Ernest H., 258n22
Keach, William, 101n18
Keiser, G.R., 148n72
Keith, A.M., 99, 101n19, 105n99
Kelly, Henry Ansgar, 85, 102n26
Kelly, Stephen, 179, 193n3
Kendrick, Laura, 110, 140n18,
   151nn88, 91
Kensak, Michael, 91, 104n65
Ker, J., 257n9
Kerby-Fulton, Kathryn, 18n2, 19n4,
   100n2, 180, 184, 193n5, 195n24
Kerrane, K., 35n20, 36n26

Kienhorst, H., 78n34
Kindermann, Udo, 35n13
Kindrick, Robert L., 227n6
Klopsch, Paul, 105n81
Kolve, V.A., 103n59
Köpf, Ulrich, 34n3
Kors, M.M., 78n34
Krueger, Roberta, 177n34
Kwakkel, Erik, 5, 6, 9–11, 74nn9–11,
    75n14, 76n23, 77nn24, 29–31,
    78n33, 79nn39–41, 44

Lactantius, 237
Laidlaw, James, 140n9, 152nn103–4,
    176n13
Laing, David, 200, 226n6
Langland, William, 80, 219; *Piers
    Plowman*, 98, 213
Leclercq, Jean, 258n22
Lem, A., 76nn18–19
Lenaghan, R.T., 228n15
Lieftinck, G.I., 77n25
Little, Katherine, 180
Livre des Cent Balades, Le, 137
Lowenstein, Joseph, 19n3
Lucan, 22
Lucubrationes Lucretianae, 237
Lucubrationes Thucydidiae, 237
*Lucubrations of Humphrey Ravelin,
    Esq., The*, 237
Luongo, F. Thomas, 151n89
Luther, Martin, 198
Lyall, R.J., 228nn14, 16
Lydgate, John, 69, 205–7, 218,
    229n25; *Siege of Thebes*, 150n83;
    Isopes Fabules, 229nn20–1, 231n46

MacDiarmid, Hugh, 227n6
Machan, Tim William, 195nn26–7,
    201, 212, 214, 216–17, 227n8,
    229nn23, 25, 230nn27, 32, 34,
    231nn42, 44, 47
Machaut, Guillaume de, 109–10, 113,
    127, 133, 138, 140n12, 152n104;
    Le Jugement du roy de Behaigne,
    140n18; *Le Livre du voir dit*, 110;
    Remede de Fortune, 110, 140n18
MacQueen, John, 227n7, 231n37
Mahoney, Dhira B., 105n86
Maidstone, Richard, 103n49
Mandeville's Travels, 219
Manly, John M., 117, 119–21, 124,
    141n22, 142n32, 143nn39–40,
    144nn44, 48, 144–5n51, 145–6n58,
    147n62
Mann Phillips, Margaret, 259nn30,
    34
Map, Walter, 4–6, 8–10, 38–47, 51n9,
    52n10, 53n19, 55nn31–4; *De nugis
    curialium*, 39–47, 48–50, 51nn1–2,
    4, 52nn10, 12, 53nn20–1
Marie de France, 205–6, 229n19
Margolis, Nadia, 176n11
Martens, Dirk, 239, 245, 250, 261n45;
    *Lucubrationum Erasmi Roterodami
    index*, 17, 255
Martial, 22, 259n29
Martianus Capella, 22, 237
Matheolus, 160; *Lamentations*, 161,
    164, 173
Matsuda, Takami, 262n50
Matthew of Linköping: *Poetria*, 25,
    35nn21–2
Maximian, 22
McCall, John P., 91, 104n62
McConica, James, 257n4
McCormick, William, 146n60
McGrady, Deborah, 5, 12–13, 108–9,
    139nn5–8, 140nn10, 12, 176n19,
    177nn23, 33, 192

McKinley, Kathryn L., 86, 98,
    102nn31–2, 105n95
Mcleod, Glenda, 176n11
Mehl, Dieter, 214, 230n36, 231n37
Meiss, Millard, 176n13
Miller, Jacqueline T., 82, 100n9
Miller, Paul, 35n13
Minnis, Alastair, 3, 5–8, 14; 18nn1–4,
    34n1, 35nn10–11, 18–19, 21,
    36nn27–32, 35–6; 39, 37nn40, 42–6,
    132–3, 152nn94–6, 196n31, 258n19
Modoin, bishop of Aubin, 86
Mombello, Gianni, 177n32
Montreuil, 175n8
Mooney, Linne R., 78n36, 112–13,
    141n23
More, Thomas, 255
Mulder, H., 77n30
Müller, Anja, 229n18
Müller, Jan-Dirk, 51n5, 53n24
Muzerelle, Denis, 73n3

Nicholas of Prato, 23
Nigellus, Ermoldus, 86
Noakes, Susan, 177n34
Nuttall, Jenni, 80, 99n2, 101n19,
    103n53, 104n66

Obermeier, Anita, 10, 11, 100nn5–6,
    13, 104n74, 106–7, 127, 139nn2–3,
    148–9n73, 153n107, 178
Olson, Glending, 129, 151n86
Origen, 243
Ouy, Gilbert, 177n31
Overgaauw, Eef, 149nn76–7
Ovid, 5, 22, 80, 85; Ars Amatoria, 10,
    23, 86–9; Epistulae ex Ponto, 85–7;
    Fasti, 86, 99, 101n19; Heroides, 86;
    Metamorphoses, 10–11, 21, 80–1, 84,
    86–8, 91, 99, 101n19, 105nn82, 97;
    Remedia amoris, 23; Tristia, 85–7, 99

Owen, Charles A., Jr, 112, 114,
    141nn22, 24, 142n29, 147n65

Pamphilus, 22
Pabel, Hilmar M., 257n5, 258n11
Palmer, Nigel, 77n28
Parkes, Malcom, 56–7, 73nn1–2,
    74n4, 128, 149n80, 149–50n81,
    176n12
Partridge, Stephen, 100n14, 140n17,
    142n31, 144n44, 145n54, 147n63
Pask, Kevin, 19n3
Patterson, Annabel, 231n47
Patterson, Lee, 95, 104n69, 105n85
Patton, Celeste A., 104n72
Pearsall, Derek, 113, 141nn22, 26,
    206, 229nn20, 22
Pecock, Reginald, bishop, 5–6,
    13–14, 18, 178–87, 192–3; Donet,
    186, 189, 196nn36–7, 197nn46–9,
    57, 59–61; Folewer, 197nn50, 53–4;
    Repressor of Over Much Blaming
    of the Clergy, 181, 186, 195n13,
    196n33, 197nn56, 58; Reule of
    Crysten Religioun, 14, 181–3, 186–7,
    190, 195nn12, 16–23, 196nn32, 35,
    38–43, 197nn51–2, 55
Pelen, Marc C., 104n72
Perry, Ryan, 179, 193n3
Persius, 22
Petrarch, 7, 31, 36n39, 237
Philip, duke of Burgundy, 136
Pinkhurst, Adam, 112–13, 141n23;
    'Adam Scriveyn,' 131
Pitard, Derrick G., 101n17
Placidus, Lactantius, 22
Plantagenet, Geoffrey, bishop of
    Lincoln, 44–6, 54n29
Pliny the Elder, 248, 259n29, 260n36;
    Natural History, 248, 259nn31–2,
    260n40

Pliny the Younger, 237, 259n31
Poor, Sara S., 18n2
Powell, Marianne, 226n2, 229n23
Powell, Stephen D., 101n17, 103n59,
   142n30
Preminger, A., 35n20, 36n26
Prosper, 22
Prudentius, 22–3
Przychocki, G., 34n5
Pythagoras, 258n21

Quain, E.A., 34n5
Quilligan, Maureen, 177n26
Quintilian, 198, 237, 247

Radelescu, Adrian, 102n36
Rand, E.K., 102n44
Ransom, Daniel, 144n44
Raybin, David, 95, 104n63, 105n83
Rayner, Samantha J., 99n1
Reedijk, Cornelis, 261n49
Reno, Christine, 177n31
Reric, Dom, 43
Revard, Carter, 127, 149n79
Reynolds, Suzanne, 35n13
Rhenanus, Beatus, 232, 235, 239, 254
Richard II, king of England, 10, 11,
   80–2, 85–6, 88–92, 95–9, 100n8,
   103n47, 111, 140–1n21
Richard the Redeless, 98
Rickert, Edith, 117, 119–21, 124,
   141n22, 142–3n32, 143nn39–40,
   144nn44, 48, 144–5n51, 145–6n58,
   147n62
Riddy, Felicity, 227n6
Riga, Peter, 22
Rigg, A.G., 35n7, 51n9
Rinuccio da Castiglione, of Arezzo,
   201, 203, 205, 228n13
Ripelin, Hugo, of Strassburg,
   79n40

Robathan, Dorothy M., 85–6,
   102nn29, 31–2
Robertson, Elizabeth, 180, 193n6
Robinson, P.R., 74n8, 75nn12–13,
   77n28
Röcke, Werner, 55n34
Ross, J., 226n3
Rouse, Mary A., 74n4
Rouse, Richard H., 74n4
Rummel, Erika, 258n18
Rust, Martha Dana, 148n71

Saenger, Paul, 155–6, 175nn5–6
Saul, Nigel, 90, 103nn51, 53–6, 58,
   104nn67–8
Savanarola, Girolamo, 8, 32
Sayce, Olive, 148–9n73
Scattergood, V.J., 104n72
Scharff, Thomas, 53n22
Scholla, A., 77nn27, 32
Schürer, Matthias, 232, 254,
   261n43
Scott, A.B., 35nn10–11, 18–19,
   36nn27–31, 35–6, 39, 37nn40,
   42–4, 46
Scott, Kathleen, 147n62
Sedulius, 22
Seibert, Harriet, 105n84
Seneca, 17, 22, 35n10, 86, 237,
   254–5
Shakespeare, William: Love's Labour's
   Lost, 236
Shirley, John, 150n84
Simpson, James, 95, 105n87, 180,
   195nn14–15
Smith, G. Gregory, 226nn3, 6
Smith, M. Ellwood, 229n18
Smith, M.M., 257n7
Smith, Richard, 226n3, 227n10,
   228n11, 257n7
Solterer, Helen, 176n18

Somerset, Fiona, 193n2
Spearing, A.C., 102n38, 214, 221, 230n35, 231n52
Staley, Lynn, 180
Statius, 22
Steele, Joseph, *The Lucubrations of Isaac Bickerstaff, Esq. (The Tatler)*, 237
Steinhöwel, Heinrich, 201, 203, 228nn14, 16, 18
Steppich, Christoph J., 257n10
Stock, Brian, 177n35
Storm, Melvin, 102n22, 103n47
Stow, George B., 103n53
Striar, Brian, 80, 85, 100n3, 102nn24, 44
Strohm, Paul, 103n47, 152n93
Suetonius, 237
Syme, Ronald, 102n36
Szirmai, J.A., 77n27

Tatlock, J.S.P., 147n62
Taylor, Andrew, 140–1n21
Terence, 22
Tertullian, 243
Thelulus, 22
Theodolph, bishop of Orleans, 86
Thibault, John C., 86, 102n37
Thomas of Woodstock, duke of Gloucester, 140–1n21
Thompson, J.J., 73n2, 75n15, 77nn26, 28
Tibullus, 22
Tobias, 22
Tokunaga, Satoko, 144n44, 145n53
Tolkien, J.R.R., 199
Trapman, Hans, 257n4
Trapp, J.B., 258n16
Trevet, Nicholas, 23, 35nn10–11, 86

Trigg, Stephanie, 132, 148n70, 152n93
Trithemius, Johannes, 258n24
Turner, Marion, 89, 103nn48, 50, 57

Usk, Thomas, 89

Valla, Lorenzo, 247
Vanautgaerden, Alexandre, 257n7
van Borssele, Anna, 241
van Maerlant, Jacob, 64–5, 70, 74n4, 78n38
van Ruusbroec, Jan, 10, 62–3, 68, 76n17
van Schoonhoven, Gerrit, 72
Varro, Marcus Terentius, 235, 237, 248, 259n29
Vaughan, Míceál F., 83, 100n12, 113–15, 120, 124, 127, 141n25, 142n29, 143nn33–6, 42, 144nn45–6, 48–9, 144–5n51, 145–6n58, 146–7n61, 147nn62, 65, 148nn68, 70, 150n83, 153n108
Vessey, Mark, 5–6, 16–18, 258nn15, 24
Vincent of Beauvais, 75n14
Virgil, 22, 201
Volz, Paul, 257n4
von Botzheim, Johann, 245, 255
von Kreisler, Nicolai, 214, 230n34, 231n52
Vredeveld, Harry, 244–5

Wachinger, Burghart, 51n6
Wallace, David, 37nn40–1, 91, 103n52, 104nn63, 69
Walsingham, Thomas, 21–3, 90; *De archana deorum*, 21, 35n7; *Prohemia poetarum*, 21, 23, 33, 35n9
Walter of Chatillon, 22

Walter of England, 223, 229n24
Watson, Nicholas, 18n2, 178, 180,
   193nn1–2
Wenzel, S., 73n3
Westervelt, L.A., 105n79
Westphal, Sarah, 56–7, 73n2
Wheatley, Edward, 101n21, 214,
   226n2, 228nn14, 17–18, 229n23,
   230nn31, 36, 231n47
Wilkins, David, 194n8
William of Moerbeke, 23, 25
Williams, Gareth D., 102nn40, 43,
   103n45–6
Wilson, Katharina, 176n11

Windeatt, Barry, 145n56
Wogan-Browne, Jocelyn, 195nn25,
   27, 196nn28–30, 34
Wood, Chauncey, 91, 103n61
Woods, H. Harvey, 226n6
Wright, Aaron E., 229n24
Wright, Thomas, 52n10
Wurtele, Douglas, 100n12

Yeager, R.F., 98, 105nn90–3

Zimmerman, Michel, 18n2
Ziolkowski, Jan M., 257n9
Zotz, Thomas, 53n24

Index of Manuscripts

Conventional sigla for manuscripts of Chaucer's *Canterbury Tales* appear in parentheses after their shelfmarks.

Aberystwyth
National Library of Wales, **Hengwrt 154 (Peniarth 392D) (Hg):** 113, 128, 143nn37, 40, 144n44, 146–7n61, 151n85, 153n108

Austin, Texas
University of Texas Library **46 (Ph¹):** 119, 124, 144n44, 144n50, 150nn82, 84; **143 (Cn):** 119, 144n50

Brussels
Koninklijke Bibliotheek, **1165–67:** 76n17; **2879–80:** 68–70; **2979:** 75n14; **3067–73:** 66, 77nn24, 31; **3416–24:** 76n17; **19295–97:** 68–9

Cambridge
Fitzwilliam Museum, **McClean 181 (Fi):** 117–18, 148n68
Magdalene College, **Pepys 2006 (Pp):** 114, 119–21, 142n31
Trinity College, **R.3.15 (Tc²):** 117; **R.3.19:** 69, 72, 75n15; **R.3.21:** 69, 72, 75n15

University Library, **Dd.4.24 (Dd):** 115, 143n37, 144n47; **Gg.4.27 (Gg):** 115–16, 119–20, 124, 128, 142–3n32, 143n34, 144nn44, 50, 144–5n51, 147n64, 150nn82, 84; **Ii.3.26 (Ii):** 117–18, 147nn64–5, 150n83; **Mm.2.5 (Mm):** 117–18

Chantilly
Musée Condé, **492–93:** 134

Chicago
University of Chicago Library, **564 (Mc):** 143n43, 146n59

Cologne
Dombibliothek, **52:** 76n21; **53:** 76n21; **54:** 76n21; **55:** 76n21

Darmstadt
Landes- und Hochschulbibliothek, **1088:** 77n32

Durham
Cathedral, **B. IV 24:** 78n35

Ghent
  Universiteitsbibliotheek, **693:**
    76n17; **1330:** 65; **1374:** 64, 74n4,
    76n23

Glasgow
  University Library, **Hunterian
  Museum U.1.1 (197) (Gl):** 118,
    121, 145–6n58, 149n74

Groningen
  Universiteitsbibliotheek, **405:** 69

Leiden
  Universiteitsbibliotheek, **Ltk. 344:**
    62, 63, 76n17; **BPL 191 A:** 79

Lichfield
  Cathedral **29 (Lc):** 117–18, 120,
    124, 144n50, 145n52, 148n68

London
  British Library, **Additional 25718
  (Ad¹):** 119, 124, 148n69, 150n83;
    Additional 35286 (Ad³): 115,
    143n38; **Egerton 2726 (En¹):**
    119; **Egerton 2864 (En³):** 119,
    124, 144n50, 148n69, 150n83;
    Harley 1758 (Ha²): 117, 124,
    145n52, 149n74; **Harley 2693:**
    35; **Harley 4431:** 108, 157,
    162, 164–7, 169–71, 176n20;
    Harley 7333 (Ha³): 142–3n32,
    143n43, 147n64, 150n84; **Harley
    7334 (Ha⁴):** 118, 120, 123, 125,
    144–5n51, 147nn62–3, 150n83;
    Lansdowne 851 (La): 117, 124,
    143n42, 150n82; **Royal 18 C.ii
    (Ry²):** 117, 124; **Sloane 1686
    (Sl²):** 142–3n32, 143n41

Royal College of Physicians, **388
  (Py):** 115

Longleat House
  29 (Ll²): 115, 143n36, 147–8n66

Manchester
  John Rylands University Library,
    English 113 (Ma): 119, 144n50,
    149n74

Munich
  Bayerische Staatsbibliothek, **Clm
  3974:** 204

Oxford
  Balliol College, **238a:** 74; **350:** 74
  Bodleian Library, **Arch. Selden
  B.14 (Se):** 117, 120, 124, 148n68;
    Arch. Selden B 26: 74; **Bodley
    414 (Bo¹):** 118, 121, 145–6n58;
    Bodley 686 (Bo²): 142n31; **Bar-
    low 20 (Bw):** 142–3n32; **Digby
    76:** 74; **Hatton donat. 1 (Ht):**
    118, 121, 145–6n58, 146–7n61,
    149n74; **Marshall 127:** 66, 77n28;
    Rawl. A.393: 148n72; **Rawlin-
    son poet. 141 (Ra¹):** 143n43;
    Rawlinson poet. 149 (Ra²): 117,
    121, 123, 145n52, 145–6n58,
    146–7n61, 149n74; **Rawlinson
    poet. 223 (Ra³):** 149n74
  Christ Church, **152 (Ch):** 115
  Corpus Christi College, **32:** 38,
    47, 48–50, 55n32; **198 (Cp):**
    115, 143nn37, 40–1; **220:**
    77n28
  New College, **314 (Ne):** 117, 118,
    147n64, 150n83
  St John's College, **94:** 148n71

Trinity College, **Arch. 49 (To):** 119, 121, 123, 144n48, 146–7n61

Paris
Bibliothèque de l'Arsenal, **8217:** 77n24
Bibliothèque Mazarine, **920:** 78n39
Bibliothèque nationale de France, **anglais 39 (Ps):** 142n31, 150n84; **fr. 605:** 176n20; **fr. 606:** 169, 176n20; **fr. 607:** 176n20; **fr. 794:** 76n23; **fr. 831:** 111; **fr. 835:** 176n20; **fr. 836:** 176n20; **fr. 848:** 169; **fr. 1584:** 110; **fr. 1586:** 110

Petworth, Sussex
Petworth House **7 (Pw):** 117–18

Princeton, New Jersey
Princeton University Library, **100 (He):** 143n43

Salisbury
Cathedral Library, **169:** 78n38

Salzburg
St Peter Stiftbibliothek, **a VIII 29:** 76n20

San Marino, California
Henry E. Huntington Library, **Ellesmere 26 C 9 (El):** 110, 113, 115–16, 119, 120, 123–5, 127–8, 137–8, 141n26, 144nn44, 49–50, 144–5n51, 145n53, 147n62, 148n70, 149n74, 149n81, 150nn82–4, 151nn85–6, 151–2n92, 153n108

St Petersburg
Academy of Sciences, **O 256:** 75n14

The Hague
Koninklijke Bibliotheek, **73 H 17:** 76n17; **128 C 8:** 75n16

Tokyo
Collection of T. Takamiya, **22 (Ds[1]):** 119, 144nn46, 50; 149n74; **32 (Dl):** 117, 121, 123, 144n46, 145n52, 145–6n58, 146–7n61

Valenciennes
Bibliothèque municipale, **170:** 76n20;

Vienna
Österreichische Nationalbibliothek, **Cod 808:** 76n20; **Cod. 13.708:** 57, 75n14

Zwolle
Stadsarchief, **Emmanuelshuizen 7:** 63